TECHNIQUES IN COMPUTER PROGRAMMING

PRENTICE-HALL INTERNATIONAL, INC., *London*
PRENTICE-HALL OF AUSTRALIA, PTY. LTD., *Sydney*
PRENTICE-HALL OF CANADA LTD., *Toronto*
PRENTICE-HALL OF INDIA PRIVATE LTD., *New Delhi*
PRENTICE-HALL OF JAPAN, INC., *Tokyo*

TECHNIQUES IN COMPUTER PROGRAMMING

PHILIP M. SHERMAN

Xerox Corporation

Prentice-Hall, Inc., Englewood Cliffs, New Jersey

To my wife, Doris

PREFACE

The title of this book, *Techniques in Computer Programming*, reflects its purpose: to describe some of the generalized techniques one may use in the planning and development of computer programs. This role may best be understood by examining my concepts of what is meant by computer programming.

Computer programming is the process of designing and writing programs for execution by a digital computer. The process involves, roughly, (a) a thorough understanding and statement of the problem to be solved, (b) selection of a method, in detail, for solving the problem, (c) analysis of the method in terms of the means whereby the computer will be used to solve the problem, (d) design of the program, (e) writing the program, (f) checking the program, (g) documenting the program. Since we are stressing techniques, steps (c) and (d) receive the great majority of the book's attention.

The process of program design and planning can be likened to engineering: programming is really program engineering. The electrical engineer, e.g., given a particular problem, draws upon his knowledge of logical circuitry, electrical circuitry, component characteristics, signal transmission, and so on. He designs equipment, deciding what technology is best suited to the problem. His approach is partially theoretical and partly experimental; it is science and art. Computer programming is much like this. We are here concerned with an introductory study of some of the technology that the programmer can draw upon as he designs his program.

In implementing this philosophy, I utilized a common language, FORTRAN, to illustrate methods by a number of simple programs that incorporate this technology. The book does not attempt to teach a programming language in depth, but is an introduction to one. Enough FORTRAN information is contained here to explain methodology; a thorough treatment of the language can be found in other texts. It should be noted, however, that no prior knowledge of

FORTRAN is required. This book is basic in that it starts from the beginning in computers, languages, and methods.

Chapter 1 introduces the computer—its organization and operation—and the concepts of programming. Chapter 2 discusses algorithms and the manner in which they are translated into programs. Chapter 3 discusses the role of flow-charting in problem analysis and program design.

Chapters 4 through 9 provide a general introduction to programming. The elements of programs and programming are treated in Chapter 4. FORTRAN is introduced in this chapter by illustration; three simple programs are given and studied, statement by statement. Chapter 5 deals with transfer of control in programs. Chapter 6 describes a hypothetical computer, the GAMMA 70, to provide an understanding of machine-level language. Chapter 7 describes the use of subroutines. This concept is treated both as a basic concept in programming and as one of the techniques in programming useful in program design. Chapter 8 discusses the process of program execution. Chapter 9 describes input-output processes with emphasis on the manner of doing this in FORTRAN. At this point in the book, the reader has sufficient background and experience to program problems of moderate complexity.

Chapters 10 through 14 are concerned with several specialized techniques that a programmer can utilize as he "engineers" his program. Symbol manipulation, useful in a certain class of problem-solving, is treated in Chapter 10. The problem of programming errors is described in Chapter 11. Roundoff errors are treated at some length; they are only of concern in numerical problems. Chapter 12 deals with data structuring problems. A variety of structures is described, with examples of the use of each. Chapter 13 describes dynamic storage allocation problems, and offers three specific approaches to the problem of allocating and freeing space in memory. Chapter 14 discusses problems in data management: the structuring of files and the storage, retrieval, and maintenance of data files.

Chapter 15 summarizes most of the text; it lists the steps in program design and development. To illustrate these steps, two problems are examined. Because of the nontechnical nature and generality of this chapter, it can be read at any time, even before the rest of the book is studied. It can then be reread periodically. The reader will, of course, get more from the material on each perusal.

To unify the material throughout the text, two particular problems are presented early and repeated on several occasions as new topics are introduced. One of these concerns the FORTRAN simulation of the GAMMA 70 and its assembler, which is discussed in Chapters 1, 6, 7, 9, and 10. The other is a student-record processing problem, discussed in Chapters 4, 5, 7, 9, and 14.

As noted, this book only serves to introduce a variety of concepts. The reader, if he is interested, should pursue these topics in the current literature.

Each technique truly represents a discipline involving continuing research and development. I would particularly suggest the Association for Computing Machinery's *Communications* and *Computing Surveys*. Its *Computing Reviews* provides extensive bibliographies of other sources.

PHILIP M. SHERMAN

Murray Hill, New Jersey
November 1969

CONTENTS

TECHNIQUES IN COMPUTER PROGRAMMING

1 COMPUTERS AND THEIR USE

The problems that must be solved in today's modern technology increase so rapidly in volume and complexity that man has turned to electronic computers for help in understanding and solving them. These machines provide the means for accomplishing these tasks quickly and accurately. Yet the problems, as thought of, often differ so vastly in format from the electronic circuit operation of a computer that a translation process is necessary. It is to this process that our attention is turned for the duration of this book.

In this chapter we shall study the basic characteristics of digital computers in an attempt to learn why they are so useful, what they can do, and how they are organized.

1.1 COMPUTER FUNDAMENTALS

The Need for Computers

Before the advent of digital computers, many problems were solved only approximately; this situation was tolerated because few means for more accurate solutions were available. The problems that were solved completely were generally small in scope and applicability. Now, more far-reaching solutions are available and, through the greater understanding thereby provided, the need for more answers grows ever more acute.

Scientific developments and discoveries yield large amounts of data in many forms. Often these data can only be processed by machines, because manual analysis would provide answers much later than the time when they would be useful. Sometimes the amount of information that must be stored for future use is staggering. The data must frequently be sorted and continually kept up-to-date. Only computers, with access to huge amounts of information, can accomplish these tasks. Records are kept about people in personnel files, about stocks in inventory files, about parts in manufacturing files, and so on, endlessly growing and multiplying.

Many complex operations must be controlled by computer, because humans cannot keep up with the demand for the calculations. Examples are chemical processes, systems of inventory control, and the control of a missile or satellite. Without computers, these systems either could not work properly or, at best, would work inefficiently at greater cost.

Besides the *need* for computers in certain areas, there is a great *desire* for the facilities a computer provides, especially for the speeds available. Airlines reservation systems can yield a response within seconds from overseas queries. Telephone systems route calls across the country, seeking optimal paths and making connections, under the control of a computer system, also within seconds. Large schools can have their students' schedules prepared by computer in minutes. We could go on; examples are almost innumerable.

Questions to be Answered

A number of questions to be answered will come to mind. Some of these are the following. What is a digital computer? What is programming? Why are computers so widely used? What kinds of problems can they solve? What is the history of computers?

What is a Digital Computer?

A computer can be viewed as a machine that executes basic operations upon symbolic representation of numbers and other quantities, under the control of a set of rules interpretable by the machine. If a problem can be stated in precise terms, comprising a number of distinct well-defined operations, it can be solved on a computer.

Computers are of two general types: *analog* and *digital*. Analog computers perform operations by representing numbers with a measure or analog; for example, 1 volt may represent 1 foot per second. As a parameter varies during the course of a calculation, its analog changes proportionately. The accuracy of representation of a number depends on the precision of the components of the analog computer. Accuracies better than within 0.01 per cent are rare. This book deals only with digital computers, and we shall say nothing more about analog computers.

Digital computers do not operate by using analogs of quantities, but deal directly with symbols, which may represent any desired quantities. When these symbols represent numbers, any desired accuracy is possible, since as many storage devices as desired may represent the number. Accuracies involving about

10 to 15 digits are readily available. In many applications, however, accuracy is not at issue, since the quantities manipulated are symbolic entities.

What is Programming?

A digital computer is constructed to operate upon information. It does so by executing a sequence of operations called *instructions*; a sequence of instructions is called a *program*. The program serves as the set of rules to be followed by the computer. For a problem to be solved on a computer, it must be analyzed into its component parts, and these parts must be transformed into a form suitable for execution, that is, into a program. This transformation is not executed manually, that is, we do not transform a problem into instructions by hand. Rather, we write a sequence of *statements* each in a form that resembles the steps of the problem, and rely upon the computer itself to translate the statements into instructions.

The term *programming* sometimes refers to the analysis of a problem and the planning of the program. The term *coding* refers to the writing of statements or instructions. Often the distinction between these tasks blurs, and we may use *programming* to refer to the complete translation process. This we shall do throughout this book.

We may look upon programming from another point of view. It is actually a process whereby the problem to be solved is translated from the form in which we think of it to a form that the computer can execute. In other words, it is a solution to the problem of communicating with the machine. This concept is at the heart of the programming task, and we shall refer to it again and again.

Why are Computers so Widely Used?

Computers are widely used because they have at least four characteristics that are very useful for solving problems. They are extremely fast, they are accurate, they can store large amounts of information with rapid accessibility, and they are capable of executing sequence of operations automatically. We can discuss these characteristics by comparison with similar features on an electromechanical desk calculator, one machine that the digital computer has largely replaced.

Because of their great speed, computers allow the solution of many problems that would otherwise remain unsolved because so much time would be needed to solve them. An electromechanical desk calculator takes about a million times as long to solve a problem as does a modern digital computer. A problem that a computer can solve in 10 minutes would thus take 80 years on a calculator operated 40 hours a week. Obviously no one (or group of people) would work so long on one problem, since its solution would be of no value. Without computers, we would not try to solve more than a small fraction of the problems we do now solve.

A direct comparison between the accuracies of a computer and a calculator is probably unfair. A computer performs sequences of operations without human intervention. In contrast, every operation on a calculator must be preceded and followed by a human task: entering numbers onto the keyboard and reading and writing a result. A comparison should be made between the computer and the human-calculator combination. A reasonable guess is that a person makes an error every thousand operations when operating a calculator. Mechanical errors in the desk calculator can be ignored by comparison. Digital computers usually run error-free for hours or days; in 1 hour a large computer can perform well over a billion operations.

It is important to note that computers do make mistakes; no machine can run forever without doing so. When a computer is used to solve a problem, there is always a small possibility that an error will occur in the machinery. Errors are usually easily detected (although their causes may be hard to discover) because they almost always lead to obviously wrong results. By regular maintenance and performance tests engineers can prevent most troubles. Little more can be said on the subject; the reader is warned.

Errors that programmers make, on the other hand, are very common. A large part of the job of programming is the detection and elimination of these errors. The subject is discussed several places in this book.

Computers have fast access to large amounts of stored information; storage area is usually referred to as *memory*. On some computers, one million numbers, each having 12 or more decimal digits, can be individually obtained within one microsecond (10^{-6} second) or less for processing. Any of billions of numbers are accessible in seconds. By contrast, a calculator can store four or five numbers, which appear on the visible registers (dials) and the keyboard; they can be stored usually only until the next operation. The main "memory" used with a calculator is the paper on which the operator writes.

The existence of a program for a digital computer is in direct contrast with the case of a calculator. In the latter machine, a list of operations remains on paper or in the operator's mind. A computer program, however, is stored within the memory of the machine. This permits the automatic execution of the program and associated processing of data. The process is automatic once the "start" button has been pushed. On a calculator, only individual arithmetic operations are automatic; each must be started by the operator.

What Kinds of Problems can Computers Solve?[1]*

If a problem can be written as a finite sequence of explicit operations, it can be solved on a computer. The question to ask is not whether a problem *can* be solved on a computer, but rather whether it is economically feasible to do so.

---

* These superscript numerals refer to bibliographic notes at the end of each chapter, which may be skipped without loss in continuity.

Programming costs are high, and problems that can readily be solved manually or with a calculator may better be done by those means.

Computer solution may be inappropriate for small problems, such as the balancing of a single checking account or the computation of one person's income tax. Banks and the Bureau of Internal Revenue use computers to perform these computations because thousands or millions of repetitions of the same problem occur. A computer is particularly useful in such situations, because one program can be used indefinitely, processing new data each time.

Another type of repetition is quite common. It involves a series of operations which compute results that are successively closer to the true answer to a problem. For example, one way to solve an algebraic equation is to guess at an answer, substitute it in the equation, and note whether the guess is too large or too small. This is followed by a better guess and further substitution. In this manner a series of guesses hopefully approaches the desired answer. This procedure is an *iterative* one.

Some problems are much more easily programmed for computer solution than others, although offhand they may seem to be more difficult. For example, the problem of evaluating a sixth-order polynomial at each of 4000 values of the independent variable is easily programmed, while the problem of translating Russian text into English is considerably more difficult to program. The reason is that the first problem can be easily stated explicitly as a sequence of operations, whereas the second cannot without a great deal of difficulty.

Certain operations can be quickly executed on a computer, whereas others that appear simpler may require more time. Consider the problems of determining the largest number of a given set of 500 four-digit numbers and of finding their sum. It probably takes a person about fifteen times as long to solve the second problem as the first, while a computer takes two to three times as long to solve the first problem. This is a disparity in human-to-computer-time ratios of about 30 to 1. The rules for addition are simpler than the rules for determining the largest number. This fact affects both computer design and the ease of programming these problems.

Computers do not operate directly upon numbers, but on their representations. The devices comprising computer memory, which are frequently magnetic cores, store physical quantities, such as voltages, magnetizations, and the like. It is convenient to think of these quantities as numbers, but more realistically we should think of them as symbols. As a consequence, we must embrace in our thinking computer manipulation of symbols which may be numbers, English words, patterns of X's, or anything else that is convenient.

The most common devices for the storage of information are magnetic cores and magnetic spots, each of which have two states. The symbols '0' and '1' are usually used to represent these states. Units of stored information are thus written as sequences of 0's and 1's, which have the appearance of binary numbers and are usually thought of as such. Frequently, computer capacity and operation is measured in terms of numbers, as though computers deal directly with them. But the computer operates upon symbols, and we must not lose sight of this fact.

What is the History of Computers?[2]

The first mechanical digital computers were built in the seventeenth century by Pascal and Leibnitz. Towards the end of that century, Jacquard devised a loom which wove complex patterns; it was controlled by punched cards. In 1812, Charles Babbage, a British mathematician, designed his "Difference Engine", which was to aid in the computation of mathematical tables. This machine was completed in 1822. In 1883, Babbage designed an "Analytical Engine", which was to be completely automatic. The machine was not built because the parts it required could not be machined with sufficient precision, but it had many elements of a modern digital computer. The operations required to solve a problem were to be punched on cards and supplied with the data. The memory was to hold 1000 numbers of 50 digits each, all stored in wheels. An ability to modify the course of calculations, depending on results obtained during the calculation, was to be incorporated by skipping cards or by moving back to earlier cards. The principles of the Analytical Engine form the basis of many modern computers.

In 1937, Professor Howard Aiken of Harvard University conceived of an electromechanical computer that was completely automatic, using the principles described by Babbage. The computer, the Automatic Sequence Controlled Calculator (known also as the Mark I), was completed in 1944 jointly by Harvard and the International Business Machines (IBM) Corporation. It could perform any specified sequence of the four basic arithmetic operations, and it allowed references to tables of previously computed results. Information was supplied on punched cards and by the setting of switches. Answers were punched on cards or written on a typewriter. A typical multiplication required about three seconds. The Mark I was in use for over 15 years.

In 1946, J. P. Eckert and J. W. Mauchley at the University of Pennsylvania were faced with the problem of processing large volumes of data on weather studies and ballistics. Clearly, high computing speeds were required. They were convinced that electronic techniques were essential for this purpose and so designed the ENIAC (the Electronic Numerical Integrator and Computer), which contained 18,000 vacuum tubes. Having no internal moving parts, it represented a great advance in computer technology. Addition required 0.2 millisecond, and multiplication required 2.8 milliseconds. Numbers had 10 decimal digits. A program was prepared by wiring of boards on the machine; the wiring was a slow process and limited the usefulness of the ENIAC.

The IBM 604 Electronic Calculator was the first computer built in quantity; 4000 were built between 1946 and 1960. The IBM Card-Programmed Calculator (CPC) incorporated the 604 in an accounting machine. Its program was stored on cards; alternate sequences of cards could be used, depending on the results obtained. Because there was no limit to the size of programs, the CPC was a very flexible computer.

In 1945, Dr. John von Neumann proposed a different type of electronic computer, one that had its program stored in its memory. Internal program storage, present in all modern computers, offers far greater programming flexibility. The computer, completed in 1950, was called the EDVAC (Electronic Discrete Variable Automatic Computer). It had twelve different instructions.

In 1945 the Digital Computer Laboratory at the Massachusetts Institute of Technology was assigned the job of building an aircraft simulator. The Whirlwind I computer was the result; it was completed in 1951. It contained 5000 vacuum tubes and 11,000 semiconductor diodes. Addition required three microseconds, and multiplication took 16 microseconds. These speeds are comparable to modern computer speeds. Because of checking features, Whirlwind I was extremely reliable. Many of the concepts incorporated in it are used in modern computers.

Computers built from the early 1950's through the early 1960's differed little in structure and operation from these earlier machines. Instruction repertoires increased greatly to the hundreds of today. The time to access computer memory and to perform operations has decreased until each approximates one microsecond or less in most large computers. By 1960, vacuum tubes in many computers were replaced by transistors, allowing the higher speeds mentioned. Internal data storage usually resides in magnetic cores, and additional storage is provided by magnetic tapes, magnetic disks, magnetic drums, and other such devices.

Computers built from the mid-sixties to the present have been termed "third-generation", a reference to the type of circuit technology used. This technology involves integrated circuitry, where circuit components are deposited, e.g., as thin films. The primary advantage in these computers is speed; in some modern computers, arithmetic operations can be performed in 100 nanoseconds (10^{-7} second).

The ever-increasing demands for convenient computing facilities has recently spurred the development of *remote terminals*. These devices are remote from the computer in the same manner that telephone handsets are remote from a central office. Through interconnections to a central computer, many users at the terminals can have access at essentially the same time. Actually, each user, who communicates his input by typing, shares the central machine, yet has the feeling he alone is using it. The computer is sharing its facilities, turning them over to each user in turn. A more efficient mode of operation results, and a user can obtain his results quite rapidly. Some of these systems utilize *time-sharing*, sharing both time and space within the computer's memory.

Another recent development in computer equipment has occurred in the area of *graphics*.[3] Cathode ray tubes, similar to television picture tubes, permit users to supply their data by drawing pictures on the CRT, using a *light pen* or other drawing device. The drawing process is aided by the computer, permitting incomplete specifications to define pictures. For example, rectangles may be defined by indicating their opposite corners. Results of computations may be displayed on the same CRT's. Since so many problems, especially in design, are formulated pictorially either in an engineer's mind or on paper, this mode of operation is very natural. Graphic techniques resulted in a giant step along the path to better communication with the computer.

The Future of Computers

It is now clear that computers will become even more widely used than at present. They are far more ubiquitous than many people realize. In addition to the applications already discussed, many others can be mentioned. Computers design automobile engines and bodies; computers plan the layouts of cities; computers check income tax forms; computers assemble electronic equipment; computers compute and prepare bills. The list is almost endless and grows continuously. Yet many difficult problems, which to us now seem as though they could be solved with the aid of computers, remain unsolved. The need for more and better-trained analysts and programmers grows at an even faster rate than the number of computers. How can the computer help us design equipment from the inception of the ideas? How can computers simulate a world-wide human system that takes food supplies, population rates, diseases, individual abilities and talents, technologies, and personalities into account, so as to help us optimize human resources for the betterment of all? These are tall orders, but the basic tools are there. All that is needed is imagination and a great deal of hard work.

EXERCISES

1. Why was problem-solving hindered before digital computers were developed?

2. Why is it so important to have some computation performed rapidly?

3. Under what conditions can a problem be solved on a digital computer?

4. What is the central part of the programming task?

5. Is much of the effort in programming involved in correcting programmer errors?

6. What are some of the characteristics of problems solved on computers?

7. Mention some of the specific tasks involved in:
   (a) Planning city layouts.
   (b) Checking income tax forms.
   (c) Computing bills.

                          *   *   *   *   *   *

8. Digital computers of many types can be found around us. Give some examples.

9. List areas, aside from those given, in which digital computers have been widely used.

10. Describe the difficulties in solving these problems on a computer:
    (a) Sorting 1,000,000 numbers, stored on magnetic tape, in increasing order of values.
    (b) Playing a game of checkers.
    (c) Translating Russian text into English.

11. Why do we say that computers do not operate upon numbers, but on their representations?

12. List the four useful characteristics of computers in order of importance.

13. In what kind of problem-solving would remote terminals be especially useful?

* * * * * *

14. What are the limitations of digital computers? How do these limitations affect the solution of problems by machine?

15. The questions asked in the text about programming and computers do not exhaust the curious reader's mind. Anticipate others that might be asked, and answer them.

16. What would appear to be the several steps in programming a problem for the computer?

17. Describe the difficulties in solving these problems on a computer:
    (a) Maintaining a personnel file for a large corporation.
    (b) Setting up a nation-wide travel reservation system.
    (c) Developing a program to design electronic systems.

18. Computers usually store information using 0's and 1's. How can this technique be used to store names, algebraic expressions, and very large numbers?

19. Make predictions about the future of computers in these areas: traffic control; record-keeping on a national scale; allocation of resources in a school, town, or city; medical diagnosis; city planning; the design of new computers.

1.2 COMPUTER ORGANIZATION

General Structure

Computers are organized functionally into a number of special units. The functions of and interactions among these units are probably best understood by analogy; the desk calculator considered in Section 1.1 also serves here.

Consider a clerk who solves an arithmetic problem on a calculator. He reads instructions written on a piece of paper, which may also contain the numbers he needs for the problem. On reading the instructions, he enters numbers into the calculator by pushing keyboard buttons. In the process of solving the problem, he reads the registers and may note on scratch paper intermediate results for use later. Subsequently, he writes down final results.

The computer is similarly organized. An *operations* unit performs addition, subtraction, and similar operations.* The program lists the operations to be performed, and a *control unit* performs these operations. Supplied data, intermediate results for later use, and final results are stored in the *memory unit* (or *memory*). Just as the clerk prepares his final results, so the computer provides results, by

---

* The term *arithmetic unit*, sometimes used here, is less descriptive.

means of *output equipment*, in an appropriate form. Analogously, *input equipment* accepts information provided by the programmer in a convenient form, converts it to the form required by the computer, and places it in the memory.

A simple block diagram of a computer, showing the interconnection of its units, is drawn in Figure 1.1.[4] Modern computers, though much more complex, are based on this simple plan. In the diagram solid lines indicate how data are moved from unit to unit for processing; this movement is termed *flow of information*. Dashed lines indicate the exercise of control of certain units over others. The program controls the control unit, which in turn controls the other units.

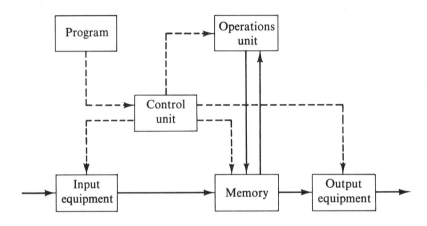

Fig. 1.1   Computer organization.

The Control and Operations Units

The control unit reads, interprets, and executes program instructions; in this way, the program exercises its control. To execute instructions, the control unit removes data from memory, places them in the operations unit, and returns the results to memory. It controls each of the several units in the computer.

Special instructions are available to effect alternate processes when decisions are required. The control unit tests for specified conditions and executes the appropriate instructions.

The control unit causes data to be read into the input equipment and read out of the output equipment, a process also under the control of the program.

The operations unit performs a wide variety of operations upon data in the memory. The unit receives the following information: (1) the operation to be performed, and (2) the operand(s) to be operated upon. For example, this information may be "multiply, x, y" or "compare, a, b". As a result, the unit provides the product or the result of the test, or whatever.

Most computers have special registers to perform arithmetic within their arithmetic unit. One common register is the *accumulator*, used for many operations.

It is similar to the dial on a desk calculator, which "accumulates" results during a calculation.

The Program

A digital computer operates automatically, under the control of the program stored within it. The program, as we have noted, consists of a sequence of instructions. It is the function of the control unit to interpret each instruction and activate whatever units are needed to perform the operation. For this reason, the program in Figure 1.1 is shown controlling the control unit, although it is not structurally part of the computer. It is loaded into memory with its data by means of the input equipment. Since the program is written for a specific problem, the effect is to create (for the time being) a special-purpose computer that solves that problem.

The problem consists of a set of instructions, as we have seen. Normally these instructions are executed in sequence, but occasionally it is necessary for decisions to be made that result in a different order of execution. Thus the computer performs different processes depending on conditions, as, e.g., when there are no more numbers to be added in a set. In a program, there may be instructions that read data, do arithmetic, make decisions, print results, and so on.

The Memory

The *memory*, also known as the *storage*, contains the program being executed, its data, and computed results. The memory consists of individual *words*, each named and referred to by a number known as its *address*. Words are addressed sequentially, but they may be referred to in any order. The time required in most computers to retrieve the contents of any word and place it in the accumulator is the same as the time to retrieve any other, and the term *random-access* applies. The computer memory referred to here is actually the *internal memory* of the computer. Most internal memory on modern computers is built of magnetic cores and is referred to as *core memory* or *core*. In this book, the word "memory" refers to core, unless otherwise qualified.

Computers also have direct access to *auxiliary memory*, which is usually much larger than internal memory, but the time to retrieve information from it is much greater. Several levels of the auxiliary memory exist, with varying sizes and access times. Auxiliary memory is not fully random-access, but has a complex structure that we shall study in later chapters.

Typically, words contain 24 to 36 bits of information, represented as binary numbers. Because such numbers are awkward, they are frequently abbreviated as octal integers. Each octal digit represents the values of three successive bits. The memory units in computers vary among machines, but most memories consist of about 4000 to 250,000 words. Some computers are organized by smaller units called "bytes", several of which normally comprise one word.

The information contained within a word is called its *contents*.* The symbol $C(x)$ is used to mean the "contents of word x". Frequently, a particular word is referred to as a *location*; the symbol $L(y)$ will mean the "location of the quantity y". Thus, if

$$C(p) = q$$

then

$$L(q) = p$$

The term *word* is sometimes used to mean the unit of information contained within a word. We shall occasionally use the term in this sense to mean the amount of the information that can be stored in a memory word. The context will make the meaning clear.

Some statements that illustrate the usage of these terms are

"A group of 500 words is used to store the data."
"Place this number at address 2000."
"The contents of location 500 is -1640."
"Locations 150 through 300 are used to store results."
"The information is stored as 750 words on tape."

We have already seen that a computer operates upon symbols often represented as integers. However, memory words may contain several types of information. The stored symbol may represent a number, an instruction, a sequence of letters, or merely be a place for a result. The contents of a word is irrelevant until a significance is attached to it by the operation performed upon it.

Whether or not it is significant, a word always exists in some state and thus can be said to contain *some* symbol or integer. When the contents of a word is retrieved, that contents remains unchanged. If a new number is stored in the word, the old value is destroyed. Thus, after the contents of one word is stored in another, the words are identical.

The GAMMA 70

An imaginary digital computer is introduced here in order that computer operation can be explained by example. This machine, the GAMMA 70, is very similar to most real computers, although its capabilities are a subset of true

---

* The word Contents may be singular or plural, and in this book its number varies with usage. Occasionally, it is more convenient to think of a word as a single piece of information; then we say "the contents is ...." At other times it is more reasonable to think of the contents of a word as several pieces of information, as when several numbers are stored in a word; then we say "the contents are ..."

computer capabilities. In succeeding chapters reference will frequently be made to this computer. It should be noted that, though hypothetical, its set of instructions and manner of operation are representative of actual machines.

The GAMMA 70 memory comprises words each containing 24 bits, each of which holds '0' or '1'. Each instruction occupies one such word.

One instruction of the GAMMA 70 computer appears in Figure 1.2, shown as a binary number. The bit positions are labeled, left to right, '0', '1', '2', ..., '23'. The 'S' bit is named to refer to a sign, to be used as described later.

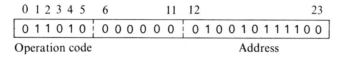

Fig. 1.2   Machine instruction (binary).

Bits '0' through '5' comprise the *operation field* and contain a 6-bit *operation code*. Each operation is identified by an operation code. The operand of the instruction fills the *address field*, which comprises bits 12 through 23. The instruction appears as in Figure 1.3. We can state that the operation code is '23' and that the operand is '2274'.

| 23 | 00 | 2274 |

The GAMMA 70 memory has 4096 (2^{12}) cells, addressed as $0000_8, 0001_8, 0002_8, \ldots, 7777_8$. Twelve bits specify an address; this is the size of the address field. This field usually refers to a location in memory. Thus, in Figure 1.3, the instruction indicates an operation upon *the contents of* location 2274_8. If '23' means divide, this instruction states, "divide by the number in location 2274".

Fig. 1.3   Machine instruction (octal).

EXERCISES

1. Suppose a clerk, who knew little or nothing about arithmetic, were to solve problems on a desk calculator. Write the several steps, in detail, needed to tell him how to solve these problems:
   (a) Add a given set of 10 numbers.
   (b) Determine the largest value of n so that $n!$ (n factorial) does not exceed 1000.
   (c) Find the first two adjacent integers whose product exceeds 500.

2. What is $C(L(q))$?

3. Why isn't the quantity in Figure 1.2 interpreted as a large number, $23,002,274_8$?

4. Why do computers have several types of memory, with different capacities and access times?

                    *   *   *   *   *   *

5. Give the forms of what seem to be reasonable instructions of these types: reading data, making a decision, and printing results.

6. Memory words may each contain two or three small numbers. What are the advantages and disadvantages of this method of storage?

7. The structure of a digital computer, outlined in this section, is certainly over-simplified. Supply further details, expanding Figure 1.1 as far as you can. Describe in some detail the physical structure of each box in that figure. Use the GAMMA 70 for specific features.

*   *   *   *   *   *

8. Why are binary numbers used as symbols in memory words, rather than decimal numbers?

9. There are certain inefficiencies of operation of the simple computer structure described. What are these? How can they be eliminated or reduced?

10. Figure 1.1 indicates nothing about the time sequencing of the several units. Consider a particular problem, such as the summation of six numbers punched on a card, and describe the manner of interaction and sequencing of the units as the problem is solved and the answer is printed.

REFERENCES

1. There are innumerable books, articles, and papers on applications of computers. The following introductory text, using the FORTRAN language as a base, covers a variety of applications:

   Charles H. Davidson and Eldo C. Koenig, *Computers: Introduction to Computers and Applied Computing Concepts*, John Wiley and Sons, Inc., 1967.

2. Many general texts on computers have a chapter devoted to the history of computing. Two excellent references are:

   R. Serrell, M. M. Astrahan, G. W. Patterson, and I. B. Pyne, "The Evolution of Computing Machines and Systems," *Proc. IRE*, **50** (1962), pp. 1039–1058.

   Saul Rosen, "Electronic Computers: A Historical Survey," *Computing Surveys*, Assoc. for Computing Machinery, **1** (1969), pp. 7–36.

   In addition, Section 1.2 of the monthly *Computing Reviews* (published by the ACM), mentioned in the Preface of this book, lists recent historical references.

3. This book does not deal with computer graphics. The following covers a good deal of the field:

   Fred Gruenberger, editor, *Computer Graphics—Utility, Production, Art*, Thompson Book Co., 1967.

   This article deals with a recent graphics system:

   Carl Christensen, Elliot N. Pinson, "Multi-function Graphics for a Large Computer System," *Proc. 1967 Fall Joint Computer Conference*, pp. 697–711.

4. The following book describes devices used in digital computers:

   Thomas C. Bartee, *Digital Computer Fundamentals*, 2nd ed., McGraw-Hill Book Co., 1966.

2 ALGORITHMS AND PROBLEM ANALYSIS

We have learned that a program, comprising a sequence of instructions, is required to operate a computer. The execution of these instructions results in the solution of the problem which has been written as the program. Prior to writing that program, however, it is necessary to develop a method for the solution of the problem and then to analyze it as a sequence of operations.

In this chapter we shall consider the task of selecting a method of solution, giving attention to the criteria of selection. Next, we shall examine the process of analysis, consider its importance, and study a number of ways by which it may be carried out.

2.1 ALGORITHMS AND PROGRAMS

What Algorithms Are[1]

If someone solves a problem in his mind or, perhaps, by writing a few notes or numbers, he may arrive at a solution without a well-defined method. That is, he may not be able to state the rules he used. For example, if he is asked to develop a three-by-three magic square, with sums of all collinear triplets the same, he may do so by a trial method. If he is further asked to do the same for squares 4, 5, 6, and 7 on a side, he probably will decide that a definite method is needed and can be sought. Indeed, such a method exists. If we consider other problems, we can often decide whether a precise method exists or does not. Consider, on the one hand, the mating of the pieces in a 1000-piece jigsaw puzzle and, on the other hand, the extraction of the square root of 35,871.

Consider now the following approach to problem solving. We have on hand a clerk who has no knowledge of any available methods nor who can devise any. He follows directions accurately, however. We must explicitly state our method to him if he is to solve a problem for us. Clearly, we can do this for solving a magic square, if we know the method. We can also do this for extracting the square root. In the case of the puzzle, however, we cannot.

Such is the situation when a programmer attempts to use a computer to solve his problem. As a consequence, he must state explicitly and without ambiguity the precise nature of the method to be used, step by step. It is to this concept that we now turn our attention.

An *algorithm* is an explicit method for the solution of a problem, giving a sequence of steps that is finite in execution and general for a variety of cases. We shall refer to the list of steps as a *procedure*, reserving the term "algorithm" for the method therein described. A computer program is also a procedure, for it is a list of steps and contains a precise description of a method of solution, written using the language of a computer for its expression.

Algorithms, particularly as applied to the computer solutions of problems, have several important characteristics:

FINITENESS. Algorithms must end after a finite number of steps. Those that do not, when translated into programs, are useless, for no problem is then solved.

DEFINITENESS. Every step in an algorithm must be defined unambiguously. This point is not generally overlooked in procedures written normally, for it is usually clear what each step means. When we consider procedures for computers, however, it is easy to introduce ambiguity unintentionally. As an example, if square roots are to be taken, a test for negative numbers is essential.

GENERALITY. An algorithm does not apply to one specific problem, but rather to one type of problem, such as summing *n* numbers or finding the largest value of a set of numbers.

PARAMETERS. Every algorithm operates upon certain quantities or *parameters* as "input" and supplies other quantities as results or "output".

From a practical viewpoint, the steps in an algorithm are generally simple in nature so that their conversion to a program is relatively straightforward. This is not an essential characteristic of an algorithm, but it is usually accepted as one.

Examples of Algorithms

Let us examine the two simple problems in arithmetic mentioned above and one other problem, developing algorithms for them. The first problem is the summation of a set of 25 positive numbers. The second problem is finding the largest number in this set. The third problem is to determine if three given numbers are in order.

Consider the summation problem. We know how to solve this problem; it is simple enough. But we now want to write an algorithm so we can have the computer solve it. Computers are built to add but two numbers at a time, so we must take this into account. What are the steps we would follow if we were to compute the sum by successively adding two numbers? We would write the first number down and add the second to it. Then to that sum we would add the third, and proceed in this manner until the last number is added.

Since we must be precise, statements like "... until the last number is added" are unsatisfactory. Rather, statements like "... until the 25th number is added" are preferred. We keep a running count of the numbers as they are added and stop when the count is 25. The count must be checked after each addition. To make the procedure read simply, we provide a sum to which we add each new number; the sum must initially be zero.

The following steps can be listed:

1. Set the sum equal to zero; set the count equal to 1.
2. Add to the sum the first number not yet added.
3. Add 1 to the count.
4. Check the count. If it is 25 or less, go to step 3; if it is greater than 25, stop.

This procedure is finite and precise. It is general in that it applies to any set of 25 numbers. The input parameters are the 25 numbers; the output parameter is the sum. A clerk who follows the procedure will perform the desired summation. Computers built to (1) add two numbers, (2) compare two numbers, and (3) continue at an earlier step or proceed to the next, depending on this comparison, can execute the procedure.

Now consider the second problem, finding the largest number. How would we do this manually? We would scan the list, beginning to end, mentally noting the largest number we have seen at any point. As soon as we see a larger one, we would remember that one instead. At the end, the last number remembered would be the largest. This process can be formalized as an algorithm. In this procedure, being formal, we shall define a variable L which, at any point in the procedure, has a value equal to the largest number yet found. The procedure:

1. Set L to an algebraic value less than the smallest number, say, zero; set the count equal to 1.
2. Compare L with the first number not yet checked. If L is the same or larger, go to step 3; if L is smaller, replace it with the new number, and then go to step 3.
3. Add 1 to the count.
4. Check the count. If it is 25 or less, go to step 2; if it is greater than 25, stop. L is then the largest number.

In both algorithms, we may note these characteristics:

(a) There is an initialization process, consisting of step 1;

(b) There is a repetitive operation in which the same steps (2 to 4) are performed once for each new number;

(c) There is a test to see when to stop. We shall examine these traits many times in the course of this book. They are very common, existing in many procedures written for the computer.

The third problem, although dealing with numbers, is not really a "numerical" problem. We are to determine if three numbers are given in order, i.e., if they are "ordered". They are considered ordered if they either increase in value or decrease in value, "left to right". For example, (25, 20, 16) are ordered; (16, 25, 20) are not. Two equal numbers are always considered ordered. This problem is not numerical because the items being checked might be names which are alphabetically ordered or people which are ordered by degree of experience in a particular field. The algorithm is the same in all cases.

Let the three numbers, as supplied, be a, b, and c. First we compare a and b. If they are equal, the set is ordered regardless of the value of c. For example, (15, 15, 30) and (40, 40, 20) are both ordered.

Then if $a \neq b$, we compare b and c. If b bears the relation (greater than, equal, or less than) to c that a bears to b, the set is ordered. Further, if $b = c$, the set is always ordered.

The algorithm:

1. If $a = b$, the set is ordered; STOP.
2. If $a > b$, and $b \geqslant c$, the set is ordered; STOP.
3. If $a > b$, but $b < c$, the set is not ordered; STOP.
4. If $a < b$, and $b \leqslant c$, the set is ordered; STOP.
5. If $a < b$, but $b > c$, the set is not ordered; STOP.

This algorithm involves many decisions and nothing else, but the tests are all simple. When a test fails, the following step is to be performed. Note that when a test succeeds, the procedure stops.

Computer Programs

Computer programs are procedures, as we noted. The structure of programs is more rigid than the informal nature of the procedures already considered, however. This is true because programs are interpreted by a computer, and a formal structure or syntax is required. The degree of formality varies among languages. Despite this difference, procedures as originally developed usually bear strong resemblances to programs written in *algorithmic languages*. Such languages, which we will study later, are so named because of this similarity.

There are other differences between problem algorithms and computer programs. Digital computers have finite memories with simply structured words that usually are fixed in size. They execute a well-defined, basically simple set of instructions. For efficient use of computers, programs must (1) be designed to take these inherent restrictions into account, and (2) be structured to reflect the algorithms developed. It is to these two points that we turn much attention in this book. In developing a computer program, we cannot simply write program instructions that carry out the steps of the procedure, if we expect the program to operate efficiently. We must develop techniques that attempt to match problem requirements with computer characteristics.

In preparing a problem for a computer it is necessary for a programmer to be explicit. All problem eventualities must be considered. If, for example, quadratic equations are to be solved, so that square roots are involved and some of the numbers may be negative, the program must include instructions for dealing with them. Because there is normally no human intervention during computer execution and because the computer cannot exercise judgment, all decisions required during execution must be programmed explicitly in advance. Whether it is performing meaningful operations or not, the computer will attempt to follow the instructions as written. The computer cannot "know", for example, that data should have been supplied in feet instead of meters or that the programmer intended negative and positive numbers to be processed differently. It cannot know these things unless it is specifically "told" about them. Because programs must be explicitly written, a programmer is forced to think about his problem in precise terms. He often gains insight into his problem that he otherwise might have missed.

Communication with the Computer

The instructions in a computer program are stored as a sequence of symbols that exist as a set of states in such physical devices as magnetic cores. The "language" of the computer, *machine language*, is embodied in these states, which indicate the operations to be performed and the associated operands. The language of the programmer's problem is a combination of English and mathematical notation. There is a great discrepancy between these two forms. The term "language barrier" describes the situation aptly.

Despite the differences, man and machine manage to communicate with one another satisfactorily. This is accomplished by a process that has several stages. First, a program is written. The coded program then must be translated into machine language; more specifically it is translated into punched cards or spots on a magnetic tape, representing instructions. This translation proceeds on the computer itself and is usually termed *compilation*. The combination of the computer and the compiler offers a programmer an "extended computer" that has, as its language, the programming language used. In other words, communication of the man with the computer is through the computer language developed for his use. The language barrier is thereby bridged. We cannot say that the barrier is fully bridged, however, for languages do not always closely match the steps in an algorithm. In these instances, programming remains a task fraught with difficulties.

EXERCISES

1. Develop algorithms to solve these problems:
   (a) Given a set of n numbers, determine the smallest number in the set.
   (b) Given three numbers, place them in order, the smallest one first.
   (c) Determine whether two given line segments on the x-axis overlap.

2. For each of the algorithms developed in Exercise 1, identify the input and output parameters.

3. In which algorithms developed in Exercise 1 are there these characteristics, listed in the text: initialization, a repetitive operation, and a test to see when to stop? What is true, in general, of algorithms that have these characteristics?

*   *   *   *   *   *

4. Develop algorithms to solve these problems:
   (a) Determine all the factors of a specified integer. (For example, if the integer is 20, the factors are 1, 2, 4, 5, 10, and 20.)
   (b) Given n numbers, determine if they are either in ascending or descending order.
   (c) Look up the telephone number of a person in the telephone book, given the name and address.
   (d) Determine if a given point (x_0, y_0) lies above or below a given line, $y = mx + b$.
   (e) Convert a given four-digit octal integer to its equivalent decimal form.

5. The algorithms written in the text are expressed in English. Prior to translation to a programming language, however, they ought to be written in mathematical terms. Do this.

*   *   *   *   *   *

6. It was stated in the text that a programmer gains insight into his problem when he writes a computer program for it. Under what circumstances might this be true? In what ways might he gain insight?

7. Develop, in simplified form, an algorithmic language that might be useful in coding the algorithms in the text and in these exercises. Consider the various types of statements that might be required.

8. Develop an algorithm for playing tic-tac-toe.

9. What are some of the factors that would have to be taken into account by a program that performed compilation?

2.2 PROBLEM ANALYSIS

Reasons for Analysis

There are several reasons why a problem should be carefully analyzed before it is programmed. First, a precise statement of the method is the result of such analysis. Second, because all steps of the procedure must be precisely stated, the programmer is forced to be accurate in that analysis. Third, the programming task is simplified if analysis is thorough. Fourth, checking the program is greatly facilitated. Fifth, future modification of the program is aided.

Though it has been made clear that the nature of a computer will affect the procedure developed for a problem, we shall not in this section consider the computer in analysis. Its effect will be taken into account subsequently.

Analysis of Two Problems

The problem of solving a quadratic equation for its two roots is analyzed. Consider the following general equation with real coefficients:

$$ax^2 + bx + c = 0$$

This is to be solved for any real numbers, a, b, and c. If a is zero, the equation is not quadratic, but is linear. Consider the linear case first.

If, in the linear case, b is also zero, then c must be zero and the case is trivial. If b is not zero, the solution is

$$x = \frac{-c}{b}$$

In the quadratic case, there are three types of solutions, depending upon the value of the discriminant D:

$$D = b^2 - 4ac$$

Then, if $D > 0$, there is a pair of real solutions, given by

$$x_1 = \frac{-b - \sqrt{D}}{2a} \quad \text{and} \quad x_2 = \frac{-b + \sqrt{D}}{2a}$$

If $D = 0$, there is one solution, given by $x = -b/2a$. If $D < 0$, there is a pair of complex solutions, given by

$$x_1 = \frac{-b - i\sqrt{-D}}{2a} \quad \text{and} \quad x_2 = \frac{-b + i\sqrt{-D}}{2a}$$

This method is straightforward. Every step of the process has been clearly indicated. As a first analysis, the following steps can be listed.

1. Determine the value of a. If it is zero, go to step 2.
2. Determine the value of b. If it is zero, the problem is trivial. If it is not zero, the solution is: $x = -c/b$. **STOP.**
3. Evaluate the discriminant: $D = b^2 - 4ac$. Evaluate the square root of the absolute value of D: $S = \sqrt{|D|}$.
4. If $D > 0$, the solution is:

$$x_1 = \frac{-b - S}{2a} \quad \text{and} \quad x_2 = \frac{-b + S}{2a}$$

If $D = 0$, the solution is:

$$x_1 = x_2 - \frac{b}{2a}$$

If $D > 0$, the solution is:

$$x_1 = \frac{-b - iS}{2a} \quad \text{and} \quad x_2 = \frac{-b + iS}{2a}$$

Thus, the problem has been formulated in four steps, in each of which formulas in a, b, and c are evaluated. While a more detailed analysis is possible here, it certainly is not necessary.

We may note these aspects of the quadratic-formula analysis: (1) Every case was treated, since anything can arise and must be accounted for. (2) An early calculation was made for the value of D, the discriminant, since it is used often; this is especially important in a computer program.

As a second example, consider the simple problem of adding two three-digit numbers, and develop an algorithm for it. Specifically, develop an algorithm for a person who only knows how to add one-digit numbers, i.e., to compute sums up to $9 + 9$. A third-grader is such a person.

Let the two numbers being added be represented as

$$a_3a_2a_1 \quad \text{and} \quad b_3b_2b_1$$

Let the sum be $c_4c_3c_2c_1$, where c_4 may of course be zero. The algorithm is the following:

1. Form a sum, $S = a_1 + b_1$, which can be written as $10t + u$. (Or, let S be represented as a two-digit number, tu.) Then, $c_1 = u$.
2. Form a new sum, $S = a_2 + b_2 + t$. (The value of t is the carry, 0 or 1, to be added to $a_2 + b_2$.) Let S be written as $10t + u$. Then, let $c_2 = u$.
3. Form a new sum, $S = a_3 + b_3 + t$, written as $10t + u$. Then, let $c_3 = u$, and $c_4 = t$.

In this algorithm, the quantities S, t, and u are given several new values as the procedure moves through the steps. The current value of each quantity, at any point, is used.

It is clear that, if there are n digits in each number, the procedure becomes highly repetitious.

The third problem is of a completely different nature than the other two. Imagine a three-by-three array, as a tic-tac-toe game, the entries being labeled $1, 2, 3, \ldots, 9$, across the rows, top to bottom, as shown in Figure 2.1. The problem is to determine whether a given set of three different integers in the range from 1 through 9 inclusive is a "collinear set". That is, determine whether the three numbers are in a straight line in the figure.

1	2	3
4	5	6
7	8	9

Fig. 2.1
An array.

There are 84 different numbers in the range 1 to 9, excluding rearrangements of the same set. Only eight of these are collinear. We could test a given set against the 84 possibilities, but this method is much too lengthy. There is a better way, one that would be much faster on (or off) a computer. These are the steps:

1. Order the set, smallest number first. Call the set (a, b, c).
2. Check for "linearity", i.e., see if

$$a - b = b - c$$

If the set is not linear, the set is not collinear in the array.
3. Check the first and last numbers in the ordered set. If the first number is 5 or 6, or the last is 4 or 5, the set is not collinear.
4. Check to see if all the numbers are even. If so, the set is not collinear.
5. At this point, any set not eliminated is a collinear set.

These rather odd-appearing steps follow from an examination of Figure 2.1. Step 2 is clear enough; linearity is necessary though not sufficient. At that point, only 16 of the 84 possibilities remain; that many sets are linear. Step 3 follows from the figure; no collinear set begins with 5, 6, 8, or 9; 8 and 9 are impossible lowest numbers in a set (since all three numbers in a set are different). Similarly, no collinear set ends with 1, 2, 4, or 5, while 1 and 2 are impossible highest numbers in a set. At this point, only 10 possibilities remain. Step 4 eliminates the remaining two noncollinear possibilities among those left.

This is certainly a roundabout way of developing an algorithm; a simpler way is to compare the set as given with the 84 possibilities, eight of which would be marked as collinear. However, our approach, though largely "experimental" (it is termed "empirical") and somewhat troublesome, is worthwhile, for it results in a much faster program. In a complex situation of this nature, the payoff as the result of an involved analysis may be much greater than here.

Data Repetition

Problems that are repetitious are, as we have seen in Section 1.1, suited to computer solution. They may be repetitious either because the same calculations are performed on many numbers or because the answers are derived in a repetitive or iterative manner. Examples of both types of problem are considered. The summation problem of Section 2.1 is a problem involving the repetition of data, where calculations are performed on all the numbers. We can express the sum as

$$S = a_1 + a_2 + \cdots + a_n$$

$$= \sum_{i=1}^{n} a_i$$

if we generalize the problem to n numbers. The summation operation in the procedure is performed on all the a_i.

A Special Symbol

Before proceeding to study other forms of the summation algorithm, a special symbol is introduced. The expression

$$b \leftarrow a$$

where a is an expression, means "replace the value of b by the value of the expression a". Thus

$$y \leftarrow x + 37$$

means "set the value of y equal to 37 more than the value of x". An arrow is used to indicate replacement rather than equality. Very commonly, a variable will be increased by 1 in a procedure; we write this as

$$i \leftarrow i + 1$$

which clearly does not mean "$i = i + 1$". The operation of replacement is, however, written as '$=$' in many programming languages. Its true meaning must be kept in mind.

Indexing

The four steps listed in the analysis of the summation problem must be translated into a form appropriate for a computer. Initially, we restate them in mathematical terms. Step 2, the heart of the process, is concerned with "the current number", the one being processed "now". If the ith number, a_i, is that one, the count of the number already summed is i at the end of step 2. With this notation, the four steps become these:

1. Set the sum equal to zero; set the count (i) equal to 1.
2. Add a_i to the sum.
3. Add 1 to the count.
4. Check the count; if it is n or less, go to step 2; if it is greater than n, STOP.

This is a more concise list of operations. The significance of step 2 changes, as the value of i changes, to permit sequencing through the entire set of numbers. The use of a count associated with a subscripted variable (a_i) is termed *indexing*. The *index* is the subscript, and it has value not only in describing repetitious operations but also in testing for termination of the process.

The four steps of the problem can be rewritten still more concisely in terms of the index:

1. $S \leftarrow 0$; $i \leftarrow 1$.
2. $S \leftarrow S + a_i$.
3. $i \leftarrow i + 1$.
4. If $i \leqslant n$, go to step 2; if $i > n$, STOP.

This last list of the steps in the summation is not only concise and explicit, it also corresponds closely to the operations that a digital computer can execute. Because indexing is so useful in expressing repetitious problems, most computers have *indexing instructions* that perform such operations as setting, modifying, and checking indices against constant values. Similarly, many programming languages incorporate an indexing feature in their structure.

It is not necessary for an index to start at 1 or to be incremented by 1. For example, assume that the 34th, 37th, 40th, ..., and 64th numbers in a list of one hundred numbers are to be multiplied together. The symbol a_i can be used to refer to these numbers. Instead of initializing a sum to zero, we initialize a product P to 1:

1. $P \leftarrow 1; i \leftarrow 34$.
2. $P \leftarrow P \times a_i$.
3. $i \leftarrow i + 3$.
4. If $i \leqslant 64$, go to step 2; if $i > 64$, STOP.

Iterative Problems

Consider the computation of the square root of a positive number to illustrate the analysis of a problem involving iteration.[2] The computation is based on this iterative formula:

$$x_{i+1} = \frac{1}{2}\left(x_i + \frac{A}{x_i}\right)$$

where x_i is the ith estimate of the square root of A, a given positive number. An initial estimate x_1 is made of $\sqrt{A}$, and a new estimate x_2 is calculated from this formula. This new value is substituted, and another estimate is calculated. The process continues until a sufficiently accurate value is derived. One criterion for testing the accuracy of an estimate is to compare its square with A; when their difference is less than a small value ε, the iteration stops.

The iterative process can be written as follows:

1. $i \leftarrow 1$; assume a value x_i.

2. $x_{i+1} \leftarrow \frac{1}{2}\left(x_i + \frac{A}{x_i}\right)$.

3. $i \leftarrow i + 1$.
4. Calculate $D = |A - (x_i)^2|$; if $D \geqslant \varepsilon$, go to step 2; if $D < \varepsilon$, STOP. The value of $\sqrt{A}$ is x_i when the process stops.

This iterative process is different in several ways from the repetitious examples considered earlier. First, sequence of data is not processed, but rather a sequence of estimates of a number is generated. Second, the subscripted variable x_i does not represent a set of numbers but rather a set of estimates of one number. Subscripting is used for a different purpose than previously. Third, the test to decide termination of the computation is not a check on the index value, but rather is a check on the current estimate of a number.

As another example, consider the determination of whether a given integer N is a prime. This can be done by dividing N by all integers up to and including the given value. If none of these divisions is evenly made, the number is prime. The procedure can be simplified by dividing only by odd numbers, after determining whether the given integer is even. Further, we need try no divisor greater than $\sqrt{N}$. If no divisor has been found that is less than or equal to $\sqrt{N}$, then none will be found that is greater than $\sqrt{N}$. This is true because dividing N by less than $\sqrt{N}$ always yields a quotient greater than $\sqrt{N}$.

The procedure can be written as below. N is the given integer. YES and NO mean that N is prime and not prime, respectively. Implied in steps 1 to 6 is the rule that if the stated condition is not true, continue to the next step. Implied also is a STOP after each YES and NO.

1. If $N = 1$, NO.
2. If $N = 2$, YES.
3. If N is even, NO.
4. If $N = 3$, YES.
5. If N is evenly divisible by the next odd number, NO.
6. If the last divisor tried (step 5) is greater than $\sqrt{N}$, YES.
7. Go to step 5.

This is an example of an iterative problem that involves no index. The criterion for stopping is the attainment of a specified value of a trial number, the current divisor.

The examples given in this section were chosen to illustrate methods of analysis and indexing, and to illustrate two distinctly different types of repetition. Although these examples are simple, their structure is similar to more complex problems, which differ primarily in the nature of the "main operation". If, for example, ten functions were all to be evaluated for n sets of variable values, the steps given for the summation problem could be rewritten for use here if, instead of step 2 (the main operation), the ten functions to be evaluated were written.

Analysis for Computers

When problems were analyzed in this chapter, no consideration was given to the nature of computers. In theory, any correct mathematical analysis is satisfactory. In practice, the characteristics of a digital computer impose restrictions both on the methods of analysis and the numbers in the computation. We shall now discuss some changes that we should make in the algorithms developed in order to be more practical.

First, let us reconsider the quadratic equation problem. Suppose the values of the coefficients, a, b, and c, differ very greatly in value, perhaps by a factor of 10^4. For example, suppose b is much greater than a or c. Then, the discriminant D is very nearly equal to b, since $D = b^2 - 4ac$. The latter term is about 10^{-8} as large as the first term and is likely to be lost in memory for most computer words can only retain about eight places of accuracy. This yields values as follows:

$$x_1 \approx \frac{-b}{a} \quad \text{and} \quad x_2 \approx 0$$

which are incorrect. The error results because the expression for x_2 involves the difference of two nearly equal numbers, computed as zero. Since the quadratic equation can be written as

$$(x - x_1)(x - x_2) = 0$$

we can, by comparing this form multiplied out to the earlier form,

$$ax^2 + bx + c = 0$$

determine that

$$x_1 x_2 = \frac{c}{a}$$

Thus, we can write a better expression for x_2:

$$x_2 = \frac{c}{a x_1}$$

Substituting the computed value for x_2, $-b/a$, in this yields

$$x_2 \approx \frac{-c}{b}$$

which is correct. The point of this analysis is that, when parameters differ by wide ranges of values, special treatment may be required in formula development.

Another way in which procedures require modification when developed for computers concerns input–output operations. There is no need, in a mathematical procedure, to be concerned with reading data or printing results. There is no need for concern over the amount of memory available. With computers, however, these may be real problems. If there is too much information to be stored in memory, some of it can be read and processed, and then more can be read, and so on, as a solution.

To illustrate these considerations, let the numbers to be summed be punched on a set of cards, preceded by one card that contains n, the number of numbers to be summed. Then the procedure can be written as follows:

1. Read n. (If no cards are left, STOP.)
2. Read $a_1, a_2, \ldots, a_n$.
3. $S \leftarrow 0$; $i \leftarrow 1$.
4. $S \leftarrow S + a_i$.
5. $i \leftarrow i + 1$.
6. If $i \leqslant n$, go to step 2; if $i > n$, go on.
7. Write S.
8. Go to step 1.

Note the changes: Step 1 reads n. Step 2 reads the n numbers; the value of n is needed so the proper number of numbers is read. Steps 3 through 6 are as before (where they were steps 1 through 4), except that, instead of stopping, the procedure continues to step 7. Step 7 causes the sum to be printed. Step 8 then causes a return to the start, to step 1. This extra step will cause new sets of numbers to be read repeatedly, as long as there are cards to be read. Even though there probably would be room in core memory for the n numbers, this approach is very common, for sometimes memory will be critical.

In the iterative square-root problem, a series of estimates x_i was calculated for the desired number ($\sqrt{A}$). We can modify the procedure by letting the symbol E represent the latest estimate at any point. Then, statement 2 of the procedure becomes

$$E \leftarrow \frac{1}{2}\left(E + \frac{A}{E}\right)$$

which indicates the replacement of an older value of E with a new one. By writing this statement instead of the other form, we imply that only one word of memory is needed for the estimates. This is the case, since only the latest need be saved. The procedure becomes the following:

1. Assume a value E.

2. $E \leftarrow \frac{1}{2}\left(E + \frac{A}{E}\right)$.

3. Calculate $D = |A - E^2|$; if $D \geqslant \varepsilon$, go to step 2; if $D < \varepsilon$, STOP. The computed value of $\sqrt{A}$ is E when the process stops.

In this form, no indexing is required.

EXERCISES

1. Using the compact notation introduced in this section, rewrite the algorithms written in the Exercises of Section 2.1.

2. Write a more detailed analysis of the quadratic-equation problem, proceeding from the given analysis.

3. Write a procedure, using index notation, to compute the sum of every fifth number in a series b_i, $i = 1, 2, \ldots, n$, starting with b_{20}.

* * * * * *

4. Consider a four-by-four array, with entries labeled 1, 2, 3, ..., 16, across the rows, top to bottom. Determine whether a given set of four different integers in the range from 1 through 16 inclusive is a collinear set.

5. Write a procedure for counting the number of integers in the range 0 through 99, 100 through 199, and 200 or greater, given 500 integers. This counting process, particularly when applied to many value ranges, results in a *histogram*.

6. Given a set of coordinate pairs for a series of points in a plane, write a procedure for counting the number of corresponding points in each quadrant.

7. Develop procedures for these extensions of the three-digit summation problem in the test, taking into account the simplification mentioned in Exercise 3:
   (a) Form the sum of two numbers, each with n digits.
   (b) Form the sum of three numbers, each with three digits.
   (c) Form the sum of m numbers, each with three digits.

* * * * * *

8. Write a procedure for determining how far apart two given days in a calendar year are, the dates being supplied as a pair of integers. For example, how many days from 4-17 (April 17) to 10-2 (October 2)?

9. A computer is fed data on the weather each day. A day may be classified as "fair", "cloudy", and "rainy". Write a procedure that computes the number of rainy days, the number of times days are rainy three days in a row, and the longest stretch of consecutive fair days. Data for one calendar year are supplied.

REFERENCES

1. Algorithms are treated at length in this book:

   Donald E. Knuth, *The Art of Computer Programming*, vol. 1, "Fundamental Algorithms," Addison-Wesley Publishing Co., 1968, especially pp. 1–9.

2. Refer to the following book for a description of the Newton iteration method, from which this equation is derived:

   Louis G. Kelly, *Handbook of Numerical Methods and Applications*, Addison-Wesley Publishing Co., 1967, pp. 20–21.

   This reference deals with the rth root of a number, for any r.

3 FLOWCHARTING

We continue our study of problem analysis by considering pictorial representations of programs, called *flowcharts*. Each operation and decision to be performed is placed in a box; the shape of each box reflects the type of process inside it: computation, decision, input–output, etc. Arrows are used to interconnect these boxes and show the sequence of operations.

The *loop*, appearing as a closed cycle of operations in a flowchart, is an important concept in programming. We shall study some of its properties.

3.1 FLOWCHARTING TECHNIQUES

The Use of Flowcharts

A problem analysis is made considerably more useful by augmenting it with a flowchart. In this form of a procedure, all operations to be performed and all paths of processing are clearly indicated.

Unless a problem consists mainly of a sequence of formulas (as in the solution of the quadratic equation in Section 2.2), the flowchart is more valuable than a listing of steps. Its value is due primarily to its pictorial nature, where procedure paths and alternatives are clearly seen. If a flowchart is sufficiently detailed, coding is very simple, for it then involves little more than converting operations into instructions. It is possible, however, for a flowchart to have so many details that the structure of the problem is obscured.

A flowchart consists of a number of boxes with directed lines interconnecting them. Statements of operations are placed within the boxes. The directed lines leaving these boxes indicate the paths of processing, that is, the sequence in which boxes are executed.

Since several people may read the same flowchart, it helps to follow conventions. Unfortunately, no universal standards exist. The following conventions are used here:

1. The statement of every operation is placed in a box. Sometimes several operations are placed in one box.
2. The sequence of operations is indicated by directed lines between boxes.
3. Each box has one line entering it and one or more lines leaving it. The operation in a box represents a process to be performed when the procedure has reached the entry point of the box. The points at which paths join before entering a box are *merge points*.
4. Several box shapes are used to identify different types of operation.

Flowchart Examples

The quadratic-equation analysis of Section 2.2 is flowcharted in Figure 3.1. The boxes are labeled to correspond to the steps in the analysis. Most of the conventions listed are illustrated in this flowchart. Notice that several shapes are used, such as rectangles, circles, and hexagons; these shapes are discussed later.

The summation problem of Section 2.2 was written as a sequence of four steps. These steps are flowcharted in Figure 3.2, where each step is placed in one box, numbered as previously. Since one of the paths leaving box 4 returns to box 2, an arrow is so drawn. The result of this path is a closed path comprising boxes 2, 3, and 4; such a closed path is called a *loop*. One traversal of all boxes in a loop is a *cycle*. There must be some way to terminate the calculations in a loop. Here the test of i at the end of the loop serves this purpose. The statement

$$i : n$$

indicates a comparison of the quantities on either side of the colon. The result of the comparison is one of two possibilities, which are indicated at the arrows leaving the box.

The problem of determining whether a given number N is prime is flowcharted in Figure 3.3. The chart follows directly from the procedure, given in Section 2.2, and its boxes are numbered correspondingly. The variable j is set to 0 or 1 if N is not prime or prime, respectively. This device, setting a variable to one of several numerical values to indicate different results, is very common in programming. Statement 5, given earlier, reads "If N is evenly divisible by the next odd number, NO." We translate "the next odd number" utilizing a variable i, whose initial value is 3, and which is incremented by 2. The results are the boxes 5.1, 5.2, and 5.3 in Figure 3.3. Note that a loop is present in this flowchart also.

Flowchart Boxes

The *operation box*, a rectangle, contains one or more operations that perform computations. Data are processed in some manner and the problem proceeds to

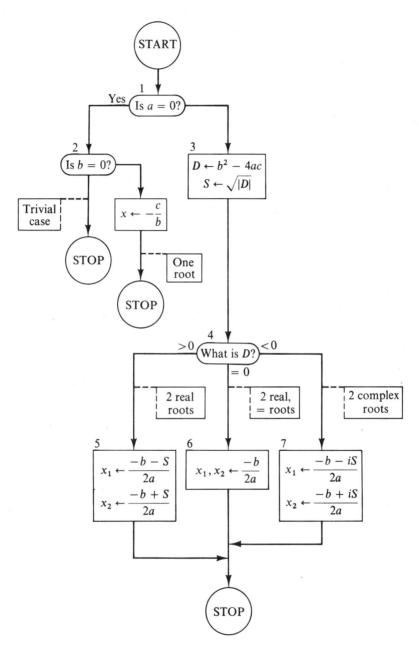

Fig. 3.1   Flowchart for quadratic equation solution.

the next box. While this description is not truly satisfactory, we can say that this box shape is used throughout a flowchart except as noted below where other boxes are used.

The statements in operation boxes may be of any form, provided they are given explicitly. In Figures 3.1 and 3.2 the following statements are used:

$$\text{`}D \leftarrow b^2 - 4ac\text{'}$$

$$\text{`}i \leftarrow i + 1\text{'}$$

The form of the statement is up to the programmer; any convenient and consistent notation is satisfactory.

Most operation boxes are used to contain the main operations in a problem, but they are also used for some indexing operations. Boxes 1, 3, and 4 in Figure 3.2 contain statements to set, increase, and test the index i, respectively.

The *decision box*, drawn variously in the literature as a hexagon, elongated oval, or a diamond, contains a question or a test, on which a decision is based. We will use an oval in this text; it is sometimes called a "mail slot". The box has two or more lines leaving it, one for each alternative path from the decision. Box 1 in Figure 3.1 and box 4 in Figure 3.2 are decision boxes containing the statements

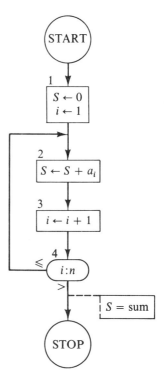

Fig. 3.2   Flowchart of summation problem.

$$\text{``Is } a \text{ equal to zero?''}$$

$$\text{``Compare } i \text{ to } n.\text{''}$$

Depending on the decision, the next operation either tests b or evaluates D (first case) or returns to step 2 or stops (second case). A statement of the type

$$\text{``Test } y\text{''}$$

may have several outcomes, depending upon the problem's structure. For example, it may be necessary to do one of four things, depending on the value of y:

If $y \leqslant 4$, take action R1;
If $5 \leqslant y \leqslant 20$, take action R2;
If $21 \leqslant y \leqslant 40$, take action R3;
If $41 \leqslant y$, take action R4.

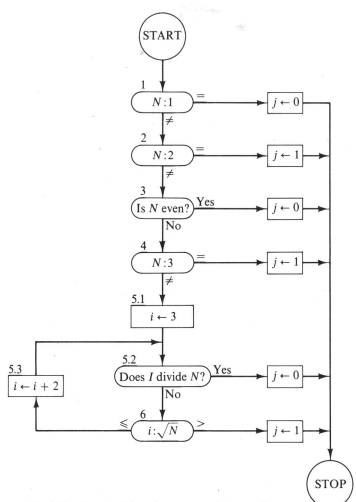

Fig. 3.3   Flowchart for prime-number determination.

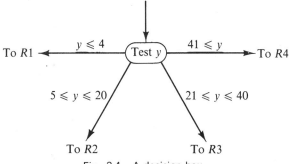

Fig. 3.4   A decision box.

The associated decision box appears in Figure 3.4. To identify the conditions under which each path is taken, these conditions should be placed next to these lines.

The *information box*, drawn as a rectangle with one side dashed, contains information not used in the calculations but which aids in understanding the flowchart. In Figure 3.1, the box containing the statement "trivial case" is one such box. It is connected to whatever arrow is appropriate, by a dashed line. Additionally, information boxes may be used to state the conditions under which control reaches a given point in the program.

The *terminal box*, drawn as a circle, contains either the word START or the word STOP (or equivalent words). These boxes indicate the starting and stopping places of the procedure. Terminal boxes appear in Figures 3.1 and 3.2.

Remote connectors, drawn as smaller circles, are used in a flowchart to avoid the use of lines that would cross the diagram and clutter the page. Two remote connectors that are labeled alike can be considered joined, that is, be the same point.

Consider the problem analyzed earlier, the multiplication of every third number in a list, starting with the 34th and ending with the 64th. Assume that the multiplied numbers are to be sorted in two lists, being placed in turn in list 1, list 2, list 1, etc. A flowchart for this problem appears in Figure 3.5. In that diagram, the circles labeled α are to be joined; after the decision box, one path returns to box 3. These are *fixed connectors*. The circle labeled β_k represents a *variable connector*; it is joined to β_1 or β_2, depending on the current value assigned to k. This value is originally set equal to 1 (in box 2) and is then changed successively to 2, 1, 2, ... by the boxes 5a and 5b. The last value determines the path taken at the β_k connector. In this way the numbers are sorted into two lists. Note that the α-connectors serve to avoid long lines, while the β-connectors do more: without them there would be no convenient way to illustrate the switching of paths.

Computer Flowcharts

In the same manner in which we considered the effect of computers on analyses (in Section 2.2), we shall consider the effect of computers on flowcharts. That is, we shall see how flowcharts should be modified when the characteristics of computers are taken into account.

Since input–output operations should be included in flowcharts, boxes are needed for them. The *input box* is sometimes drawn in the shape of a punched card, since most input is supplied in this manner. The variables for which values are read are listed in the box, as in Figure 3.6, where values for X, Y, and a list a_i, $i = 1, 2, \ldots, n$ are read.

The *output box* is sometimes drawn as in Figure 3.7, which represents a piece of paper quickly torn off a computer printer. As with the input box, the variables to be printed are listed in the box. If a sentence, or part of one, is to be printed, it is written within quotation marks as an item in the list of variables, as

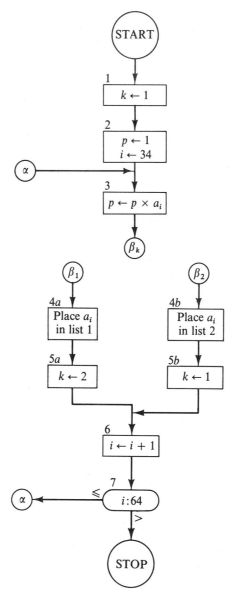

Fig. 3.5   Flowchart of multiplication and sorting.

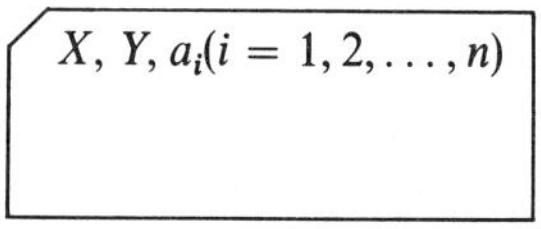

$$X, Y, a_i(i = 1, 2, \ldots, n)$$

Fig. 3.6   An input box.

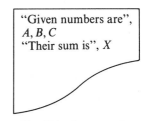

"Given numbers are",
A, B, C
"Their sum is", X

Fig. 3.7   An output box.

in Figure 3.7. If, for example, we assume values for A, B, and C, and their sum is X, the printed lines might appear as follows:

> GIVEN NUMBERS ARE 509 378 222
>
> THEIR SUM IS 1109

The algorithm given in Section 2.2 that included reading and printing would be flowcharted as in Figure 3.8, numbered to correspond with that procedure. The outer loop, which returns the procedure to step 1, is shown. The input box is shown with two arrows leaving it, implying the decision of whether any more cards remain.

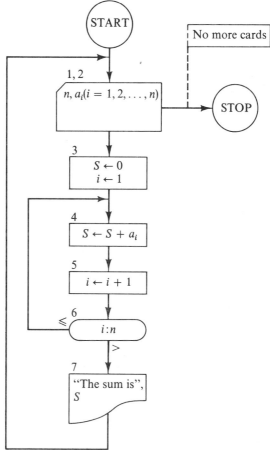

Fig. 3.8   A more complete flow-chart of summation problem.

EXERCISES

1. What is the advantage in using specific flowchart conventions, such as those used in this section?

2. What features of flowcharts have not been given specifically by convention?

3. Modify Figure 3.1 to indicate the variables read and the various results printed. Supply output boxes for each exit from the procedure. There are five, identified by information boxes. Supply printed text to identify the type of result.

*   *   *   *   *   *

4. What is the value of S at the STOP box in these flowcharts?

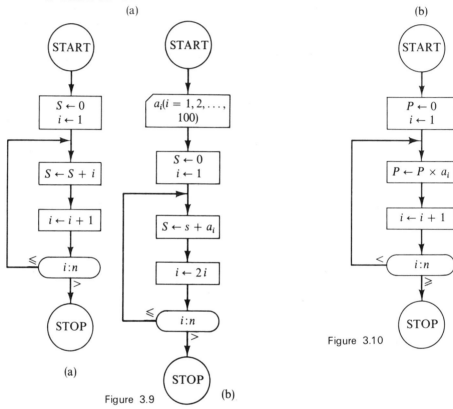

Figure 3.9

Figure 3.10

*   *   *   *   *   *

5. It was stated that flowcharts vary widely in their degree of detail. Yet it is also true that a given flowchart is equally detailed throughout. Why?

6. A correctly drawn flowchart has certain features regardless of the problem it represents. What are they?

7. Draw flowcharts for the algorithms developed in these exercises in Section 2.1: Exercises 1, 4, and 8.

8. Correct the errors in these flowcharts.
   (a) Compute the product of the a_i (see Figure 3.11).
   (b) Determine if any two successive numbers in the set a_i are equal (see Figure 3.12):

9. In addition to those computer features introduced, what others might be included into flowcharting to reflect computer characteristics? Consider features of importance to the analysis.

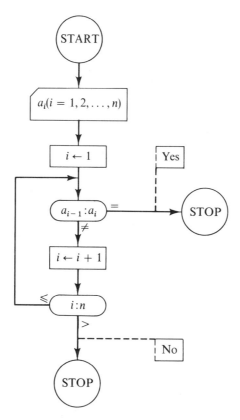

Figure 3.11

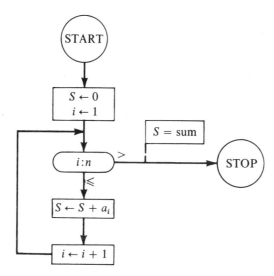

Figuro 3.12

3.2 LOOPS

Types of Loops

Within a loop some means for its termination must be present. Once each loop cycle some form of this question must be asked: "Should computation within the loop be stopped?" The flowcharts with loops already studied have such tests.

Loops may be classified according to the manner in which their cycling is stopped. At least these five types can be listed:

1. Loops having a number of cycles implied by the statement of the problem. (The flowchart in Figure 3.5 is an example, for it is known that exactly 11 loop cycles will occur.)
2. Loops having a number of cycles that is a variable, supplied as part of the data. (The summation of n numbers, where n is given with the data, flowcharted in Figure 3.2, is an example.)
3. Loops having a number of cycles determined during problem execution. (An example is offered by this problem: Given 100 numbers, determine the sum of the positive numbers. The number of positive numbers is determined during the run.)
4. Loops that terminate when a searching or other operation proves successful. (An example is the following: Given a list of 100 numbers, identified as a_i, $i = 1, 2, \ldots, 100$, locate the number x in the list, if it is present. Upon a match, when $x = a_i$ for some i, the loop terminates.)
5. Loops that terminate when a quantity achieves a certain value or other characteristic. (The iterative problem, where the square root is determined, is an example. The loop terminates when the difference between the square of the current guess and A is less than ε.)

The Iteration Box

A number of examples of loops have been studied. In nearly all cases, the termination test has been placed in the loop so that it occurs *after* the computation. We are safe in doing this unless the possibility exists that the number of loop cycles may be zero. In many real problems, this possibility *does* exist and we must be on the alert for it. Figure 3.2, the flowchart for the summation problem, could be revised so that it appears as in Figure 3.13. The test "compare i to n" occurs immediately after initialization, where i is set to 1. Then, if $n = 0$, the test immediately terminates the loop before any summation can occur. In the older version, Figure 3.2, at least *one* loop cycle will always be executed.

An alternate way around the difficulty is simply to add another box before the loop, that states "is $n = 0$?" and sends control to STOP if the answer is "yes".

The several indexing operations in many of the flowcharts in this chapter may be grouped together. These operations are initialization, modification, and

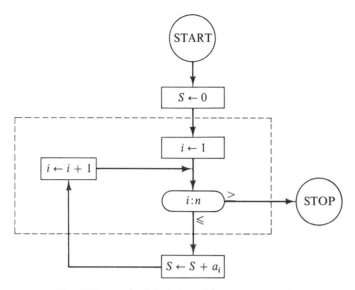

Fig. 3.13   Revised flowchart of summation problem.

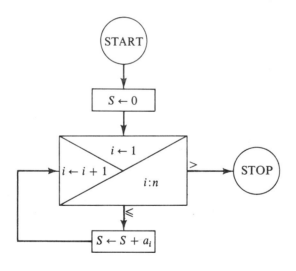

Fig. 3.14   Revised flowchart, grouping index operations.

testing of the index. Thus, we can redraw Figure 3.13 as in Figure 3.14. The large dotted box contains the three index operations. Next, these three can be drawn as a single *iteration box*, as in Figure 3.15.*

---

* The *iteration box* is given, in another form, in "The Language of Computers", B. A. Galler, McGraw-Hill Book Company, 1962.

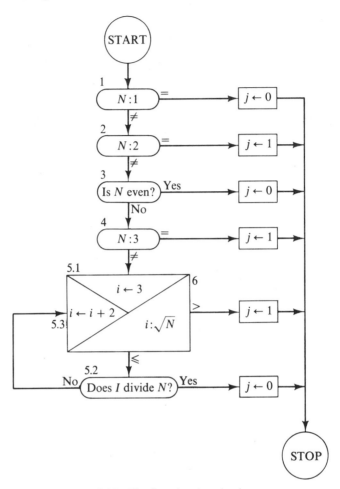

Fig. 3.15   The flowchart iteration box.

An iteration box cannot be used in all flowchart loops. As we have seen, not all loops terminate when the value of the index reaches a particular value. However, when this is true, and when an index is initialized and incremented regularly by an integer (which need not remain fixed throughout the computation), this device is useful.

The flowchart in Figure 3.3, determination of whether a number is prime, is revised in Figure 3.16, where an iteration box is used. The same box numbering of Figure 3.3 is used. Now the termination test occurs before the division test (lowest box) rather than after, as previously. This change, however, does not lead to error. Rather it saves one division because the division test need not occur if i exceeds $\sqrt{N}$.

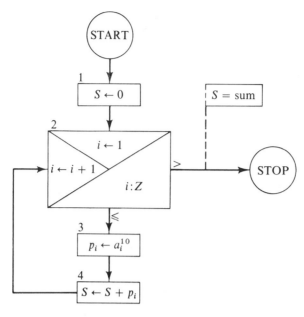

Fig. 3.16   Revised flowchart for prime numbers.

Nested Loops

In many problems one loop is *nested* within another one. This occurs when a loop contains a box with a repetitious process that itself can be drawn as a loop.

Consider the following problem, which can be flowcharted with two nested loops. Given Z numbers, find the sum of the tenth powers of the numbers. This problem is flowcharted in Figure 3.17, with the computation of p_i, the tenth power of a_i, placed in a single box. This computation is repetitious and can be set up as a loop itself, as shown in Figure 3.18, as an inner nested loop. Box 3 in Figure 3.13 has been expanded into boxes 3.1, 3.2, and 3.3 of Figure 3.14.*

Note that the inner and outer loops have the same structure. It is necessary to use a different index (j) for the inner loop, which must be initialized once each outer-loop cycle. Thus the index j cycles from 1 to 10 between each unit increase of the index i, just as the digit position in a car odometer cycles through ten digits between changes in the tens' digit.

Some flowcharts contain three or more nested loops. The flowchart techniques just explained can be extended to these cases. Generally one index per nested loop is necessary.

---

* In general, computation of powers by this repetitious approach is unsatisfactory. The value of x^{10}, e.g., can be computed in four multiplications, if x^2, x^4, and x^8 are initially computed, in that order.

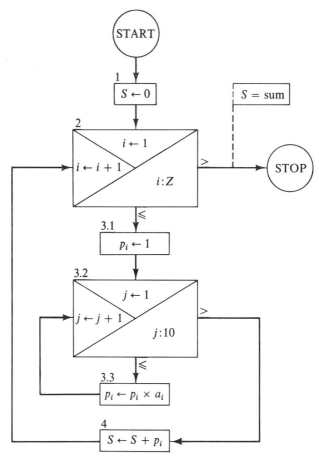

Fig. 3.17 First flowchart of nested-loop problem.

EXERCISES

1. Give other examples of each of the five loop types.

2. Which loop types would be present in the flowcharts for these problems:
   (a) 100 numbers are given; determine which exceed 500.
   (b) 100 numbers are given; compute the average in succession of the first two numbers, of the first three numbers, etc., until the average first exceeds 100.
   (c) n numbers are given; determine their product.
   (d) Compute the factorial of a given number.
   (e) 100 numbers are given; determine if three in a row are all positive.

3. Give the general form of an iteration box, including the nature of each of the entries.

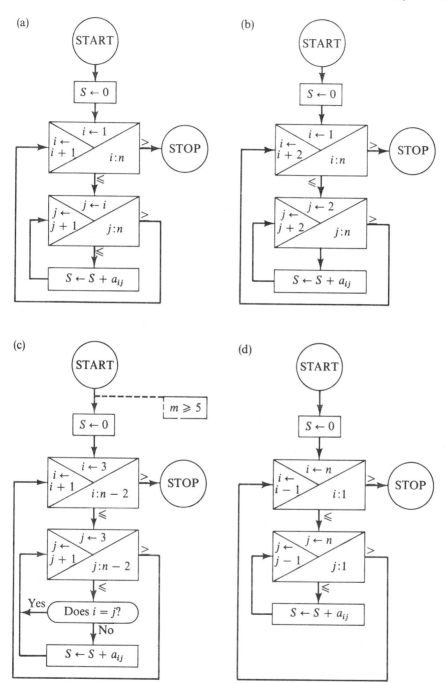

Fig. 3.18   Second flowchart of nested-loop problem.

4. If a procedure has nested loops, with indices i, j, and k, and numbers of loop cycles equal to m, n, and p, respectively, how many times will the innermost loop cycle in all? the next-to-innermost loop cycle?

* * * * * *

5. Given an ordered list of numbers, $a_1, a_2, \ldots a_i, \ldots a_{100}$, such that $a_i < a_{i+1}$ for all i, and a number b, find the value of i such that a_i has the closest value to b among the 100 numbers.

6. Given a rectangle in a plane, with sides parallel to the axes, specified by its lower-left corner (x_0, y_0), its width (w), and its height (h), determine which of 500 given points (x, y) lie within it, on its border, and outside it.

7. Given two matrices A of order $m \times n$ and B of order $n \times p$, calculate their sum C and product D:

$$c_{ij} = a_{ij} + b_{ij}, \qquad d_{ij} = \sum_k a_{ik} b_{kj}$$

8. In which problems given in the text (or other problems) can an iteration box not be used?

9. An array of elements a_{ij}, $i = 1, 2, \ldots, n$, $j = 1, 2, \ldots, n$, from a matrix is processed. In each of the following flowcharts, indicate what sum is computed.

4 ELEMENTS OF PROGRAMMING

This chapter introduces the basic concepts involved in programming a computer, by reference to (1) statements within a programming language and (2) information as stored and processed within a computer. We accomplish this study by examination of a specific language, FORTRAN IV, which is one of a series of languages (FORTRAN) in very wide use. While we cannot learn all there is to know about programming by the study of but one language, its study nonetheless provides us with exposure to a wide range of programming techniques. In this chapter, we briefly examine the language and develop a basis for its further study and its use in solving problems in many areas of application.

4.1 ALGORITHMIC LANGUAGES[1]

Nature of the Languages

FORTRAN is an *algorithmic* language. Such languages are perhaps misnamed, for all programming languages can be used to write algorithms. What the term really means is that when algorithms are written out, their steps can readily be translated into statements in these languages. This is true because algorithmic-language statements are very much like mathematical statements. Other terms frequently used to characterize these languages are *problem-oriented*, *procedural*, and *higher-level*. All are descriptive of the languages.

Most algorithmic languages were developed primarily for problems where formula evaluation is the prime task. Language statements were developed to resemble such formulas very closely. These are called *arithmetic* or *assignment* statements, for they assign values to variables. Other types of statements, less problem-oriented, are also required, as for input–output, data-moving, and decision operations. Still others are required for certain descriptions of data. We shall study each of these statement types.

Algorithmic languages have at least two important characteristics: (1) They are "natural" to a particular problem class or classes. The statements are close to the statements we would want to write in procedures. Mathematical notation has long been used to describe ways of solving problems. Algorithmic languages make use of this notation and thus have a natural appearance. (2) They are "formal", which means that statements obey rules of syntax. This is necessary because a computer translator must translate statements into machine language. When these rules are disobeyed, translation may be impossible. The syntax rules may be simple or complex, but they must be present.

Program Statements

What is the nature of a programming statement? It is difficult to answer this question in general, but we can say that statements are the basic operational units of a program. They can be likened to sentences, which are the units in a natural language (such as English). Statements may be short and include one operation and one operand, such as in the GAMMA 70 language. This is similar to writing, "Face the house. Turn right. Walk ten steps. Turn left. Walk 25 steps. Stop." On the other hand, statements may be long and imply a number of operations, translatable perhaps into a dozen machine instructions. This is similar to writing, "Walk to the back of the house." The intent is the same as before, but the statement is more concise. The latter statement is comparable to an algorithmic language statement. The former statement is comparable to a machine language instruction. A *compiler* translates algorithmic language programs into machine language.

In the problem analyses in Chapter 2, it was necessary at times to refer to specific steps within an algorithm. If, e.g., we are through with step 6 in a process, we may want to return to step 2. Thus we say, "If . . . , go to step 2." In the same manner, program statements must have names or *labels* if we wish to refer to them within the program.

The concept of the *flow of control* through a program is vital to a language. It is usually implied, in the absence of statements to the contrary, that control passes from one statement to the next in sequence (the one written below it). That is, statements are executed in sequence as written. If this sequence is to be changed, statements to the contrary (such as " . . . go to step 2") must be present. If this occurs, a *transfer of control* is said to take place.

Another trait common to programming languages is the distinction usually made between what might be called *declarations* and *commands*. A declaration is a statement that is not executed, i.e., is not translated into machine code. Rather it is a statement about the nature of the variables (whether they are real, complex, etc., how many subscripts they have, and so on), about the setting aside of space needed for data, about the nature of the data to be read, etc. In other words, a declaration describes the structure of the program and its variables. A command is a statement that is executed, one that performs an operation upon data or transfers control within the program.

Language Versatility

Although algorithmic languages were originally developed for numerical problem-solving, they have proven to be more versatile than that. They can be used in problem areas where data are not numbers and where operations are not arithmetic. This point is well illustrated in the text by examples. When FORTRAN, for example, proved deficient several years ago, it was extended in certain directions to encompass broader statement types. Further, it has been used in a wide variety of ways in different kinds of problems, as we shall see.

EXERCISES

1. Identify each statement below as one of these types: declaration, arithmetic, input–output, or decision:
   (a) Read a, b, c.
   (b) If $i \leqslant n$, go to step 6.
   (c) $D \leftarrow \sqrt{b^2 - 4ac}$.
   (d) X is a complex number.
   (e) $i \leftarrow i + 1$.
   (f) Write "The sum is", S.
   (g) There are 100 numbers in the set a_i.

2. What is a data-moving statement?

* * * * * *

3. Why are algorithmic languages also called "problem-oriented"? "procedural"? "higher-level"?

4. Translate these statements into a series of "basic" statements, in the manner of a compiler (decide what "basic" ought to mean in each case):
   (a) Drive to my house, three blocks away.
   (b) Find the first page of the book that contains the word "algorithm".
   (c) Determine R. C. Jones' telephone number, given the phone book.

* * * * * *

5. It is stated that FORTRAN has been used in a wide variety of ways in different kinds of problems. What are some kinds of operations, besides evaluating formulas, that we might wish to perform in solving problems? (Consider some of the problems studied in this book and others mentioned in passing.)

6. Consider the process of compiling a program, translating it into machine-language instructions. What are some of the problems that we would have to be concerned with in developing a compiler?

4.2 FORTRAN[2]

FORTRAN is the oldest and most widely used algorithmic programming language. It was developed in 1956 to serve as an aid in writing problems largely involving the evaluation of formulas. It has been very successful in this and, after several improvements, has evolved into FORTRAN IV, described here. The language is introduced by illustration. Three problems are coded in FORTRAN and a detailed study is made of every part of the programs.

First Example

The first problem to be solved is this: Compute the volumes of a number of cylinders, given data on the radius and height of each cylinder. The analysis is simple: If the radius is r and the height is h, the volume is given by

$$V \leftarrow \pi r^2 h$$

The FORTRAN program (let us call it CYLVØL) is the following:

```
 8   READ (5,10) RADIUS, HEIGHT
     VØLUME = 3.1416 * RADIUS**2 * HEIGHT
     WRITE (6,11) RADIUS, HEIGHT, VØLUME
     GØ TØ 8
10   FØRMAT (2F10.2)
11   FØRMAT (10HØRADIUS = F6.2, 13H    HEIGHT = F6.2,
     1 13H    VØLUME = F11.2)
     END
```

This program reads a card containing the radius and height for one cylinder, computes the volume, and prints the radius, height, and volume in this format:

```
RADIUS =    12.32   HEIGHT =    61.07   VØLUME =    29120.59
```

This process repeats until no data cards remain.

Let us study each statement in this program.

1. 8   READ (5,10) RADIUS, HEIGHT
   (a) '8' at the left is a label for this statement. The label is needed because reference is made to this statement by the fourth statement (see below), whence control passes to statement 8.
   (b) 'READ' identifies the type of statement. This is a command to read one card and place its contents into memory.
   (c) '(5,10)' provides two items of information. The '5' refers to the medium from which data are read. In this case, we mean punched

cards. The '10' is a reference to a statement describing the format of the data card. We shall study that statement below.

(d) 'RADIUS, HEIGHT' is a list of the variables in this program which are to be given the values on the card. The first value is assigned to RADIUS and the second is assigned to HEIGHT.

2. VØLUME = 3.1416 * RADIUS**2 * HEIGHT

This is a formula to be evaluated; given the radius and height, the volume is to be computed. This is an *arithmetic assignment* statement. The '*' represents multiplication; the '**' represents exponentiation. A constant is required, having the value 3.1416, which is π. The '=' represents the assignment process and is equivalent to the left arrow used earlier. VØLUME is to be assigned the value computed by multiplying 3.1416 by the square of the value of RADIUS by the value of HEIGHT. (The slash in the 'Ø' distinguishes it from zero.)

3. WRITE (6,11) RADIUS, HEIGHT, VØLUME

(a) 'WRITE' identifies this statement as a command to write one line.

(b) '(6,11)' indicates, by the '6', that the output is to be printed and, by the '11', that a statement with that label describes the format of the line printed.

(c) 'RADIUS, HEIGHT, VOLUME' is a list of the variables in this program whose values are to be printed.

4. GØ TØ 8

This is a command to transfer control to the statement with label '8', that is, the first statement. This return to an earlier statement forms a loop so that calculations can be repeated. Since the first statement involves a READ statement, the loop is repeated with new data, i.e., new values for RADIUS and HEIGHT. Loop termination occurs when no more data are present; then the READ statement "fails", i.e., the program stops.

5. 10 FØRMAT (2F10.2)

(a) '10' is the label, referred to by the READ statement. This statement applies to that READ statement and describes its data.

(b) 'FØRMAT' identifies the type of statement, which is a declaration.

(c) '(2F10.2)' describes the format of the data. The 'F' states that the items are *floating-point* numbers, i.e., a number written with a decimal point. (Floating-point numbers are discussed in detail later.) The '10' indicates that 10 columns on the card are allotted for each number. The '.2' indicates that the data have two decimal places to the right of the decimal point. The '2' to the left of the 'F' states that the format *specification* 'F10.2' is to be applied twice in succession, i.e., to each of the two items. In summary, each data card has this appearance:

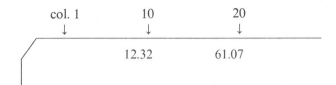

In other words, columns 1–10 contain the value of RADIUS, and columns 11–20 contain the value of HEIGHT.

6.`11   FØRMAT (10H0RADIUS = F6.2, 13H   HEIGHT = F6.2
    1   13H   VØLUME = F11.2)

(a) '11' is the label, referred to by the WRITE statement.

(b) 'F6.2' (in two places) describes the format for printing the values of RADIUS and HEIGHT, listed in the WRITE statement. This specification states that each of these values will be allotted six print spaces on a line, with two digits to the right of the decimal point, as shown earlier on the sample printed line.

(c) 'F11.2' has a similar meaning. Since it is the third specification given, it applies to the third variable listed in the WRITE statement (VØLUME). Because the result will be a larger number than the input values, 11 print positions are allowed. Note that the 'F6.2' and 'F11.2' specifications impose a limit on the size of the numbers that can be printed, namely 999.99 and 99999999.99.

(d) '13H   HEIGHT = ', a string of characters that includes several blanks, represents information that is to be printed exactly as shown. This is known as *literal* information. The 'H' in this string indicates that fact, and the '13' states that 13 characters are to be printed (four blanks, the word 'HEIGHT', a blank, an equals sign, and another blank). Because of its position in the FØRMAT statement, this string is to be printed between the values of the variables RADIUS and HEIGHT, as shown in the sample printed line given before. Note that the included blank spaces are used for clarity in reading the printed output.

(e) '13H   VØLUME = ' has a similar meaning.

(f) '10H0RADIUS = ' also has a similar meaning but includes an extra character, '0', following '10H'. This is a signal to the printing device that the line is to be printed after skipping one line. The result, if several lines are printed, is double spacing. The '0' is not printed; it is an example of *carriage control.*

(g) The '1' which begins the second line of this statement indicates that the line is part of the statement just before it. The second card is a *continuation card.*

7. <u>END</u>

      The statement, required in all FORTRAN programs, indicates the end of the deck.

      Little need be said on the structure of this program, CYLVØL, because it follows readily from a description of the procedure: read RADIUS and HEIGHT, compute VØLUME, print all three variables, and return to repeat the process. Planning is needed in deciding how the data are to be punched and how the printed line is to appear. FØRMAT statement 11 must be carefully prepared in order that all spacing and text information appear as planned. When algorithms and flowcharts were developed in Chapters 2 and 3, no attention was paid to card and printer formats, but in coding, these details become very important.

      At the end of Section 3.1, in Figure 3.8, there are two features that show up in this program. First, at the read operation one arrow indicates a reading failure due to the absence of further cards. This situation occurs in the program. Second, in the output box (box 7) some words are listed as part of the material printed. In the program here, the literal information in the FØRMAT statement 11 corresponds to those words in quotes.

      While CYLVØL is extremely simple, it is functionally complete. Indeed, if we wanted to compute the volume of 25,000 cylinders, we would find it very useful. The program contains statements for reading data, performing calculations, and printing results. It contains a loop for repeated calculations. Any other program we write will contain each of these aspects but will undoubtedly be a good deal more complex.

FORTRAN Cards

      A FORTRAN program is composed of a sequence of statements, generally punched one to a card, in an 80-column format. Statement labels are integers, from 1 through 99999, placed anywhere in columns 1–5. Column 6 of the first card of a statement must be blank or contain '0'. If a statement takes more than one card, part of it may be placed on one or more successive cards, called *continuation cards*. All continuation cards must contain a nonzero character in column 6; usually the sequence '1', '2', ..., is used in that order. The statements themselves appear in columns 7 through 72. Blanks within statements are ignored by the compiler, except when they occur in literal character strings (as in FØRMAT statements). Blanks may be used to improve readability. They are frequently used, e.g., within arithmetic expressions and in input–output variable lists, as shown in this chapter.

Second Example

      We turn next to the problem of determining whether a given number is prime, last flowcharted in Figure 3.12. Statements in the following program,

PRIME, are labeled to match the boxes in that figure; the box numbers are multiplied by 10 throughout to convert them to labels

```
C     PRIME
C     THIS PRØGRAM DETERMINES WHETHER A GIVEN NUMBER
C     IS PRIME N
C     READ (5,101) N
C     CHECK TØ SEE IF N IS ØNE.
   10 IF (N .EQ. 1) GØ TØ 90
C     CHECK TØ SEE IF N IS TWØ.
   20 IF (N .EQ. 2) GØ TØ 91
C     CHECK FØR N EVEN.
   30 IF (2 * N/2 .EQ. N) GØ TØ 90
C     CHECK TØ SEE IF N IS THREE.
   40 IF (N .EQ. 3) GØ TØ 91
C     SET I TØ 3.
   51 I = 3
C     CHECK FØR FINAL TEST ØF I.
   60 IF (I − SQRT(N)) 52, 52, 91
C     DØES I DIVIDE N.
   52 IF (I * N/I .EQ. I) GØ TØ 90
C     ADD 2 TØ I.
   53 I = I + 2
      GØ TØ 60
C     HERE IF NUMBER IS NØT PRIME.
   90 J = 0
      WRITE (6,200) N
      STØP
C     HERE IF NUMBER IS PRIME.
   91 J = 1
      WRITE (6,201) N
      STØP
  101 FØRMAT (I5)
  200 FØRMAT (1H0 I5 23H IS NØT A PRIME NUMBER.)
  201 FØRMAT (1H0 I5 19H IS A PRIME NUMBER.)
      END
```

This program might print these results, if given a series of integers as data:

```
  6 IS NØT A PRIME NUMBER.
101 IS A PRIME NUMBER.
  1 IS NØT A PRIME NUMBER.
 79 IS A PRIME NUMBER.
```

Once again, we study the program, examining particularly those statements that introduce new concepts.

1. C   THIS PRØGRAM DETERMINES WHETHER A GIVEN NUMBER

    This is a comment, so identified by 'C' in column 1. Comment cards
    are printed by the compiler but are not processed. Comments
    should be used generously throughout a deck for documentation
    purposes.

2. 10   IF (N .EQ. 1) GØ TØ 90

    This is a *logical IF statement*. It states that, if the value of N is equal
    to 1, control passes next to statement 90. (Statement 90 corresponds
    to the case where J is set to zero.)

3. 30   IF (2 * N/2 .EQ. N) GØ TØ 90

    This logical IF statement states that, if N is even, control passes to
    statement 90. The peculiar expression '$2*N/2$' uses the property
    of integer division that the quotient is an integer and the remainder is
    lost. If several values of N are substituted in this expression and
    integer division is used, we see that the expression equals N only if
    N is even.

4. 60   (I − SQRT(N)) 52, 52, 91

    (a) The expression 'SQRT(N)' means the square root of N. SQRT is a
    "built-in" operation and the programmer may use it as shown. Its
    value here is $\sqrt{N}$.
    (b) This is an *arithmetic IF statement*. It states that, if the expression
    in parentheses is negative, zero, or positive, then control passes to
    statement 52, 52, or 91, respectively. In other words,

    $$\text{if } I \leqslant \sqrt{N}, \text{ control passes to statement 52;}$$

    $$\text{if } I > \sqrt{N}, \text{ control passes to statement 91.}$$

5. STØP

    This statement directs the computer to stop execution and not to go
    on to the next statement.

6. 101 FØRMAT (I5)

    The 'I' in this statement indicates that the data being read are integers,
    each occupying five columns on a card.

We should make some further remarks about the program. First, note that
all the cases in the flowchart (Figure 3.15) where J is set to zero or one are grouped
into two statements, numbers 90 and 91, respectively. This saves some coding,
though the program does not then run faster. Second, greater efficiency would
result if the SQRT operation were not present in the loop; refer to Figure 3.12 to

see this. The square-root operation takes relatively long to perform; as the program is written it would be computed once for each comparison of I with $\sqrt{N}$. A "dummy variable", say NRØØT, should be computed at the start and this value used in statement 60. Here, the suggestion requires more coding but uses less execution time.

Once again, the program follows directly from the flowchart, for that diagram is fully detailed. It is just a matter of converting the decision boxes to IF statements and the formulas to arithmetic statements. Again, some planning is required in development of the formats and associated statements.

Third Example

A college must keep records on its students. Among these records are student grades that must be averaged, say once a term or possibly at any given time. It is desired that a cumulative average of all grades received to date be computed. We shall assume that grades are punched eight to a card, with three columns allotted for each grade. Since grades have a maximum value of 100, this suffices. A single extra card precedes the grades, containing an integer in columns 1 to 3, the number of grades to be processed. The summation process in this program is the one analyzed and flowcharted earlier. This program is STREC1 (first version of student-record system).

```
      C    STREC1
      C    THIS PRØGRAM CØMPUTES THE AVERAGE ØF A NUMBER
      C    ØF GRADES, AND PRINTS THE AVERAGE. ALL GRADES
      C    ARE FIRST PRINTED.
             INTEGER GRADES, SUM, AVER, NUMBER
             DIMENSIØN GRADES(80)
             WRITE (6,49)
             READ (5,50) NUMBER
             READ (5,50) (GRADES(I), I = 1, NUMBER)
             WRITE (6,51) (GRADES(L), L = 1, NUMBER)
             SUM = 0
             DØ 35 J = 1, NUMBER
         35  SUM = SUM + GRADES(J)
             AVER = SUM / NUMBER
             WRITE (6,60) AVER
             STØP
         49  FØRMAT (15H1THE GRADES ARE)
         50  FØRMAT (8I3)
         51  FØRMAT (8I5)
         60  FØRMAT (16H0THE AVERAGE IS I5)
             END
```

If there are 35 grades, the output may look as follows:

```
THE GRADES ARE
   83   84   90   99   96   88   87   90
  100   97   95   88   86   97   80   75
   88   89   95   98   96   93   97   90
   80   75   85   95   99   88   89   93
   86   89   99
THE AVERAGE IS   90
```

Before we analyze this program, some comments should be made about its structure. First, the number of grades NUMBER is read in. Then the grades are read. Enough cards are read to provide the proper number of grades. When all grades are read, their sum is computed and the average is taken and finally printed.

1. INTEGER GRADES, SUM, AVER, NUMBER

   This statement declares that the listed variables are integer variables, that the quantities stored as those variables are integers. In the absence of declarations to the contrary, FORTRAN considers variables whose names begin with the letters I, J, K, L, M, and N, to be integer variables. Others are assumed to be floating-point numbers, described in the next section. To vary this notation, one must use a *type statement*, of which the one above is an example.

2. DIMENSIØN GRADES(80)

   The expression 'GRADES(80)' indicates that GRADES is the name of a subscripted (indexed) variable set of size 80; this set is termed an *array*. (Eighty words in memory are set aside for up to 80 values.) All subscripted variables in a program must be declared to be dimensioned.

3. WRITE (6,49)

   This WRITE statement does not include a variable list, hence no variable values are printed. It merely states that the format 49 should be used, i.e., that the 15 characters there should be printed.

4. READ (5,50) (GRADES(I), I = 1, NUMBER)

   (a) The expression 'GRADES(I)' indicates the subscripted variable GRADES, having the subscript or index 'I'. As in mathematics, the expression is a general one, referring to the Ith member or word in the array GRADES.

   (b) The expression 'I = 1, NUMBER' means that the index I is to take on the sequence of values from 1 through the value of NUMBER, all integer values considered. Thus, the entire sequence inside the second parentheses states that values are to be assigned to a sequence of GRADES entries.

5. DØ 35 J = 1, NUMBER

(a) 'DØ' identifies this as a looping and indexing statement. A sequence of statements, called the *range*, is identified as those belonging to this loop. The range here comprises all statements following the DØ through statement 35. The range is thus two statements long.

(b) The loop defined by the statement has one index associated with it, J, given in the statement. The significance of the DØ statement is that all statements in the range are to be executed repeatedly, once for each implied value of J. These values are given by the expression 'J = 1, NUMBER' as in the READ statement above. If NUMBER has the value 35, e.g., the loop will be executed 35 times, which here computes the sum of the 35 grades.

6. 49   FØRMAT (15H1THE GRADES ARE)

(a) The '1' following the first 'H' is the carriage control character; it indicates that the material is to be printed as the first line on a new page.

(b) This statement includes no specifications for the format of a variable, since, as we noted, the WRITE statement referring to it has no listed variables.

7. 50   FØRMAT (8I3)

Since this format specification calls for eight integers, each occupying three columns on a card, the data must be so punched. In general, however, we have more than eight grades; our dimensioning on GRADES allows up to 80 grades to be processed. The number of grades actually to be processed is given by NUMBER, read in before the grades are read. The second READ statement calls for 35 grades, e.g., if NUMBER is 35. What happens is that the format specification here is used and reused until the 35 grades are read, i.e., five cards will be read, eight grades taken from each of the first four and three grades taken from the fifth. In other words, the FØRMAT statement describes the data format on *one* card, while the READ statement states the number of values to be read.

8. 51   FØRMAT (8I5)

This statement has the same significance as the last one above, except that it applies to writing. Eight grades will be written per printed line, as in the sample output given earlier.

Nature of FORTRAN

This chapter began with an introduction to the "nature of algorithmic languages". At this point, the reader is advised to reread Section 4.1 with these examples in mind. In particular, it should be clear that FORTRAN is both "natural" and "formal". The statements in these examples are close to the mathematical statements we would write in their procedures. (One notable exception to this is the statement that determines whether a number N is even. Here we take advantage of the way in which integer division works.) The formality of FORTRAN is partially embodied in the descriptions of the several types of statements encountered. The rules described cannot be disobeyed, or else the compiler would have trouble translating, if it could do this at all.

EXERCISES

FORTRAN was introduced in this section; many of its features were illustrated by example. These features are best learned, however, by doing, and these examples incorporate all of them. By writing programs for each of the problems below, the student will use each of the features and learn them. These programs should be run on the computer; in that way the planning, writing, and testing of programs will all be experienced.

The methods of analysis and flowcharting covered in Chapters 2 and 3 should also be utilized in this programming effort.

1. Compute the areas of a series of triangles, given the base and height of each on one card. Print the results.

2. Read 10 numbers from a card, and print the largest number.

3. Determine the square root of the sum of five given floating-point numbers, and print the answer. If the sum is negative, however, print an appropriate comment.

4. Create a printed table of squares, cubes, square roots, and factorials of the integers from 1 through 10.

5. Given, on each of two cards, the values of m and b in two linear equations of the form $y = mx + b$, solve the pair of equations for x and y.

         *   *   *   *   *   *   *

6. Given an integer in base ten, convert it to its equivalant in base eight. Do the reverse. Print both given and computed values, properly identified.

7. Given 200 integers, determine how many are less than zero, equal to zero, and greater than zero, printing these three counts.

8. Given 200 integers, determine how many values fall in each of these ranges: 0–9, 10–19, 20–29, ..., 90–99. Print the counts.

9. Given 200 integers, considered to form an ordered sequence as read, determine how many times a number is greater than both its predecessor and its successor. Print the count and each of these local maxima.

10. Given 200 integers, find the largest number, the smallest number, the sum of the numbers, and the average of the numbers. Examine the array of integers just once. Print the results with appropriate titling.

         *   *   *   *   *   *   *

11. Given a point (x, y), determine if (a) it lies above a given line ($y = mx + b$), (b) within a given circle (of radius R at x_0, y_0), inside a given triangle (vertices at

x_i, y_i, $i = 1, 2, 3$). In each case, the parameters defining the line, circle, or triangle are supplied with the point as data. Print appropriate results.

12. The price of an item and a certain amount of money to pay this price are given. Determine the change to be returned, if any, indicating precisely how many pennies, nickels, dimes, etc., are to be returned. The top price is $10.00.

4.3 INFORMATION IN COMPUTERS

Types of Data

Within a digital computer, it is possible to process data in different ways. The circuitry of the computer allows it to process integers and floating-point numbers differently, for example. Through an appropriate selection of instructions, we also may cause a program to process other classes of data. Among the several types of data of interest, all of which are described below, are these: integers, floating-point numbers written both with and without a power of ten, and strings of characters which may be letters, digits, or otherwise. Other types of data, used in particular problems, can be identified, but programming languages are generally limited to these.

Integers

Integers are whole numbers, written without decimal points. They may of course be given in any base, but most common in computing are those in bases two, eight, and ten, known as binary, octal, and decimal integers, respectively. Because of memory word limitations, integers are commonly limited in size to something like 10 or 12 digits.

Floating-Point Numbers

The range of numbers that can be stored in each memory word of a fixed-word-length computer is limited because the number of stored digits is limited. Consider a computer capable of storing signed 10-decimal-digit numbers, one to a word. (We use the decimal system for illustration because of its familiarity.) Although 10 significant digits can then be stored for each number, the implied accuracy is deceiving. In one problem, for example, the numbers 0.0000345, 67.8, and 7895671 may all be present. We may place the decimal point anywhere within a word, but regardless of its position, the three numbers cannot all be stored with full accuracy.

For correct processing, the decimal points must be in effect aligned, as in manual arithmetic:

$$0.0000345$$
$$67.8$$
$$7895671.$$

Fourteen places for decimal digits are required to hold all three numbers in the manner shown. This difficulty can be bypassed by scaling, however, by applying a scale factor, a power of 10, to each number:

$$0.0000000345 \times 10^3$$

$$0.0000000678 \times 10^9$$

$$0.0007895671 \times 10^{10}$$

In this form the decimal points are aligned, but 10 places are sufficient for all the numbers. It is necessary, however, to store the power of 10. (Since the base of the exponent is always 10, that information need not be stored.)

More commonly, numbers are stored in computers in normalized form, with fractions having a nonzero digit immediately to the right of the point:

$$0.3450000000 \times 10^{-4}$$

$$0.6780000000 \times 10^2$$

$$0.7895671000 \times 10^7$$

When arithmetic operations occur in computers, the results are usually normalized. This feature of automatically normalizing and keeping track of the powers of 10 is termed *floating-point operation*. The number stored by such operation is a *floating-point number*. In many programming languages, floating-point numbers are termed *real* numbers.

Complex Numbers

Numbers stored in computer memory are never intrinsically complex. If we have a problem involving complex numbers, we must store them as real number pairs, representing the real and imaginary parts of the complex numbers.* Generally, two adjacent words store these two parts as floating-point numbers. Computers do not operate upon complex numbers as though they were complex.

As an example of a complex operation, consider the multiplication of $a + bi$ and $c + di$:

$$(a + bi)(c + di) = ac - bd + (ad + bc)i$$

We must perform the complex multiplication by performing four separate real multiplications, two real additions, and a real subtraction. The two real numbers $ac - bd$ and $ad + bc$ are stored as the answer. Fortunately, some programming languages enable us to avoid these complications by allowing complex notation.

---

* The term "real", as used in this section, differs from its use earlier (floating-point).

Alphanumeric Information

In computer programming, there is a class of data having no counterpart in mathematics. Frequently, in computer processing, it is necessary for a program to check for a particular word. An example, the process of translating a FORTRAN program into machine instructions involves, among other things, seeking the end of the program. This requires a search for the word END. Therefore, that sequence of characters is needed as a "constant" in the translating program. Such a sequence of characters, which might include digits and arithmetic or punctuation symbols, is called an *alphanumeric string* or *Hollerith string*. When such a string is stored in a memory word, each character is encoded as a set of bits and can therefore be written as an octal integer. Six to eight bits are commonly used to encode each character.

The literal strings within format statements, discussed in Section 4.2, are in a sense alphanumeric constants, though they are not so identified. In future programs, we shall see better examples of such constants.

We will study alphanumeric strings at length in later chapters, but we can now describe some of the operations that are commonly performed on these strings. Alphanumeric strings are searched for the appearance of a given *substring* or part of a string. For example, if we are analyzing a FORTRAN statement so that it can be translated (into machine code), we may look for or identify a specific variable, say GRADES. In addition, substrings are often combined to form larger strings. We may count the number of appearances of a given character in a string, determine if a given character occurs before another, or may substitute one substring for another in a string.

Logical Quantities

The truth of the expression in a logical IF statement must be checked, so that the decision can be made. The value of such expressions is either "true" or "false". This concept applies to variables as well as expressions; any variable may be considered to be *logical* and thereby have values of truth or falsity.

EXERCISES

1. Give examples of problems in which each type of data described appears.

2. In what situations would integers be preferred to floating-point numbers? the reverse?

3. Why are floating-point numbers used in computers?

4. Given two complex numbers, $a + bi$ and $c + di$, write expressions for addition, subtraction, and division of these numbers, separating real and imaginary parts as in the text.

* * * * * *

5. Give other examples of alphanumeric strings as data. When would they be used?

6. Since we operate upon numeric quantities in a program, it seems reasonable to operate upon alphanumeric strings. Is this indeed reasonable? If so, what operations might be performed?

7. Consider a normalized floating-point number, such as this one:

$$0.8538672952 \times 10^{-2}$$

Not all of the information in this expression need be stored in memory as the number. What can be dispensed with? Devise a convenient, compact way to store floating-point numbers in memory words. Assume either a word with 32 bits or a word with 10 digits.

4.4 ELEMENTS OF ALGORITHMIC LANGUAGES

We have already studied several examples of FORTRAN coding in some detail, in a general manner. Now we study the language somewhat more formally, summarizing and extending the concepts learned to algorithmic languages in general. Much of the material in this section is true of all such languages, while some is peculiar to FORTRAN. Where no specific reference is made to FOR-TRAN, the concepts are widely applicable in programming.

Constants

Most programs require the use of constants, quantities whose values do not change during execution. For example, in the prime-number program in Section 4.2, the constants 1, 2, and 3 are required. The number 1 has been used elsewhere for index initialization.

We have encountered two types of constants in FORTRAN: integers and real constants. An integer consists of up to 11 digits written without a decimal point. If the integer is negative, a minus sign must appear. Examples of integers are:

$$0 \qquad -450 \qquad 567000000$$

A FORTRAN real constant is written either as (1) a sequence of up to nine decimal digits with a decimal point or (2) a sequence of up to nine digits with or without a decimal point followed by an integer (an exponent) written after E. The exponent is a power of 10 and may be negative. The absolute value of the exponent may be as great as 38 (or greater in some versions of FORTRAN). Examples of real numbers are:

$$35. \qquad .00378 \qquad .015E-2$$

The last of these numbers is 0.015×10^{-2}.

Another type of constant in FORTRAN is the alphanumeric or Hollerith constant, written in either of two forms:

$$wHxxx\ldots xxx \quad \text{or} \quad \text{'}xxx\ldots xxx\text{'}$$

where w is the number of characters (x's) in the constant. In the second form, which is available only on certain computers, the string of characters in the constant is delimited by quotes.

Variables

In mathematics, when we wish to refer to a number that may take on different values throughout a problem or when we do not know what value a number has, we assign it a name and call it a *variable*. The same thing is done in programming languages. Variables, referred to by name, may assume many values during the running of a program. Additionally, the variable name in a program is also the name of the location of the variable in memory or of the locations if the variable is an array.

In mathematics, we use a single letter to represent a variable; sometimes the letter is subscripted or superscripted. In computer languages, however, combinations of letters, digits, and other characters are used as variable names. The juxtaposition (concatenation) of two letters usually forms the name of a new variable, as in ab. The variable ba is a different variable. Very commonly, letter combinations that form words or near-words are used because of their mnemonic content. Examples are SUM, RESULT, and GRADES.

It is necessary that each variable in a program be identifiable as to type, so that the compiler can compile the correct instructions. Computers have both integer and floating-point arithmetic operations, and the intent must be clear in all variable uses. Sometimes the nature of the variable indicates its type; more commonly, declarations are needed.

A FORTRAN variable may have one to six digits or letters, of which the first must be a letter. If the first letter is I, J, K, L, M, or N, the variable is considered of integer type. If the first letter is other than one of these six, the variable is considered as real. By the use of *type* statements, these conventions may be overruled and variables may be declared of other types. The statements used include INTEGER and REAL. These words are followed by a list of variables, separated by commas, as in the third FORTRAN example.

Variables may also be *logical*, with values .TRUE. or .FALSE. as mentioned before. The value of a logical variable is then acted upon, as in a "logical IF" statement.

Subscripted variables are signified by placing subscripts in parentheses. Thus, the sequence $X_1, X_2, \ldots, X_{10}$ would be written as

X(1), X(2), . . . , X(10)

One may also refer to higher-dimensional arrays, by using two or more subscripts in parentheses. Subscripts need not be integers. They may be combinations of integers and variables, though of a form no more complex than 4*M-10. Each subscripted variable requires the presence of an associated DIMENSIØN statement in FORTRAN, placed early in the program.

Functions

In mathematics it is common to refer to several functions by a symbology generally understood. Thus, we may write sin x, arcsin x, or log x, without bothering to write out the equivalences of the functions as polynomials. The 'x' in each case is the *argument* of the function; the value of the function depends upon the value of x. The argument may be complex; it may be an algebraic expression or a function itself: sin $(x^2 + y^2)$, log (sin x).

The same concept extends to algorithmic languages with a similar notation. There, arguments are usually given in parentheses, so we would write sin (x), arcsin (x), etc. FORTRAN allows this notation, and the programmer can assume that certain "built-in" functions will be understood and properly treated. Specifically, a function in FORTRAN is a separate program, coded in advance, that the programmer can use by supplying the required arguments. We shall study this process in detail in Chapter 7.

Among the built-in functions in FORTRAN are these:

Square root of x	SQRT(X)
Logarithm of x to the base e	ALØG(X)
Sine of an angle x, given in radians	SIN(X)
Cosine of an angle x, given in radians	CØS(X)
Exponential of x (e^x)	EXP(X)
Arctangent of x	ATAN(X)

Operations and Expressions

Programming languages generally have provision for the four arithmetic operators, for exponentiation, for certain "relations", and for logical operations. Other operations are indicated functionally. There is, in mathematics, a set of rules for the performing of operations in an arithmetic or algebraic expression. Within a programming language, these rules must be extended in order that a well-defined syntax be available. We review here the manner of writing mathematical expressions in a way that conforms to programming conventions, and then we review the corresponding syntax in FORTRAN.

We define now a *procedural* mathematics notation, one that largely conforms to standard mathematics but which also anticipates the requirements of programming languages. In this notation, algebraic expressions are formed in the usual manner, by appropriately combining constants, variables, functions, operators, and parentheses. These restrictions are added:

1. Every operation must be explicitly indicated by an operator. Juxtaposition of variables cannot be used to indicate multiplication.
2. Functions are indicated with arguments in parentheses. Such expressions as "sin x" lead to error in a language where blank spaces are ignored.
3. Evaluation of expressions proceeds by a set of precedence rules, which state which operations have precedence over which others. These rules are discussed below.

As examples of rules (1) and (2), consider the following, where the expressions on the left should be written as shown on the right:

$$\text{Normal form} \qquad\qquad \text{Procedural form}$$

$$A = 4\pi r^3/3 \qquad\qquad A \leftarrow 4 \times \pi \times r^3/3$$

$$m = \sin x + \cos e^x \qquad m \leftarrow \sin(x) + \cos(e^x)$$

$$c = a(b + |x|) \qquad\qquad c \leftarrow a \times (b + \text{abs}(x))$$

Most programming languages require special notation for indicating raised and lowered symbols (superscripts and subscripts), since characters are on the same level of printing. There does not seem to be any need, however, to force this restriction on our procedural language.

The indexing notation introduced earlier, is useful in our procedural language. To refer to an array of subscripted variables, we use this notation:

$$(a_i ; i = 1, n)$$

This implies all the members of the array, from a_1 through a_n. If we want to indicate every other member, we would write

$$(a_i ; i = 1, n, 2)$$

as in FORTRAN. Similarly, we may use any desired subscript increment. To refer to sequences of two subscripts, we use a nesting notation, as in the following:

$$(a_{ij} ; i = 1, n ; j = 1, m)$$

where the implication is that the i-index, whose range is given first, varies more rapidly than the j-index, so we mean the sequence

$$a_{11}, a_{21}, \ldots, a_{n1}, a_{12}, a_{22}, \ldots, a_{n2}, \ldots, a_{nm}$$

If we want the j-index to vary more rapidly, we must write

$$(a_{ij} ; j = 1, m ; i = 1, n)$$

Before considering the rules of operator precedence, let us introduce other common operators. *Relational* operators express the relationship between expressions. Six common operators are present in most programming languages: "equal to", "not equal to", "less than", "greater than", "less than or equal to", and "greater than or equal to". Generally, relationships are tested for truth or falsity, some action being taken on this decision. For example, we may write, as we did in the second FORTRAN example,

$$\text{if } (n \neq 1) \text{ go to } 90$$

The relationship tested may of course be more complex:

$$\text{if } (a^2 + b^2 + c^2 \geqslant r^2 x(\sin(x))^2) \, t = 0$$

This states that if the relationship is true, t is to be set to zero, and not otherwise.

The *Boolean* operators, "not", "and", and "or", are also common in programming languages. They are used to combine variables and expressions that have values "true" and "false". They are used in conjunction with relational operators to permit even more complex relationships to be established and tested. Consider the following:

$$\text{if } (r > 0 \lor s > 0) \text{ go to } 100$$

The symbol '$\lor$' means "or". Here, if either (or both) r or s is greater than zero, control goes to 100. The other symbols used are '$\land$' for "and" and '$\neg$' for "not".

Having introduced the several types of operators that occur in most algorithmic languages, we now consider the precedence rules. The rules can be stated concisely by this table, where operations higher in the list have precedence greater than those lower:

1. Unary operation.
2. Function reference.
3. Exponentiation.
4. Multiplication and division.
5. Addition and subtraction.
6. All relational operations.
7. "Not".
8. "And".
9. "Or".

This list means, for example, that multiplication is performed before addition. This is a commonly-known algebraic rule. *Unary operators* are '+' and '−' signs that sometimes accompany numeric or algebraic symbols, to indicate their signs. We have seen examples of function references with arguments in parentheses, such as 'sin (x)'

Accompanying this table is the rule that parentheses may be introduced around any part of an expression to specify the order in which operations are to be performed. If used, they overrule the precedence rules above.

The rules defining our procedural expressions apply to FORTRAN as well. The only difference is that FORTRAN uses a different notation for operators. The four arithmetic operators in FORTRAN are '+', '−', '*', and '/'. Exponentiation is given by '**'. There is no ambiguity in the double asterisk, because FORTRAN disallows successive operators. Function references are given as in the procedural language. Relational and Boolean operators are written as capital letters with delimiting periods: '.EQ.', '.NE.', '.LT.', '.GT.', '.GE.', '.LE.', '.NOT.', '.AND.', and '.OR.'. An *arithmetic expression* involves only the arithmetic exponentiation, and function operators. A *logical expression* involves constants, logical variables, relational operators, or Boolean operators as well. The value of a logical expression is either '.TRUE.' or '.FALSE.'.

When FORTRAN expressions are constructed, care must be taken to avoid mixed-mode combinations. In general, real and integer quantities may not be combined. For example, $A + J$ is illegal if A is real and J is integer. An exception to this rule occurs with exponentiation; a real variable may be raised to an integer power. Some FORTRAN processors do allow mixed expressions, however. In this event, integers are usually first converted to real quantities and then the operations are performed. The programmer must be aware of such conventions. Full details on mixing variables of other types (complex, logical, etc.) are generally given in specific FORTRAN manuals.

Integer Arithmetic

Special attention must be paid to what is called "integer arithmetic" with regard to division. This was introduced in the second FORTRAN example. The term implies that the result of an arithmetic operation will be an integer, with no associated fractional part. Operands in this arithmetic are also integers. This causes no problem in any arithmetic operation but division, where the result of dividing one integer by another is not always integral. However, if integer arithmetic is being used, the result will be made integral; the fraction (or remainder) is simply dropped. Thus we have

$$\frac{5}{2} = 2$$

In many programming languages, where an expression involves integers, integer arithmetic is used. One must be wary of this process. Consider this example:

$$6 \times 3/4 = ?$$

By the rules of evaluation, this means $(6 \times 3)/4$, which is 4 (in integer arithmetic).

However, we might intend $6 \times (\frac{3}{4})$, which is 0, or even $(\frac{6}{4}) \times 3$, which is 3. The ambiguity must be resolved by the proper use of parentheses, as shown. Thus, if a particular order of computation is desired, parentheses may be useful or necessary.

It should be noted that sometimes the consequences of integer arithmetic are used to advantage. For example, the expression

$$n - n/2 \times 2$$

takes on the values 1, 0, 1, 0, ..., for successive integer values of n. Another example appears in the second program.

Assignment Statements

Computation in a program written in an algorithmic language is accomplished in the *assignment statements*, in which a variable is assigned a value. Such statements have the form

$$y \leftarrow f(x_1, x_2, x_3, \ldots)$$

where f is a function of the variables x_i. The purpose of this statement is to assign a value to y, using the current values of x_i. The values current are the values of the variables at the time the statement is executed.

In FORTRAN, assignment statements are written as follows:

$$y = f$$

where f is an expression whose value is to be assigned to y.

Declarations

Some statements within a program describe the data in some manner. These are termed *declarations* and involve the allocation of space for arrays, identification of variable types, or description of data. They are not executable statements.

Space allocation statements are required so that sufficient room may be set aside for storage of arrays. Space requirements must be given when the program is coded. In FORTRAN, space allocation is given by the DIMENSIØN statement, where each dimension of an array is given within parentheses.

Variables may be of several types, as we have seen. Sometimes conventions apply such that the name of the variable identifies its type. In other cases, specific statements are used. In FORTRAN, the initial letter determines the variable type in the absence of *type* statements. Variables with names beginning with I, J, K, L, M, or N are taken as integers; other variables are taken as real. Among the

type statements are REAL, INTEGER, and COMPLEX. The variables so identified are listed after the type name:

INTEGER ARC, SUM, TØTAL

Descriptions of data are needed when information is to be read into memory
or printed from memory. Descriptions include information on the type of data
(integer, real, alphanumeric), the width of the data, i.e., the number of columns, and
the number of items. In FORTRAN, this information is supplied in FØRMAT
statements. We have seen how integers and real numbers are specified, using
specifications of these forms:

Iw   Fw.d

The first specification signifies integers of width w, while the second signifies real
numbers of width w and with d decimal places to the right of the decimal point.
If there are sequences of like fields in succession, an integer n may precede these
specifications:

nIw   nFw.d

Thus, '5I6' means that five integers of 6 columns each appear on a data card.
FORMAT statements also permit the specification of line spacing in a printout.
These characters have the following meanings when used as initial characters in
an output format:

Character	*Meaning*
(blank)	single spacing
0	double spacing
1	new page

The use of the character is "carriage control".

EXERCISES

1. Write the following numbers in normal mathematical forms:
   (a) 267E-2   (b) .0004E-3
   (c) 6700E-3   (d) .00444E5
   (e) 88.88E0   (f) .999E2

2. Which of the following are illegal FORTRAN variable names?
   (a) TABLE   (b) TABBLE
   (c) 9000   (d) H9000
   (e) LØØPSIZE   (f) LP SIZE
   (g) 9XYZ   (h) TAB.LE
   (i) X/2   (j) T8ABLE
   (k) TBALE   (l) ITEM(2)

3. List the elements in the order implied by these arrays:
   (a) $(a_{ij}; j = 1, 3; i = 1, 3, 2)$
   (b) $(a_{ijk}; i = 1, 3; i = 1, 5, 2; k = 8, 9)$

4. Which expressions below have illegal subscripts?
   (a) B(3 − 1)   (b) B(3*I)
   (c) B(I*J*K)   (d) B(B(I))
   (e) B(5*I − J)   (f) B(I*J)

5. If *A*, *B*, and *C* are real variables, and *I*, *J*, and *K* are integer variables, which of the following FORTRAN expressions are illegal?

   (a) A − C   (b) A/J
   (c) (A*B)/(I + J)   (d) A**I
   (e) I**A   (f) (A + B)**(I − J)

6. Under what conditions does control go to 100?
   (a) if (*x* < 2 ∨ *y* > 5) go to 100
   (b) if (*x* < 2 ∨ *y* > 5 ∧ *z* = 3) go to 100

7. Evaluate the following expressions, given these values: $A = 2.0$, $B = -2.5$, $C = 1.0, D = -3.0$.
   (a) A − B * C/(2. + D)   (b) (A − B) * C/(2. + D)
   (c) (A − B) * (C/(2. + D)   (d) A − B * (C/2.) + D

8. Evaluate these expressions, using integer arithmetic, given these values: $I = -2$, $J = 5, K = -1$.
   (a) I/J + K   (b) J/I − K
   (c) J/(I/K)

9. Describe the format of the cards read by each of these format statements:
   (a) 100 FØRMAT (6I5, 4F6.1)
   (b) 100 FØRMAT (4I3, F8.0, 3I2, 2F5.2)

                    *   *   *   *   *   *

10. Remove the redundant parentheses in each of the following expressions:
    (a) $(((x − y) × (a^2) + (b/c)^2)/2)$
    (b) $(x + (a × b))/(a − b) + (x^2/\sin(x))$
    (c) $(x < y + 2 ∧ x > z − 2) ∨ (a = 3) ∧ b > c$

11. Write FORTRAN logical expressions to describe these conditions:
    (a) *A* is greater than *Y*, and either *C* is zero or *D* is greater than *Z*.
    (b) *X* is greater than −3 but less than +3.
    (c) *Y* is equal to one or more of the odd numbers between 4 and 10.
    (d) *A* exceeds *B* and *B* exceeds *C*, or *B* is less than *C* and *C* is less than *A*.

12. Evaluate each of the following logical expressions using the sets of values given below them. Assume *I*, *J*, and *K* are integers while *A*, *B*, and *C* are real numbers. The expressions are .TRUE. or .FALSE.
    (a) I/J .GT. 10 .ØR. A .LE. B
       (1) I = 20, J = 2, A = 8.0, B = 6.5
       (2) I = 20, J = 3, A = 8.0, B = 8.0
       (3) I = 30, J = 2, A = 8.0, B = 5.0
    (b) (I*J/K .GT. 5 .ØR. J .EQ. 10) .AND. .NØT. (A .NE. B .ØR. B .EQ. C)
       (1) I = 4, J = 2, K = 2, A = 10.0, B = 12.0, C = 12.0
       (2) I = 20, J = 10, K = 5, A = 10.0, B = 10.0, C = 12.0
       (3) I = 20, J = 12, K = 5, A = 10.0, B = 11.0, C = 12.0
       (4) I = 2, J = 2, K = 2, A = 10.0, B = 11.0, C = 12.0

REFERENCES

1. The following book discusses many algorithmic languages from the point of view of their history, structure, and utility:

   Jean E. Sammet, *Programming Languages: History and Fundamentals*, Prentice-Hall, Inc., 1969.

2. There have been many books published on FORTRAN. One or more should be consulted to supplement the introductory treatment given here. See, for example, the following:

   Elliott I. Organick, *A FORTRAN IV Primer*, Addison-Wesley Publishing Co., Inc., 1966.

   Charles P. Lecht, *The Programmer's FORTRAN II and IV*, McGraw-Hill, Inc., 1966.

5 TRANSFER OF CONTROL

This chapter reviews the concepts of flow of control and transfer of control through a computer program. Many of these concepts were introduced in earlier chapters, particularly in Chapter 4, where a few coding examples illustrated transfer of control. We shall here expand these ideas, and correspondingly enlarge the scope of coding to illustrate further their inclusion in a program. We shall consider conditions under which control is transferred, the manner of constructing loops, and the use of indexing for control.

5.1 CONTROL STATEMENTS

Nature of Control Statements

Control statements involve the flow of control through a program and may change this flow. They may be unconditional, indicating a transfer of control always, or conditional, indicating a transfer under stated conditions. The former can be written as

$$\text{go to } m$$

where m is the label of the statement to which control is to go.
The conditional form is

$$\text{if } p \text{ then transfer to } m$$

where p is a condition to be met for a transfer to statement m to occur. Sometimes this is generalized to

$$\text{if } p_i \text{ then transfer to } m_i$$

where the p_i and m_i represent a multiplicity of conditions and statement labels. Another form of conditional transfer is given by

$$\text{if } p \text{ then } q$$

where q is a statement to be executed if condition p is met. If p is not met, control passes to the next statement. A generalization of this form is the following:

$$\text{if } p \text{ then } q \text{ else } r$$

where r is another statement, to be executed if condition p is not met.

In FORTRAN, the unconditional transfer is this statement:

$$\text{GO TO } m$$

We have studied two forms of conditional transfers. One is the arithmetic IF:

$$\text{IF } (a)\, n_1, n_2, n_3$$

where a is an arithmetic expression and n_i are statement labels. Control passes to n_1, n_2, or n_3 if the value of a is less than, equal to, or greater than zero, respectively. The other is the logical IF:

$$\text{IF } (t)\, s$$

where t is a logical expression and s is an executable statement though not another logical IF or a DØ statement. If t has the value .TRUE., statement s is executed. If t has the value .FALSE., control passes to the following statement.

Another type of control statement is the *computed GO TO* statement, which permits a multiple branch at a point in a program. Control passes to one of any named statements in the program. The statement is of the form

$$\text{GO TO } (n_1, n_2, \ldots, n_k),\, i$$

where the n_j are statement labels in the program and i is an integer variable. Control passes to statement n_i, depending upon the value of i. Thus, in this statement

    GØ TØ (20, 25, 35, 40), L

control passes to statement 20 if $L = 1$, to statement 25 if $L = 2$, etc.

Uses of Control Statements

We have seen how the IF statements are used to make decisions based on the values of expressions. Let us here consider several examples of the uses of these statements.

Example 5.1. Consider again the grade records of our imaginary college, averaged in GRADAV. A student is considered for admission to an honor society if his average exceeds 85 and he has taken at least 20 courses without a failure (under 60) or if his average exceeds 90 and he has taken at least 10 courses:

```
IF (AVER .GT. 85 .AND. NUMBER .GE. 20 .AND. LØGRAD .GE. 60
   .ØR. AVER .GT. 90 .AND. NUMBER .GE. 10) . . . .
```

where LØGRAD is his lowest grade to date.

Example 5.2. Given values for M, D, and Y, representing the month, day, and year of a given data (in integer form), determine whether the triplet (M, D, Y) is legal. Assume that only twentieth-century dates are given.

We can delineate four cases: when the number of days is 28, 29, 30, or 31. A flowchart appears in Figure 5.1. To test these cases, we can write complex conditional statements. The program (to test date):

```
C    TDATE
     INTEGER M, Y, D
C    CHECK TØ SEE IF ANY NUMBER IS ZERØ ØR NEGATIVE.
     IF (M .LE. 0 .ØR. Y .LE. 0 .ØR. D .LE. 0) GØ TØ 99
C    CHECK FØR 31 DAYS.
     IF ((M .EQ. 1 .ØR. M .EQ. 3 .ØR. M .EQ. 5 .ØR. M .EQ. 7
    1       .ØR. M .EQ. 8 .ØR. M .EQ. 10 .ØR. M .EQ. 12)
    2       .AND. D .GT. 31) GØ TØ 99
C    CHECK FØR 30 DAYS.
     IF ((M .EQ. 4 .ØR. M .EQ. 6 .ØR. M .EQ. 9 .ØR. M .EQ. 11)
    1       .AND. D .GT. 30) GØ TØ 99
C    CHECK FØR 29 DAYS.
     IF (M .EQ. 2 .AND. Y .EQ. (Y/4)•4 .AND. D .GT. 29)
    1       GØ TØ 99
C    CHECK FØR 28 DAYS.
     ,IF (M .EQ. 2 .AND. Y .NE. (Y/4)•4 .AND. D .GT. 28)
    1       GØ TØ 99
C    CHECK MØNTH.
     IF (M .GT. 12) GØ TØ 99
C    CHECK YEAR.
     IF (Y .GT. 99) GØ TØ 99
     PRINT 100
     STØP
```

```
 99   PRINT 101
      STØP
100   FØRMAT (15H DATE IS LEGAL.)
101   FØRMAT (17H DATE IS ILLEGAL.)
END
```

A note on the use of the expression '(Y/4)*4' is appropriate. This expression is equal to Y if and only if Y is divisible by 4, a fact we need to know in the program.

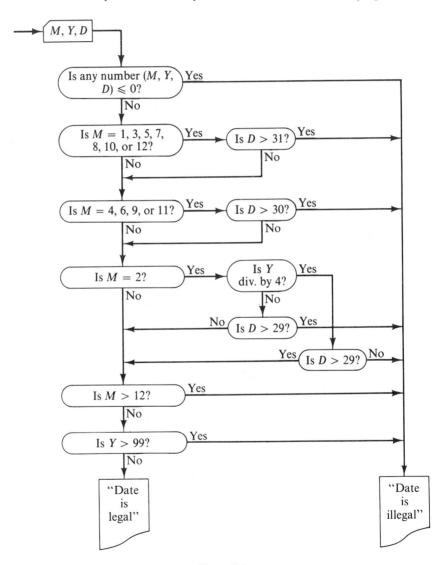

Figure 5.1

Example 5.3. Given a list of coordinate pairs (x, y), n in number, determine the number of points lying in each of the four quadrants. Assume, for simplicity, that no points lie on either axis. The problem is flowcharted in Figure 5.2.

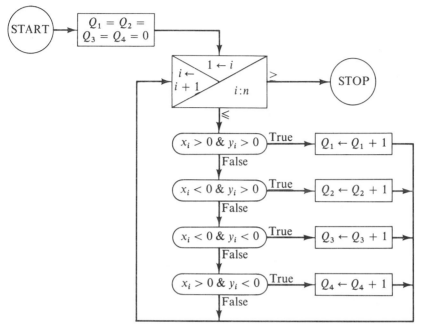

Fig. 5.2.   Quadrant counts.

The program segment:

```
C     QUADCT
      DØ 10 I  = 1, N
      Q1  = 0
      Q2  = 0
      Q3  = 0
      Q4  = 0
      IF (X(I) .GT. 0 .AND. Y(I) .GT. 0) QI  = Q1 + 1
      IF (X(I) .LT. 0 .AND. Y(I) .GT. 0) Q2  = Q2 + 1
      IF (X(I) .LT. 0 .AND. Y(I) .LT. 0) Q3  = Q3 + 1
      IF (X(I) .GT. 0 .AND. Y(I) .LT. 0) Q4  = Q4 + 1
   10 CØNTINUE
```

Note that, in this program, each case passes through all IF statements, even if an early one is successful. This is inefficient, and the process could be speeded up.

EXERCISES

1. Construct sequences of FORTRAN statements to realize the following situations; do these two ways, once with a logical IF and once with an arithmetic IF.

(a) If X exceeds Y but is less than Z, set C equal to 1.
(b) Set Q equal to the larger of A and B.
(c) If Q and R are both greater than 1, set S equal to their sum; otherwise set S equal to their difference.

2. How can the code in Example 5.3 (QUADCT) be made more efficient, as suggested in that example?

3. Extend QUADCT to supply, in addition, a count of the number of given points greater than unit distance from the origin (i.e., outside a unit circle at the origin).

* * * * * *

4. Construct sequences of FORTRAN statements to realize the following situations; do these two ways, as in Exercise 1.
(a) If X is less than zero, set Y equal to zero; if X lies between zero and one (or equals either value), set Y equal to one; if X exceeds one, set Y equal to zero.
(b) Set Q equal to the largest of A, B, and C, unless one of these three exceeds 25.
(c) If Q, R, and S are each in the range -1 to $+1$ inclusive, replace the largest of these by the sum of the three values and proceed to statement 50. Otherwise simply proceed to statement 60.

5. Given a set of students' grades punched on cards as described in the third example (STREC1) in Chapter 4, write programs to solve these problems:
(a) Determine the grades above 90, listing these.
(b) Determine a "merit rating", equal to twice the number of grades over 90, plus the number of grades from 81 to 90, minus the number of grades from 65 to 70, minus twice the number of grades under 64.
(c) A student is "cum laude" if his average exceeds 85, is "summa cum laude" if his average exceeds 90 without failures (under 65), and is "magna cum laude" if his average exceeds 95 without any grades below 80. Rank the student into one of these classifications, if appropriate.

6. Describe the types of decisions that are best handled by arithmetic IF's and those best handled by logical IF's.

5.2 LOOPS

Significance of Loops

We have seen the significance of a program loop; it expresses the repetitive nature of a problem. Virtually every computer program is repetitive in some way or in many ways. A loop indicates that a sequence of operations is to be repeated a number of times, a change in the index or a subscript occurring each cycle. As a result, either a sequence of variables is processed, or an operation is performed several times on one quantity.

Indexing Statements

Indexing statements are usually associated with looping operations. Loop execution involves the initialization, modification, and testing of an index. The following indexing statement encompasses these operations:

$$\text{do } n \text{ for } i = iv, fv, inc$$

which means, "execute statements from this one through statement n, varying the index from an initial value iv to a value not exceeding the final value fv, modifying the index by the increment inc each cycle."

FORTRAN has a statement in this form, as follows:

$$DØ\ n\ i = iv,\ fv,\ inc$$

where n, i, iv, fv, and inc have the same significance as before.

The index must be a nonsubscripted integer variable. The last three parameters must each be integers or nonsubscripted integer variables, having positive nonzero values. Sometimes, the value fv is not matched by the index; in that instance, the final value of the index is the largest value not exceeding fv. In other words, fv acts as an upper limit on the index.

After each execution of the sequence of operations, which is termed the *range* of the DØ statement, the index is modified and a test is made to see if the loop is to be terminated. This is the case when i first exceeds fv. If the value of fv is not exceeded, control returns to the start of the sequence for another repetition. These actions are diagrammed in Figure 5.3, a modification of the iteration box. Note that the initialization box is displaced from its usual position. This is the case because processing occurs *before* index testing.

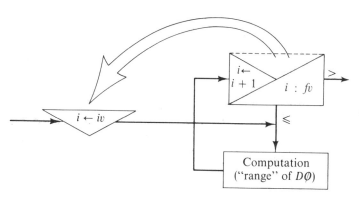

Figure 5.3

Because of where the index is tested, the DØ range is always executed at least once. In some instances, this may be erroneous, for zero loop cycles may be required. If this case is a possibility, a test prior to the DØ statement should be added:

```
IF (N .EQ. 0) GØ TØ 77
DØ 60 I = 1, N

     ·
     ·
     ·
60   CØNTINUE
70   ·
     ·
     ·
```

If the increment in a DØ statement is unity, the value may be omitted for then the FORTRAN compiler will assume it is unity; these statements state the same thing:

```
DØ 50 J = 1, 10
DØ 50 J = 1, 10, 1
```

The CØNTINUE statement in FØRTRAN is a dummy statement that does nothing more than provide a place to put a label. The last statement of a DØ range may not be a GØ TØ statement, an arithmetic IF statement, or another DØ statement, and so the CØNTINUE statement is frequently used when one of these statements would otherwise be the last statement in the range. It is good practice to use the CØNTINUE statement regularly, for then it is less likely to be omitted when it is required. Thus we write the array:

```
    DØ 35 J = 1, NUMBER
    SUM = SUM + GRADES(J)
35  CØNTINUE
```

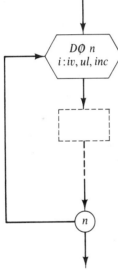

Fig. 5.4. DO-loop flow-chart convention.

Within a DØ range, there are some restrictions on jumps. A jump into a DØ loop from outside the range is not allowed, nor is a jump from within the range to the DØ statement. A jump may occur from within the range to outside the loop, in which case the loop index retains its current value as control leaves the loop. If the loop terminates by a final index test (the normal case), the index cannot be assumed to have any particular value upon exit.

In order to have flowcharts conform more nearly to DØ-statement form and to simplify them, a new type of box is introduced. This box is drawn as a hexagon, as in Figure 5.4, and contains the loop parameters. These parameters, including the index, are shown in the second line in the box; the range is indicated in the first line by giving the label of the last range statement. As before, if the increment is 1, it may be omitted. The circle near the bottom acts as a decision box at the end of the loop range.

Nested Iterations

Many problems containing a loop actually contain an inner loop within that loop. We saw an example earlier, where the sum of the tenth power of Z numbers was computed. That problem is coded here.

Example 5.4. Write a program that sums the tenth power of a set of numbers, using nested loops. (The tenth power of a number can be written in a single statement, but we shall use an inner loop.) Assume the numbers are written four to a card, 12 columns each, with three places to the right of the decimal point in each number. On the first card, ending in column 5, is the number of such numbers.

```
C    SUM10
C    THIS PRØGRAM CØMPUTES THE SUM ØF THE TENTH PØWER
C    ØF A SET ØF NUMBERS.  TWØ NESTED LØØPS ARE USED.
     REAL BUF, SET, SUM, PØWER
     INTEGER NUMBER
     DIMENSIØN BUF(4), SET(100)
     WRITE (6,10)
     READ (5,20) NUMBER
     READ (5,30)  (SET(J), J  =  1, NUMBER)
C    FØRM SUM BY CØMPUTING TENTH PØWERS AND THEN SUMMING.
     SUM  =  0
     DØ 90 I  =  1, NUMBER
     PØWER(I)  =  1
     DØ 91 J  =  1, 10
     PØWER(I)  =  PØWER(I) ∗ SET(I)
 91  CØNTINUE
     SUM  =  SUM  +  PØWER(I)
 90  CØNTINUE
     WRITE (6,30) SUM
     STØP
 10  FØRMAT (1H1)
 20  FØRMAT (4F12.3)
 30  FØRMAT (12H THE SUM IS 12F.3)
     END
```

Note that the inner loop, DØ range 91, does not use the inner index J. This is true because J is used only for counting to 10, so that the tenth power is computed.

Example 5.5. Given a two-dimensional integer array, 10×10 in size, determine the sum of the elements in the upper triangular area, above the diagonal. Assume the integers are punched 10 to a card. The array is depicted in Figure 5.5, with the upper triangle shaded. We determine the sum of the triangle's elements by finding the sum of the shaded portion of each row, and then by summing these row sums. Let i be the row index, j be the column index, and a_{ij} be an element. We can see that, for each row, j runs from a value one greater than the row number to the value 10. For example, in the first row, j runs from 2 to 10. Thus the DØ parameters for a j-loop, i.e., for summing one row, are $(i + 1, 10, 1)$. Then,

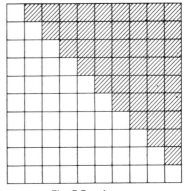

Fig. 5:5.   An array.

the index i runs from 1 to 9. The flowchart appears in Figure 5.6. In the inner loop, the row sum r_i is computed. In the outer loop, the total sum S is computed. Note that in this problem, in contrast to the earlier nested-loop problem, the inner index has an initial value that is variable; it is a function of the outer index. The FORTRAN program (TRSUM1) appears below.

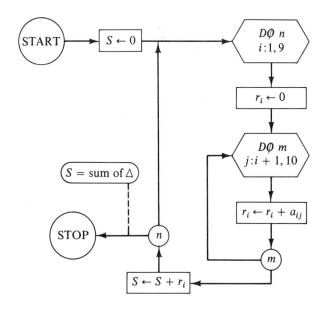

Fig. 5.6.   Summing array elements.

```
C     TRSUM1
C     THIS PRØGRAM SUMS THE UPPER TRIANGULAR AREA.
      INTEGER A, R, S
      DIMENSIØN R(10), A(10,10)
      READ (5,101) ((A(I,J), I = 1, 10), J = 1, 10)
      WRITE (6,103) ((A(I,J), I = 1, 10), J = 1, 10)
      S = 0
      DØ 10 I = 1, 9
      R(I) = 0
      I1 = I + 1
      DØ 20 J = I1, 10
      R(I) = R(I) + A(I,J)
   20 CØNTINUE
      S = S + R(I)
   10 CØNTINUE
      STØP
      WRITE (6,102) S
```

```
101  FØRMAT (10I5)
102  FØRMAT (32H0THE ARRAY UPPER TRIANGLE SUM IS I8)
103  FØRMAT (12H1THE ARRAY IS/(10I5))
     END
```

The following additional features should be noted.

1. I1 = I + 1

   The parameters in a DØ statement cannot be expressions; i.e., 'DØ 20 J = I + 1, 10' is not allowed. Hence, we use a dummy initial value set by this assignment statement.

2. 103 FØRMAT (12H1THE ARRAY IS/(10I5))

   A slash (/) is used to separate two parts of the format. In this usage, it means that the first part, up to the slash, is used for the first line, while the second part, in its own parentheses, is used thereafter for all future lines, until the output list in the WRITE statement is exhausted. Thus 10 integers will be printed on each line.

EXERCISES

1. What is the final value of the index I as each of the loops defined by these DØ statements is completed, assuming no transfers out of the loops.
   (a) DØ 20 I = 1, 10
   (b) DØ 20 I = 1, 10, 2
   (c) DØ 20 Ø = 6, NUMBER, 5
      where NUMBER has the value 75

2. What is wrong with each of these statements?
   (a) DØ 30 I = 2, 10, −2
   (b) DØ 30, J = 1, 100
   (c) DØ 30 K = −1, 10, 1
   (d) DØ 30 K = J + 2, M, L
   (e) DØ 30 K = J, M(1), L

3. Consider a 10 × 10 array, A, whose elements are named as in Example 5.5. Write loops to perform these summations.
   (a) Sum of the main diagonal elements.
   (b) Sum of the Ith row elements.
   (c) Sum of the Jth column elements.
   (d) Sum of the diagonal from upper right to lower left.

*   *   *   *   *   *

4. Write FORTRAN programs to sum the elements of a 10 × 10 array enclosed in the following areas of the array; include input-output statements.
   (a) In the lower triangular area (below the diagonal).
   (b) In the outermost square of the array, i.e., the elements at the four edges.
   (c) In a checker board's black squares. i.e., in alternate positions in both directions.

(d) In an octagon-shaped area that excludes the 10 elements nearest each corner (of which each 10 elements form a right triangle).

5. Write a FORTRAN program that sums the elements in a three-dimensional array, $10 \times 10 \times 10$.

6. Write a FORTRAN program that sums the elements in a three-dimensional array but which excludes all elements on any diagonal passing through the center of the cube.

5.3 BRANCHING

The term *branching* refers to the flow of control at a decision point that has several possible outcomes.

> **Example 5.6.** Code a branch point that sends control cyclically to statements 10, 20, 30, and 40, repeating that sequence indefinitely. We can set a variable X to the values 1, 2, 3, and 4, then repeat, and use a computed GØ TØ to achieve the desired result. To restore X to 1 after it has reached the value of 4, we can reassign it an initial (zero) value:

```
    INTEGER X
    X = 0
    .
    .
    .

    X = X + 1
    GØ TØ (10, 20, 30, 40), X
    .
10  .
20  .
30  .
40  X = 0
    .
    .
```

> **Example 5.7.** Let us again consider the student grades of Chapter 4, but with additional information in the records. The records have thus far comprised, for each student, a set of punched cards, with eight grades punched per card (in three columns each), preceded by a count (on one card) of the number of grades.
>
> These records would be more meaningful if they contained such information as student names, classes, and major fields. Let us therefore assume one card is added before each of the cards above, and that our records comprise information on many students. The first card has this format:
>
> > Columns 1–30: student last name, first name, middle initial
> > Columns 31–32: class, in two digits
> > Columns 35–38: major subject, four-letter code

Thus, typical records might be these:

```
1                           31    38
↓                           ↓     ↓
SMITH,  KAREN  R.           69   ENGL
JØHNSØN,  RØBERT  S.        70   MECH
HAMILTØN,  ALEXANDER        70   PHYS
```

Two spaces are skipped between the last two items for readability. These spaces must be taken into account in the FØRMAT statements.

The problem here is to read in all the data on each student, and decide whether he is to be considered for membership in an honor society. The rules for admission require these minimum averages, among other qualifications:

For freshmen:	90 average
For sophomores:	88 average
For juniors:	86 average
For seniors:	85 average

A program is to be written that determines which students meet these requirements and prints the lists, with their classes, majors, and averages. Now we shall use floating-point computations for more accurate average determination. Using integer arithmetic, as in Chapter 4, leads to roundoff errors.

After each student's average is computed, a branch is made on the value of the variable CLASS, which is reduced from its actual value (69, 70, 71, or 72) by the number 68. Thus CLASS has a modified value of 1, 2, 3, or 4. Because of the changes, we rename the program.

```
C    STREC2
C    THIS PRØGRAM DETERMINES WHETHER A STUDENTS MEETS THE
C    MINIMUM AVERAGE REQUIREMENTS FØR CØNSIDERATIØN FØR
C    MEMBERSHIP IN HØNØR SØCIETY.
        INTEGER NAME(8), NUMBER, CLASS, MAJØR
        REAL GRADES(80), SUM, AVERAGE
        WRITE (6,30)
   10   READ (5,40) NAME, CLASS, MAJØR
        CLASS = CLASS  −  68
        READ (5,50) NUMBER, (GRADES(I), I = 1, NUMBER)
        SUM  =  0.
        DØ 35 J  =  1, NUMBER
   35   SUM  =  SUM  +  GRADES(J)
        AVER  =  SUM / FLØAT(NUMBER)
C    DETERMINE CLASS ØF STUDENT.
        GØ TØ (91,92,93,94), CLASS
C    SENIØR (CLASS ØF 69).
   91   IF (AVER .LT. 85.0) GØ TØ 10
        GØ TØ 99
```

```
C   JUNIØR (CLASS ØF 70).
   92   IF (AVER .LT. 86.0) GØ TØ 10
        GØ TØ 99
C   SØPHØMØRE (CLASS ØF 71).
   93   IF (AVER .LT. 88.0) GØ TØ 10
        GØ TØ 99
C   FRESHMAN (CLASS ØF 72).
   94   IF (AVER .LT. 90.0) GØ TØ 10
        GØ TØ 99
C   HERE IF STUDENT IS TØ BE LISTED.
   99   WRITE (6,60) NAME, CLASS, MAJØR, AVER
        GØ TØ 10
   30   FØRMAT (1H1 9X, 12HSTUDENT NAME 10X, 5HCLASS 5X,
      1      5HMAJØR 5X, 5HAVER.)
   40   FØRMAT (7A4,A2, I2, 2X, A4)
   50   FØRMAT (13/(8F3.0))
   60   FØRMAT (1H0 7A4,A2, 3X, I2, 7X, A4, 5X, F4.1)
        END
```

The output from this program might begin as follows:

STUDENT NAME	CLASS	MAJØR	AVER.
SMITH, KAREN R.	69	ENGL	88.5
JØHNSØN, RØBERT S.	70	MECH	94.2
HAMILTØN, ALEXANDER	70	PHYS	90.2
. . .	. . .		

Several additional features of FORTRAN are introduced in STREC2. These are explained below.

1. INTEGER NAME(5), NUMBER, CLASS, MAJØR

   (a) The dimensions of the array NAME are given in the INTEGER statement, rather than in a separate statement. This is allowable; it is a convenience and is a reasonable extension of that statement. The statement is a declaration, and two types of attributes of the array NAME are given by it: The array is of size 5, and it is of type integer.

   (b) The array NAME, though declared to be of size 5, actually is used for one item, the name of a student. Although the name is composed of several parts (first name, etc.), we conceptually think of it as a unit that occupies five words, each holding six characters. In a computer holding more or less characters per word, different dimensioning would be required.

   (c) Alphanumeric information, of which a name is an example here, may be declared in most compilers to be either real or integer.

2. REAL GRADES(80), SUM, AVER

> This is another example of dimensioning within a type statement. In these two declarations, all the variables are declared to be of one type or the other, though they need not be. For example, SUM would be taken as real, while NUMBER would be taken as integer, in the absence of these declarations. It is good programming practice, however, to so declare all variables.

3. 10   READ (5,40) NAME, CLASS, NUMBER

> The array NAME is listed as a single variable here, rather than as

$$(NAME(J), J = 1, 5)$$

> If every member of a declared array is to be listed in a READ or WRITE statement, the indexing may be omitted. The implication is that every member is included. If only three of the five members were intended, e.g., indexing would be required.

4. AVER = SUM / FLØAT(NUMBER)

> (a) The divisor in this expression uses the built-in function FLØAT to convert the contents of word NUMBER to a floating-point (real) number so that the division can take place using real arithmetic, to eliminate most roundoff error.
>
> (b) Because of the real arithmetic, some changes were made in the code in Chapter 4. SUM and AVER are declared as real variables. NUMBER could also have been declared to be real, but it need not be.
>
> (c) The format specification used to read the grades is discussed below.

5. GØ TØ (91,92,93,94), CLASS

> This is a computed GØ TØ statement and sends control to one of four routines, one for each class.

6. 30   FØRMAT (1H1 9X, 12HSTUDENT NAME 10X, 5HCLASS 5X,
   1   5HMAJØR 5X, 5HAVER.)

> A new code is introduced here, 'X'. This indicates, for a WRITE statement (as here), that spaces are to be skipped. Thus, before the heading 'STUDENT NAME' nine spaces ('9X') are to be left on the line. Similarly, ten spaces are to be left between that heading and 'CLASS', and so on.

7. 40   FØRMAT (7A4,A2, I2, 2X, A4)

> (a) The 'X' here, used with a READ statement, indicates that spaces are to be ignored on reading. Thus two spaces ('2X') on a card, between the integer (I2) and the next item (A4) are to be ignored.
>
> (b) Another new code, 'A', is used here. It refers to alphanumeric information. The specification '7A4,A2' means that eight words (array

NAME) are to be given the values in eight successive fields, the first seven with four characters each and the last with two characters. In keeping with our concept that the name is a 30-character string, a more appropriate specification would be 'A30'. However, that is not correct. The '4' indicates that four characters are to be stored in each word, a common limit.

8. 50   FØRMAT (I3/8F3.0))

The specification for reading numbers is '8F3.0'. This implies eight real numbers, each three columns on a card, with no digits after the decimal point. This is the format of the data cards, where integers are actually used. A decimal point need not appear in numbers to be read as real, provided the FØRMAT statement includes the 'F' code. Thus, '85' will be read as though punched as '85.0', in this case. (If, on the other hand, the specification were '8F3.1', then '85' would be read as '8.5'.)

EXERCISES

1. Write a program sequence that causes flow of control to this sequence of program labels, using a computed GØ TØ statement: 10, 20, 30, 40, 30, 20, 10, 20, ...

2. Write a program segment to send control to one of the nine labels shown in the table below. In this table, control goes to 10 if $x = 1$ and $y = 1$, to 20 if $x = 2$ and $y = 1$, etc.

TABLE 5.1

y: \ x:	1	2	3
1	10	20	30
2	40	50	60
3	70	80	90

3. Using computed GØ TØ's, write program segments to accomplish these tasks:
   (a) Given a set of integers, count those divisible by 5.
   (b) Given a set of numbers, find three sums: the sum of the 1st, 4th, 7th, . . . ; the sum of the 2nd, 5th, 8th, . . . ; the sum of the 3rd, 6th, 9th, ...
   (c) Given a card punched with digits in columns 1 to 80, count the number of times each digit appears.

* * * * * · *

4. Given a set of integers over a wide range of values, compute a "logarithmic" histogram as follows: Count the number of integers having one digit, the number having two digits, the number having three digits, etc. Use a computed GØ TØ to branch to the counting sequences.

5. Under what circumstances and in what kind of problems is a computed GØ TØ the best device for branching? In many situations, IF statements are preferable.

6 A DIGITAL COMPUTER

In Chapter 1, the GAMMA 70, an imaginary digital computer, was introduced. The computer's memory consists of 4096 memory words, addressed as 0000_8, $0001_8, \ldots, 7777_8$. Each word contains 24 bits, numbered 0 through 23. In this chapter, these characteristics and others will be examined in a great deal more detail. The purpose in studying this computer is to understand in some depth the processes by which digital computers actually operate to solve a problem. While studying a FORTRAN program illustrates the method whereby an algorithm is converted into a computer program, this does not supply an appreciation of machine operation.

6.1 MACHINE LANGUAGE

Basic Instructions

We continue our study of the GAMMA 70 by introducing some of its instructions, thus studying the nature of machine language. These instructions are typical of those in any small digital computer. The instructions here have one operand each, referred to by its address. Hence, this computer is a *single-address* machine. A special register is available for the accumulation of results; this is the *accumulator*, referred to in Section 1.2.

Two fundamental instructions are required for moving a number into the accumulator from memory and for the reverse:

	Code (octal)
Place a number in the accumulator.	10
Store a number from the accumulator.	11

Recall that each instruction is identified by a two-digit (6-bit) code and that the addresses of operands appear as four-digit (12-bit) fields. Thus,

$$10 \ 00 \ 2000$$

means "place the contents of location 2000_8 in the accumulator".

In addition, arithmetic instructions are needed; in each of these cases, the result of the operation is left in the accumulator, replacing the number originally there:

Add a number to the accumulator.	20
Subtract a number from the accumulator.	21
Multiply the number in the accumulator by another.	22
Divide the number in the accumulator by another.	23

Besides these operations, it is necessary also to read data into memory and to print results. We have the following:

Read one number from a card and place it into memory.	40
Print the value of one number in memory.	41

Finally, we must also be able to stop the computer:

Stop.	00

For the input-output instructions, let us assume that the format F10.2 always applies, i.e., 10 columns on the card and 10 positions on the printed line are used.

A Simple Problem

Let us consider a problem already coded in FORTRAN in Chapter 4, computing the volume of a cylinder:

$$V \leftarrow \pi r^2 h$$

We can write a computer program in machine language for the GAMMA 70, using octal notation. The program (CYLVØL-M, for machine language) is below, with the location in memory of each instruction indicated at the left:

Location	Instruction	Remarks
0000	40 00 0011	Read the value of r into location 0011.
0001	40 00 0012	Read the value of h into location 0012.
0002	10 00 0013	Put the value of π into the accumulator, getting it from location 0013.
0003	22 00 0011	Multiply π by r, leaving the product in the accumulator.
0004	22 00 0011	Multiply the number in the accumulator by r again.
0005	22 00 0012	Finally, multiply by h, obtaining $\pi r^2 h$.
0006	11 00 0014	Store the result, V, in location 0014.
0007	41 00 0014	Print the result, V.
0010·	00 00 0000	Stop.

A few comments are necessary here. The operand addresses in these instructions are 0011 through 0014. Each of these four locations has been set aside for data, of which three kinds are represented. First, we have given data, r and h, supplied by the user when the program is run. Second, we have a constant, π, which is part of the program. Third, we have a location set aside for the result, V. The program, nine instructions long, is stored in locations 0000 through 0010.

One aspect of running this program is missing. We must load the program itself into memory, before we can execute it. The details of such an operation are complex, in general. However, we can assume that a man who operates the computer pushes a button on the machine that causes cards from the card reader to be loaded into memory, starting with the first instruction at location 0000. When the last card is loaded, the computer is instructed to start executing the program at location 0000. Although this is a simplification of the true operation, it illustrates the technique. With this operation, the complete process of loading and executing a program is described. In Chapter 8, this process will be discussed in greater detail.

EXERCISES

1. Write programs in machine language for the GAMMA 70 to solve the following problems:
   (a) Given three numbers, a, b, and c, compute the value of x:
   $$x = a + b + c$$
   (b) Given three numbers, a, b, and c, compute the value of y:
   $$y = a^2 + b^2 + c^2$$

   (*Hint:* After a^2 is computed, its value must be stored temporarily in a word in memory; the same is true for b^2.)

   *   *   *   *   *   *

2. With the instructions given, it is not possible to solve a problem like the quadratic-equation problem of Chapter 4. What additional instruction(s) might be needed?

3. With the instructions given, it is not possible to set up a loop that will terminate as desired. What additional instruction(s) might be needed?

   *   *   *   *   *   *

4. Assuming the instructions were available, write a program to add 100 numbers, using a loop, assuming the numbers were already in memory, at locations 1000_8 through 1143_8.

5. What additional instructions would be useful to solve the following problems, using machine language?
   (a) Determine the largest number in a set.
   (b) Place in increasing order the numbers in a set.

6. Write machine-language segments to perform the evaluation of these FORTRAN expressions:
   (a) $X = Y ** 3$
   (b) $X = (A + B)(C - D)/(M * N)$
   (c) $X = (A*B + C*D * E*F) ** 2$

6.2 CONTROL AND PROGRAM EXECUTION

Control

For understanding the manner in which a sequence of instructions in a program is executed, the concept of *control* is important. To appreciate this concept, let us examine the execution of instructions.

At a given instant, exactly one instruction is being either interpreted or executed. "Being interpreted" means that the type of the instruction is being determined by the control unit and the instruction operand is being identified. For example, suppose that the instruction at location 0002 is being interpreted; assume the instruction (in a GAMMA 70) is the following:

$$22001002$$

The control unit must identify these parts of this instruction: "multiply" (given by operation code 22) and "contents of location 1002". It then sends signals to the operations unit, which performs the multiplication.

While an instruction is being interpreted and executed, its address (here 0002) is located in the *address register* (AR).* Control is said to be "with" or "at" that instruction. After each instruction is executed, the C(AR) is normally increased by 1. Then the next instruction to be executed is the one located at the next address in memory. Let us now consider the possibility that different sequencing occurs.

In Section 2.1, the problem of summing 25 numbers was analyzed. Step 5 of the analysis reads as follows:

"Check the count. If it is 25 or less, continue at step 3; if it is greater than 25, stop."

Such a statement clearly requires a test. Special test (or *decision*) instructions are available on all computers. They are of the form, "if a given number is positive, jump to location X; if it is negative, go on to the next instruction in sequence." To "jump to location X" means to execute next the instruction at location X, i.e., to send control directly to location X. Such an instruction is termed a *jump, transfer,* or *branch* instruction.

If an instruction is of jump type, there may be a change in the normal sequencing of control. The address in the AR may be changed to the value given in the instruction. Consider this instruction, assumed at location 0100: "Jump to location 0200 if a particular number is positive; go on to the next instruction if it is negative." Just before this instruction is executed, the C(AR) = 0100. After it is executed, if the number is positive, the C(AR) = 0200; the next instruction executed is the one at 0200. If the number is negative, the C(AR) = 0101.

---

* This register is also known as the *location counter, instruction counter,* and *program address counter.*

We see from this example that the C(AR) actually determines which instruction is to be executed. Either that address is increased by 1, or it changes as directed by the instruction. This sequencing of control is called *flow of control.* If the C(AR) is changed by other than 1, there is a *change of control.* This is a jump, as defined earlier.

Clearly, the GAMMA 70 needs jump instructions if it is to be able to make decisions and create loops. The following instructions are available:

Jump unconditionally.   30
Jump if the accumulator is greater than zero; continue
   in sequence if it is zero or negative.   31

A Problem with a Loop

Let us again consider the problem of summing 25 numbers. For simplicity, we shall assume that all the numbers are in memory, in locations 0022_8 through 0052_8, inclusive. We have a jump instruction that can be used to test and terminate the loop.

The instruction 31 (above) causes a jump if the accumulator is greater than zero, and so no jump occurs if it is zero or negative. We need some means of counting the loop cycles. Thus we set aside a counter in memory (location 0016_8), in which we keep a count of cycles. Because of the manner in which the jump instruction works, coding is easiest if that counter is initially set to 25 and is then decreased by one each time a number is summed. When zero is reached, the jumps stop and the summation is at an end.

We have another problem. If we think about the problem of summing 25 numbers starting at location 0022, we realize we would need, at the start, this instruction:

$$20 \ \ 00 \ \ 0022$$

Subsequently, to add numbers from 0023, 0024, ..., we need instructions as follows:

$$20 \ \ 00 \ \ 0023$$

$$20 \ \ 00 \ \ 0024$$

$$\cdot \quad \cdot \quad \cdot$$

But if we include each of these instructions within the program, we ignore the convenience of the loop. Rather, we must somehow change the original addition instructions above to the later instructions in turn. We can do this by treating the instruction as a number to be increased by one each loop cycle.

Now we sum up the summation process by noting that in each loop cycle, we must do the following:

1. Add one number to the sum.
2. Modify the addition instruction.
3. Decrease the counter by one.
4. Test for termination of the loop.

We must set aside certain locations in memory for constants and for the sum. Let location 0017_8 contain zero, 0020_8 contain 1, and 0021_8 be used for the sum.

The program (call it SUM-M) appears as follows:

Location	Instruction	Remarks
0001	10 00 0017	Place zero, from location 0017, in the accumulator (AC).
0002	11 00 0021	Place zero into location 0021, to be used for the sum.
0003	10 00 0021	Place sum in AC.
0004	20 00 0022	Add one number to the sum.
0005	11 00 0021	Store sum in location 0021.
0006	10 00 0004	Place add instruction (location 0004) in the AC.
0007	20 00 0020	Add 1 to the instruction.
0010	11 00 0004	Store modified instruction back in 0004.
0011	10 00 0016	Place counter (0016) in the AC.
0012	21 00 0020	Subtract one from the counter.
0013	11 00 0016	Store modified count back in counter.
0014	31 00 0003	Jump back to location 0003 if the AC > 0, i.e., if not all 25 numbers have been summed.
0015	00 00 0000	Stop.

In this program, the four steps listed before the program have these counterparts in the program:

Step 1: instructions at 0003 through 0005;
Step 2: instructions at 0006 through 0010;
Step 3: instructions at 0011 through 0013;
Step 4: instructions at 0014.

As in the previous example, we had to assign memory space for constants, results, and data. The block of words from 0022 through 0052 contained the data, while locations 0016 through 0021 were used for constants and the result. It should be evident that these assignments were made after the instructions (without their operand addresses) were written. Only then was it known how long the program was. These other items are located after the program.

The problem of reading in data has been ignored. Using only the GAMMA 70 instructions available to us, we would have to punch each of the 25 numbers on a separate card and use a reading loop similar to the addition loop here for reading these cards.

The task of doing coding in the manner described is tedious, but in the next section we shall see that much has been done to improve the situation.

Program Execution

The address register (AR) of a computer contains the address of the instruction being executed. As soon as the C(AR) is interpreted, the contents of the word whose address is in the AR is obtained for execution, being placed in another register, the *instruction register* (IR). For example, referring to the program in the last section, initially the C(AR) = 0001, the starting address of the program. Then, the C(IR) becomes 10000017_8, the instruction located at 0001.

We can outline the process of instruction interpretation and execution as follows:

1. The AR is set to the starting address of the program, which we call S_0. (We can assume for the present that S_0 is supplied with a program, or that there is a standard value for S_0, such as 0000.) Once this is done, the computer acts under the control of the program.
2. Place the instruction located at C(AR) into the IR.
3. Interpret the instruction, obtaining its operation code and operand (in the operation and address fields, respectively).
4. Execute the instruction, by obtaining the operand needed and thus perform the operation.
5. Place the next instruction address in the AR: If the instruction is not a decision type or if a test fails, simply increase the C(AR) by 1; otherwise, set the C(AR) to the value given in the instruction.
6. Return to step 2.

This process continues until a stop occurs, at which time program execution has been completed. If the program is properly written, the correct answers will have been obtained.

Let us consider some of the instructions of the GAMMA 70 and examine steps 4 and 5 in some detail. We consider the following instructions, listed here with symbolic names for reference purposes:

Instruction	Description	Op. Code
LOAD	Place a number in the AC.	10
STORE	Store a number from the AC.	11
ADD	Add a number to the AC.	20
READ	Read a number.	40
STOP	Stop.	00
JUMP	Jump unconditionally.	30
JMPGZ	Jump if the AC is > 0.	31

The other instructions (subtract, multiply, divide, write, identified as SUBT, MULT, DIV, and WRITE) are similar to some of these. Each of these instructions is listed, with its execution stage and AR-setting stage, in Table 6.1. The symbol A represents the contents of the instruction address filed, i.e., the location of the operand. Thus, 'C(A)' means the contents of the operand address, or the operand itself.

TABLE 6.1

Instruction	Execution	Setting AR
LOAD	AC ← C(A)	AR ← C(AR) + 1
STORE	A ← C(AC)	AR ← C(AR) + 1
ADD	AC ← C(AC) + C(A)	AR ← C(AR) + 1
READ	A ← an item read	AR ← C(AR) + 1
STOP	Stop	—
JUMP	(None)	AR ← A
JMPGZ	Test the C(AC):	
	if > 0 ...	AR ← A
	if ⩽ 0 ...	AR ← C(AR) + 1

The operations in the table should be understood. Consider a LOAD instruction, such as the following:

Location	Instruction
0010	10 00 2000

At location 0010, there is an instruction that says, "Load the contents of location 2000 in the AC." Thus, A has the value 2000 and 'C(A)' means the quantity stored in 2000. That quantity is placed in the AC. That is the meaning of the expression, 'AC ← C(A)', in the first line of the table. At the same time, since the C(AR) was 0010, it is changed to 0011, as indicated by 'AR ← C(AR) + 1'. Other lines in the table can be similarly interpreted.

We can see that, in most cases, the C(AR) is simply increased by 1. Only in the case of decision instructions, when a transfer of control is involved, does the AR change to the value given in the instruction itself. Since that value is 'A', the expression 'AR ← A' signifies this operation.

Figure 6.1 illustrates the manner of execution of the several instructions in the GAMMA 70. The diagram is a simplification of the operation of that (or any) computer. This process is worth studying, as we have done, because of the understanding gained of the manner in which a digital computer operates. In the next section, we shall actually build a model of the GAMMA 70, so that programs written for it can be executed.

The simple diagram of computer organization in Figure 1.1 is shown with some details added in Figure 6.2. This figure also serves to summarize the information in this chapter on the GAMMA 70.

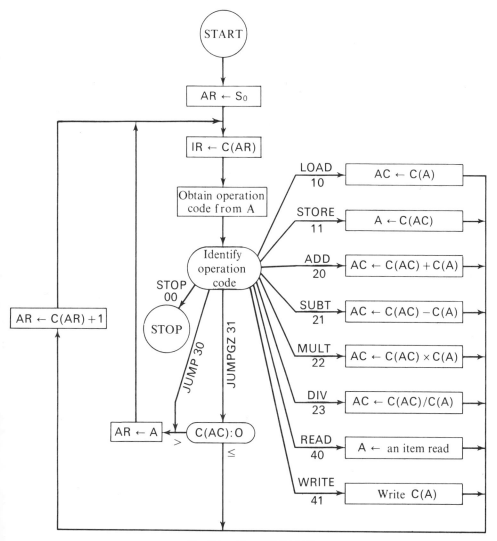

Fig. 6.1.   The GAMMA 70.

EXERCISES

1. Complete Table 6.1, adding the instructions SUBT, MULT, DIV, and WRITE.

2. Devise other useful decision instructions and indicate in what type of programs they would be of value.

3. Some computers have an instruction, "add one to memory", which adds the number 1 to a specified memory location. Assuming the existence of such a GAMMA 70 instruction, with an operation code of 27, recode the program to add 25 numbers.

*   *   *   *   *   *   *

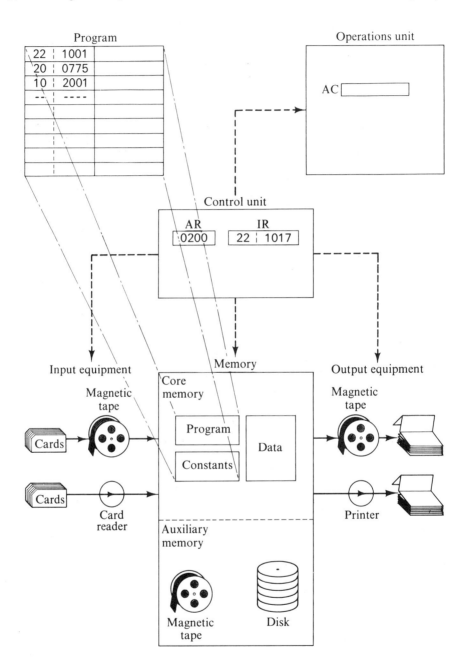

Fig. 6.2.   Computer organization (with details).

4. Complete the coding of the problem in this section by including a reading loop that reads the 25 numbers; also add a WRITE instruction for the result. Note that new assignments of constants and data will have to be made.

5. Write programs in GAMMA 70 machine language for the problems below. Make assignments of space as required. Assume that the data are already in memory.
   (a) Given a set of numbers, determine the largest one. Code this without a loop, for four numbers, as flowcharted in Chapter 3. Code this also using a loop, for 100 numbers. (*Hint:* To compare two numbers, compute their difference and use the decision instruction.)
   (b) Given four numbers, print them in increasing order of value.

6. Add further to Table 6.1, imagining these instructions to exist: Jump if AC is zero, do not jump otherwise; add the number in the AC to a specified location (A) in memory, putting the sum in that location; clear (set to zero) the AC.

* * * * * *

7. The program developed in this section has one major fault. If it were used a second time with new data, the addition instruction (at location 0004_8) would fail to add the numbers, since that instruction was modified many times. Rewrite the program so that it can be used indefinitely. (Note that the coding added by Exercise 2, above, may need such modification.)

6.3 SIMULATION OF THE GAMMA 70

Simulation[1]

It is sometimes desirable to be able to write a program for one computer and execute it on another. This is true if the former machine does not exist, the case of the GAMMA 70. We can do this by means of an *interpretive program* (or *interpreter*), located in the computer being operated. We say that the computer whose program is being interpreted is being *simulated*.

The program to be interpreted is placed in the memory of the simulating or *host* computer. The contents of the fields in the interpreted instructions are examined. The operations and operands of those instructions are interpreted and executed by the host computer. In this manner, the given program can be simulated and therefore run.

We are here interested in a variation of this technique. We will write an interpretive program in an algorithmic language that will execute a machine-language program. The simulated computer is the GAMMA 70.

Writing a Simulator

Let us consider the design of a simulator, which we call SIM70. Both the interpreter and the simulated program are in the memory of the host computer. It is necessary, at the start of the simulation, to provide the interpreter with the starting location of the program. This location is placed in a simulated address register (AR). Control is then considered to be at the instruction whose address is in

AR. This is not strictly true, since control never actually passes to the simulated program. The starting instruction is interpreted and executed, and control "passes" to the next instruction, and so on. If a transfer of control occurs, then the proper address is placed in AR. Otherwise, the C(AR) is increased by 1. Throughout the simulation, control remains with the interpreter, and AR guides the execution of the simulated program.

Each simulated instruction is interpreted by an analysis of its fields. For the GAMMA 70, this means interpretation of the operation and address fields. Each operation is executed by sending control to an appropriate routine within the interpreter.

The operation of the GAMMA 70 was partially sketched in Figure 6.1. Now we shall write a program to realize that flowchart and thereby simulate the operation of any program written for that hypothetical computer.

First, consider the format of the data cards. Each card represents one GAMMA 70 instruction in machine language, with eight octal digits. Since the digits are octal, they must be so interpreted. Some FORTRAN compilers permit data fields to be so translated, provided that the 'Ø' format specification is used. 'Ø' is used in the manner of the 'I' specification. Each card may contain an instruction in this form:

32002274

Since the two fields (operation code '32' and address '2274') are truly separate entities, they will be read separately. In order to skip the unused middle field ('00'), we may use the format specification '2X', which indicates that two characters are to be skipped. Following the last card, to indicate the end of the program, we punch a string of eight 7's: 77777777.

Next, let us consider the storage of data, which in this case is the simulated program. Since the GAMMA 70 has 10000_8 or 4096 words of memory, we allot just that many words in the host memory. However, since we are going to accept two fields per instruction, let us place each of the two instruction fields in a separate word. Thus we allot an array 4096×2, called PRØG. A picture of the simulated memory is shown in Figure 6.3. This memory is the array PRØG. The numbers shown in the array represent a program; the program is the one coded in Section 6.2, which computes a sum of numbers. The number pair in parentheses in each entry of PRØG represents the subscripts of the entry; these are written in octal to correspond to the earlier program.

	Op. codes	Addresses
	(1,1) 10	(1,2) 0017
	(2,1) 11	(2,2) 0021
PRØG array	(3,1) 10	(3,2) 0021
	(4,1) 20	(4,2) 0022
	⋮	⋮
	(17,1) x	(17,2) 0
	(20,1) x	(20,2) 1
	⋮	⋮

Fig. 6.3. Simulated memory.

In locations 0017_8 and 0020_8, in the program and in Figure 6.3, are stored two constants, 0 and 1, respectively. For simplicity, we can read in constants the same way as we read in instructions. Using the 'Ø2,2X,Ø4' specification described above, the program places these constants in PRØG(K,2), where K is some number. If constants exceed four octal digits, they will not be read correctly, due to the '2X' in the format specification. Thus we must limit the constants and data to integers no greater than 7777_8 (4095) in this simulation. Furthermore, they must be positive. In the lower part of Figure 6.3, the constants 0 and 1 are shown, in PRØG(17,2) and PRØG(20,2). We ignore the quantities in PRØG(17,1) and PRØG(20,1), shown as 'x', for they are meaningless.

The program in Figure 6.3 would appear as follows on punched cards:

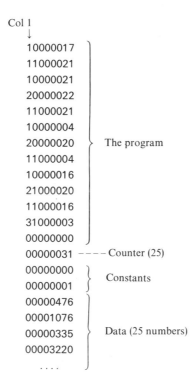

```
Col 1
  ↓
  10000017  ⎫
  11000021  ⎪
  10000021  ⎪
  20000022  ⎪
  11000021  ⎪
  10000004  ⎪
  20000020  ⎬  The program
  11000004  ⎪
  10000016  ⎪
  21000020  ⎪
  11000016  ⎪
  31000003  ⎪
  00000000  ⎭
  00000031  ────Counter (25)
  00000000  ⎫
  00000001  ⎬  Constants
  00000476  ⎫
  00001076  ⎪
  00000335  ⎬  Data (25 numbers)
  00003220  ⎪
    . . . .  ⎭
```

The following statements read the program into the host memory; ACCUM simulates the GAMMA 70 accumulator. Let us start the program at location 0001.

```
C    SIM70-1
     DIMENSIØN PRØG(4096,2)
     INTEGER START, PRØG, ACCUM, AR
C    READ IN PRØGRAM.  START PRØGRAM AT 0001.
```

```
  1  START = 1
     K = START
  2  READ (5,101) INSØP, INSAD
101  FØRMAT (Ø2,2X,Ø4)
     IF (INSØP .EQ. 63) GØ TØ 3
     PRØG(K,1) = INSØP
     PRØG(K,2) = INSAD
     K = K + 1
     GØ TØ 2
  3  . . .
```

In this sequence, K is an index which always contains the program location into which an instruction is to be stored. We are assuming that the first instruction read is also the first to be executed. This is a convenience, though not a necessity. The two statements involving the array PRØG store the two portions of a simulated instruction into that array. Those two portions were read into INSØP (instruction operation) and INSAD (instruction address), before being stored in PRØG. The end-of-program signal, the '77777777', is identified by the test for 63 in the IF statement. (An octal 77 is a decimal 63.) The sequence above loops until the end-of-program card is hit, at which time control passes out of the loop.

If 'Ø'-conversion is not available in a particular compiler, then the octal conversion must be programmed. This is not difficult to do. One only has to use this formula:

$$N = \cdots + 8^3 \times d_3 + 8^2 \times d_2 + 8 \times d_1 + d_0$$

where the d_1 are the digits of the octal integer. We read the octal integer in as separate digits and apply this conversion. The early part of the program above is rewritten as follows (after declaring D1, D0, . . . integers):

```
  1  K = 1
  2  READ(5,101) D1, D0, DD3, DD2, DD1, DD0
101  FØRMAT (2I1,2X,4I1)
     INSØP = 8 * D1 + D0
     INSAD = 512 * DD3 + 64 * DD2 + 8 * DD1 + DD0
     IF (INSØP .EQ. 63) GØ TØ 3
```

The next step is to consider the program execution. First, we set AR to the starting location, which is 0001. Then we obtain the operation and address, placing these in IRØ and IRA, representing jointly the instruction register, IR. To determine which operation code we have, a sequence of IF statements may be used. If $C(IRØ) = 10_8$, then the instruction is LØAD; if it equals 11_8, then the instruction is STØRE; etc. The legal GAMMA 70 operation codes (in octal) are 00, 10,

11, 20, etc., but the tests in the logical IF's must be in decimal. The complete set of codes is the following:

Instruction	Operation Code	
	Octal	**Dec.**
STØP	00	0
LØAD	10	8
STØRE	11	9
ADD	20	16
SUBT	21	17
MULT	22	18
DIV	23	19
JUMP	30	24
JMPGZ	31	25
READ	40	32
WRITE	41	33

The sequence of coding that executes the simulated program is the following:

```
C    EXECUTE THE SIMULATED PRØGRAM
   3   AR = START
   4   IRØ = PRØG(AR,1)
       IRA = PRØG(AR,2)
C    DETERMINE THE ØPERATIØN CØDE AND EXECUTE
C    STØP (ØPCØDE = 00).
       IF (IRØ .EQ. 0) STØP
C    LØAD ACCUMULATØR (ØPCØDE = 10).
       IF (IRØ .EQ. 8) ACCUM = PRØG(IRA,2)
C    STØRE ACCUMULATØR (ØPCØDE = 11).
       IF (IRØ .EQ. 9) PRØG(IRA,2) = ACCUM
C    ADD (ØPCØDE = 20).
       IF (IRØ .EQ. 16) ACCUM = ACCUM + PRØG(IRA,2)
C    SUBTRACT (ØPCØDE = 21).
       IF (IRØ .EQ. 17) ACCUM = ACCUM − PRØG(IRA,2)
C    MULTIPLY (ØPCØDE = 22).
       IF (IRØ .EQ. 18) ACCUM = ACCUM * PRØG(IRA,2)
C    DIVIDE (ØPCØDE = 23).
       IF (IRØ .EQ. 19) ACCUM = ACCUM / PRØG(IRA,2)
C    JUMP UNCØNDITIØNALLY (ØPCØDE = 30).
       IF (IRØ .EQ. 24) GØ TØ 90
C    JUMP IF AC GREATER THAN ZERØ (ØPCØDE = 31).
       IF (IRØ .EQ. 25) IF (ACCUM) 80, 80, 90
```

```
C    READ A NUMBER (ØPCØDE = 40).
        IF (IRØ .EQ. 32) READ (5,102) PRØG(IRA,2)
   102  FØRMAT (F10.2)
C    WRITE A NUMBER (ØPCØDE = 41).
        IF (IRØ .EQ. 33) WRITE(6,103) PRØG(IRA,2)
   103  FØRMAT (1H F10.2)
C    INCREMENT AR BY 1 (NØN-JUMP).  BACK FØR NEXT INSTRUCTIØN.
    80  AR = AR + 1
        GØ TØ 4
C    SET AR TØ JUMP VALUE.  BACK FØR NEXT.
    90  AR = IRA
        GØ TØ 4
        END
```

Comments on this program are appropriate. First, we may note that the two statements at label '4' fetch the operation code and operand address. Since AR contains the address of the instruction to be executed, PRØG(AR,1) contains the operation code of that instruction, and PRØG(AR,2) contains the operand address. IRØ and IRA are set equal to these two items, respectively.

Next, we see that, since IRA has a value equal to the operand address, PRØG(IRA,2) contains the operand itself. Therefore, this subscripted variable appears in each statement that executes a simulated nontransfer instruction. Each operation is thus performed on PRØG(IRA,2) which contains four simulated octal digits. In the case of the transfer instructions, AR may be set to the value of IRA, the operand address.

If the test for an operation code succeeds, the simulated execution will take place. Then, because of the way the program is written, all other tests will also be made until statement 80 (or 90) is hit. This results in some running inefficiency, which can be eliminated.

This completes the design of the GAMMA 70 simulator, as far as that computer has been defined. Later, we shall extend the simulator so that the GAMMA 70 can be more easily coded. We have already seen that writing in machine language is difficult. The next step is to introduce certain symbolic coding features.

EXERCISES

1. How does an interpreter differ from a compiler? When would each be used? What is the main advantage in using an interpreter?

2. Identify three tasks performed in the coding for the GAMMA 70 that normally are performed by computer hardware.

3. Estimate how much slower a simulated computer such as the GAMMA 70 would run than the computer itself.

4. Negative numbers were excluded in this simulation. How could they be considered?

*   *   *   *   *   *

5. Punch on cards the programs written in octal machine language for the GAMMA 70, as exercises for Section 6.2, using the format described in this section. Run these programs, using the simulator given, debugging them until they are correct.

6. Include in the GAMMA 70 simulator the instructions defined for Exercise 5 of Section 6.2. Write a program using these new instructions and run it with the simulator.

7. Modify the simulator so that one may locate a program at any point in memory, e.g., let the first instruction be located in location 1000_8 instead of 0001_8. To accomplish a proper loading and execution of the program, the starting location must be supplied with the program. Let this be punched on one card, in columns 1 through 4, given prior to the program itself.

8. Rewrite the code that simulates the program execution so that it is more efficient when running. Insert jumps (GØ TØ's) so that not all tests are made each time.

6.4 HIGHER-LEVEL CODING

Symbolic Coding

We have seen how tedious it is to code using machine language. Because of this, higher-level languages are used. We have also seen how simply FORTRAN can be used to code programs. Summing 25 numbers in FORTRAN requires three statements, once data are in memory. Using GAMMA machine language, thirteen instructions, each with eight digits, are needed.

Coding at the machine level has many advantages and, despite the existence of FORTRAN, continues to be used in a number of situations. Code compiled from algorithmic programs tends to be inefficient, for the generality of the approach has to take many possibilities into account. Machine-level coding can be "hand-tailored" to the problem at hand and thus can be made very efficient. Furthermore, there are many operations that simply cannot be done well at all in FORTRAN. (Other programming languages have provisions for such operations.) Among these are manipulation of bits within words and characters within strings. (We shall examine such operations in later chapters.) When FORTRAN is so used (and we shall do this), the result is often a slower running program that requires much space. We should note, however, that in this book we are not directly concerned with these problems and shall use FORTRAN to develop techniques, bypassing most considerations of efficiency.

Machine coding is not really done in machine language (using octal numbers), however, for it is too tedious. Rather, symbols are used for the names of operations and for memory locations. We will use the operation names given in the last section. Clearly it is easier to use 'STORE' and 'JUMP' than to remember '11' and '31'. Similarly, it is easier to refer to a location 'TWO' than to a location called '1002' which contains 2. Furthermore, when a reference is made to a location in memory, the address of that location must be assigned at the end if numeric addresses are used. If new instructions are added, the address must be changed. If symbolic addresses are used, however, we can refer to 'TWO' and not give any thought to where the location really is. Later, that location is assigned in sequence when needed. If extra instructions are added later, no changes need be made in references to 'TWO'.

Let us examine a program using *symbolic coding*, as the process is called, and compare the two techniques. Consider the formula evaluation (CYLVØL-M) in Section 6.1, where the volume of a cylinder was computed. Let 'RAD', 'HT', 'PI', and 'VØL' be the symbols used for radius, height, pi, and volume, respectively. The program (now called CYLVØL-S) is written as follows:

Location	Instruction		Remarks
0000	READ	RAD	Read the value of r into location RAD.
0001	READ	HT	Read the value of h into location HT.
0002	LØAD	PI	Put the value of π into the AC, getting it from location PI.
0003	MULT	RAD	Multiply π by r, leaving product in AC.
0004	MULT	RAD	Multiply by r again.
0005	MULT	HT	Finally, multiply by h, obtaining $\pi r^2 h$.
0006	STØRE	VØL	Store the result in location VØL.
0007	WRITE	VØL	Print the result.
0010	STØP		

The program as written consists only of the material under "Instruction". The locations are assigned by the program that translates the symbolic form to machine language, the *assembler*.

The program is not complete, for we must still assign the locations for the data read, the constant (pi), and the result. We do this by using a special kind of operation, a *pseudo-operation*, used to indicate to the assembler that special action is to be taken. Here the special action is to assign a floating-point number of given value to the location given, as here:

PI NUMBER 3.1416

The complete program is the following:

START	READ	RAD	Read the values of r and h.
	READ	HT	
	LØAD	PI	Form $\pi r^2 h$ in AC.
	MULT	RAD	
	MULT	RAD	
	MULT	HT	
	STØRE	VØL	Store result.
	WRITE	VØL	Print result.
	STØP		

```
RAD     NUMBER 0
HT      NUMBER 0
PI      NUMBER 3.1416
VØL     NUMBER 0
        END
```

The name START was added to the first instruction to illustrate that we may give that location a name and that it is the first instruction. The four pseudo-operations, using NUMBER, are placed directly after the instructions to be executed. The assembler will assign them to four words directly after the STØP instruction, i.e., to locations 0011 through 0014. We use NUMBER even when we do not know the value, as with RAD, HT, and VØL, because we must assign a word for each. (In FORTRAN, such preassignment of locations is unnecessary.) Finally, we use END to signify the end of the deck to the assembler.

Now we can see the advantages of symbolic coding over machine-language coding. We can see that if extra instructions were added, we do not have to worry about renumbering words for other instructions or for the data.

As another illustration of symbolic coding, let us consider the summation problem, coded in Section 6.2. That program (now called SUM-S) might be written as follows, using symbolic coding:

```
START   LØAD    ZERØ        Set SUM to zero.
        STØRE   SUM
LØØP    LØAD    SUM         Place SUM in AC.
ADIN    ADD     SET         Add one number to SUM.
        STØRE   SUM
        LØAD    ADIN        Place addition instruction in AC.
        ADD     ØNE         Add one instruction.
        STØRE   ADIN
        LØAD    CTR         Place counter in AC.
        SUBT    ØNE         Subtract one from counter.
        STØRE   CTR
        JMPGZ   LØØP        Jump back if last number not summed.
        STØP
ZERØ    NUMBER  0
SUM     NUMBER  0
ØNE     NUMBER  1
CTR     NUMBER  0
SET     BLØCK   25
        END
```

This program resembles the earlier one, but there are some differences. This one contains a jump to an earlier point in the program (labeled LØØP). A block of memory words has to be set aside for the 25 numbers to be used. The pseudo-operation BLØCK directs the assembler to do this, and gives the name SET to the first of these 25 words.

This program is clearly easier to write than the machine-language program given earlier. Digital computers have other instructions that simplify the task still further. One very important one is automatic indexing, that allows a computer to take into account subscripts on arrays in an automatic fashion. With this feature, the nuisance of having to modify instructions, something we did in this program, is avoided.

Even though this symbolic program is much easier to write than if machine code is used, and even though automatic indexing makes things easier yet, we cannot avoid noting that FORTRAN is easiest of all. Consider this program:

```
       SUM = 0
       DØ 10 I = 1, 25
   10  SUM = SUM + SET(I)
```

This code adds the 25 numbers of array SET, precisely what the symbolic-code program does! Nonetheless, we study symbolic programming to understand digital computers better, to study programming techniques used for program translators, and to study simulation methods.

Program Assembly

An assembler is used to translate symbolic coding into machine language. The task of converting symbolic operations and addresses is straightforward. For operations, the process involves looking in a table for each symbol and then replacing it with the numerical operation code. For addresses the process is somewhat more complicated, since the choice of symbols is up to the programmer, but it is still essentially a replacement problem.

The assembly process, the conversion of a symbolic source program to a machine-language object program, consists of two phases or *passes*. In the first pass, the instructions and data words in the program are assigned locations as they are encountered; symbols that are used to name some of these words are entered in a *symbol table*. For example, for the second symbolic program above, this table would be created:

Symbol	Location
START	0000
LØØP	0002
ADIN	0003
ZERØ	0015
SUM	0016
ØNE	0017
CTR	0020
SET	0021

In the second pass, the complete instruction is assembled; its two parts, operation code and address, are entered. The complete symbol table, for the entire program, is sorted and available at the start of the second pass. In Chapter 7, we shall develop an assembler that will accept symbolic programs.

This is really a gross simplification of the process, but we shall not in this text work extensively with assembly. There are many extensions to this simple process. It is possible, e.g., to specify a specific area of memory into which a program is to be loaded, to specify octal numbers as well as decimal numbers as constants, to set aside areas of memory for the storage of constants that are more than just one word in size, and so on.

Source and Object Programs

A program that is supplied to a translator is called a *source program*; the language used is a *source language*. FORTRAN and symbolic programs for the GAMMA 70 are examples. The result of the translation process is an *object program* in an *object language* or machine language. The output of a FORTRAN compiler is an object program that will run on the computer for which the compiler was written.

When a program is run, its object program with its data are loaded into computer memory and executed. We shall study this process of execution in greater detail in Chapter 8.

EXERCISES

1. Consider the two passes described, which together form the assembly process. Expand the descriptions of what takes place in each pass.

2. If FORTRAN is so much easier to use, is there any reason for using symbolic languages?

3. In the assembly programs given in this section, explain the difference between the STOP and the END cards.

*   *   *   *   *   *

4. Using symbolic code, rewrite the programs written in the exercises for Section 6.3.

REFERENCES

1. The following book describes one language for simulation:

   H. M. Markowitz, B. Hausner, and H. W. Karr, *SIMSCRIPT: A Simulation Programming Language*, Prentice-Hall, Inc., 1963.

7 SUBROUTINES

Very often, a sequence of program statements constitutes a procedure that is frequently used. In such a case, the sequence is usually identified as a separate routine called a *subroutine*. It is alternately called a *procedure* or a *subprogram*, though slightly different connotations are associated with these terms. When a subroutine is defined, it is given a name and its *arguments* are identified. Its arguments are its variables, i.e., those items that vary from use to use, much in the way that a function has parameters. In this chapter we shall study the nature of subroutines, as well as their purpose and use.

7.1 THE PURPOSE OF SUBROUTINES

Extensions of the Language

In any programming language, there are several different statement types. It may be convenient to a programmer that a new statement, one that performs a specific well-defined task, become available. By defining a subroutine to execute that task, he may accomplish just that. Suppose, for example, that he wished to write a statement that would call for computing the sum S of the elements in the upper triangular area of an array, coded in Section 5.2. We might write the statement in the form

$$S \leftarrow \text{trisum}(A,m)$$

where "trisum" is the name of the process, A is the name of the array, and m is the dimension of A. We write the expression as a function, whose "value" is the desired answer, S. The function has two parameters.

To incorporate this statement into the language, we must code "trisum" as a subroutine, identifying its arguments. We have studied a flowchart and a program

110

for this procedure in Section 5.2. Now we wish to make use of the subroutine, adding it to our language.

An alternate form of writing the statement is this:

$$\text{execute trisum}(A,m,S)$$

where "execute" implies execution of the subroutine. The result, S, is treated as another argument of the function. As we shall see, FORTRAN permits either form. These statements are termed subroutine *calls*.

A distinction should be made between these two forms of calls. The first implies that a *value* is returned, as with a function. We may include that value in an expression, as here:

$$A \leftarrow B + \text{trisum}(A,m)$$

The second implies that an operation is performed; in the example this operation is "trisum", determining a triangular sum. No value in such cases is necessarily returned. This type is better exemplified by this call:

$$\text{execute sort}(B,n)$$

which states that an array B of size n is to be sorted.

In both of these types of statements, a new capability is in effect added to the programming language. Once a subroutine has been created and its call has been established, a new operation is available to the programmer, and so the language has been extended.

Simplification of Code

Without the use of subroutines, operations such as "trisum" and "sort" would have to appear in their entirety everywhere those operations were needed. This would result in a great deal of duplication of code, as sequences of instructions would be repeated with but few changes. The use of subroutines avoids this difficulty, greatly reducing the effort in coding.

Library Development

As programmers write subroutines of general value, these programs can be made available to others. A library of subroutines can be created that is usable by many programmers. The work of one person can be utilized by many, particularly if the subroutine performs a commonly-used operation. Most computer installations provide "mathematics" libraries including matrix operations, trigonometric functions, sorting of numbers, and so on. Provision for calling many of these is imbedded within most computers.

Program Development

We have seen that, in developing a computer program, we perform a sufficiently detailed analysis, perhaps written as a flowchart. What is "sufficiently detailed" varies, of course, from problem to problem, from user to user, and from language to language. If we write in an algorithmic language, we may be able merely to write a statement that calls for the square root, as in

```
QRØØT  =  A  +  SQRT(Y**3)
```

Were it not for that SQRT call, we might detail that operation, as was actually done in Section 2.2. Similarly, we might want to order the numbers in a list, as implied by a call to "sort" given earlier. If such a subroutine did not exist, we would have to code it. Once this was done, however, the call could be written as though "sort" were part of the language.

Subroutines can be coded and debugged independently of the programs that use them; the latter are called *main* programs. By isolating the work involved, the programmer decreases the chances for errors to occur in main programs. Once subroutines are debugged, their code need not be considered again; they act as single instructions or extensions of the language. Further, the main programs are simpler to code and debug. The result of this isolation of individual tasks makes the task of program development more efficient.

Another advantage to identifying such operations as subroutines is that, with tasks so isolated, they can be assigned to the several members of a programming project. Because of their relative independence, subroutines coded by a number of people can be more readily combined than would otherwise be the case. A measure of coordination is required in this approach, however, in ways that will become clear.

Finally, we may note that when a program must be studied in the future for possible modification or extension, the re-educational process (or educational process with a new programmer) can be aided by the use of the subroutines. The several tasks of the program are more readily identified as to function in this approach.

EXERCISES

1. Several reasons for using subroutines have been given. Which seems to be the most significant, and why?

2. What are some functions or operations that could reasonably be coded as subroutines?

3. When would each of the two forms of subroutine calls be used?

7.2 THE CHARACTER OF SUBROUTINES

Transfer of Control

A particular subroutine appears only once in memory, although it may be called many times by one or more programs. When the subroutine is used, control must be sent to it, and then later control must be returned to the main program.

To study the problem of transfer of control, let us consider a subroutine call:

execute trisum (A,m,S)

The manner of control transfer is illustrated in Figure 7.1. Control passes to "trisum" from each of three calls. Control returns to the main program to each of three points, just after the calls, the actual route taken being determined by the contents of the *return register*, described below. The boxes labeled I, II, III, and IV represent sequences of instructions in the main program.

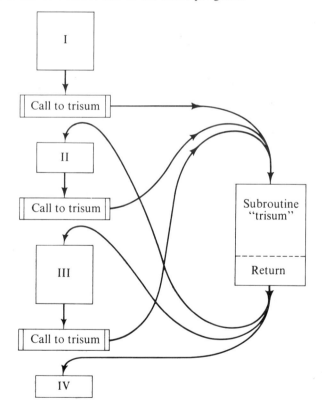

Main program

Fig. 7.1.   Flow of control to and from a subroutine.

Control is transferred to a subroutine by means of a *calling sequence* at the point in the program where the call to the subroutine occurs. Commonly, one memory location in the calling sequence is assigned to hold each call parameter. Since parameters are frequently variables (rather than constants), those locations contain references to the parameters, rather than the parameters themselves. For example, if a symbol ARRAY is given, its location is compiled into the calling sequence.

Consider the transfer of control from the point of view of the subroutine. It obtains control from the calling program, performs its task, and then must return control. To do this, it must retain the point in the calling program from which control came. Let us consider the GAMMA 70, and add two new instructions to our repertoire:

	Code (octal)
Subroutine jump.	32
Subroutine return.	33

The first instruction, "subroutine jump", is a jump with a special extra task. It enables the subroutine to store the location from which control came, i.e., where the "subroutine jump" instruction was located in the program. It does this by storing the location's address in a *return register*, available for this purpose. The second instruction, "subroutine return", returns control to the main program.

Consider the following GAMMA 70 calling sequence for the call given above:

Locations	Instructions	Remarks
0220	32 00 1020	Transfer to subroutine.
0221	00 00 2000	First argument (A).
0222	00 00 3000	Second argument (m).
0223	00 00 3001	Third argument (S).

Let us analyze this calling sequence. Control passes to the subroutine, located at 1020. Since there are three parameters, the subroutine must be coded to return to four locations beyond the call within the main program, wherever that call is located. The number stored in the return register, 0220, is increased by four within the subroutine, becoming 0224, the location to which control eventually returns, when the "subroutine jump" instruction is executed within the subroutine.

The two new instructions and the technique described for transferring control to and from the subroutine are, of course, imaginary, but they are quite similar to those used in computers.

Figure 7.1, although not truly a flowchart, resembles one. A new type of box is introduced there, a rectangle with double vertical sides. This box will be used for subroutine call operations and represents the calling sequence. Normally, the name of the subroutine and the parameters supplied with it will be entered in the box.

Transfer of Information

Besides control being transferred to the subroutine, the parameters must also be transferred. As we have seen, the calling sequence contains the addresses of those parameters. For example, in the calling sequence above for "trisum" given in GAMMA 70 code, the array A is located starting at location 2000, the argument m is at location 3000, and the argument S is at location 3001. These locations are thus "known" to the subroutine and by appropriate instructions are extracted from memory. We will not examine the machine-language details by which this is accomplished.

Subroutines may be called with expressions supplied as parameters. In that event, it is necessary for the value of that expression to be computed before control passes to the subroutine. For example, the statement

$$\text{execute trisum } (A, 2 \times r, S)$$

would mean that the dimension of the array is given as twice the value of r. The compiler would have to compile instructions that would compute $2 \times r$, store its results temporarily some place, with the address of that place in the calling sequence, and then permit control to pass to the subroutine.

Standardization

If we are to use subroutines written by others, or by ourselves, it is necessary to standardize the manner in which they are called and the way in which they supply results. All subroutines written need not have the same format, but a standard must be set for each. Although each subroutine may have its call format different from all others, it helps one's memory when similar subroutines have similar call formats.

Consider the two subroutine calls mentioned:

$$\text{execute trisum } (A, m, S)$$

$$\text{execute sort } (a, n)$$

The first call includes three parameters, which must be written in the order given, for the subroutine is coded to interpret its given parameters as array name, number of columns, and sum, in the order shown. Similarly, the second call supplies the list name, then the list size.

Standardization of another type must be established for each subroutine. The form of the data must be standardized. Consider a two-dimensional array which can be stored with row elements in succession in memory or with column elements in succession. The data format clearly must be standardized in one form or the other. Numbers may be stored in floating-point or integer form. They might be stored singly or two to a word. Once again, a standard storage scheme must be established and assumed.

To illustrate that a variety of forms for a given subroutine can be used, consider the "trisum" subroutine. The parameters of the array could have been stored so that only two need be given:

execute trisum (A,S)

The other parameter, m, could be stored in memory in the location just *preceding* the array A. The subroutine would, of course, have to be so written. The advantage would be that the call is simplified, but this parameter would have to be stored in that location. There is no general rule for designing subroutine calls; their formats are dictated by convenience.

The need for standardization of the form and location of the parameters and their sequence in the call should be clear. Even if correct subroutines are used improperly, chaos can result.

EXERCISES

1. It was stated that, for a given subroutine, the calling sequence is standardized. However, it is possible to have a variable calling sequence for a subroutine. How could this be accomplished?

2. When, for a given subroutine, would a variable calling sequence be useful?

3. Write calling sequences for subroutines that perform the following tasks:
   (a) Determine the largest number in a given set.
   (b) Determine whether a given set of numbers has its sum greater than 1000.
   (c) Given a paragraph of text, determine which word is the longest and identify the word.

* * * * * *

4. Write a segment of machine-language code (for the GAMMA 70) to perform this "execute" statement:

execute trisum $(A,2 \times r,S)$

   discussed in the text. This code should include instructions that properly determine "$2 \times r$" and then comprise the calling sequence.

5. There may be an advantage in complete standardization of calling sequences, so that all have one fixed length. How can this be accomplished with a variable number of arguments permitted?

6. The transfer of subroutine arguments was considered in the text. Write GAMMA 70 code that extracts these arguments from a calling sequence and places them in a subroutine. Consider the "trisum" subroutine.

7. Write code, as in Exercise 6, to return the result of "trisum" to the main program.

7.3 WRITING SUBROUTINES (I)

FORTRAN Subprograms

In FORTRAN, subroutines are called *subprograms*, and two types are recognized: FUNCTIØN and SUBRØUTINE. Subprograms can be compiled separately, and their variable names are independent of any variables in the main program or in other subprograms.

'FUNCTIØN' Subprograms

A FUNCTIØN subprogram defines a function; it is written as a separate program:*

FUNCTIØN name $(x_1, x_2, \ldots)$

.

.

name = expression

.

.

END

where the name of the subprogram and its list of arguments x_i, which are names local to this program, appear in the FUNCTIØN statement. These arguments are dummy variables, as in a mathematical function, and must be nonsubscripted FORTRAN variables. A value must be given to name somewhere in the subprogram, as indicated by the assignment statement. FUNCTIØN subprograms are called with functional notation. These subprograms correspond to the first form of subroutine call considered in Section 7.1.

Use is made of a FUNCTIØN subprogram simply by writing the function name and its arguments to be applied:

$$\text{name } (y_1, y_2, \ldots)$$

This call appears in an assignment statement as though it were a variable. That variable is considered to have the value computed by the subprogram. The arguments y_i given in the call may be expressions of any form, provided they match the mode of corresponding dummy arguments. This list of arguments must be ordered exactly as the dummy arguments are ordered.

We shall extend the flowchart conventions to accommodate subroutines, including both the FUNCTIØN and SUBRØUTINE types. Instead of a START

---

* From this point on, the following convention will be used to illustrate the form of certain cards in a general way: capital letters (as "FUNCTIØN") stand for themselves, while small letters (as "name") stand for a substitutable parameter. References to the latter are underlined.

Fig. 7.2. Sub-
routine boxes.

box, a circle or oval appears at the start with the subroutine name and its parameters, as shown in Figure 7.2. RETURN boxes are used in place of STOP boxes.

Example 7.1. Write a FUNCTIØN subprogram BIG that determines the largest number in a given list.

The simplest approach is to assume that the first number is the largest and store it away. Then, compare that number with the next, and save the larger. Then, compare that number now stored with the next, and so on, each time storing away the larger in the comparison. After the last number has been checked, the largest number in the set will have been obtained. A flowchart appears in Figure 7.3. The numbers of which we assume there are no more than 1000, are $a_1, a_2, \ldots$. In Figure 7.3, the largest number at any point is assigned to BIG. There are n numbers in the given set. The parameters (a and n) are shown in the top circle.

The FORTRAN program is the following where the arguments are the list and its size:

```
    FUNCTIØN BIG(A,N)
    DIMENSIØN A(1000)
    BIG = A(1)
    DØ 10 J = 2,N
    IF (A(J) .GT. BIG) BIG = A(J)
10  CØNTINUE
    RETURN
    END
```

We may note the following about FUNCTIØN subprograms in general: (1) A RETURN statement is required at the point in the subprogram where control is to be returned to the calling program; two or more RETURN statements may be given. (2) The name of the subprogram is also a variable in the subprogram; we can consider the subprogram to be an extended function definition where a variable is given a value. (3) The subprogram variables are dummies, bearing no particular relationship to variables in the program calling it.

The following statement is an example of the use of this subprogram:

$$\text{ITEM} = 2 + \text{BIG(LIST,50)}$$

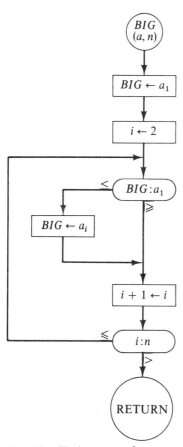

Fig. 7.3. The largest number.

This call will add 2 to the largest number in the LIST sequence, assigning the value of the sum to ITEM.

Example 7.2. Write the TRSUM1 program (Example 5.5) as a FUNCTIØN subprogram, generalizing the array to any size up to 100.
The subprogram:

```
FUNCTIØN TRSUM2(A,M)
INTEGER A, R, TRISUM
DIMENSIØN R(100), A(100,100)
TRISUM = 0
M1 = M − 1
I1 = I + 1
DØ 10 I = 1, M1
R(I) = 0
DØ 20 J = I1, M
20   R(I) = R(I) + A(I,J)
10   TRISUM = TRISUM + R(I)
RETURN
END
```

This is the same program as previously, except that the variable 'S' was renamed "TRISUM" and the size was made 'M'.

Simulation of an Assembler

A simulation of GAMMA 70 operation was written in Section 6.3. The input to that program is a machine-language program. Let us extend that simulator using subroutine techniques, so that programs written in symbolic code can be simulated as well. We can view this modification in one of two ways: (1) we now have an assembler (called GAP, for GAMMA assembly program) that converts symbolic code to machine language, or (2) we have extended the scope of the GAMMA 70 by permitting a symbolic program to be accepted by it. Either viewpoint is acceptable, because both descriptions apply. In the real world, normally only (1) would make sense, for an assembler usually produces a machine-language intermediate program as a separate process.

Example 7.3. Let us assume a specific format for GAP programs, as follows:

> The label shall begin in column 1;
> the operation code shall begin in column 8;
> the address shall begin in column 16.

The simulator must have these modifications: (1) symbolic operation codes must be accepted and converted to their numeric equivalents; (2) a symbol table must be created in Pass 1 and used in Pass 2 to convert symbolic addresses to numeric ones. We only consider the first of these tasks now.

For conversion of operation codes, we require a "dictionary" of equivalences, one we have seen already:

Symbol	Octal	Decimal
STØP	00	0
LØAD	10	8
STØRE	11	9
ADD	20	16
SUBT	21	17
MULT	22	18
DIV	23	19
JUMP	30	24
JMPGZ	31	25
READ	40	32
WRITE	41	33

We convert the given symbol, placed in SYMØP (symbolic operator), to its octal equivalent, stored in INSØP, as previously (see Section 6.3). We want this conversion to be given by a FUNCTIØN subprogram, called thus:

INSØP = ØPCV(SYMØP,ERR)

where ØPCV means operator conversion. If ERR is returned with the value 1, then an illegal code was given.

To accomplish this conversion, we require identification of alphanumeric strings, such as 'STØP', 'LØAD', etc. For this purpose, alphanumeric constants must be stored within the program for comparison.

To store within a program required constants of any type, we can make use of a special declaration statement in FORTRAN. We accomplished this in symbolic language by a pseudo-operator NUMBER of Section 6.4. We take a temporary diversion to learn of the method in FORTRAN.

DATA Declarations

The DATA declaration "preassigns" any desired constants to named variables. The declaration is of the following form in its simplest case:

$$\text{DATA } n_1, n_2, n_3, \ldots / v_1, v_2, v_3, \ldots /$$

where the n_i are names of constants and the v_i are the values of these constants. For example, we may write

DATA NAME,X(1),ITEM(2,2,2)/75,−2.01,2/

which has the same effect as writing

NAME = 75
X(1) = −2.01
ITEM(2,2,2) = 2

While we can write these three executable statements, we expend some execution time if we use them. The declaration, however, is nonexecutable, having an effect only during compilation.

   If some or all the elements of an array are to be given, we may utilize the DØ-loop form, as here:

   DATA   (X(I), I = 2,6)/2.2,3.2,4.9,5.0, −0.5/

If several values in succession are repeated, we may use the form $k*v_i$ when k repetitions occur, as in:

   DATA   (X(I), I = 2,6)/5.8,3*4.4,2.0/

which assigns 4.4 to X(3), X(4), and X(5).

   In the example above, we need alphanumeric constants. To place these in a DATA declaration we write them in the form

                        wHxxx . . x   or   'xxx . . x'

where xxx . . x is the constant and w is a count of its characters. The second form can be used only on certain compilers. Examples with alphanumeric constants are these:

   DATA   NAME,ITEM,(TITLE(I), I = 1,3)/5HMARY,3HHAT,14HCLØTHING ITEMS/

or, alternatively,

   DATA   NAME,ITEM,(TITLE(I), I = 1,3)/'MARY','HAT','CLØTHING ITEMS'/

The assignment of the characters to words in memory depends upon the number of characters C stored in a word. This varies among computers, but the usual numbers are 4, 6, or 8. If the string is C characters long, one full word is used. If the string has fewer than C characters, one word is used, the string is left-justified (usually), and the balance of the word is filled out with blanks. If the string has more than C characters, then C characters are assigned to each variable named on the left in the DATA declaration, until enough words are used. The declarations above yield the following assignments, if $C = 6$ (☐ represents a blank):

NAME	M A R Y ☐ ☐
ITEM	H A T ☐ ☐ ☐
TITLE(1)	C L Ø T H I
TITLE(2)	N G ☐ I T E
TITLE(3)	M S ☐ ☐ ☐ ☐

In this book, however, we shall assume that $C = 4$.*

---

* This restriction of a maximum of four characters per word does not preclude the use of the programs in this text on computers allowing six characters per word. The format declaration 'A4' will work on the latter, though it will be wasteful of space in each word storing alphanumeric data.

If the DATA declaration is absent from a particular computer, assignment statements may be used, as shown above. The last DATA statement above may be replaced with

```
NAME  =  'MARY'
ITEM  =  'HAT'
TITLE  =  'CLOTHING ITEMS'
```

Simulation of an Assembler (continued)

Now we can develop our subprogram. We search an array (SYM) of alphanumeric constants, having been given a symbol. Then we extract its numeric equivalent from another array (NUM). If the ith elements of the two arrays represent corresponding values (symbolic and numeric operations) we can utilize the index that locates the symbol in the first array to "point" to the corresponding numeric value in the second array. This is a common technique for identification of a given item and its subsequent translation to another form. A flowchart appears in Figure 7.4. The END card of the simulated program is associated with octal 77 or decimal 63, as before. We allow for the case of an erroneous operation code. If all entries fail to match, an error exists; E is then set to 1. The program:

```
        FUNCTIØN ØPCV(ØP,E)
        DIMENSIØN SYM(12), NUM(12)
        DATA (SYM(I),I=1,12)/4HSTØP,4HLØAD,4HSTØR,4HADD,4HSUBT,
     1       4HMULT,4HDIV ,4HJUMP,4HJPMG,4HREAD,4HWRIT,4HEND /
        DATA (NUM(I),I=1,12)/0,8,9,16,17,18,19,24,25,32,33,63/
        E = 0
        DØ 10 J = 1,12
        IF (ØP .EQ. SYM(J)) GØ TØ 20
   10   CØNTINUE
        E = 1
        RETURN
   20   ØPCV = NUM(J)
        RETURN
        END
```

For simplicity, note that each operation symbol is treated as a four-character code, sometimes including a blank. The rest of the symbol (if any) need not be considered.

Let us generalize the reading portion of the simulator to allow the simulated program to be stored anywhere in memory (PRØG). We can do this by supplying the starting location as a new item of data, as a four-digit octal address. Then, we modify the card format to the one described. As a result, this portion of the

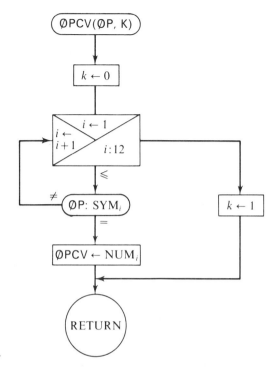

Fig. 7.4.   Conversion of code.

simulator becomes the following, where new or modified statements are underlined:

```
C    SIM70-2
        DIMENSIØN PRØG(4096,2)
        INTEGER START, PRØG, ACCUM, AR
C    READ IN PRØGRAM.
    1   READ (5,100) START
  100   FØRMAT (Ø4)
        K = START
    2   READ (5,101) SYMØP, INSAD
  101   FØRMAT (7X,A4,4X,Ø4)
        INSØP = ØPCV(SYMØP,ERR)
        IF (INSØP .EQ. 63) GØ TØ 3
        IF (ERR .EQ. 1) GØ TØ 70
        PRØG(K,1) = INSØP
        PRØG(K,2) = INSAD
        K = K + 1
        GØ TØ 2
    3   . . . .
        .
        .
   70   . . . . (error condition)
```

EXERCISES

1. What does it mean to say that a subroutine's variables' names are independent of variables in other programs? Why are a subroutine's variables characterized as "local"?

2. How would Figure 7.3 be modified to have the subroutine determine the smallest number in the list? The second largest number in the list?

3. If a new GAMMA 70 instruction were to be introduced, say JUMPZE (jump if zero), how would the ØPCV subprogram be modified?

4. Suppose an octal address were given to the SIM70-2 program as a three-digit number. What would happen?

*   *   *   *   *   *

Write FUNCTIØN subprograms to realize these functions:

5. The functions in Figure 7.5, called Y1 and Y2.

6. Determination of the number of entries in a given vector equal to a given quantity S. The function is called:

    EQUAL(VECTØR,S)

7. Determination of the number of entries in a given vector that exceed a given quantity, R, considering only the Mth entry through the Nth entry inclusively. The function is called

    CØUNT(VECTØR,M,N,R)

    where 'VECTOR' represents the name of the vector.

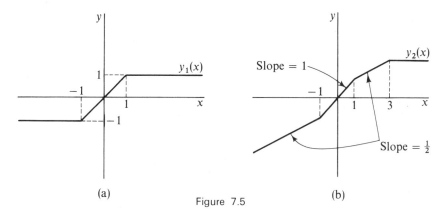

(a)   Figure 7.5   (b)

8. A chess knight's move checking function is required. Assume the board is numbered from 1 through 64 across each row and then row after row. Given the numbers representing the original and the intended new positions, return the value -1 if the move is illegal and $+1$ if the move is legal. The call is

    KNIGHT(P,N)

    where P is the original position and N is the new position.

7.4 WRITING SUBROUTINES (II)

'SUBRØUTINE' Subprograms

SUBRØUTINE subprograms are used in FORTRAN for the description of processes to be performed upon data. They correspond to the second form of subroutine call considered in Section 7.1. A value is not necessarily returned; an example is the case of a sorting operation. The arguments of the subroutine are the input parameters and, if any, the output parameters. Within the SUB-RØUTINE subprogram the point at which control returns to the calling program must be specified; a RETURN statement is used. The subprogram has this form:

$$\text{SUBROUTINE name } (x_1, x_2, \ldots)$$

.
.

$$\text{RETURN}$$

.
.

$$\text{END}$$

where the <u>name</u> of the subroutine and its list of dummy arguments x_i are given in the first statement. The arguments are nonsubscripted variables or constants. There may be any number of RETURN statements present; all return control to the same point in the calling program.

Within the main program, a SUBRØUTINE subprogram is called by this statement:

$$\text{CALL name } (y_1, y_2, \ldots)$$

As with FUNCTIØN subprograms, the arguments y_i may be any expressions of the same type as corresponding dummy arguments. The list of arguments must be ordered exactly as in the SUBRØUTINE statement.

A Sort Subroutine

A sort procedure, as mentioned earlier, is an example of a process that should be written as a subroutine. It is an example of an operation on a set of numbers.

Example 7.4. Write a sort subroutine.

We will develop a very simple sorting procedure, one that orders numbers in ascending values by interchanging numbers when an adjacent pair is out of order. By doing this continually, the numbers can be sorted. A flowchart of the procedure appears in Figure 7.6. The array of elements being sorted is $(a_i; i = 1, n)$. The method involves two nested loops and has a structure very similar to the *trisum* procedure of Section 5.2. Within the inner (j) loop, one array entry is compared with each entry following it; the index limits on this loop are thus $i + 1$ and n, where i is the index of the entry being compared. When it is found that $a_i > a_j$, the two entries are reversed. After the inner loop is completed as a result, the smallest entry among those examined ends up as the earliest of those entries.

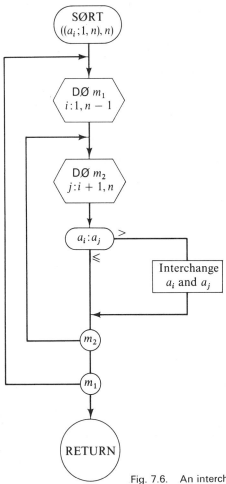

Fig. 7.6.   An interchange sort.

Within the outer loop, the index i is varied so that a new entry a_i is compared with all entries following it. When this loop is completed the numbers are all in ascending order from the start of the array. The index limits on i are 1 and $n - 1$. A program is the following:

```
C    A SØRT SUBRØUTINE
     SUBRØUTINE SØRT (ARRAY,NUM)
     DIMENSIØN ARRAY(100)
```

```
      NUM1 = NUM - 1
      DØ 20 I = 1, NUM1
      I1 = I + 1
      DØ 20 J = I1, NUM
      IF (ARRAY(I) .LE. ARRAY(J)) GØ TØ 20
      TEMP = A(I)
      A(I) = A(J)
      A(J) = TEMP
   20 CØNTINUE
      RETURN
      END
```

This subroutine is callable by a main program, such as the one given below, TSØRT (test sort). That program, which can be used for testing SØRT, reads in data, calls SØRT, and writes the result, a sorted list.

```
C    TSØRT
C    THIS PRØGRAM TESTS THE SØRT SUBRØUTINE.
     DIMENSIØN X(100)
     READ (5,100) SIZE
     READ (5,101) (X(I), I = 1, SIZE)
     WRITE (6,102)
     WRITE (6,103) (X(I), I = 1, SIZE)
     CALL SØRT (X,SIZE)
     WRITE (6,201)
     WRITE (6,103) (X(I), I = 1, SIZE)
 100 FØRMAT (N3)
 101 FØRMAT (8F8.2)
 102 FØRMAT (26H1THE NUMBERS AS GIVEN ARE)
 103 FØRMAT (1H0 8F8.2)
 201 FØRMAT (24H0THE SØRTED NUMBERS ARE)
     END
```

In the SØRT subroutine above, a maximum array size of 100 was assumed and the DIMENSIØN statements in that routine and the calling program are so written. Setting a fixed size in this manner limits the efficiency of the subroutine in two ways. First, for smaller lists, space is wasted. Second, for larger lists, the subroutine is of no value. Most FORTRAN processors permit a subroutine to be defined with variable dimensions whose values are to be supplied with a call. To accomplish this, the DIMENSIØN statement in the subroutine is replaced by the following:

```
DIMENSIØN ARRAY(NUM)
```

Thus the dimension NUM is supplied as an argument in the call. It is still necessary, however, for the dimensioning in the main program to be explicitly given.

A Set of Subroutines

We have already done a small amount of processing of student records, but in an actual situation, a great deal more would be done. The record processing shall be extended here, utilizing the subroutine concept. As we already know, when a computation problem can be broken into several small procedures realized by separate subroutines, program development and operation is more efficient. Let us consider the development of a small set of subroutines.

Example 7.5. Change the student-record processing program by extending data to include these specifics on courses: credits, course number, course title, and term taken. Compute a weighted average for each student, taking into account the number of credits for a course. In addition, print each student's top five grades. Finally, modify the requirements for admission to the honor society by adding minimum requirements on lowest grade achieved, and apply these rules to each student.

The number of courses completed shall remain on one card, but let each grade received by a student be placed on a single card with the following format:

Columns   1–4 : course number
Columns   7–36 : course title
Column   38 : credits
Columns 40–42 : grade
Columns 44–46 : term taken

Thus, typical records might be these:

```
                                  38        46
                                   ↓         ↓
    M104   ELEMENTS ØF MECH ENGG    3   88  F69
    P106   PRØGRAMMING TECHNIQUES   3   93  S70
    S200   MECH ENGG SHØP           1   85  S70
```

The weighted average is the sum of the products of grades and credits, divided by the total number of credits. The method for computing the average that was used in Example 5.8 thus has to be modified. A SUBRØUTINE subprogram shall be written that supplies this weighted average; the call is

CALL   WAVER1 (AVG,CREDS,GRADES,NUMBER)

where CREDS is an array of credits for the courses, GRADES is an array of grades for the courses, and NUMBER is the number of courses. The required subprogram is the following:

```
C    THIS FUNCTIØN CØMPUTES A WEIGHTED AVERAGE.
     SUBRØUTINE WAVER1 (CR, GR, N)
     DIMENSIØN CR(80), GR(80)
     WSUM = 0.
     CRSUM = 0.
```

```
      DØ 10 J = 1, N
      WSUM = WSUM + CR(J)*GR(J)
  10  CRSUM = CRSUM + CR(J)
      WAVER = WSUM / CRSUM
      RETURN
      SUM
```

Next we must determine a student's top five grades. Clearly a sort routine can be useful here. The SØRT subroutine of Example 7.4 can be used provided a modification is made. Since we need only sort the top five grades, we can stop the sorting process short of full sorting. The SØRT program, however, places smallest values first while we are here interested in largest values first. We can turn the process around as needed simply by interchanging a_i and a_j whenever it is true that $a_i < a_j$ (see Figure 7.6). This involves changing the IF statement in the SØRT routine; let the program then be called BSØRT1 (for backward sort).

We are not done with BSØRT1, however, for we wish to be able to stop the sorting after a specified number of entries, say m, have been sorted. This can be accomplished by having the number m be the upper limit on index i. In that case, only the first m passes through the procedure occur, resulting in the m largest entries being placed at the head of the array. The program:

```
C   A BACKWARD SØRT RØUTINE THAT
C   YIELDS THE LARGEST M VALUES.
      SUBRØUTINE BSØRT1(ARRAY,NUM,M)
      DIMENSIØN ARRAY(80)
      NUM1 = NUM - 1
      DØ 20 I = 1, M
      I1 = I + 1
      DØ 20 J = I1, NUM
      IF (ARRAY(I) .GE. ARRAY(J)) GØ TØ 20
      TEMP = A(I)
      A(I) = A(J)
      A(J) = TEMP
  20  CØNTINUE
      RETURN
      END
```

We are not done with BSØRT1, however, for we wish to be able to stop the ship in the honor society. Let these rules be as follows:

For freshmen: 90 average and no grade below 70
For sophomores: 88 average and no grade below 65
For juniors: 86 average and no grade below 60
For seniors: 85 average and no grade below 50

Clearly a method for determining the lowest grade of a student is needed. In

Example 7.1 a FUNCTIØN subprogram BIG determined the largest of a given array of numbers. We need, as before, to turn the procedure around:

```
FUNCTIØN  SMALL1(A,N)
DIMENSIØN  A(80)
SMALL  =  A(1)
DØ 10 J  =  2, N
IF  (A(J) .LT. SMALL)  SMALL  =  A(J)
10   CØNTINUE
END
```

This is the last subroutine required for the problem.

CØMMØN Storage

Three subprograms have been developed for the student problem: WAVER1 for computing a weighted average. BSØRT1 for determining the largest m values in an array, and SMALL1 for determining the smallest value in an array. The subprograms process much data in common, e.g., each process the grades, utilizing in addition the number of grades. We have already seen the need for very carefully structuring the data transmitted between a main program and its subroutines. There must be agreement on sequence of variables, on types of data, and on dimensionality of data between the programs. This requirement necessitated writing properly structured calling sequences.

Certainly our processing problems here are quite simple; in most large programming systems there are many subroutines with perhaps quite complex calling sequences. FORTRAN provides a facility to aid in the problem of communication among main programs and subroutines. This involves the allocation of a CØMMØN area of memory, to be shared by several programs. A CØMMØN declaration may be used to list those variables, simple and dimensioned, that are to be stored in the CØMMØN area. As a result, if two or more programs each declare the same variables to be so stored, those variables need not be listed as arguments in subroutine calls. Values are automatically shared by the several programs. Whenever any CØMMØN variable is assigned a new value by one of the sharing programs, that value becomes immediately available to the other sharing programs.

The CØMMØN declaration is the following:

$$\text{CØMMØN arg}_1, \text{arg}_2, \ldots$$

where $\underline{\text{arg}_i}$ are the variables to be stored in CØMMØN. If any of these variables are dimensioned arrays, the dimensions can be given in this statement.

Example 7.6. Modify the student-grade subroutines, using CØMMØN. In that problem, the variables to be shared are shown diagrammed in Figure 7.7. These variables

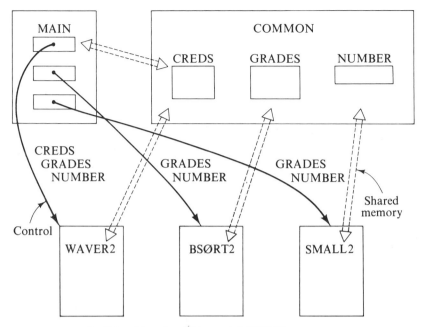

Fig. 7.7.   Shared variables and CØMMØN storage.

are CREDS, GRADES, and NUMBER, the array of course credits, the array of course grades, and the number of courses, all applied to one student. The three subprograms can now be written as follows:

```
      SUBRØUTINE WAVER2(AVG)
      CØMMØN GR(80), N, CR(80)
      WSUM  =  0.
      CRSUM  =  0.
      DØ 10 J  =  1, N
      WSUM  =  WSUM  +  CR(J)*GR(J)
10    CRSUM  =  CRSUM  +  CR(J)
      AVG  =  WSUM / CRSUM
      RETURN
      END

      SUBRØUTINE BSØRT2(M)
      CØMMØN ARRAY, NUM
      DIMENSIØN ARRAY(80)
        (as before)

      RETURN
      END
```

```
      FUNCTIØN  SMALL2(A)
      CØMMØN  DUMMY  (80),  N
      DIMENSIØN  A(80)
      SMALL  =  A(1)
      DØ  Z0  J  =  2,  N
      IF  (A(J)  .LT.  SMALL)  SMALL  =  A(J)
   10 CØNTINUE
      END
```

We note the following:

1. Variables listed in CØMMØN statements may have their dimensions given there as well.
2. The variable AVG could have been included in the CØMMØN area, but we chose not to do so.
3. The variable M represents an integer, supplied in the main program, and so does not belong in the CØMMØN area.
4. FUNCTIØN subprograms have one argument; hence, the variable A is listed as the argument, even though its counterparts (GR and ARRAY arrays) are located in the CØMMØN area. Space would be more efficiently used if the array were common than if N were, but it is more logical to supply A as the argument.
5. Space is allocated in the CØMMØN area to the variables as listed, the same assignment of space being made in all programs. As a result, space is assigned as follows in the CØMMØN area.

Main pr.	In WAVER2	In BSØRT2	In SMALL2	Space
GRADES	GR	ARRAY	DUMMY	80 locations
NUMBER	N	NUM	N	1 location
CREDS	CR	—	—	80 locations

Thus, e.g., the variable GRADES(1), GR(1), ARRAY(1), and DUMMY(1) in the four programs share the same location in memory. DUMMY is a dummy area, required so that N in SMALL is identical to NUMBER in the main program. In BSØRT2 and SMALL2, no use is made of an array for course credits, so the CØMMØN statements are shorter.

The main program needs to be almost completely rewritten; it requires a CØMMØN declaration also. In the main program, the CØMMØN variables are GRADES, NUMBER, and CREDS. (Reference should be made to Example 5.7 for comparison.)

```
C   STREC3
C   THIS PRØGRAM SUPPLIES THE FØLLØWING INFØRMATIØN
C   ØN EACH STUDENT:  STUDENT NAME, CLASS, MAJØR, LIST
C   ØF CØURSES, AVERAGE, TØP 5 GRADES, LØWEST GRADE,
C   AND QUALIFICATIØN FØR HØNØR SØCIETY.
      INTEGER NAME(8), NUMBER, CLASS, MAJØR
```

```
          INTEGER CØURSE(80), TERMS(80), TITLES(80,8)
          REAL GRADES(80), CREDS(80), AVER, LØGRAD
          CØMMØN GRADES, NUMBER, CRED
C    START NEW PAGE.
   10    WRITE (6,100)
  100    FØRMAT (1H1)
C    READ A STUDENTS RECØRD.
          READ (5,101) NAME, CLASS, MAJØR
  101    FØRMAT (7A4,A2, I2, 2X, A4)
          WRITE (6,102) NAME, CLASS, MAJØR
  102    FØRMAT (8H0NAME: 714,A2, 8H CLASS: 12,
        1     8H MAJØR: A4)
          CLASS = CLASS - 68
C    READ NUMBER ØF GRADES, THEN THE GRADES.
          READ (5,103) NUMBER
  103    FØRMAT (I3)
          DØ 11 I = 1, NUMBER
   11    READ (5,104) CØURSE(I), (TITLES(I,J), J = 1,8),
        1     CREDS(I), GRADES(I), TERMS(I)
  104    FØRMAT (A4, 1X, 7A4,A2, 1X, F1.0, 1X, F3.0, 1X, A3)
C    DETERMINE STUDENT AVERAGE. PRINT IT.
          CALL WAVER(AVER)
          WRITE (6,105) AVER
  105    FØRMAT (23H0CØURSE GRADE AVERAGE: F4.1)
C    DETERMINE 5 TØP GRADES. PRINT THEM.
          CALL BSØRT(5)
          WRITE (6,106) (GRADES(I), I = 1, 5)
  106   FØRMAT (23H0THE 5 TØP GRADES ARE: 5F5.0)
C    DETERMINE LØWEST GRADE.
          LØGRAD = SMALL(GRADES)
C    DETERMINE CLASS ØF STUDENT.
          GØ TØ (91,92,93,94), CLASS
C    SENIØR (CLASS ØF 69).
          IF (AVER .LT. 85.0 .ØR. LØGRAD .LT. 50.0) GØ TØ 200
          GØ TØ 201
C    JUNIØR (CLASS ØF 70).
          IF (AVER .LT. 86.0 .ØR. LØGRAD .LT. 60.0) GØ TØ 200
          GØ TØ 201
C    SØPHØMØRE (CLASS ØF 71).
          IF (AVER .LT. 88.0 .ØR. LØGRAD .LT. 65.0) GØ TØ 200
          GØ TØ 201
C    FRESHMAN (CLASS ØF 72).
          IF (AVER .LT. 90.0 .ØR. LØGRAD .LT. 70.0) GØ TØ 200
          GØ TØ 201
```

```
C   HERE IF STUDENT DØES NØT QUALIFY.
 200   WRITE (6,107)
 107   FØRMAT (25H0STUDENT DØES NØT QUALIFY.)
       GØ TØ 10
C   HERE IF STUDENT DØES QUALIFY.
 201   WRITE (6,108)
 108   FØRMAT (19H0STUDENT QUALIFIES.)
       GØ TØ 10
       END
```

We note that not all the variables in this program are in a CØMMØN area. For example, CØURSE, TITLE, and TERM are not so located because these items are not processed by any of the subroutines. Another point to note is the nature of the TITLES array, which is two-dimensional. We are only concerned with a one-dimensional array of titles, but alphanumeric entries often require several words, as we have seen in the past. We here have eight-word entries, hence the extra dimension of '8'. Each entry is represented by the sequence 'TITLE(I,J), J = 1, 8'.

Multiple Subroutine Entries

When two or more similar subroutines are used by programs, it may be more efficient in terms of space to combine the functions of the several subroutines in one subroutine. In order that different calls to the subroutine yield different results, multiple entries to the subroutine can be created and used. In FORTRAN, this is accomplished by supplying a unique name to each entry point and a set of arguments for each. Functionally, one may think of the several entries as calls to different subroutines. When control passes to the subroutine at one of the entry points, control within the subroutine proceeds to that point.

Example 7.7. We can utilize this capability in the sort programs written. We have studied SØRT, BSØRT, BIG, and SMALL. The functions of all four of these subroutines can be combined. First, we note that the SMALL procedure is equivalent to a sort of one pass only, while the BIG procedure is equivalent in the same way to BSØRT. The primary difference between SØRT and BSØRT is that in the comparison test the IF statement differs. We can set up two IF statements, only one being used for each process. To do this, an internal variable K can be initialized upon entry and checked just prior to the IF statement; control can then be sent to the proper test. Another, though minor, difference is that BSØRT requires a third argument that is the number of items to be sorted. That argument is 'M' and in the case of SØRT 'M' is implicitly assumed to be equal to the length of the list, 'NUM'. We can combine all of these features in the following program, GSØRT (general sort), where ARRAY and NUM are placed in a CØMMØN area:

```
C   A GENERALIZED SØRT RØUTINE.
C   FØRWARD AND BACKWARD SØRTING IS PØSSIBLE,
C   THE LATTER TØ A SPECIFIED PØINT, AND
```

```
C    DETERMINATIØN ØF SMALLEST AND LARGEST
C    ENTRIES IS PØSSIBLE.
     SUBRØUTINE GSØRT
     CØMMØN ARRAY(80), NUM
     M = NUM
     GØ TØ 5
     ENTRY SMALL
     M = 1
  5  K = 1
     GØ TØ 10
     ENTRY BIG
     M = 1
     ENTRY BSØRT (M)
     K = 2
 10  NUM1 = NUM − 1
     DØ 20 I = 1, M
     I1 = I + 1
     DØ 20 J = I1, NUM
     GØ TØ (11,12), K
 11  IF (ARRAY(I) .LE. ARRAY (J)) GØ TØ 20
     GØ TØ 15
 12  IF (ARRAY (I) .GE. ARRAY(J)) GØ TØ 20
 15  TEMP = A(I)
     A(I) = A(J)
     A(J) = TEMP
 20  CØNTINUE
     RETURN
     END
```

The manner of calling SMALL and BIG is different than previously, where these procedures were coded as FUNCTIØN subprograms. This means that the functional use of SMALL in the main program above is replaced by the statements

```
CALL SMALL
LØGRAD = GRADES(1)
```

since the SMALL entry leads to placing the smallest value of the array in ARRAY(1).

EXERCISES

1. Give examples of subroutine calls with and without output parameters. Indicate why the latter are not needed in some cases. Note that it was pointed out that there may be no output parameters.

2. How does the time of execution of the SØRT subroutine vary with the number of items sorted?

3. What are the advantages and disadvantages of using CØMMØN storage?

4. Why can different names for the same arrays in CØMMØN be used in different subroutines?

*   *   *   *   *   *

5. Write subroutines to realize the operations below on a set of numbers. Assume the numbers lie in the range 0 through 200 inclusive, and that they are to be read from cards punched 10 numbers to a card with a count card first.
   (a) Return the subscript of the first appearance of the value 100 (i.e., if $a_i = 100$, what is i?).
   (b) Return a count of the number of values greater than 100.
   (c) Remove all duplicated values in the set.
   (d) Return the mode, the most frequently occurring value.

6. Write a subroutine MERGE that, given two sorted lists of numbers, combines them into a single sorted list. The call is:

   CALL MERGE(ARR1,N1,ARR2,N2,ARR3)

   where the given arrays are ARR1 of size N1 and ARR2 of size N2, and ARR3 is the name of the merged list.

7. Provide extra facilities to the record-processing program, as follows:
   (a) Print the title of the course in which each student received the lowest grade.
   (b) Print the reason for a student's failure to qualify for the honor society, i.e., either because of average or lowest grade.

8 PROGRAM EXECUTION

We have learned how to design and build programs to realize a number of procedures of numerical and nonnumerical nature. In chapters to follow, additional techniques will be introduced that are useful in developing programs. We have also studied the GAMMA 70 and developed some understanding of the way in which a program is executed at the machine level. In this chapter we turn to the task of executing programs in a computer, and study what processes occur to bring this execution about. The chapter does not deal with programming methods but should deepen our understanding of the manner in which programs can be made to solve our problems.

In order that a computer solve a problem by executing a program, these steps must occur: (1) the program and its data must be placed in memory, (2) the program must be executed, and (3) the answers must be supplied. In addition, prior to these steps, the source program must be translated into an equivalent object program. We shall study details of each of these operations here.

8.1 THE RUNNING OF PROGRAMS

Several Approaches

There are at least three distinct approaches to running programs on a computer, each of which involves all of the steps outlined just above. *Batch processing* refers to the sequential running of programs, one after another. *Multiprogramming* involves the permanent sharing of computer memory among several programs as each or part of each is executed in turn. *Time-sharing* is similar to multiprogramming except that both space and time are allocated as needed for the optimal execution of a number of programs.

Batch Processing

Batch processing involves the execution of programs in sequence, the full resources of the computer being available to one program for its operation. A program is placed in computer memory, where it is executed. Results are then supplied. The next program is loaded, and the process repeats in this manner.

Batch processing may be accomplished in *on-line* operation, where information on punched cards is placed directly into memory by input-output equipment; computed results are later printed directly on a printer. On-line operation is normally not used for batch processing, because during the reading of cards and writing on paper, the computer is otherwise idle. These input-output operations are relatively very slow and would result in great inefficiencies on a large computer.

In order to achieve a better match between internal computational speeds and input-output speeds, magnetic tape is often used in an on-line manner. In this approach, punched cards are read onto magnetic tape at a time prior to the transfer of the information from the tape into memory; this approach is termed *off-line* operation. Any length of time may elapse from tape-loading time to memory-loading time, as well as between memory-reading time and print time. Information transfer between the outside world and computer memory proceeds at about 100 times the rate as when on-line processes are used. On-line batch processing is accomplished by loading a tape off-line with a number of programs, perhaps 10 to 100. Then the tape acts as an "input tape" as the computer proceeds to execute each, in turn. At the same time, the results of all of these programs are supplied to an "output tape", which is printed at a later time. The result of this means of operation is a more efficient use of large computers.

A feature added to computers in recent years improves large-machine efficiency even more. Input-output processes can be handled by *channels* that permit reading directly into memory without the use of the central control unit. Special channel commands are executed independently of the control unit for reading from a magnetic tape into memory; these commands are executed at the same time as internal instructions are executed, resulting in greater efficiencies. The same activity occurs during output processes; different channels are used for input and output and so can be in action simultaneously.

There is still another approach to batch processing, one that involves the use of a remote terminal. We noted already, in Chapter 1, that terminals are input-output devices located remotely from a central computer. Many terminals, perhaps several hundred, can be linked to the central machine. In this approach auxiliary memory is associated with each terminal; information is typed at the terminal into that memory. This method of operation is particularly important when a great deal of information must be transferred into or out of the computer. The process of loading, execution, and returning results from programs is very simlar to the off-line procedure described. The difference is that input is supplied on a typewriter instead of punched cards, and output is returned on the same typewriter. The "turn-around time", the interval from the time information is supplied to the time results are returned, is generally much less than with off-line operation. On the other hand, much more elaborate auxiliary memory and bookkeeping methods for keeping track of all users are required. There is, thus, a tradeoff of convenience and money.

Multiprogramming[1]

Multiprogramming differs from batch processing in one important respect: When a program is being executed, it has the full internal resources of the computer but only occupies as much space in memory as it requires. At any given time, memory is partitioned among a number of programs, generally less than 10 in number, but only one program is actually executed at a time. As soon as any program requires an input-output operation, control passes to another program, the channels being brought into execution as required. At a given time, several programs may be actively involved in input-output processes while one is being executed.

The concept of multiprogramming offers great potential for making use of computer resources, both in time and in memory. A little thought, however, reveals that to use these resources optimally requires a careful scheduling algorithm. Programs vary in space requirements, in execution times, in requirements for auxiliary memory, and in input-output processes. It is desirable that as much space in memory as possible be in use at any given time, yet programs as they are supplied by input equipment are mixed in all attributes, in general. The scheduling algorithm must take into account current available space and decide which of several waiting programs to load into that space. In this environment, users are required to supply with their programs estimates on space and running times. These data are used by the scheduling program to select proper programs to be run at proper times. The problem is clearly too complex for us to dwell upon in depth here.

Time-Sharing[2]

Time-sharing is quite similar to multi-programming, with these differences. First, a portion of memory is not set aside for a program during the duration of its stay in memory. Rather, the space may be used by another program (or programs) if that is in the interests of overall system efficiency. Subsequently, when that original program is to continue its execution, it is reloaded into memory, perhaps in another portion of memory. Second, a program may be broken into separable portions if it is very large, so that only one portion at a time is in memory undergoing execution. When that portion is completed, another will be brought in, though during this loading process, execution passes to another program. The effect of all this memory and time swapping is a better utilization of all resources, for much flexibility can be incorporated. At the same time, overhead costs climb because of the enormous amount of bookkeeping required. To the user, at a remote terminal, the effect is that of having the machine to himself, for computer speeds are so great compared to human speeds that the bottleneck tends to become human reaction time to the last computer result on the typewriter. The same effect can be achieved in multiprogramming, of course, but now hundreds rather than a dozen users are involved with one machine.

Because of the great number of programs involved in the time-sharing processes, each is usually run for a finite amount of time, say 50 milliseconds, before its chance is up and the control passes to another program. Of course, input-output operations cause a switch of control as well. Thus, a program that requires three seconds of processing time may require 30 seconds or more in total elapsed time. This may seem like a long wait and indeed under certain circumstances it is, but a programmer is likely to segment his program into a lot of small pieces under a system like this, so turn-around times become very small.

Interaction

The term *interaction* is one that covers a number of processes that occur on-line. Interaction may imply remote batch processing, multiprogramming, or time-sharing. More significantly, the man "interacts" with the computer, i.e., after he makes a response (types in data, for example) he waits for the computer in turn to make its response. People will wait at a terminal, and hence interact, for varying amounts of time before they find they will walk away and return later for results. If a response is only one second in coming, anyone will wait. If a response is one minute in coming, a user will have the patience to wait if he expects a relatively significant amount of information back. He may even wait five minutes for a large amount of information. He will not wait, however, for 30 minutes (unless he is remarkably tolerant), nor will he wait five minutes if all he then gets is a small result that may demand a succession of similar waits for similar results. Certainly these comments are generalizations, but they indicate the tone of what seems to be human reaction to remote terminal operation.

Another significance to interaction is the term itself. A program can be written in segments such that control returns to the user after each so that he can monitor the progress of the program, deciding upon the next step. That next step may be the supplying of new or modified data, it may be a return to the last segment for another iteration on the same original data, or it may be the running of the next segment in sequence. This approach tends to lead to a very flexible system wherein the best talents of man and machine are each optimally used, interactively.

EXERCISES

1. In what kinds of problems would each of these approaches to program execution be useful: batch processing, multiprogramming, and time-sharing? Give examples.

2. Name some considerations in the scheduling problem for multiprogramming.

3. Consider the other tasks involved in the three approaches. What needs to be done?

8.2 OPERATING SYSTEMS

Generalities

In the last section we examined the several methods whereby programs are loaded into memory and caused to be executed in some sequence. The sequencing used depends, of course, on the processing scheme, be it batch processing, multi-programming, or time-sharing. The loading of programs into memory, the passage of control among them, and their execution are all controlled by the *operating system* (or simply *system*). The system is always present in memory and is the master controller of all of the executive and bookkeeping operations needed to cause the computer to function properly under the conditions described. The system performs many other functions as well as these; in this section, we shall briefly examine each of its functions.[3]

Control Cards

A programmer will call upon the operating system to perform a number of tasks, both within programs and as separate "calls" to the system. The separate calls are given as *control cards* and are usually called *commands* (a general term). These commands are in the nature of language statements and as such have their own format. They each consist generally of a task name and a list of parameters associated with the task. Some of the command types are listed here:

1. To indicate a translation (e.g., via FORTRAN or an assembler).
2. To indicate data cards.
3. To identify specific magnetic tapes.
4. To request a specific amount of memory space.
5. To indicate required execution time.
6. To load a program.

We may note that tasks 4 and 5 are of interest to the scheduler that assigns programs to memory under multiprogramming.

Program Translation

Before any program can be run on a computer, it must be translated from source language to object language. This is done by an assembler or a compiler. It is the job of the operating system to call into memory the appropriate translator when a translation is requested. Generally, a programmer has several options when making the call, such as whether to print the object deck in equivalent symbolic form, whether to provide an object deck, and whether to load the compiled deck into memory for subsequent execution. The last-named task, where an object deck is immediately loaded into memory and executed, is a separate process that follows translation. The two operations often follow in sequence.

Because the system permits program translation, it must have access to auxiliary memory on which the translators are stored. To the system, the translators are simply programs to be executed themselves, using data that are the statements in an object deck. However, because the translation operation is so frequently performed, the translating programs are considered to be an extension of the operating system.

Program Loading and Linking

The operating system does not itself execute programs; the computer hardware does that job. The system, however, must perform a number of functions associated with program execution. After the system scheduler has determined when and where a program is to be loaded into memory in a multiprogramming or time-sharing system, it loads the program. Most commonly, several programs are loaded into memory at one time; these might be a main program and several associated subroutines. These programs were assembled or compiled independently of each other and must be interconnected after they are loaded into memory, so that they can properly call one another.

The linkage problem is that of interconnecting programs. As an example, in a main program, there may be a call as follows:

CALL SØRT(A,N)

There is a subroutine SØRT, let us say, and it is necessary that the calling sequence in the main program be properly set for the transfer of control to SØRT. A jump instruction to SØRT is required, yet the main program has no intrinsic knowledge of where SØRT is loaded in memory. This is the linkage problem.

The usual method of linkage is approximately as follows:

1. On compilation (or assembly), each object deck is given a "symbol table" that lists all subroutines called, with the places in the program that called them.
2. On compilation, each subroutine is given its name in symbolic form. (Remember that, during compilation, symbolic information is translated to machine form; it is important that the subroutine *name* is retained symbolically.)
3. The system, as it loads programs into memory, keeps a table that indicates all loading locations of programs. This table lists the memory address of the entry points of all subroutines.
4. The system, after loading programs, then modifies the calling sequences, using the table, so that jumps to actual subroutine entry points can occur.

This is a simplification of the true procedure, but it reflects the general technique of linkage.

Relocation

In Chapter 6, we examined machine-language programs and discussed the starting point of such programs. The starting location S_0 was assumed to be 0001, but may in fact be any location in memory. In fact, if we consider that a number of programs may be compiled independently yet be run together as a set, we realize that each cannot be compiled to load at 0001. In fact, there is no information available to each program during compilation that enables *any* particular assignment of memory locations to be made.

One method used to assign memory locations is called *relocation*. The term implies that only relative word locations are assigned to instructions as they are compiled, and that these assignments are relocated upon memory loading. The process works in a manner best explained by illustration. Assume that a main program requires 2000_8 locations, and that three associated subroutines require 1000_8, 600_8, and 500_8 locations. During compilation, each object program is generated as though its starting point is 0001, resulting in these tentative memory assignments:

Program	Memory Assignment
Main program	$0001-2000_8$
Subroutine I	$0001-1000_8$
Subroutine II	$0001-0600_8$
Subroutine III	$0001-0500_8$

When the programs are loaded into memory, they are placed in sequence, one being loaded after another. The resultant actual memory assignments become these:

Main program	$0001-2000_8$
Subroutine I	$2001-3000_8$
Subroutine II	$3001-3600_8$
Subroutine III	$3601-4200_8$

We say that there is a *relocation constant* associated with each program; this is the amount added to each assigned address. Here, the constants are 0000, 2000, 3000, and 3600 for the four programs. Programs compiled in the manner just described are *relocatable*. Programs compiled as described in Chapter 6, with specific memory assignments, are *absolute*.

Input-Output Processes

The processes of input and output are fundamental to the task of computing. We have studied the statements within FORTRAN that can be used by a programmer to indicate these processes within a program. Each statement is compiled into a subroutine call; the parameters of the subroutine are the variables listed and the associated format statement. Because input-output processes are so common, they are invoked by subroutine calls and are normally placed under the control of the operating system. Thus, upon entry to these subroutines, control passes to the system.

Control of input-output processes implies a great deal more than merely the act of reading information from magnetic tape and the act of writing it thereon. In the several types of computer systems discussed in Section 8.1, there are input-output complexities of varying degree. The proper timing of input-output channels, of allocation of space for input-output use and programmer use, the transmission of the proper information between terminals and programs in core when there is a multitude of users—all of these processes are part of the input-output facility of the operating system.

Input-Output Devices

A variety of computer memory devices exists for reading, writing, and storing information. These devices vary in the speed with which they can be read and written upon, in the amounts of information they can store, and in the manner in which information is organized on them. We will consider a few such devices.

Magnetic tapes are reels normally 12 inches in diameter on large computers, with 2400 feet of tape on each. Such a reel can hold about 10 to 20 times as much information as the largest core memories. Reading and writing occur at rates up to about 150,000 characters per second. Information is linearly strung out along the length of a tape, so that the tape must be rewound from its present position to any specific desired position for reading. Thus the access time may be relatively large; it can approach one minute. If information is to be read in sequence into memory, tape storage is efficient, but if information must be selectively read in a random manner from a file, magnetic tape is a poor storage medium.

Magnetic disks store information much in the manner of phonograph records, except that their surfaces are perfectly smooth. Information is stored in concentric circles of high density. Disks may be mounted permanently or may be removable. The latter form offers the advantage of the establishment of a large library of programs and data, stored as tapes are stored on shelves or racks. In all disk units, read-write heads are lowered over selected tracks on the disks, which are rotated continuously at high speed. There may be but one head for each disk surface, or there may be many heads for the surface. In large disk units, dozens of disks are stacked upon each other, with both surfaces of each disk available for storage. Because of the organization of information on a disk, the access time is only the time it takes the read-write head to move over the selected track or the time it takes for one disk revolution, whichever is greater. Reading and writing times are comparable to those for magnetic tape, though are generally somewhat higher. We may ask, if disks have so much less access time, why ever use tapes? The answer is simple: Today at least, magnetic disks are considerably more expensive than magnetic tapes. Nonetheless, in many applications, particularly those performed on-line, disk input-output is preferable.

Magnetic drums provide the most rapid access of all auxiliary memory units. Read-write heads exist for channels around the drum. Characters are read or written at rates up to 3,000,000 per second. Drums are useful in time-sharing systems where portions of programs must be brought into memory at great speeds. Total memory capacity is relatively low.

A number of other memory devices of lesser importance are available. We cannot consider all of them here. In all magnetic storage media, information is stored as a series of tiny magnetized spots, each spot representing '0' or '1' (as in core memory).

Data Management

We have seen that information may be linearly stored on magnetic tape, it may be stored as a set of equally accessible small linear portions on magnetic disk or drum, or it may be stored in a randomly accessible manner in core memory. Furthermore, problems encompass a great variety of types and formats of data, some more suitable to one of these storage forms and some more suitable to another. It is important that a programmer have facilities that enable him to match his problem's structure with the storage structures available on a computer. These facilities must give him the ability to structure his stored data in any desired manner, the ability to store and retrieve the data easily and efficiently, and the ability to edit or update the stored data in many different ways. The term that encompasses these processes is *data management*. The data management function is partially performed by the operating system, though many tasks in this area may be performed by subroutines not physically within the system. In any event, the system has a major responsibility in the data management area. We shall return to data management in a later chapter.

Subroutine Library

In the very same manner that calls to system input-output subroutines are contained within a program, calls to many other system subroutines may be used. We have seen how certain mathematical functions may be called within FORTRAN; SIN(X), ABS(X), and EXP(X) are examples. As with input-output, these compile into calls for system subroutines. Generally, a collection of such mathematical routines are placed in a *mathematical library* under the control of the operating system.

Aids to Debugging

Most operating systems provide aids to debugging programs. These generally include the capability for calling for a printout of a portion of memory, so that intermediate results can be examined. They also provide for the stopping of a program partially through execution for the same purpose. Programmer requests for these aids are made either through certain subroutine calls or through control cards. Debugging aids, and errors in general, are discussed at length in Chapter 11.

EXERCISES

1. How would multiple entry points be handled by a linking program?

2. Compare absolute and relocatable methods of program assembly, with regard to the advantages of each.

3. What are some ways to organize data on a disk that take advantage of the way in which that kind of memory is physically constructed?

4. Name some data management tasks.

8.3 THE COMPILATION PROCESS

The process of translating algorithmic-language statements into machine form is termed *compilation*.[4] Such translation usually involves conversion of a statement into a number of machine instructions. The program that does the compilation is called a *compiler*. The term FORTRAN applies both to a language in which programs are written and to the compiler that translates those programs.

The compilation process resembles assembly in that symbolic entities are replaced by numeric ones, translated into bits when placed in core memory. It translates source code into object code. However, there is a significant difference in that algebraic expressions are translated into a sequence of machine instructions that, when executed in memory, evaluate the indicated expressions. We have seen how powerful some FORTRAN statements are, frequently combining a number of indexing operations or a number of arithmetic or logical operations. It is the task of the compiler to unravel these statements, converting them to code.

We can briefly consider the compilation process here. Let us assume, for simplicity, that an algebraic expression without parentheses is to be translated. Here is such an expression:

$$X = A * B + C/D - G$$

The hierarchy of operators is important; two levels are represented here: (1) first, multiplication (∗) and division (/); (2) second, addition (+) and subtraction (−). Since we must perform '∗' and '/' before '+' and '−', it is necessary that each of these operators be identified and located. Further, since we must insert, as operands, the symbols 'A', 'B', ..., these must also be identified and located. For this purpose, a *scan* is performed, which is a search from one end of the character string to the other, which identifies each part or *token* of the expression.

Once the scan is completed and all tokens identified, subexpressions must be converted to code. A *subexpression* is a sequence of n operands separated by $n - 1$ operators at the same level, such as '$A * B$' above. It may include surrounding parentheses. More specifically, those subexpressions whose operators are at the highest level must be so converted. Here, these are '$A * B$' and 'C/D'. Note that the third term in the expression is a single operand, 'G', rather than a subexpression, yet it must be considered at the same level as the ' $*$ ' and '$/$' subexpressions. These subexpressions are converted to code and given temporary identifiers, as indicated here:

$$x_1 \leftarrow A * B \qquad \begin{array}{ll} \text{LØAD} & \text{A} \\ \text{MULT} & \text{B} \\ \text{STØRE} & \text{X1} \end{array}$$

$$x_2 \leftarrow C/D \qquad \begin{array}{ll} \text{LØAD} & \text{C} \\ \text{DIV} & \text{D} \\ \text{STØRE} & \text{X2} \end{array}$$

New form of expression:

$$X = x_1 + x_2 - G$$

The next step is to identify subexpressions at the highest level remaining, that is, at the '$+$' and '$-$' level:

$$X \leftarrow x_1 + x_2 - G \qquad \begin{array}{ll} \text{LØAD} & \text{X1} \\ \text{ADD} & \text{X2} \\ \text{SUBT} & \text{G} \\ \text{STØRE} & \text{X} \end{array}$$

Since this level is the last one remaining, the result is the named variable on the left in the expression. The compiled code is the sequence of instructions shown to the right above, 10 instructions long. Actually, the object deck consists of *binary* instructions, ready for loading directly into memory, but the compiler will list the equivalent symbolic code, shown here, in the printed compilation output.

This compilation process is a simplification of the complete operation, but it is indicative of the approach taken. There are other complexities that modify the course of action:

1. There is a more extensive hierarchy of operation levels than shown above. We have already studied such a precedence list.
2. Parentheses may be introduced around any subexpression to specify the order in which operations are to be translated. If used, they overrule the hierarchy precedence.

If the compiler were to follow the method given in the translation process, some inefficiencies would occasionally result. For example, a particular portion may exist more than once in an expression. Its repeated evaluation wastes space and execution time. For example, in the expression

    Y = (A+2.*B)/F − A+2.*B + H

the portion 'A + 2. * B' occurs twice. The code for this sequence need only exist once in the code. Some compilers will detect this repetition and behave appropriately. If, of course, the second appearance is written 'B * 2. + A', the compiler will not detect the duplication. In any event, the programmer can avoid the problem by the use of a preliminary statement which evaluates the portion. This approach was taken in examples earlier in this chapter.

All program translators provide messages or *diagnostics* to the programmer on the legality of the source statements. Compilers traditionally provide many different diagnostics. For example, the GE 600 series FORTRAN IV compiler has a library of over 280 different diagnostics. These will appear, as needed, in the printed listing of the source program. If errors are serious enough, compilation is suppressed. Sometimes, the diagnostics are but warnings, given because of the possibility of actual error.

REFERENCES

1. This book on real-time computer systems is valuable in general terms for program design:
   James Martin, *Design of Real-Time Computer Systems*, Prentice-Hall, Inc., 1967.
2. The following book discusses time sharing and its application in several areas:
   James R. Ziegler, *Time-Sharing Data Processing Systems*, Prentice-Hall, Inc., 1967.
3. Operating systems of various types are described in the following:
   Saul Rosen, editor, *Programming Systems and Languages*, McGraw-Hill Book Co., 1967, pp. 513–730.
4. These are two references dealing with the compilation process:
   Saul Rosen, op. cit., pp. 181–358.
   Robert L. Glass, "An Elementary Discussion of Compiler/Interpreter Writing," *Computing Surveys*, **1** (1969), pp. 55–77.

9 INPUT-OUTPUT PROCESSES

We have seen that a computer program requires input ("read") and output ("write") statements. Input-output statements distinguish computer programs from mathematical algorithms, since the latter need not state that data are to be read, what their formats are, etc. Here we are dealing with a machine, however, and must be concerned with how human information is translated into a form usable by the machine, and vice versa. This chapter summarizes what we have learned about input-output and introduces some new language features.

Input processes are concerned with some problems that differ from output processes, and so we consider these two in separate sections. However, many operations are common to the two; these include problems concerned with data formating, which we study first.

9.1 DATA FORMATS

Records of Data

A *record* is a unit of data; it has no standard definition. It is defined here as that amount of information that is read by the execution of a single read statement or written by the execution of a single write statement. Thus, the statement

$$\text{read, } a, b, x_1, x_2$$

will read four numbers; this unit of data is a record.

Sets of records are referred to as *files*. Within a file, an order of records exists, for we are able to identify a first, next, and last record. The data within a record are subdivided into *fields* (also called *elements* or *entries*).

Fields of Data

A field, part of a record, is the smallest unit of data referred to by a program. If a string of digits, for example, constitutes a field, we cannot (by definition) extract a portion of that field. If the string comprises three fields, then we can refer to three adjacent portions. A given string on a card may include one, two, or more fields, depending upon the coding that refers to it.

A data field has four primary attributes of interest: (1) its name; (2) its size or length, measured in number of bits or characters; (3) its type, such as decimal integer, octal integer, floating-point number, etc.; and (4) its value. Another attribute, applicable more to the record than the field itself, is the position within the record, measured by a count of the bits, characters, or fields from the start of the record. Consider the record in Figure 9.1, with character positions indicated above the data. Fields are named below the data: NAME, COST, NO., and DATE. These fields occupy positions 1–19, 20–25, 26–30, and 33–38, respectively. Positions 31 and 32 are unused. The NAME field is alphanumeric, the COST field is floating-point, the NO. field is decimal integer, and the DATE field is alphanumeric. We may note that the DATE field could have been considered to comprise three fields (one each for month, day, and year) if that were preferable.

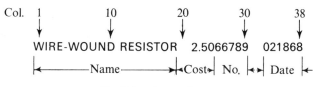

Fig. 9.1.   A record.

Lists of Variables

If we are to read or write a record, we must refer to the fields within it. We must also refer to the variables within a program so that their values can be related to the record fields.

The variables within a program are involved in an input-output operation are given in a *list* within the input-output statement. If we wish to refer to an array of variables, we indicate the sequence in the usual manner, e.g., $(a_i; i = 1, n)$. Thus, we may write

$$\text{read, } x, y, (b_j : j = 2, 20, 2), z$$

which would assign values to x, y, b_2, b_4, b_6, ..., b_{20}, and z. As a record is read, the numbers within its fields are associated in sequence with the list of variables. The same is true on output.

In FORTRAN, it is necessary to supply, in addition to the list of variables, a number referring to the device from which data are read, as the input tape, a card reader, etc., or the device on which data are to be printed, as the output tape, card punch, etc. Consistent with common convention, we shall use '5' and '6' to refer to the input and output tapes, respectively, the normal input-output media. The read statement is of the form

$$\text{READ (device, format) list}$$

where device is normally '5' as indicated, format is the label of an associated FØRMAT statement, and list is the list of variables. An example is the following:

```
      READ  (5,100)  X,  Y,  Z
100   FØRMAT  ( . . . . . )
```

The FØRMAT statement contains information on the format of the X, Y, and Z fields.

The entries in a list of variables may be any of the following, which are followed by examples:

1. A variable name: A, LIST, XARRAY.
2. A subscripted variable: T(1), M(I, J), N(2 * I).
3. An array: ARRAY (declared in DIMENSIØN statement).
4. An array segment: (B(J), J = 1, 7), ((B(I, J), J = 1, 5), I = 1, 5).

If a subscript is a variable, as in case (2), that variable must have an assigned value at the time the statement is executed. In declared arrays, as in case (3), no indexing in the input-output statements is needed; by implication, every element of the array is involved. In array segments (portions of arrays), Case 4, subscript values are given by the DØ-form of the parameters.

The general form of an array segment is given by

$$(V(I), I = F, L, D)$$

where F is the first value of the index I, F is the last value, and D is the difference in successive values of the index, as in a DØ statement.

There are these special cases to consider:

1. A subscript may be given a value by the READ statement itself. For example,

```
READ  (5,100)  X,  Y,  I,  A(I)
```

will give a value to A(6) if I is assigned the value 6 by the input process.
2. Two arrays may be combined in a list:

```
WRITE  (6,77)  (X(I),  Y(I),  I = 1,3)
```

Here, the variables are these, in this order:

```
X(1),  Y(1),  X(2), . . . ,  Y(3)
```

A few comments on the storage scheme for arrays should be given. When a two-dimensional array is read into memory, the entries are stored *columnwise* in memory, i.e., in the order $A(1, 1)$, $A(2, 1)$, $A(3, 1)$, ..., $A(m, n)$ for an array A. When a three-dimensional array is read into memory, the entries are in this order: $B(1, 1, 1)$, $B(2, 1, 1)$, $B(3, 1, 1)$, ..., $B(1, 2, 1)$, $B(1, 3, 1)$, ..., $B(m, n, p)$. In general, the leftmost subscript varies most rapidly, and the rightmost varies least rapidly.

FORMAT Statements

In FORTRAN, a FØRMAT statement is used to indicate the format of each field of data transferred in or out of memory, giving field sizes and types. A FØRMAT statement consists of a sequence of codes, special characters, and alphanumeric strings. These entities are utilized in the same sequence as the variables in the input-output statements.

Conversion codes for numeric data take on three forms:

Iw indicates integer conversion, with a field width w in the record;

Fw.d indicates floating-point conversion, with a field width w in the record and d digits to the right of the decimal point;

Ew.d indicates floating-point conversion as with 'Fw.d', but with printed exponents of the form 'E $\pm$ n'.

In these codes, w and d are always integers. In addition, one conversion code exists for alphanumeric data:

Aw indicates reading or writing of a string of w characters. Normally, w is limited to a number from 4 to 8.

As illustration of the use of these codes, consider these examples:

I3 indicates conversion of an integer from or to a field of three characters' width.

F7.3 indicates conversion of a real number from or to a field of seven characters' width, with three characters in the decimal fraction.

E9.2 indicates conversion of a real number from or to a field of nine characters' width, with two characters in the decimal fraction and with the exponent printed (as '.4565E + 02').

A4 indicates reading or writing an alphanumeric string of four characters.

Examples of FØRMAT statements are these (all must have labels, which are referred to by READ or WRITE statements):

```
80  FØRMAT (I3, I3, F7.3, F7.3)
99  FØRMAT (I4, F2.0, E9.3, E9.3, E9.3)
```

Associated input-output statements will normally list four and five variables, respectively, as here:

```
READ  (5,80)  I, J, A, B
WRITE (6,99)  K, X, Y, Z, V
```

The conversion codes within a FØRMAT apply in sequence, one to one, to the variables named within the input-output statements and to the read or printed record, as we noted earlier.

When two or more adjacent codes are identical, they may be combined with a count. For example, the FØRMAT statements given above may be written as follows:

```
80   FØRMAT (2I3, 2F7.3)
99   FØRMAT (I4, F2.0, 3E9.2)
```

Special attention should be given to the 'Aw' conversion code, for alphanumeric input-output. Let us assume that w may be no larger than 4; this limit means that no more than four alphanumeric characters can be placed into one memory word. Suppose we wish to read a string of 34 characters:

```
FØURSCØRE AND SEVEN YEARS AGØ, ØUR
```

We clearly require nine words in which to store these characters; the last of these nine will hold two characters. The codes are 'A4,A4,A4,A4,A4,A4,A4,A4,A2' which can be abbreviated as '8A4,A2'. Thus we see that multiple codes can be used with alphanumeric input-output, but the '8' here does not indicate eight different numbers or eight different fields. Our assumed limit of four defines fields of four characters. If we think in terms of four-character fields, the usage of the codes is consistent with the other codes. What we in fact have is a 34-character field.

It is possible for the number of conversion codes to be greater or less than the number of variables in the input-output list. Consider first the case of more codes than variables. In this case, when the list of variables is exhausted, the remaining codes are simply ignored. Thus one FØRMAT statement may be used with several WRITE statements each with a different number of variables, giving some flexibility to the coding. Consider now the other case, with more variables than codes. The sequence of codes in a statement applies to one record, so that additional records must be read (or printed) until the list is satisfied. Consider these statements.

```
     READ  (5, 22) A, B, C, D, E
22   FØRMAT (F7.3, F4.2)
```

Since there are five variables to be assigned values but only two codes in the format, three cards must be read to satisfy the list. The values of *A* and *B* appear on the first card, the values of *C* and *D* appear on the second card, and the value of *E* appears on the third card.

A special symbol, the slash (/), is used within a FØRMAT statement to indicate the end of a record for both input and output. Thus, within the statement, two different format sequences may be used to read cards or print lines with different formats. We may write

    23   FØRMAT (F7.3, I4, I6/ F6.3, 2F6.1)

If this statement were used repeatedly to read cards, it would apply the two sequences alternately to cards read. In a like manner, three or more sequences, separated by slashes, may be used as needed.

It is also possible to write a FØRMAT statement so that one sequence of codes applies to the first record, while a second sequence applies to subsequent records. The form is the following:

    n FØRMAT (sequence-1/(sequence-2))

An example is the following:

    100   FØRMAT (5F9.3/(8F9.3, 2I5))

Used for input, this statement indicates that the first card has '5F9.3' conversion, while subsequent cards have '8F9.3,2I5' conversion.

EXERCISES

1. The text refers to four attributes present in all data fields. Where in a FORTRAN program are these attributes to be found?

2. Given that a data card has the integers 1 through 9 punched in columns 2, 4, ..., 18 and that format statement 100 is (9I2), indicate the values assigned to all the variables listed in the following READ statements:
   (a) READ (5,100) (X(I), I = 1, 4), (Y(I) = 1, 5)
   (b) READ (5,100) (X(I), Y(I), I = 1, 3)
   (c) READ (5,100) ((X(I,I), I = 1, 2), J = 1, 2)

3. Indicate data cards punched for the following format statements:
   (a) 10 FØRMAT (3I4, 2A4, I6)
   (b) 20 FØRMAT (2(I2, A4), 5E6.2)
   (c) 30 FØRMAT (4F8.2, 2A4/5I6)

4. Write the list of variables which would appear in a WRITE statement if the following were to be printed from a two-dimensional 8 × 8 ARRAY:
   (a) The complete array.
   (b) The central square, four on a side.

(c) The upper triangular portion, above the main diagonal.

(d) The full contents of alternate rows, starting with the first row.

(e) The positions in the array to which a chess queen, placed at ARRAY(I,J), is permitted to move, considering the array to be a chessboard.

5. Write the FØRMAT statements for reading or writing data as specified in the following:

(a) Six numbers are punched on a card, each with code 'F10.5', and are to be read into a 2 × 3 array called ARRAY.

(b) 100 numbers are to be printed, 10 to a line, with code 'F10.5', from a 10 × 10 array called TABLE.

6. Write sequences of code, including DØ-loops as required, for reading or writing data in the following:

(a) Data are to be read into a 10 × 10 array, INPUT, but with a variable amount of data. The array size of the data is punched on the first card as two numbers each with code 'I3', and the array elements follow, one row on each card.

(b) The contents of a 45-word vector are to be printed on nine lines, with one number on the first line, two numbers on the second, and so on. The conversion code is 'I8'.

9.2 READING DATA FIELDS

Conversion of Data

Let us now consider several types of data punched on cards and the manner of reading them into memory.

INTEGER CONVERSION (I). Numbers without decimal points are read with I-conversion. The numbers, including signs, may occupy any portion of a field; '+' signs may be omitted. Any blank spaces within the field are interpreted as zeros; a blank field is considered to contain zero. The following statements apply to the card in Figure 9.2:

```
      READ (5, 100) K1, K2, L1, L2
100   FØRMAT (I3, I5, I7, I4)
```

The numbers read into memory have these values: $+953$, -648, $+32,800$, and $+888$.

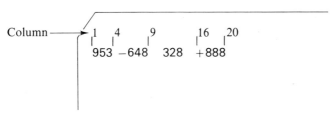

Fig. 9.2.   A card with integers.

REAL CONVERSION (F). The 'F' code is used to read real (floating-point) numbers, punched without an exponent. The number is punched according to the rules for integers, except that the decimal point may appear. Upon conversion into memory, the number is stored as a floating-point number. The value of 'd' in the conversion code 'Fw.d' is taken as the number of positions allotted to the fractional part of the number, counting from the rightmost position of the field. The following statements apply to the card in Figure 9.3:

```
      READ (5, 101) A1, A2, B1, B2, C
101   FØRMAT (F8.3, F5.0, F6.2, F5.3, F5.3)
```

The numbers read into memory are these: $+33.672$, $+207.$, $+63.40$, $-.634$, and $+12.14$. We note the following: (a) Field B1, the third field, is interpreted as $+63.40$ because 'd' has the value 2 and the blank space at the right of that field is blank (or zero). (b) The fractional character count of the last conversion count (3) disagrees with the punched fractional character count (2); the latter prevails.

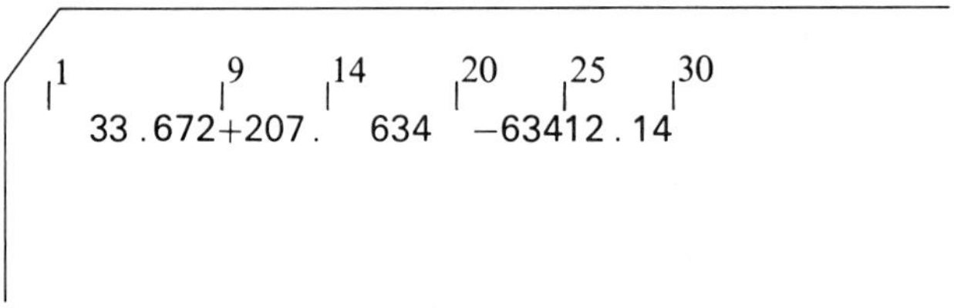

Fig. 9.3. A card with real numbers.

REAL CONVERSION (E). The 'E' code is also used to read real numbers, those punched with an exponent. The exponent is a power of ten, written as an integer following the letter 'E'. Negative exponents require a sign before their values; positive exponents do not. In other respects, E-conversion is similar to F-conversion. The following statements apply to the card in Figure 9.4:

```
      READ (5, 111) D, E, F, G, H
111   FØRMAT (E10.4, E7.2, E7.0, E13.2, E10.3)
```

The numbers read into memory are these: -4.3678×10^2, $+3.67 \times 10^{-2}$,

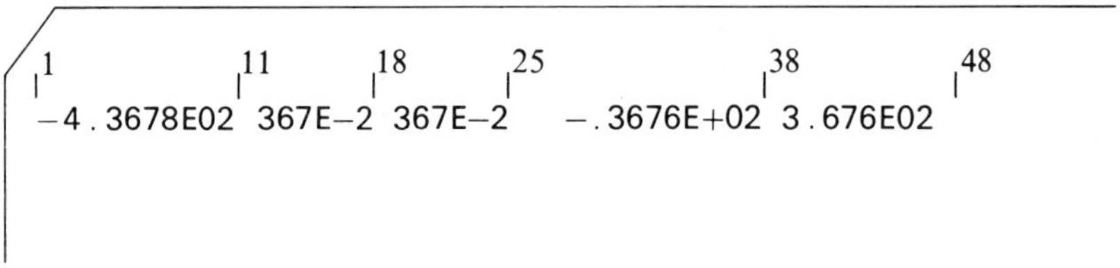

Fig. 9.4. A card with real numbers with exponents.

$+367 \times 10^{-2}$, $-.3676 \times 10^2$, and $+3.676 \times 10^{20}$. Again, when the fractional part of a punched number disagrees in count with a code, the punched form prevails. Note that when a number is not right-justified in a field, as in the last number, its interpreted exponent will be too large (10^{20} here).

Alphanumeric Data

The 'A' code is used to read alphanumeric data into memory. As we have seen, a maximum value of 'w' in the code 'Aw' exists for any given processor; we shall assume the value 4. The following statements apply to the card in Figure 9.5:

```
      READ (5, 200) A, B, C
200   FØRMAT (A4, A2, A3)
```

```
 |1        |5 |7   |10
 |         |  |    |
 WØRDIS  20
```

The first item, 'WORD', fills one memory word. The second item, 'IS', does not fill a word, but is left-justified. The word thus contains 'IS □ □' after reading. Finally, the third word contains '□20'.

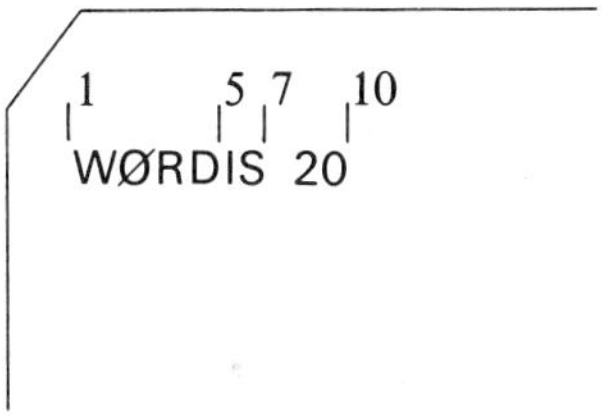

Fig. 9.5.   A card with alpha-numeric data.

Suppose the 34-character string mentioned in Section 9.1 is to be read. Assume the statements for this purpose were these:

```
READ (5, 300) (TEST(I), I = 1,9)
300   FØRMAT (8A4, A2)
```

Since the string is to be considered as a single field, we assign its value to the array TEXT. After execution of the READ statement, TEXT contains the following:

Location	Contents
TEXT(1)	F Ø U R
TEXT(2)	S C Ø R
TEXT(3)	E □ A N
TEXT(4)	D □ S E
TEXT(5)	V E N □
TEXT(6)	Y E A R
TEXT(7)	S □ A G
TEXT(8)	Ø , □ Ø
TEXT(9)	U R □ □

Skipping Fields

A special format code is used for skipping columns or fields on a card upon reading. It may be desirable or necessary that this be done, for a given data card could be used by different problems requiring extraction of different data. The code is of the form 'wX', where w is an integer, representing the number of columns to be skipped. An X code is not required to indicate the skipping of the balance of the card after the last code. An example of its use is given by these statements:

```
    READ (5, 333) A, B, C
333  FØRMAT (6X, F10.3, F9.3, 8X, F8.0)
```

These statements apply to the card in Figure 9.6. The two skipped fields are marked in the figure.

The 'X' code may also be used for output statements. The code 'wX' states that w spaces on a line are to be skipped, i.e., the left blank, at the point at which the code appears.

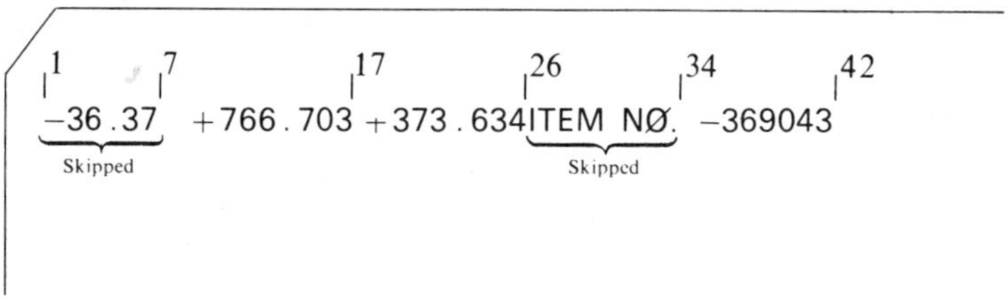

Fig. 9.6.   A card.

Variable Formats

In all the examples we have studied, the format description of data appeared within the program. As a consequence, it was necessary always to supply data in accordance with the FØRMAT statements. Greater flexibility can be built into a program if the data format is supplied during program execution. In that case, the format may vary from application to application, while the program itself remains unchanged.

It is possible in FORTRAN to supply the format as data itself, given as an alphanumeric string and read with code 'A'. Suppose, for example, some data had the format sequence

```
(2I6, 3X, 5F10.3, I4)
```

This string has 18 characters and will occupy five words if four characters are stored per word. We can read this string, including parentheses, into memory with these statements:

```
    READ (5, 44) DATAF
44  FØRMAT (5A4)
```

provided we appropriately declare the array DATAF in a dimension statement. We recall that an array may be given in a READ list simply by giving its name.

Once the format is read into memory, we may now use it in the following manner:

READ (5,DATAF), I, J, (X(K), K = 1,5), N

Summarizing, we do the following: declare an array to be used to store the format sequence (in a DIMENSIØN statement), read the format into the array, and finally read the data, referring to the array as the format. We may represent the coding symbolically:

DIMENSIØN array (m)

.
.
.

READ (5, n) array
n   FØRMAT (mA4)

.
.
.

READ (5, array) variable-list

where $\underline{m}$ is the size of the array for the format, and $\underline{n}$ is the statement label. We assume here a four-character-per-word storage arrangement.

EXERCISES

1. Given the cards as punched at the left in the cases below and the FØRMAT statements at the right below, give the values of the variables A, B, I, and J if the input statement is the following, applied to all cases:

READ (5, 100) A, B, I, J

Cards	FØRMATs

(a)
```
  1    5     10    16      20
  22.00  −600   80    −450
```
100   FØRMAT (F6.1,F5.1,I5,I4)

(b)
```
  1    5     10    15      20
  .67E−1   6E2  TITLE  SAM
```
100   FØRMAT (E8.2,E4.1,2A4)

2. Write FØRMAT statements to supply values to a real array B, as in this READ statement:

READ (5, 200) (B(J), J = 1, M)

where M is an integer in memory when the READ statement is executed. All numbers appear with three places to the right of the decimal point. Each of the cases below is to be considered.

(a) Values of B are punched eight to a card, in adjacent fields, starting in column 1. Each field is eight columns wide.

(b) Values of B are punched six to a card, in fields separated by five blank spaces, starting in column 4. Each field is six columns wide.

(c) Values of B are punched seven to a card, as follows: columns 1–6, 8–13, 15–20, 25–30, 40–45, 47–52, and 60–65.

(d) Values of B are punched alternately five on one card then six on the next, as follows: on the first card, in adjacent fields, starting in column 2, eight columns per field; on the second card, in fields separated by three blanks, starting in column 9, seven columns per field.

(e) Values of B are punched eight on the first card and six on all succeeding cards, as follows: on the first card, in seven-column fields separated by one blank, starting in column 5; on the other cards in columns 1–8, 9–16, 20–27, 29–36, 40–47, and 56–64.

9.3 WRITING DATA FIELDS

Conversion of Data

We shall now turn our attention to the problem of generating lines of printed output and the conversion processes involved in printing fields of data. Again, we consider the several types of data.

INTEGER CONVERSION (I). Integers are printed at the extreme right of their fields, i.e., they are right-justified, and the unused positions are left blank. No decimal points are printed, and minus signs are printed if the integers are negative. Assume we have the numbers $+468$, -2689, -4, and $+3344$ in memory. The following statements apply to them; the printed line appears in Figure 9.7:

```
     WRITE (6, 200) J1, J2, J3, J4
200  FØRMAT (I5, I8, I2, I2)
```

Two points should be noted:

1. The last code, 'I2', was insufficient for the printing of the four-digit value of J4, so only the two rightmost digits were printed.

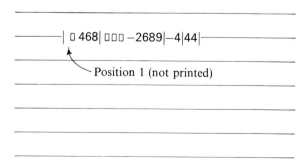

Fig. 9.7.   A printed line with integers.

2. Only four of the five positions allotted for the first integer are "printed"; actually only three digits appear. The first character of a printed line (here, a blank) is used in a special way.

The first character is used to control the movement of the paper just prior to the printing of the line. This character is termed the "carriage control" character. Its usage is as follows:

Character	Significance
( ) Blank	Single space
0	Double space
1	Start new page

Thus, for example, a record whose first character is '0' causes the carriage to be double-spaced before that record is printed. We shall discuss later how the carriage control characters are incorporated into a printed record.

REAL CONVERSION (F). Numbers are printed right-justified in their fields, a decimal point appearing in accordance with the value of 'd' in the conversion code. Minus signs are printed; plus signs are not. If a number has a magnitude less than one, a zero is usually printed to the left of the decimal point. If a real number must be truncated to meet the 'd' specification, roundoff occurs to the least significant digit printed. Assume that these numbers are to be printed: $+45.06$, $-.4567$, -589.0, 0. These statements apply; the printed line appears in Figure 9.8:

```
    WRITE (6, 201) A, B, C, D
201 FØRMAT (F10.3, F9.3, F9.2, F8.2)
```

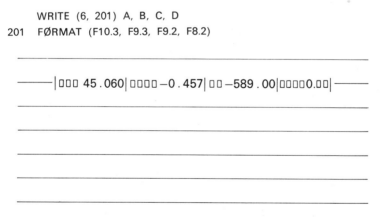

——|□□□ 45.060|□□□□ −0.457|□□ −589.00|□□□□0.00| ——

Fig. 9.8.   A printed line with real numbers.

REAL CONVERSION (E). Numbers are printed right-justified in their fields, with a decimal point and an exponent. The usual form of the printed field is

$$-0.\,\mathrm{xx}\ldots\mathrm{xxE}-\mathrm{ee}$$

where '−' means a minus sign or a *blank* (if the number is negative or positive, respectively); 'xx ... xx' refers to the 'd' digits of the decimal fraction, and 'ee' refers to the exponent (to the base 10). Note that seven character positions in addition to 'd' positions are required. Numbers are rounded off as with F-conversion. Assume that these numbers are to be printed: +45.06, −.004567, −589.0, and +2.0. These statements apply; the printed line appears in Figure 9.9:

WRITE (6, 202) A, B, C, D

202 FØRMAT (E13.4, E10.2, E13.4, E10.3)

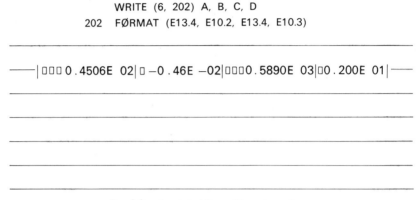

Fig. 9.9.   A printed line with real numbers.

Alphanumeric Data

The 'A' code is used to write alphanumeric data. The writing technique follows the reading technique very closely, a sequence such as 'mA4' normally being used (under our four-character assumption).

A more common situation, however, is the printing of textual information as commentary, heading, or warning information to the programmer or user. As examples, consider the following:

"THE ITERATIØN HAS CØNVERGED."
"DATE   PAYMENT   INTEREST   TAXES"
"DIVISIØN BY ZERØ ATTEMPTED."

The first might appear at the successful conclusion of a program segment. The second might be the heading information for four columns of results. The third might represent an error condition. As another example, it may be desirable to intermingle textual information and computed results, as here:

"THE SUM IS xxxxx; THE PRØDUCT IS xxxxxxxx."

Here, the 'xx ... xx' sequences represent the computed numbers.

When the alphanumeric information to be printed is constant and can so be incorporated into a program, the 'H' code can be utilized within a FØRMAT statement. Such information can be placed anywhere within a printed line by its proper insertion in the statement. The H-specification is given in the FØRMAT sequence as any code is given, and its appearance will be, as usual, in the proper sequence. The specification takes the form

$$wHxxx \ldots xxx$$

where $\underline{w}$ = the count of the number of characters to be printed, all of which (represented by 'xxx ... xxx') must immediately follow the 'H'. All characters to be printed, which may include blanks, must appear in the sequence and be counted in 'w'. (This is the one exception to the rule that blanks in a FORTRAN statement are ignored by the processor.) The alternate form

$$H`xxx \ldots xxx'$$

may be used on some computers.

As an example, suppose SUM and PDT were the two variables (declared integers, let us say) to be printed in the line given above. The appropriate statements would be:

```
    WRITE (6, 55) SUM, PDT
55  FØRMAT (12H THE SUM IS I5, 17H; THE PRØDUCT IS I8, 1H.)
```

We note the following:

1. The first alphanumeric character is a blank, representing carriage control.
2. The w characters following the H code are all printed as shown, including the punctuation.
3. Commas following H-fields may be omitted, but commas following other codes are required.
4. The blanks required in the output statement are included in the H-fields.

Format of Printed Data

We have considered the problem of converting internally stored data to an appropriate form upon printing, e.g., integers, real numbers with and without exponents, and alphanumeric strings. We have paid little attention, however, to the problem of locating printed items across a line and down a page.

Page formating is important, for the printed page is to be read and should therefore be appropriately structured. Columns of information should be properly spaced and titled, and the pages should be properly headed and possibly labeled with page numbers. We consider some of these problems in this section.

Line spacing can be handled by carriage control codes, as we have seen. The slash (/) in a format terminates a printed line, so that two or more slashes in succession lead to blank lines. Thus, the format

    55   FØRMAT (1X, 6E10.3//1X, 3E10.3)

causes a blank line to appear between the two printed lines. The double slash leads to a blank record which implies single spacing of a blank line, or double spacing. In general, *n* successive slashes within the body of a FØRMAT statement cause *n* − 1 blank lines between printed lines. A slash at the end leads to one blank line, for a blank record is implied at the end. If *n* slashes appear at the end of a FØRMAT statement, *n* blank lines result. We can also reason that *n* slashes at the start of a FØRMAT statement lead to *n* blank lines. Thus, we are not limited to single and double spacing of printed material.

Spacing across a line can be achieved in three ways: (1) by use of an extra large count in a conversion code, as 'F20.4' to give the effect of 14 blank columns when a code of 'F6.4' is adequate; (2) by use of an H-field with imbedded blanks, as '14H   ' to give the 14 blank columns; or (3) by use of the 'wX' code which causes *w* columns to be skipped on the printed line, as '14X' to give the same 14 blank columns. Of course, any combination of these methods can be combined in a single FØRMAT statement.

Variable Formats

The variable-format technique described in Section 9.2 is applicable to output as well. It is useful if the format of the output varies with the data read. We have already noted one feature of FØRMAT statements that permits one such type of variation. If items to be printed vary in number but remain constant in format type, a maximum-count conversion code—e.g., '10F10.3'—can be used for any number of items no greater than the maximum.

EXERCISES

1. Assume these values for the named variables:

$$K = 50, \qquad P = +486.06, \qquad Q = -.00374$$

Write exactly what would be printed by the use of this statement:

WRITE (6, 300) K, P, Q

and each of these FØRMAT statements:

(a) 300   FØRMAT (1X, 13HRESULTS: K = I4, 3X,
                  3HP = F8.3, 3HQ = F8.4)

    (b) 300   FØRMAT (18H TEST RUN NUMBER I3//4X,

                  13HTEMPERATURE F8.2,

                  17HDEG. F   CØEFF. E11.3)

2. Write FØRMAT statements which will print the 120 values of the array TABLE in the following formats. Assume the entries of ARRAY are real numbers no greater than 1000, and that only two decimal places are significant. Use double spacing.
   - (a) Print 10 values to a line, utilizing most of the 120 columns of the page, uniformly spaced across the page.
   - (b) Print alternately seven and eight values to a line, allowing at least five blanks between numbers. The printed lines are to be aligned vertically.
   - (c) Print five values to a line, but precede each value with a count of the value, as follows:

      1– 567.89   2– 374.09   3– 452.00   4– 333.55   5– 200.01

      6– 427.11   7– 469.22   8– 576.11   9– 289.33   10– 998.06

    Clearly some additional coding beyond the WRITE and FØRMAT statements is required.

3. Write a program that computes the square roots of integers from 1 through 100. Print each number on a line with its root; the latter should be accurate to three decimal places. The lists of output should be approximately centered in the first 50 columns of the page, as should appropriate list headings and a page title. Only 50 pairs of numbers should appear on a page.

4. Write a program that reads 100 real numbers, punched 10 to a card, with values in the range from -10 to $+10$. Print out the numbers, 10 to a line, but if the absolute value of any number is less than 0.1, replace its value with the word 'TRACE'. (*Hint:* Use the variable-format technique, inserting the word TRACE as the value of one of the variables printed, with an appropriate FØRMAT change.)

9.4 REPORT PREPARATION

The Problem

    When we considered the format with which data are to be printed, we paid some attention to the matters of spacing the data and the inclusion of alphanumeric descriptive information. That is, if we computed a sum, we did not merely print the sum:

    4520.678

Rather, we added a few words of explanation:

    THE SUM IS 4520.678

If we are preparing a lengthy printout, showing much data tabulated in several columns, we must give much more consideration to the design of the page to be printed. In such situations, the printout is often referred to as a "report" and the planning of its format may be called "report preparation"; the term "report generation" is commonly used.[1]

Some of the considerations in report preparation, aside from data field specifications, are as follows:

1. Page titling.
2. Page numbering.
3. Tabs (location of data columns).
4. Column titles.
5. Line spacing.
6. Overall height and width (number of lines and characters in a line).
7. Page footings.

Consider the report in Figure 9.10. The following can be said about it under the headings above.

1. The page titling comprises two lines, which can be realized by these statements:

```
    WRITE (6, 100)
100   FØRMAT (23X, 17HSALES JANUARY 1968//19X, 24HELECTRØNIC SALES DIVISIØN)
```

It is possible that the date is a variable, supplied with the data. For complete generality, this would be done. We could read this data as follows:

```
    READ  (5, 50) (DATE(I), I = 1,3)
50   FØRMAT (3A6)
```

Then the output statements would become:

```
    WRITE  (6, 101) (DATE(I), I = 1,3)
101   FØRMAT (23X, 6HSALES 3A6//19X, 24HELECTRØNIC SALES DIVISIØN)
```

2. Page numbering here is located near the bottom of the page. Each time a page is ended, a page counter, say PGCNT, must be increased by one and printed:

```
    PGCNT = PGCNT + 1
    WRITE (6, 108) RNUM, PGCNT
108   FØRMAT (8H REPØRT RNUM, 7H, PAGE PGCNT, 1H.)
```

The value of RNUM (report number) must also be supplied, of course.

SALES JANUARY 1968

ELECTRØNIC SALES DIVISIØN

ITEM	NUMBER	CØST	SØLD	TØTAL
STEREO RECEIVER	66H002	120.50	3	361.50
LR–2 SPEAKER	33Q200	64.95	5	324.75
FM TUNER	34Q001	122.50	2	245.00
MC75 75-WATT AMPLIFIER	20H990	205.75	1	205.75
MC50 50-WATT AMPLIFIER	20H980	163.50	1	163.50
MC25 25-WATT AMPLIFIER	20H970	110.00	4	440.00
3-WAY SPEAKER SYSTEM	44L005	64.95	5	324.75
MØDEL 25 TURNTABLE	20Z775	55.75	2	111.50
MØDEL 35 TURNTABLE	20Z776	66.60	3	199.80
4TX CARTRIDGE	88Z000	2.75	12	33.00
BUMPER ANTENNA	66A335	13.25	20	265.00
WIRELESS INTERCØM NØ. 33	50W200	32.50	8	260.00
WIRELESS INTERCØM NØ. 34	50W201	37.50	9	337.50
TUBE TESTER MØDEL 10	20T202	20.00	5	100.00
TUBE TESTER MØDEL 15	20T204	22.40	4	89.60
CD–S PHØTØCELL	18S000	1.59	40	63.60
SE PHØTØCELL	18S100	5.55	10	55.50

TØTAL CØST   3580.75

REPORT 378, PAGE 16.
02/05/68

Fig. 9.10.   A report.

3. The five columns of tabulated information involve the following statements:

        WRITE (6, 106) (ITEM(I), I = 1,6), NUMBER CØST, SØLD, TØTAL
    106   FØRMAT (1H0 6A4, 4X, A6, 2X, F8.2, 3X, I4, 2X, F9.2)

The tab positions, allocation of space along the line to data fields, and space between fields are all implied by the above FØRMAT statement. It is necessary to draw a "picture" first of the desired format of a line. The picture may appear as follows, where X's are used to indicate the extent of the several fields on each line:

    XXXXXXXXXXXXXXXXXXXXXXXXX   XXXXX XXXXX.XX   XXXX XXXXXX.XX

After the line format has been decided upon, as in the above, the FØRMAT statement can be written (statement 106, above).

4. Column titles are provided by a single FØRMAT statement:

```
102   FØRMAT (//7X, 4HITEM, 18X, 6HNUMBER, 5X, 4HCØST, 5X, 4HSØLD, 4X, 5HTØTAL)
```

5. Line spacing here is double and is provided by the '0' carriage control code in format 106.

6. The height of the printout in Figure 9.10 is 48 lines and is here assumed to be the allowable height. This allows 17 full printed lines of sales information. If fewer such lines are printed, we can still require that the last two lines remain at the bottom (see item 7). Line width in this printout is 61 characters (exclusive of the carriage control code). This value is taken into account in item 3, above, as the format is determined. This value also helps determine several other FØRMAT statements, specifically numbers 101, 102, and 107.

7. The page footings here consist of the last three lines of the figure. The first of these, giving the total cost, is to be located two lines after the last sales line. A summation is involved. The second footing is "REPØRT 378, PAGE 16", and is located on the third line from the bottom in all cases, even if less than 17 full lines of information are to be printed. Finally, the third footing, the date, must be on the last line always. The date itself may be obtainable from the computer, as is the case in some installations, or alternately may be supplied with the data.

EXERCISE

Write a complete program to supply printed reports in the form illustrated in Figure 9.10. Assume the data to be printed are stored in memory at the time the report is to be prepared, in these arrays: ITEM(250), NUMBER(250), CØST(250), SØLD(250), and TØTAL(250). Up to 250 lines of data (excluding headings and footings) may then be printed. As before, no more than 17 lines of data may be printed on a page.

The program is to allow for any number of printed lines of data up to 250, and therefore a count must be made as lines are printed. The same headings are to appear on each page of the report, and the same report number and date are to appear in the footings on each page. The page number is to begin at '1' and proceed in sequence. The total cost is to appear only on the last page of the report. In all other respects, the format of the report follows the specifications given above, under items 1 to 7.

9.5 FILES OF INFORMATION

Files in Auxiliary Memory

A file was defined as an ordered set of records. We may consider a deck of cards to be a file, with individual cards as records. We may also consider data in memory as a file. Still another type of file, the type usually referred to when the term "file" is used, can be identified. Such a file exists in auxiliary memory, on magnetic tape, disk, or drum. We shall consider such files here, referring only to magnetic-tape files. Such files are conceptually simpler, because of the nature of tapes, than other files. The concepts studied here apply equally well to other media, which will be studied subsequently.

We can define three general classes of files on magnetic tape. First, a *scratch file* is a temporary one, created during a computer run and not used after the run is over. Second, an *input file* is one that is read during a run by a program; it generally contains data that were stored in the file previously, either by the same program or by another program. Third, an *output file* is one that is created during a run yet saved for future use, perhaps as an input file later.

The form of the READ and WRITE statements allows for the designation of devices from which or to which data may be transmitted. We can interpret the device designator as a file designator. Thus, if we write

    READ (5,100), . . .

we mean that file 5 supplies the input data. File 5 has been, throughout this text, the input tape for off-line operations. In other words, punched cards were read onto a tape off-line, and this tape was later treated as the input tape; the programmer may consider file 5 to be a deck of cards. File 5 can be said to be the *system input tape*, the tape considered as the normal source of input data. In an analogous manner, file 6, the output tape for off-line operations, is said to be the *system output tape*. This file is used for printing on paper, and the programmer may consider it simply to be a printout.

We can be more general by using other tape designators as file names. Typically, six to twenty such files are available to a program. This means, physically, that there are that many tape units upon which one tape can be mounted at a time. There is of course no limit to the number of tape files generated, if one has enough magnetic tapes. A tape unit is designated as an input, an output, or as either input or output file. Furthermore, some tapes are considered to be "BCD" and others "binary". BCD tapes are simply those we have been considering; they may be printed if desired. Binary tapes may not be printed for their data are not formatted or converted. As an example, a real number on a BCD tape may appear as '750.28', whereas on a binary tape it would appear in exactly the same form as it does in memory as a floating-point number, with a sign bit, several bits for the exponent, and other bits for the fractional part. In other words, a binary tape is created without any conversion; a stream of bits from memory cells is transmitted to the tape.

Since there is no conversion involved in using a binary tape, an input or output statement requires no reference to a FØRMAT statement. The READ and WRITE statements appear as follows:

READ (unit) list

WRITE (unit) list

where <u>unit</u> is an integer, the number of the file. At any computer installation, there is a standard assignment of tape units to files. This assignment varies among installations, but it might appear as in Table 9.1. Here, files 5 and 6 are as designated

TABLE 9.1

Tape unit	Purpose	Mode
1	Input or output	BCD
2	Input or output	BCD
3	Input or output	Binary
4	Input or output	Binary
5	Input	BCD
6	Output	BCD

previously: the system input and output files (or tapes), respectively. Files 1 and 2 are BCD tapes that can be used for either input or output, as the programmer desires. Files 3 and 4 are binary tapes that can also be used for input or output. The operating system will provide some protection for files 5 and 6, for they are used by a number of programmers in a batch-processing system. Since these are public files, a programmer should not be able to write on file 5 nor to read file 6. The system prevents this from happening and usually provides commentary if either action is attempted.

In all **READ** and **WRITE** statements, the unit may be given symbolically, provided the variable named is given a correct value. In this way, the output file written on, for example, may be changed during a run. Thus, if we write

    WRITE (FILE, 106), X, Y, Z

we can place results on several files by varying the value of FILE during the run.

Tape Operations

There are three statements in **FORTRAN** that are used to perform tape manipulation operations. Each is of the form

    operation   unit

where <u>operation</u> is END FILE, REWIND, or BACKSPACE, and <u>unit</u> is the file number or variable.

END FILE is used to indicate the end of a file on a tape. On printing, the printer must be directed when to stop printing. Tapes are used over and over again, and there is frequently no way of indicating the end of current meaningful information without an end-of-file indicator. The indicator is also useful for reading, for the same reason. When the system files (5 or 6) are written, the end-of-file indicator is provided by the computer installation.

REWIND is used to return a tape to its starting point. Again, since tapes are reused, the only way to be certain that all desired information can be read from a tape is to rewind it both before writing on it and reading it later. A programmer is prevented from rewinding the system input and output tapes.

BACKSPACE is used to back up the specified file one record, i.e., so that the record just read is in position to be read again. The statement is not used very much, except for rereading information that is known to have been read incorrectly, since tape files are usually read in record sequence, from the start. A programmer is prevented from backspacing files 5 and 6 by the operating system.

Scratch Files

Scratch files may be created under these circumstances:

1. When so much information is generated during a run and is later reduced in quantity by processing, that some must be stored outside core temporarily.
2. When much data must be processed in two or more passes, i.e., when all the data must be processed from start to finish more than once yet cannot all fit in core, so that the information must be temporarily stored outside.
3. When it is convenient to store the results of processing by a series of programs in one run outside core, so that later programs can retrieve these intermediate results for further processing.

In all these cases, of course, auxiliary memory is required because there is insufficient core memory. With a large enough core, scratch files are not needed.

Referring to Table 9.1, we see that files 3 and 4 are available for scratch purposes. (We may also use files 1 and 2, but they involve conversion, which is unnecessary.) We can return to the GAMMA 70 assembler, GAP, considered in Section 7.3, and continue the task of writing that assembler. To help in this task, we use a scratch file.

Example 9.1. In Example 7.3, two new tasks for the simulated GAMMA-70-and-GAP were mentioned. The first of these, converting symbolic operation codes to numeric form, was coded in that example. We turn now to the second task, that of writing Pass 1 and Pass 2. In Pass 1 a symbol table must be created. In Pass 2 this table must be used to convert symbolic addresses to numeric equivalences. Since we must pass twice through the input data, the symbolic instructions, a scratch file (file 3) will be used.

Pass 1 involves storing a pair of entries in the symbol table every time a label is given in a symbolic instruction; this pair is the location and the label. Thus, we must check the label field (assumed to be four columns) to see if it is nonblank; the label field begins in column 1. If a label is given, the current value of K, the location into which an instruction is to be stored (see Section 6.3), and the label must be stored in the symbol table, STABLE. In the program, STABLE is defined as a two-dimensional array, 500×2, since entries are two words each. An index J identifies the current entry in STABLE.

Normally, **K** is·increased by one each time an instruction is read, for each occupies one word. The pseudo-operation BLØCK, however, requires several words to be used for storage, and **K** must then be increased by the number of words. The effect of thus increasing **K** will be to set aside the requisite number of words. We shall bypass this problem now, returning to it later in Chapter 10, because we need a new capability not yet studied.

The early part of the reading portion of the assembler, including Pass 1, follows; SYMAD is the symbolic address. As previously, new or changed statements are underlined.

```
C    SIM70-3
     CØMMØN STABLE
     DIMENSIØN PRØG(4096,2), STABLE(500,2)
     DATA BLANK/4H    /END/3HEND /
     INTEGER START, PRØG, ACCUM, AR
C    READ IN PRØGRAM.
  1  READ (5,100) START
100  FØRMAT (Ø4)
     K = START
     J = 1
     REWIND 3
C    PASS 1.
  2  READ (5,101) LABEL, SYMØP, SYMAD
101  FØRMAT (A4,3X,A4,4X,A4)
     WRITE (3) SYMØP, SYMAD
C    CHECK FØR LABEL FIELD BLANK.
     IF (LABEL .EQ. BLANK) GØ TØ 20
C    NØNBLANK . . . ENTER INTØ SYMBØL TABLE.
     STABLE(J,1) = K
     STABLE(J,2) = LABEL
     J = J + 1
20   K = K + 1
C    TEST FØR END.
     IF (SYMØP .EQ. END) GØ TØ 21
     GØ TØ 2
21   END FILE 3
```

We may recall the following: (1) scratch file 3 is used to store the cards (except the label) after they are read for Pass 1, for eventual use in Pass 2; the REWIND and END FILE instructions are used as required, and a WRITE statement stores the cards on file 3; (2) the label, operation, and address fields are located in columns 1–4, 8–13, and 16–19, respectively, assuming four- or five-character symbols.

Pass 2 consists merely of reading the cards again (except for the label) from file 3, converting the symbolic operation and address, and entering these in the PRØG array, as was done in Example 7.3. A function ADCV, for converting symbolic ad-

dresses to numeric form is required; the symbol table STABLE is to be used. The code
is very much as it was before:

```
C    PASS 2.
C    RESET PØINTER TØ PRØG ARRAY.
     K = START
C    READ FILE 3.
 22  READ(3) SYMØP, SYMAD
     IF (SYMØP .EQ. END) GØ TØ 3
     INSØP = ØPCV(SYMØP,ERR)
     INSAD = ADCV(SYMAD,ERR)
     IF (ERR .EQ. 1) GØ TØ 70
     PRØG(K,1) = INSØP
     PRØG(K,2) = INSAD
     K = K + 1
     GØ TØ 22
  3  ....
```

This code, interestingly enough, accommodates the NUMBER pseudo-
operation, described in Section 6.4, provided the numeric value given is an integer, and
provided "NUMBER" is converted to zero in the ØPCV function. (That function
can easily be extended to include this.) If, e.g., this card is processed

```
     SEVEN   NUMBER   7
```

the entries in the PRØG array will be

```
     PRØG(K,1) = 0
     PRØG(K,2) = 7
```

These entries are correct, for numbers to be processed are supposed to be stored in
PRØG(K,2).

Input and Output Files

The input data for all the programs considered thus far have been supplied
on punched cards, loaded off-line onto the system input tape. We have briefly
considered the possibility of supplying data at a terminal, but this approach is
basically the same as supplying data on punched cards; there is essentially just a
difference in timing in these approaches. In a similar vein, all output results have
been supplied to the system output tape and printed later, off-line, or were supplied
to a terminal.

A very common situation is the case of a file of information kept on magnetic tape or other auxiliary medium, rather than on cards. If a collection of data
is to be modified or updated a number of times and processing is required each
time, it may be much more convenient to store the information in this way. Loading
information into memory is much faster, and updating the information is frequently
easier.

Consider the file of student records that we have been writing programs for. The file of interest contains the records for all students currently enrolled at the college; these are the records of all courses taken to date. If the college has 2000 students and the average number of courses taken by a student to date is 20, then there are over 40,000 cards in the file. Each term it might be necessary to add the grades of 10,000 new courses. Each school year it might be necessary to delete the grades of 500 students, as they graduate, and add records for 500 new students, anticipating adding grades from them later. Since we have the computer at our disposal for doing the calculations described in earlier chapters, we can readily use the computer for updating the file. Clearly this is far easier than keeping a file of 40,000 cards and manually adding and deleting cards.

A file on magnetic tape would be satisfactory for the student record processing problems, since we normally search the data from one end to another. We shall consider this form of storage. In this chapter, we shall not be concerned with the problem of originally creating the tape file nor with updating it. We will treat these problems in Chapter 14, on data management. We shall, however, modify our earlier code to allow reading a tape file of student records, an example of an input data file.

Let us consider the generation of an output file by the student record programs. Certainly, if all we wish to do is calculate the several items required in Example 7.5, there is no need to create an output file. The input file would require no changes and would simply serve as the input file the next time the programs were used. However, suppose the student file is to have added the items calculated each time by STREC3 (Example 7.5): the weighted average, the five top grades, and an indication of whether a student qualified for the honor society.

Example 9.2.   Write a program (STREC3.1), a modification of STREC3, that updates these three added records:

1. The weighted average, in format F4.1.
2. The five top grades, in format 5F5.0.
3. '*Y*' or '*N*', if the student qualified or not.

The program is to replace the old values in these records by new ones, computed on the basis of new data in the file. The assumption is made that other programs bring all the other records up-to-date, that we are only concerned here with the three new records. (More likely, a set of editing programs, as described in Chapter 14, would be used for these functions.)

The new output file becomes the input file for the next run of this program. Both the input and output files are to be BCD, so that they can be printed if desired.

To accommodate the modified approach, the following changes must be made in the main program of Example 7.5:

1. The data must be read from the input file, which we will assume is file 3.
2. The three added records for each student on the input file must be read in order to "get past them", but not processed.

3. The new values of these records for each student must be added to the output file.

4. All the other student records on the input are placed, unchanged, on the output file.

The revised program is the following:

```
C    STREC3.1
C    THIS PRØGRAM SUPPLIES THE FØLLØWING INFØRMATIØN
C    ØN EACH STUDENT: STUDENT NAME, CLASS, MAJØR, LIST
C    ØF CØURSES, AVERAGE, TØP 5 GRADES, LØWEST GRADE,
C    AND QUALIFICATIØN FØR HØNØR SØCIETY.   A TAPE FILE
C    IS UPDATED BY ADDING NEW INFØRMATIØN ØN AVERAGE,
C    TØP 5 GRADES, AND QUALIFICATIØN.
         INTEGER NAME(8), NUMBER, CLASS, MAJØR
         INTEGER CØURSE(80), TERMS(80), TITLES(80,8)
         REAL GRADES(80), CREDS(80), AVER, LØGRAD
         CØMMØN GRADES, NUMBER, CREDS
C    START NEW PAGE.
   10    WRITE (6,100)
  100    FØRMAT (1H1)
C    READ A STUDENTS RECØRD.   WRITE ØN ØUTPUT FILE.
         READ (3,101) NAME, CLASS, MAJØR
         WRITE (4,101) NAME, CLASS, MAJØR
  101    FØRMAT (7A4,A2, I2, 2X, A4)
         WRITE (6,102) NAME, CLASS, MAJØR
  102    FØRMAT (8HØNAME: 7A4,A2, 8H CLASS: I2,
        1       8H MAJØR: A4)
         CLASS = CLASS − 68
C    READ NUMBER ØF GRADES, THEN GRADES.   WRITE ØN FILE.
         READ (3,103) NUMBER
         WRITE (4,103) NUMBER
  103    FØRMAT (I3)
         DØ 11 I = 1, NUMBER
         READ (3,104) CØURSE(I), (TITLES(I,J), J = 1,8),
        1       CREDS(I), GRADES(I), TERMS(I)
   11    WRITE (4,104) CØURSE(I), (TITLES(I,J), J = 1,8),
        1       CREDS(I), GRADES(I), TERMS(I)
  104 FØRMAT (A4, 1X, 7A4,A2, 1X, F1.0, 1X, F3.0, 1X, A3)
C    BYPASS THREE ADDED RECØRDS ØN INPUT FILE.
         DØ 20 J = 1, 3
   20    READ (3)
C    DETERMINE STUDENT AVERAGE.   PRINT IT AND PUT ØN FILE.
         CALL WAVER(AVER)
         WRITE (4,205) AVER
```

```
    205 FØRMAT (F4.1)
C   DETERMINE 5 TØP GRADES.  PRINT AND PUT ØN FILE.
        CALL BSØRT(5)
        WRITE (6,106) (GRADES(I), I = 1,5)
    106 FØRMAT (25H0THE 5 TØP GRADES ARE: 5F5.0)
        WRITE (4,206) (GRADES(I), I = 1,5)
    206 FØRMAT (5F5.0)
C   DETERMINE LØWEST GRADE.
        LØGRAD = SMALL(GRADES)
C   DETERMINE CLASS ØF STUDENT.
        GØ TØ (91,92,93,94), CLASS
C   SENIØR (CLASS ØF 69).
        IF (AVER .LT. 85.0 .ØR. LØGRAD .LT. 50.0) GØ TØ 200
        GØ TØ 201
C   JUNIØR (CLASS ØF 70).
        IF (AVER .LT. 86.0 .ØR. LØGRAD .LT. 60.0) GØ TØ 200
        GØ TØ 201
C   SØPHØMØRE (CLASS ØF 71).
        IF (AVER .LT. 86.0 .ØR. LØGRAD .LT. 60.0) GØ TØ 200
        GØ TØ 201
C   FRESHMAN (CLASS ØF 72).
        IF (AVER .LT. 90.0 .ØR. LØGRAD .LT. 70.0) GØ TØ 200
        GØ TØ 201
C   HERE IF STUDENT DØES NØT QUALIFY.
    200 WRITE (6,107)
    107 FØRMAT (25H0STUDENT DØES NØT QUALIFY.)
        WRITE (4,207)
    207 FØRMAT (1HN)
C   HERE IF STUDENT DØES QUALIFY.
    201 WRITE (6,108)
    108 FØRMAT (19H0STUDENT QUALIFIES.)
        WRITE (4,208)
208 FØRMAT (1HY)
        GØ TØ 10
        END
```

Note that the records on the output file do not include a carriage control character; hence, formats 101, 103, and 104 can serve for both input and output. Formats 105–108, however, include commentary that is not needed on the output file, so that formats 205–208 are used for that purpose.

We pointed out earlier that the process of updating the file by adding new course records is not under consideration here. Between successive uses of this program, another program is needed for this operation. We shall consider this problem and others related to it later.

EXERCISES

1. Write the subroutine ADCV, which converts symbolic addresses to numeric form. The subroutine was mentioned in Example 9.1.
2. Write a GAP program that can be supplied to the assembler of Example 9.1, and assemble the program and run it. Choose a simple problem of the type studied in early chapters: adding a set of numbers, sorting numbers, finding the largest, etc.
3. Outline a set of programs to solve these problems for the student record processing problem:
   (a) Permit adding new course records.
   (b) Permit correction of specific grades in courses.
   (c) Permit deleting old course records.
   Consider the task of defining the commands the user would use in requesting these operations. These would be subroutine calls.

4. Assume that a program has to be written involving two "old" tape files of data, where two "new" such files are to be generated, replacing the old. During processing, two scratch tapes are needed. The system input tape will be used, as normal, to supply the program, and the system output tape will contain certain output information for printing.
   (a) Make assignments of tapes 1, 2, ... to each tape file involved in this program.
   (b) Write the input-output statements required, including imaginary lists of variables.
   (c) Flowchart the program, being specific on input-output and general on any processing that might be performed.

5. Include in SIM70-3 the following additional features:
   (a) A check to see if a symbol in the location field was used twice (a "multiply-defined symbol").
   (b) A check to see if a symbol is referred to in the address field of an instruction that is absent from all location fields (an "undefined symbol").

REFERENCE

1. IBM has developed a system (RPG) for the generation of reports:
IBM Corporation, *System/360 Operating System Report Program Generator Specifications*, Form C24-3337, Data Processing Division, White Plains, N.Y., 1965.

10 SYMBOL MANIPULATION

We have noted that many problems put on the computer are nonnumerical, i.e., they involve operations that are not predominantly arithmetic in nature. Most of the statements written in an algorithmic-language program represent formula evaluations when a numerical problem is being solved. This is not true in non-numerical problems. In the latter, the processes generally treat the data as symbols of one form or another, and the operations performed on these symbols involve searching, sorting, structuring, rearranging, and the like. We shall, in this chapter, deal with symbols of a particular kind. The processes we perform on them are termed "symbol manipulation".

The symbols we are here concerned with comprise strings of alphanumeric characters. The basic unit of data is a single character, while the items of data actually processed are ordered sets or strings of such characters. The processing is thus also termed "string manipulation". [1]

10.1 ELEMENTS OF SYMBOL MANIPULATION

The Data

The data we consider in this chapter are alphanumeric characters. Each item of data processed is a *character string*, an ordered set of characters. Because such strings may be of variable length, we associate with each a *character count*. The characters in the string may be any of the allowed characters in a computer's character set: letters, digits, arithmetic operators, punctuation marks, and so on. For example, there are 47 characters in the FORTRAN basic character set: the 26 letters of the alphabet, the 10 digits, the blank, and these 10 arithmetic and punctuation characters:

$$= + - */ (), . \$$$

The character count of a string S shall be m. The characters are labeled $c_1, c_2, \ldots, c_m$. Physically, in memory, we shall store the count in the first location of the one-dimensional array S, and store the characters in sequence beginning in the second location. Thus, we have these assignments of space:

Location	Item
$S(1)$	m
$S(2)$	c_1
$S(3)$	c_2
$\vdots$	$\vdots$
$S(m + 1)$	c_m

We shall not pack several characters in one word, though they would fit, because we want to be able conveniently to refer to each character separately. Thus, we store one character per word.

We shall use a convenient notation for reference to character strings and operations upon them. Let us name a string by a capital letter, e.g., 'P', and name its constituent characters by corresponding small letters, e.g., $p_1, p_2, \ldots, p_m$ if its count is m. A contiguous portion of a string is called a *substring*. The substring consisting of the ith through jth characters of P is written $p_{i,j}$.

We may write the contents of a string by listing its characters in succession, placing the string in quotation marks. A character count, given in parentheses at the left, is optional. Thus we may write

```
R  =  'FØURSCØRE AND SEVEN YEARS AGØ'
S  =  (37)'NØW IS THE TIME FØR ALL GØØD MEN TØ'
```

Operations

The variety of processes performed on character strings is not very great; processes are quite simple in concept. They include the following:

1. Searching a string for a given substring.
2. Searching a string for a sequence of substrings.
3. Locating the first appearance of a given character.
4. Counting the appearances of a given character or substring.
5. Combining strings to form new strings.

From these and other basic processes can be built much more complex processes that are very useful in many areas of problem solving. We shall consider some processes in detail in this chapter.

A common operation performed upon strings is concatenation; one string is concatenated to another by placing one at the end of the other, forming a longer string whose length is the sum of the lengths of the original strings. Concatenation is indicated by a double vertical bar: ‖. Thus, for example, let

```
P = (8)'AMERICAN'
Q = (8)' STØRY. '
```

Then

```
P ‖ Q = (16)'AMERICAN STØRY. '
```

Frequently, we wish to search a string for the first appearance of a given character or one of a set of given characters (see 3 above). Having found it, we then wish to break the original string into two portions, the substring prior to the character and the substring following it. If the sought character, called the *break* character, is c and the original string is P, let the resultant strings (separated by c in P) be Q and R. We may write

$$Q, R \leftarrow P/c$$

We can define a kind of subtraction, as follows. If a substring S is present in a string P, then the statement

$$R \leftarrow P - S$$

defines a new string R consisting of P with the first appearance of S deleted; if S is not present in P, then R is identical with P. After deletion, the "gap" is closed up. Thus, let

```
P = (27)'ØUR FATHERS BRØUGHT FØRTH'
S = (6)'FATHER'
```

Then

```
P - S = (21)'ØUR S BRØUGHT FØRTH'
```

If we wish to indicate the deletion of all appearances of S from P, we write

$$R \leftarrow P - \Sigma S$$

which is a shorthand form of

$$R \leftarrow P - S - S - S - \ldots$$

which states that S should be repeatedly "subtracted" from P. Thus, let

```
P = (27)'ØUR FATHERS BRØUGHT FØRTH'
S = 'Ø'
```

Then

    P − ΣS = (24)'UR FATHERS BRUGHT FRTH'

Applications

Now that we have briefly examined the kinds of data we are now dealing with as well as some fundamental operations upon them, we consider a few uses of symbol manipulation.

Program translators accept, as input, statements written in programming languages. These statements are character strings and must be analyzed. We have already briefly examined the process of compilation in Section 8.3, where we noted that an algebraic expression must be scanned from one end to the other, so that tokens can be identified. Constants, variable names, and arithmetic operators (including the equals sign) are the tokens in an assignment statement. This separation into tokens is accomplished by repeatedly applying the following rule

$$T, E_{i+1} \leftarrow E_i/(+, -, *, /)$$

for a range of values of i. After each such breakdown, T contains the variable or constant just extracted. The operators are also extracted by this process, if properly identified. We have not considered such complications as exponentiation or parentheses in this oversimplified analysis, but the utility of string manipulation processes should be evident. We shall code a simple such process in detail later in this chapter, as an adjunct to the GAP assembler.

Another area that utilizes symbol manipulation techniques is that of natural language translation. Computers have been widely used to translate Russian text into English, for example. As a first approximation, a simple substitution of one word for another, utilizing a dictionary, provides a translation. However, so much of the meaning depends upon context that much more analysis is required. The processing that takes place is of the type we have been discussing in this chapter. Yet another area of a similar nature is that of analyzing prose for language content. Detailed studies of old texts have been made for authorship identification. Distributions of certain words and phrases have been determined and compared with distributions of known authors. Once again, techniques in symbol manipulation are required.

Subroutines

We shall now consider the development of a few elementary subroutines for string manipulation. In succeeding sections, we shall make use of these subroutines. We require subroutines that read strings, write strings, and test for given characters or substrings. These are developed below.

Example 10.1. Write a subroutine READST that reads a character string from a card and stores it in memory. The card is punched with the string beginning in column 1.

We must use the format code '80A1' in order to place each character in its own location. The subroutine call is the following:

    CALL READST(STRING)

where STRING is the name of the string read. The subroutine:

```
    SUBRØUTINE READST(STR)
    DIMENSIØN STR(81)
    READ 100, (STR(I), I = 2, 81)
C   SET THE CØUNT.
    STR(1) = 80
    RETURN
100 FØRMAT (80A1)
    END
```

Note that the calling program must provide a DIMENSIØN statement of size 81 for the string. The subroutine sets the count in STR(1) at 80, since 80 columns are read from the card.

This routine fills an 80-character string, but in many instances, the read string may be far fewer characters, say 20 or 25. In later processing, much time would be wasted if we were to scan 80 characters most of which were blank. Let us therefore introduce a new procedure, TRIMST, which improves efficiency.

Example 10.2. Write a routine TRIMST that removes all trailing blanks from a given string. That is, all blanks in sequence at the "right" are to be deleted. For example, this string

    (80)'THIS IS A STRING ØF INPUT DATA.

becomes this trimmed string

    (31)'THIS IS A STRING ØF INPUT DATA.'

which has 31 characters. The subroutine call is the following:

    CALL TRIMST(STRING)

where STRING is the string to be trimmed.

To accomplish the task, we must begin checking at the extreme right (the last character) and work backwards. The procedure:

```
    SUBRØUTINE TRIMST(STR)
    DATA BLANK/1H /
    DIMENSIØN STR(81)
C   FETCH THE CØUNT.
    M = STR(1)
```

```
C    CHECK LAST CHARACTER.
    1  IF (STR(M+1) .NE. BLANK) GØ TØ 2
C    IF BLANK, REDUCE STRING.
        M = M - 1
        GØ TØ 1
C    RESET CØUNT.
    2  STR(1) = M
        RETURN
```

In the reducing loop, we continually check the last character of the string (as it is reduced), decreasing it by one character as long as the new "last" character is blank. The count is reset.

Example 10.3. Write a subroutine WRITST that prints a character string as a single line.

The subroutine:

```
    SUBRØUTINE WRITST(STR)
    DIMENSIØN STR(78)
C    ØBTAIN THE CØUNT.
        N = STR(1) + 1
        WRITE 100, (STR(I), I = 2, N)
        RETURN
  100  FØRMAT (1H, 78A1)
        END
```

The variable N here and henceforth is one more than the count m, needed because of the storage scheme.

We can now develop two searching routines, useful in determining whether given characters or substrings are present.

Example 10.4. Write a subroutine TESTCH that tests a given character string for the appearance of a specified character. If that character is present, the index (subscript) of its first appearance is returned as the value of P. (We say that P is a *pointer* to that character.) If the character is absent from the string, P is set to zero. For the sake of generality, we permit the search to begin at any specified index Q.

The subroutine call is the following:

```
    CALL TESTCH(STRING,Q,CHAR,P)
```

where STRING is the string searched, Q is a pointer to the starting index, CHAR is the location of the character sought, and P is the pointer. A flowchart appears in Figure 10.1. The characters in the string are c_i, and the given character is C. The character C is compared with each c_i until a match is found, whence the index pointer P is set. If the string is exhausted and no match is found, P is set to zero.

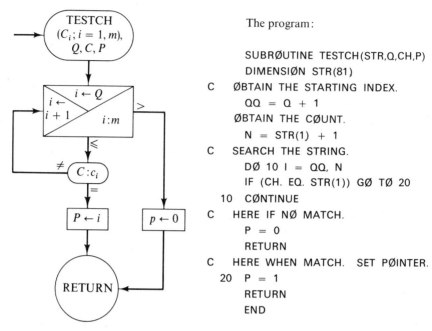

The program:

```
        SUBRØUTINE TESTCH(STR,Q,CH,P)
        DIMENSIØN STR(81)
C       ØBTAIN THE STARTING INDEX.
        QQ = Q + 1
        ØBTAIN THE CØUNT.
        N = STR(1) + 1
C       SEARCH THE STRING.
        DØ 10 I = QQ, N
        IF (CH. EQ. STR(1)) GØ TØ 20
   10   CØNTINUE
C       HERE IF NØ MATCH.
        P = 0
        RETURN
C       HERE WHEN MATCH.  SET PØINTER.
   20   P = 1
        RETURN
        END
```

Fig. 10.1.   The TESTCH subroutine.

Example 10.5. Write a subroutine TESTST that tests a given character string for the appearance of a specified substring. The search begins at index Q. If that substring is present, the index of the first character of its first appearance is returned. If the substring is absent, the pointer P is set to zero.

The subroutine call is the following:[2]

CALL TESTST(STRING,Q,SUBSTR,P)

where SUBSTR is the name of the substring sought. Let the substring characters be $t_1, t_2, \ldots, t_u$.

The search can be accomplished in two phases:

1. A search for the initial character of the substring within the string, using the TESTCH subroutine.

2. A test of the following characters in the string to see if they match the following characters in the substring.

In the event that phase 2 fails (i.e., after an initial match is found, a mismatch is found in subsequent comparisons), it is necessary to return to phase 1, restarting the search at the character following the initial match previously.

A flowchart appears in Figure 10.2. The starting index Q is saved as QQ, since internally it is modified (for the TESTCH call). If the substring is greater than the balance of the string yet to be tested, there is no reason to continue the search. That is, if $u > m - QQ + 1$, we stop. Otherwise, TESTCH is then called; the search is always for the first character of the substring, t_1. If P is zero, the substring is absent. If the substring is a single character, the routine ends at this point, the problem being a single call to TESTCH.

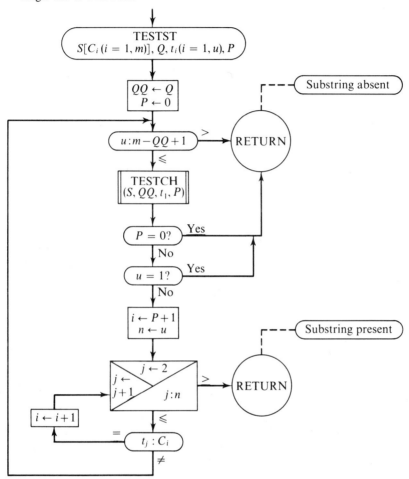

Fig. 10.2.   The TESTST subroutine.

If the substring contains more than one character, a test must now proceed for the balance of the substring (phase 2), so a search is begun, starting with a comparison of c_{P+1} with t_2. If all the t_j match the $u - 1$ string characters from that point, the substring is present. If not, then we must begin again with phase 1, now starting the search with the $(P + 1)$th character of the string S, so QQ is reset.

The program:

```
SUBRØUTINE TESTST(STR,Q,SUB,P)
DIMENSIØN STR(79), SUB(79)
QQ = Q
P = 0
```

```
C   CHECK FØR SHØRT STRING BALANCE.
   5  IF (SUB(1) .GT. STR(1) − QQ + 1) RETURN
      CALL TESTCH(STR,QQ,SUB(2),P)
      IF (P .EQ. 0) RETURN
      IF (SUB(1) .EQ. 1) RETURN
C   SET STRING INDEX AND SUBSTRING CØUNT.
      I = P + 2
      N = SUB(1) + 1
C   SEARCH FØR REST ØF SUBSTRING.
      DØ 10 J = 3, N
      IF (SUB(J) .NE. STR(I)) GØ TØ 15
  10  I = I + 1
C   SUBSTRING MISMATCH.   RESET QQ FØR TESTCH.
      QQ = P + 1
      GØ TØ 5
      END
```

EXERCISES

1. What other operations might we want to perform on strings?

2. What are the subroutine calls associated with the operations given for Exercise 1?

3. What other applications involve the processing of strings of characters?

*   *   *   *   *   *

4. Write a subroutine RETRST (read and trim string) that accomplishes both the READST and TRIMST operations.

5. Write a modified READST subroutine, called READLS, that reads long strings from several cards in succession. Let a '$' act as the end-of-string indicator; the string, which may be up to 10 cards long, ends just prior to that mark.

6. Write a subroutine LISTST that is similar to the WRITST subroutine, differing in that the name of the string and its character count are given as well. The format used in this section for indicating string contents is to be used. Thus, we might write

```
NAME = ( 5)'HENRY'
TEXT = (22)'CØNTENTS ØF THE STRING'
```

Write a modified LISTST subroutine that excludes the character count. In both cases, the name of the string, in alphanumeric form, must be given; the call is (e.g.)

```
CALL LISTST(STRING,6HSTRING)
```

Note that the string name is given as an alphanumeric constant.

7. Given a string TEXT in memory, write subroutines to perform the following tasks:
   (a) Count the number of appearances of a specified character.

(b) Determine if the character 'A' occurs at any place after the character 'B'. If so, return pointer to 'B'.

(c) Determine if the characters 'A', 'B', and 'C' occur in that order, though not necessarily adjacently.

(d) Identify the most frequently occurring character.

(e) Determine if any letters of the alphabet occur exactly three times and identify them.

8. In an arithmetic expression, parentheses must balance. If a counter is used to keep track of the level in the expression, being increased by 1 if a left parenthesis is hit and being decreased by 1 if a right parenthesis is hit, that count must never become negative and must be zero at the end of the expression. Write a subroutine TSTPAR that performs these tests.

9. Write a subroutine that deletes from a string all appearances of a given substring.

* * * * * *

10. A "concordance" is a tabulation of certain key words appearing in a body of text, with reference to their specific appearances. Write a program that prepares such a concordance. Select 10 key words for the search. Let the data be punched so that no words are hyphenated and so that sentences are grouped into "sections". The tabulation must list the sections in which each appearance occurs. Each section is identified by a card with 'S' in column 1 and the section number in columns 2–4; the balance of this card is blank. Key word counts must be given. The output ought to look something like this:

Key words	Section	Count
TABLE	1	2
	3	1
	5	3
CHAIR	2	4
	3	2
:	:	:

11. The TESTCH subroutine seeks a specific character. The subroutine might be more useful if it permitted a test for any one of a set of given characters. Write a modified subroutine TESTCS (test for characters) with this call:

```
CALL TESTCS(STRING,Q,CHARS,P)
```

where CHARS is a character string and all other arguments are as in TESTCH. The pointer P, upon return, points to the first appearance of any one of the characters in CHARS.

10.2 READING VARIABLE-FORMAT DATA

The Scanning Problem

We shall now consider a problem that is properly a topic for a chapter on input operations, yet which involves string manipulation. It offers an example of the use of such techniques to ease the data preparation problem.

We considered, in Section 9.2, the problem of reading data with a format that was considered "variable" by the program reading it. That is, the format description of the data accompanied the data in the cards. In this section, we consider something more general than that: we permit the data format to be truly variable, even from card to card. Such data are often termed *formatless*.

Let us consider an example of variable-format data. Suppose we wish to supply a sequence of integers to a program. We could supply them as we have described earlier, as shown in Figure 10.3, where a format code 'I8' is used. Alternately, we could avoid this rigid format and simply list them, in sequence, separated by commas and ending, let us say, with a period, as shown in Figure 10.4. We see immediately the advantage of the latter format. It is far easier to punch. It is easier

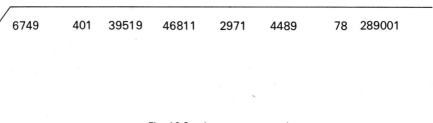

6749   401   39519   46811   2971   4489   78   289001

Fig. 10.3.   Integers on a card.

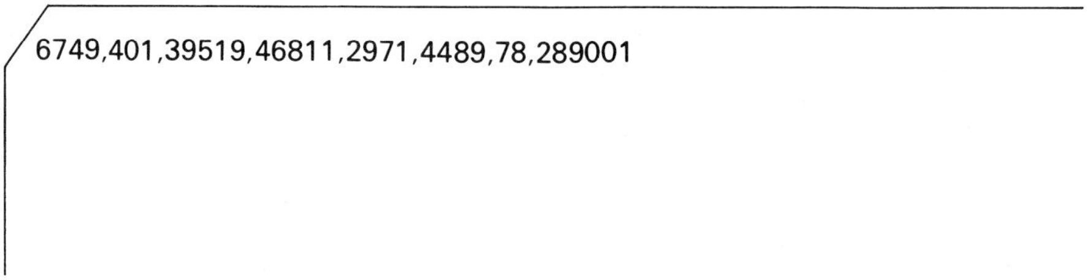

6749,401,39519,46811,2971,4489,78,289001

Fig. 10.4.   Integers on a card.

to check, for we need not worry about right-justification in fields, as is required in Figure 10.3. But FORTRAN does not allow us to so format our data. We can circumvent this problem by scanning the data and extracting the contents of each field. The "fields" must now be interpreted as those sequences of characters delimited by the left end of the card, by commas, and the period. We shall refer to scanning and extracting information from such variable fields as "the scanning problem".

We must be sure we realize the difference between such truly variable-format data and the "variable-format" case considered earlier. Here, there is no fixed format at all; the fields are variable in length from one instance to the next. Earlier, the format was only variable in the sense that the program could accept any format. But after the format information was read prior to the data, the reading problem was the same as in the fixed-format case (until the format was changed by further reading of format descriptions).

Extracting Variable Fields

We shall now consider the problem of extracting the contents of the variable fields described. Let us assume that such a sequence appears on a card as follows: with all fields separated by commas and ending with a period, with no blank spaces intervening. Then to extract a field, we start with the character just after a comma, and extract the substring ending just before another comma or a period. We might note that this process does not depend upon having digits in the fields, so any fields written can be extracted this way.

It is clear that we can utilize the string-manipulation techniques introduced in Section 10.2. In addition, we need a subroutine to extract a specified substring from a given string. The substring is specified by giving the indices of its terminal characters. This subroutine will be used to extract a field delimited by commas.

Example 10.6. Write a subroutine EXTRSS that removes a substring from a given string, thereby creating a new string. The call is

    CALL EXTRSS(STRING,FC,LC,NEWST)

where STRING is the original string, FC and LC are integers which are the indices of the first and last characters of the substring, and NEWST is the name of the new substring. For example, assume we have

    STRING = 'THIS IS A STRING ØF INPUT DATA.'

Upon executing

    CALL EXTRSS(STRING,9,16,TEXT)

we will have

    TEXT = 'A STRING'

Let us call the created string T with entries t_j. If f and l are the first and last character indices of the given string S with entries c_i, we move characters as follows:

$$t_2 \leftarrow c_f$$
$$t_3 \leftarrow c_{f+1}$$
$$\vdots \quad \vdots$$
$$t_{l-f+1} \leftarrow c_l$$

A flowchart appears in Figure 10.5. In the iteration box in that flowchart, the index i runs from f through l. At the end of the string generation, t_1 (the character count in T) is set to its proper value, $l - f + 1$. The program:

    SUBRØUTINE EXTRSS(STR,F,L,NEW)
    INTEGER F,L
    DIMENSIØN STR(100), NEW(100)

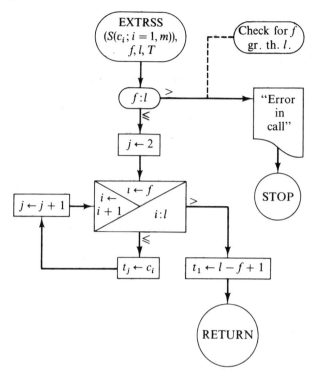

Fig. 10.5.   EXTRSS subroutine.

```
C    CHECK FØR 'F' GREATER THAN 'L'.
     IF (F .GT. L) GØ TØ 10
C    MØVE SUBSTRING TØ NEW STRING.
     J = 2
     DØ 20 I = F, L
 20  NEW(J) = STR(I)
     NEW(1) = L - F + 1
     RETURN
 10  WRITE(6,100)
100  FØRMAT(15H1ERRØR IN CALL.)
     STØP
     END
```

Now we can return to our original problem, that of extracting the fields of a variable-format data sequence.

Example 10.7. Write a subroutine EXTRAC that extracts the fields on a card which are separated by commas and terminate with a period.

We must first consider the locations of the extracted fields, which we consider to be substrings. It is perhaps simplest to make use of CØMMØN storage. We must create an array of strings, since we do not wish to use a new name for each string created. The number of strings, as well as the length of each, is a variable. Let us assume that each field is no greater than 15 characters and that there are no more than 20 fields in a given sequence. This statement is required in both the main program and the subroutines:

CØMMØN FIELD(20,16)

With this statement, we need not list the names of the extracted fields in the SUB-RØUTINE argument list. As previously, we place character counts in the first positions, i.e., in FIELD(1,1), FIELD(2,1), ...

We extract fields as follows:

1. Using TESTCH, with Q (the starting index) = 1 and the sought character a comma, locate the first comma.
2. Using EXTRSS, move the substring from the starting character through the character just before the comma to a new position.
3. Repeat steps 1 and 2, until no comma is found. Then, seek a period in the string and form a new string.

The process is flowcharted in Figure 10.6. Note that Q is initially set to 1 but thereafter is set to P + 1, where P is the pointer whose value is returned by TESTCH. The call

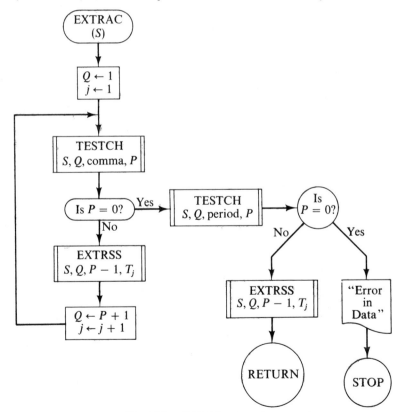

Fig. 10.6.   EXTRAC subroutine.

to EXTRSS has the arguments (S,Q,P − 1,T$_j$), where S is the given string and T$_j$ is the set of created substrings. Actually, EXTRSS moves substrings to a temporary buffer TFIELD, from which the substrings are then moved to FIELD. The string moved runs from Q through P − 1, i.e., one character before the comma or period. The program:

```
      SUBRØUTINE EXTRAC(STR)
      DIMENSIØN STR(100), FIELD(20,16), TFIELD(16)
      CØMMØN FIELD
      INTEGER P, Q
      DATA CØMMA/1H,/PERIØD/1H./
      Q = 1
      J = 1
C   LØCATE END ØF FIELD.
    5 CALL TESTCH(STR,Q,CØMMA,P)
C   IS THIS LAST FIELD.
      IF (P .EQ. 0) GØ TØ 30
C   MØVE FIELD (SUBSTRING).
      CALL EXTRSS(STR,Q,P−1,TFIELD)
C   MØVE TØ FIELD ARRAY.
      DØ 10 I = 1,16
   10 FIELD(J,I) = TFIELD(I)
      Q = P + 1
      J = J + 1
      GØ TØ 5
C   END ØF STRING.
   30 CALL TEXTCH(STR,Q,PERIØD,P)
C   TEST FØR ØMITTED PERIØD.
      IF (P .EQ. 0) GØ TØ 40
C   MØVE LAST FIELD.
      CALL EXTRSS(STR,Q,P−1,TFIELD)
      DØ 35 I = 1,16
   35 FIELD(J,I) = TFIELD(I)
C   ERRØR.
   40 WRITE(100,6)
  100 FØRMAT (15H1ERRØR IN DATA.)
      STØP
      END
```

At the conclusion of this subroutine, the fields shown in Figure 10.4 are stored in the array FIELD as shown below; note that one character is stored per word and that the kth extracted field is given by (FIELD(j, k); $j = 2, m_k$), where $m_k =$ the count of the kth field:

FIELD(1,1) = 4,   FIELD(2,1) = '6',   FIELD(3,1) = '7',
                  FIELD(4,1) = '4',   FIELD(5,1) = '9';
FIELD(1,2) = 3,   FIELD(2,2) = '4',   FIELD(3,2) = '0',
                  FIELD(4,2) = '1';   ...

EXERCISES

1. The use of a free format for punched data illustrates the difference between an approach that eases the burden of the user and one that eases the burden of the programmer. Comment on this tradeoff.

2. Illustrate other tradeoffs, in other examples.

*   *   *   *   *   *

3. The EXTRAC subroutine is somewhat specialized in that it is written under the assumption that the field separators are all commas. Generalize the subroutine so that any two specified characters may be used as field separators and field terminator, respectively. Add two arguments to the subroutine call which are the locations of these two characters. In addition, add another argument, the location of a count of the number of fields extracted.

10.3 PROGRAM TRANSLATION

Data Conversion

We have already considered the problem of translating a symbolic program into numeric form. In Section 9.5, a GAP program with symbols given for both operation codes and addresses was translated. We did not consider all aspects of the assembly process in that section because of complexities in certain of the operations. Now that we have studied some symbol manipulation processes, we are ready to tackle more of those problems.

In almost any symbolic program, as in almost any FORTRAN program, numeric quantities appear. When read into memory, these quantities cannot be read with 'I' or 'F' conversion codes if they are intermingled with alphanumeric information. As an example, we may have the expression 'X + 3' in a FORTRAN statement or, as we shall shortly see, in a symbolic program. The only way we can analyze such expressions in general is to read them as alphanumeric strings, scan them, and then extract the numeric parts; here the numeric part is '3'. We have seen how this can be done using the EXTRAC subroutine of Section 10.2.

Once numeric quantities have been extracted, we must convert them to an equivalent numeric form. Until this conversion is accomplished, the characters in the number are simply alphanumeric quantities, stored one to a word. They are symbols and not numbers. To consider this conversion process, let us assume that each word in the computer has 32 bits and that each character occupied eight bits. Thus a word can hold four characters. Suppose the number '635' was read and extracted by the EXTRAC subroutine. The character count is three, and this number appears in binary form in the first word of an array, called ITEM. The storage of the string ITEM appears as in Figure 10.7. The character fields of 8 bits each are shown in ITEM(2) to ITEM(4). The 'x' in three fields per word indicate that we are not concerned with their contents. The count '3' is stored as a binary three, while the characters '6', '3', and '5' are stored as alphanumeric characters, not as binary integers.

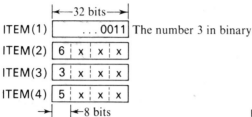

Fig. 10.7.   A string ITEM.

As a result of conversion of the number to a true numeric quantity, we will have the configuration shown in Figure 10.8. The number 635 is the number 1173_8 or the number 1001111011_2. Thus the *converted* number is in this latter form.

$$.... 001001111011$$

Fig. 10.8.   A converted number.

This type of conversion is common. It is in fact the process that the input-output portion of an operating system must execute in reading data from cards if 'I' conversion is requested. The opposite procedure is used in output conversion.

We now develop a subroutine for this conversion, for we shall need it for our assembly simulator.

Example 10.8. Write a subroutine ABCØNV (alphanumeric-to-binary conversion) that accepts a string of alphanumeric digits, including a character count, and converts it to a binary number. The call is of the form

CALL ABCØNV(ASTRNG,BWØRD)

where ASTRNG is the given alphanumeric string, of no more than four characters (for simplicity), and BWØRD is a word into which the binary equivalent is to be located.

Before describing the conversion method, we shall make the following simplifying assumption: the alphanumeric encoding of a digit is the binary equivalent of that digit. Thus, e.g., the character '6' is encoded as '00000110' in binary. (This method of encoding digits is in fact used in some computers.) If this assumption is made, then we need only compute this sum:

$$a_1 + 10 \times a_2 + 100 \times a_3 + 1000 \times a_4$$

where the number to be concerted is represented as '$a_4 a_3 a_2 a_1$'. The a_i are of course the eight-bit field values, under our assumption. The required subroutine follows:

```
        SUBRØUTINE ABCØNV(A,B)
        INTEGER A(5), B
C    FETCH THE CØUNT.
```

```
         N = A(1)
C    INITIALIZE THE RESULT, MULTIPLIER.
         B = 0
         K = 1
C    INITIALIZE INDEX TØ CHARACTERS.
         J = N + 1
C    GENERATE SUM.
         DØ 10 I = 1, N
         B = B + (A(J)/256**3)*K
         J = J - 1
   10    K = K * 10
         RETURN
```

Let us examine this program. Since we are summing, B must initially be set to zero. Each character is to be multiplied by a different power of 10; K is that multiplier. K is initially 1, but it is multiplied by 10 each time (in statement 10). The first character to be processed is the last in the string, for it is the units' digit. Its index is given by 'N + 1', where N is the character count. In the loop, we successively multiply the characters, right to left, by increasing powers of 10. Decreasing J by one each loop cycle accomplishes the right-to-left processing. Since each digit is 24 bits to the left of where it should be, we must first divide each by 2^{24} or 256^3.

It was noted in Chapter 9 that the BLØCK pseudo-operation of the GAP assembler required a facility not then available. The needed facility is the ability to read a variable-length field and interpret it. The BLØCK pseudo-operation's address field is an integer of one to four digits. We can interpret this integer, by using the ABCØNV subroutine, if we can store it as a string of characters.

There is another problem, however; GAP symbolic cards are read with the format (A4,3X,A4,4X,A4). Thus the address field is read with A4 and is stored in memory in a single word. However, alphanumeric strings are stored one character per word. As a consequence, it is necessary that we develop a subroutine that "unpacks" an alphanumeric string from a single word into a string of words. We write that subroutine next.

Example 10.9. Write a subroutine UNPACK that, given an alphanumeric string packed in a single word, unpacks the string into the normal string format, including a character count. We shall assume that the string may have up to four characters. Further, the string is assumed to be entirely of nonblank characters, so the first blank in the given word marks the end of the string. An example of a given string in location ITEM and the resultant string in array LIST is shown in Figure 10.9. The call to the subroutine is the following:

```
    CALL UNPACK(WØRD,STRING)
```

where WØRD contains the given string, and STRING is the location of the unpacked string. The program:

Fig. 10.9.   Unpacking a string.

```
      SUBRØUTINE UNPACK(W,S)
      DATA   BLANK/4H000 /
      INTEGER W, S(5)
C   UNPACK CHARACTERS.
      DØ 10 J = 1, 3
      S(6−J)  =  W * 256**(4−J)
   10 W = W − S(6−J) / 256**(4−J)
      S(2) = W
C   CHECK FØR BLANKS AND SET CØUNT.
      DØ 20 J = 2, 5
      IF (S(J) .EQ. BLANK) GØ TØ 30
   20 CØNTINUE
      S(1) = 4
      RETURN
   30 S(1) = J − 2
      RETURN
```

As in ABCØNV, we use multiplication and division by power of 256 to shift characters left and right, respectively. The first DØ loop causes each character to be shifted to the leftmost character position and stored in the array A, as required. As the index J increases, the power of 256 decreases in that loop. After a character is located in A, it is deleted from the given location W by the last statement in that loop; this is effected by shifting the character back to its original position and subtracting it from W. At the end of the loop, all that remains in W is the leftmost character; it is placed in A(2).

In the second loop, blanks are checked for, and a character count is set. The loop exits normally to the statement after 20 if no blanks are present; the character count is then 4. The loop exits early if a blank is found, and the count is properly set.

Now we can return to the problem of the BLØCK pseudo-operation. We will utilize the two subroutines just introduced.

Example 10.10. Modify Pass 1 of the GAP assembler to allow for the BLØCK pseudo-operation.

After a symbolic card is read, as was done in the program in Example 9.1, we must test for the presence of the BLØCK pseudo-operation. If it is found, UNPACK is called to generate an alphanumeric string, and ABCØNV is used to convert the numeric value. As a result, Pass 1 becomes the following:

```
C    SIM70–4
C    PASS 1.
          DATA BLØCK/4HBLØC/BLANK/4H     /END/3HEND /
          INTEGER VALUE, SIZE
      2   READ (5,101) LABEL, SYMØP, SYMAD
    101   FØRMAT (A4,3X,A4,4X,A4)
          WRITE (3) SYMØP, SYMAD
C    CHECK JØR LABEL FIELD BLANK.
          IF (LABEL .EQ. BLANK) GØ TØ 20
C    NØNBLANK ... ENTER INTØ SYMBØL TABLE.
          STABLE(J,1)  =  K
          STABLE(J,2)  =  LABEL
          J  =  J + 1
C    CHECK FØR BLØCK PSEUDØ-ØPERATIØN.
          IF (SYMØP .NE. BLØCK) GØ TØ 20
          CALL UNPACK(SYMAD,VALUE)
          CALL ABCØNV(VALUE,SIZE)
          K  =  K + SIZE
          GØ TØ 22
     20   K = K + 1
C    TEST FØR END.
     22   IF (SYMØP .NE. END) GØ TØ 2
          END FILE 3
```

Relative Addressing

There is another aspect of assembly that needs attention. The addresses that we can currently convert are those consisting of a single symbol. Very often, it is desirable to be able to use an address of the form 'LØC+n', where LØC is an address and n is an integer. For example, reference may be made to two addresses in a program that are in sequence. If the first is 'LØØP', the second may be called 'LØØP+1'. Without this approach, a separate symbol would be required for the second location.

Another, related addressing problem is that of referring to an instruction two instructions after the current one, for example. This would be useful if a particular instruction was to be skipped. Again, we can introduce a new label and refer to it, but it is easier to use a special mark to mean "this instruction". Let us use the asterisk (∗) for that mark. Thus, if we have

```
          JMPGZ    ∗+2
          JUMP     BACK
          LØAD     X
```

then control goes from the JMPGZ instruction directly to the LØAD instruction, because the address '*+2' means two beyond this (the JMPGZ) instruction.

In this section, then, we shall address this problem: Given a simple algebraic expression of the form 'a Ø b', where 'Ø' is an operator (+, −, *, or /), evaluate it. The quantities 'a' and 'b' may be symbols, integers, or the special mark '*'. The values of any symbols that appear are to be used as addresses, as we noted.

Example 10.11. Write a subroutine EVAL that evaluates an expression of the form 'a Ø b', where 'a' is a symbol, 'Ø' is an operator, and 'b' is an integer. The input is a string consisting of a single symbol or such an expression, and the output is the value of the expression. The symbol table STABLE is available through CØMMØN.

The call shall be as follows:

```
CALL EVAL(STRING,VALUE)
```

where STRING is the given string and VALUE its value.

We shall assume that only correct expressions are supplied to EVAL, that no error-checking is required.

The steps in evaluating the expression, given in string form, are these:

1. In the given string, locate the operator. If there is none, then a single symbol is present.
2. Break the given string into two parts, each with one operand. (One operand occurs before the operator; the other occurs after the operator.)
3. Replace the first operand with its numeric value. If the operand is '*', replace it with the current value of the address register (AR).
4. Evaluate the expression by executing the indicated operation.

Several string-manipulation routines developed in this chapter shall be used in EVAL. To check for and locate the operator, the TESTCH subroutine is used; one call is written for each possible operator. The EXTRSS subroutine is used to extract the second operand, the integer, if it is present. The symbol is converted using ADCV as previously, while the integer is converted using ABCØNV. Finally, a new subroutine, PACK, is required for forming a one-word symbol out of the string, so that ADCV can be used.

```
      SUBRØUTINE EVAL(S,VAL)
C    S IS THE GIVEN STRING.
C    S BECØMES FIRST ØPERAND, T IS SECØND ØPERAND.
C    ADD, SUBTRACT, MULT, DIV REPRESENTED BY 1, 2, 3, 4.
      CØMMØN STABLE, K
      DIMENSIØN S(13), T(7)
      INTEGER ØP, PØP
      DATA PLUS/1H+/MINUS/1H−/TIMES/1H*/DIVBY/1H//
      CALL TESTCH(S,2,PLUS,PØP)
      IF (PØP .NE. 0) GØ TØ 31
```

```
           CALL  TESTCH(S,2,MINUS,PØP)
           IF (PØP .NE. 0) GØ TØ 32
           CALL  TESTCH(S,2,TIMES,PØP)
           IF (PØP .NE. 0) GØ TØ 33
           CALL  TESTCH(S,2,DIVBY,PØP)
           IF (PØP .NE. 0) GØ TØ 34
C     HERE IF NØ ØPERATØR FØUND (PØP = 0), HAVE SYMBØL ØNLY.
           GØ TØ 50
C     ADDITIØN.
       31  ØP = 1
           GØ TØ 40
C     SUBTRACTIØN.
       32  ØP = 2
           GØ TØ 40
C     MULTIPLICATIØN.
       33  ØP = 3
           GØ TØ 40
C     DIVISIØN.
       34  ØP = 4
           GØ TØ 40
C     EXTRACT ØPERANDS IF TWØ.
       40  CALL EXTRSS(S,PØP+1,S(1),T)
           S(1) = PØP - 1
C     CHECK FØR * AS SYMBØL.
       50  IF (S(2) .NE. TIMES) GØ TØ 51
           INSAD = K
           GØ TØ 52
       51  CALL PACK(S,SYMBØL)
           INSAD = ADCV(SYMBØL,ERR)
       52  IF (PØP .EQ. 0) GØ TØ 60
C     CØNVERT INTEGER.
           CALL ABCØNV(T,INT)
C     EVALUATE EXPRESSIØN.
           GØ TØ (61,62,63,64) ØP
C     HERE IF SYMBØL ØNLY.
       60  VAL = INSAD
           RETURN
C     HERE IF ADDITIØN.
           VAL = INSAD + INT
           RETURN
C     HERE IF SUBTRACTIØN.
           VAL = INSAD - INT
           RETURN
C     HERE IF MULTIPLICATIØN.
```

```
      VAL = INSAD * INT
      RETURN
C   HERE IF DIVISIØN
      VAL = INSAD / INT
      RETURN
      END
```

These comments may be made on this subroutine:

1. PØP (pointer to operator) locates the operator, if present, and is used to separate the two operands via EXTRSS.
2. If '*' is present, it is simply replaced by the value of K, which represents the address register (AR) at the current point in assembly.

Evaluation of the expression given as the address of a symbolic instruction must take place in Pass 2 of the assembly, as did symbol conversion previously (in Example 9.1). Pass 1 must be modified also, for we must read the address in as a string, using format '12A1'. The location SYMAD must be replaced by an array. Pass 1 and Pass 2 are modified to become the following:

```
C   CHECK FØR LABEL FIELD BLANK.
C   SIM70-5
C   PASS 1.
      DATA BLØCK/4HBLØC/BLANK/4H    /END/3HEND /
      CØMMØN STABLE, K
      INTEGER VALUE, SIZE, SYMAD
      INTEGER PØP, ØP
      DIMENSIØN SYMAD(13), NUMBER(8)
  2   READ (5,101) LABEL, SYMØP, (SYMAD(I), I = 2,13)
101   FØRMAT (A4,3X,A4,2X,12A1)
      SYMAD(1) = 12
      WRITE (3) SYMØP, (SYMAD(I), I = 2,13)
      IF (LABEL .EQ. BLANK) GØ TØ 20
C   NØNBLANK ... ENTER INTØ SYMBØL TABLE.
      STABLE(J,1) = K
      STABLE(J,2) = LABEL
      J = J + 1
C   CHECK FØR BLØCK PSEUDØ-ØPERATIØN.
      IF (SYMØP .NE. BLØCK) GØ TØ 20
      CALL UNPACK(SYMAD,VALUE)
      CALL ABCØNV(VALUE,SIZE)
      K = K + SIZE
      GØ TØ 22
 20   K = K + 1
C   TEST FØR END.
```

```
    22  IF (SYMØP .NE. END) GØ TØ 2
        END FILE 3
C   PASS 2.
C   RESET PØINTER TØ PRØGRAM ARRAY.
        K = START
C   READ FILE 3.
    22  READ (3) SYMØP, (SYMAD(I), I = 2,13)
        CALL EVAL(SYMAD,SYMVAL)
        INSØP = ØPCV(SYMØP,ERR)
        IF (SYMØP .EQ. END) GØ TØ 3
        IF (ERR .EQ. 1) GØ TØ 70
        PRØG(K,1) = INSØP
        PRØG(K,2) = SYMVAL
        K = K + 1
        GØ TØ 22
    3   . . .
```

Note that now, in Pass 2, EVAL supplies the numeric value of the address, SYMVAL, and that ADCV is called within EVAL and so is not called here.

EXERCISES

1. In Figure 10.7, the first '3' is stored as a binary number, while the other three digits are stored as alphanumeric characters. Why is this done?

2. Some computers store six characters per word. What changes would have to be made in the methods and programs of Examples 10.8 and 10.9 to accommodate such computers?

3. Complex expressions, using parentheses, are usually permitted in assembly languages. In a qualitative way, describe the effect of allowing such expressions on the EVAL program. For example, consider $2 * (X + 2)$.

4. The processing of algebraic expressions is quite different for algebraic languages and for symbolic languages. (The former was discussed in Section 8.3.) What are the differences?

* * * * * *

5. Rewrite the EVAL subroutine, utilizing the TESTCS subroutine of Exercise 8, Section 10.2. Note that, in this case, when control returns from TESTCS, it will be necessary to test the character found to determine what it is.

6. Include in EVAL the possibility of one more operator, exponentiation, as given by '**'. Now the operator test must be extended, for two characters must be checked.

7. Write a PACK subroutine, whose call is

    CALL PACK(STRING,WØRD)

    where STRING is a given string of no more than four characters, and WØRD is the location into which the string is packed.

8. In Example 10.8, the assumption was made that the forms of alphanumeric digits were simply the binary equivalents of the digits. This is not necessarily the case. Modify ABCØNV for a more general situation, where this is not true.

* * * * * *

9. Add additional coding to EVAL to check for errors in the written expression. Include tests: (a) for an operator other than the four allowed; (b) for an initial operator; (c) for a symbol as the second operand.

10. Rewrite UNPACK and PACK so that strings of arbitrary length may be unpacked and packed. Call these new routines UNPAKS and PACKS. The calls are these:

```
CALL  UNPACKS(WØRDS,STRING)
CALL  PACKS(STRING,WØRDS)
```

where WØRDS is the packed form with a character count in WØRDS(1), and STRING is the unpacked form in the usual string format.

REFERENCES

1. A language developed specifically for string or symbol manipulation is SNOBOL:
   Allen Forte, *SNOBOL3 Primer: An Introduction to the Computer Programming Language*, M.I.T. Press, 1967.
   Several symbol manipulation languages are discussed in the following:
   Saul Rosen, editor, *Programming Systems and Languages*, McGraw-Hill Book Co., 1967, pp. 359–511.

2. Many of these subroutines are adapted from the following book:
   School Mathematics Study Group, *Algorithms Computations, and Mathematics*, Stanford University, 1966.
   They were developed for that book by the author.

11 ERRORS IN PROGRAMMING

The subject of errors in programming deserves considerable treatment because a great deal of time is spent in eliminating them. Errors can be introduced into a program at every step of the program-writing process. In this chapter we shall consider a number of different types of errors and ways of identifying them.

11.1 TYPES OF ERRORS

Sources of Errors

Errors can be categorized into two general classes: *unconscious* and *conscious*. The first class includes those due to programmer errors and to computer malfunctions. Programmer errors are called *bugs*, and the process of identifying them is *debugging*. The second class includes a variety of errors introduced because of the limitations of the computer and because of approximations made in the methods programmed on the computer.

Errors in Problem Formulation

The first possible source of error is the statement of the problem itself. This cannot be considered an error in programming, for a program can be correctly written that solves the wrong problem. Since most people tend to overlook this possibility, this error can be most wasteful, for sometimes only when improper results are obtained can the error be detected. We shall call these *definition errors*.

Once the problem to be solved has been defined, it is possible to select a method that is erroneous, either for the particular set of data to be processed or for all data. For example, an iterative method for solving an equation may diverge. Sometimes an iterative method may yield a correct solution but very slowly. We cannot say, in this case, that the program is in error, since the correct answer is obtained, but certainly the programmer's judgment is questionable. Errors in the selection of a method are *algorithmic errors*.

Errors in Analysis

A very common type of error occurs when a problem is analyzed and a flowchart is created. Such errors are *analysis errors* and occur when the analysis is faulty or incomplete. For example, recall the solution of a quadratic equation, a problem considered in Chapter 2. A number of special cases must be treated. The coefficients a and b must be checked to see if they are zero, otherwise an analysis error results. If data were supplied wherein a and b were not zero, the error would go undetected until they were zero. Further, we must check the sign of the number whose square root is to be extracted. That number must be positive, since computers deal directly only with real numbers, and we must treat complex numbers in a special way. Failure to check the sign is an analysis error. In general, it is necessary to account for all possible values of the supplied data, since anything might be supplied as data.

Frequently, definition and algorithmic errors are not detected until coding is well under way or even completed. Analysis errors, however, can sometimes be readily detected if an attempt is made to reconstruct the problem from its flowchart.

Another type of error associated with the analysis of a problem is a *logical error*. Logical errors are similar to analysis errors, but are those related primarily to carelessness in the layout of a method in detail. Examples are the following:

1. Interchange of two or more of the paths leaving a decision box.
2. Use of an improper test for termination of a loop.
3. Inclusion of the wrong number of loop cycles.
4. Improper or omitted loop initialization.
5. Improperly drawn arrow, as to the wrong box.
6. Incrementing of an index by the wrong amount.

Both analysis and logical errors may result from an improper understanding of the method, which are errors difficult to detect.

If a flowchart is drawn, it must be carefully checked. The boxes in a flowchart must have certain features: only one box can normally be entered from the outside, all boxes must have at least one entering path and one leaving path, all decision boxes must have at least two paths leaving, and so on. A flowchart, in addition to being structurally correct, must correspond to the original problem. It is necessary to trace all paths of control to see that they are taken under the

correct conditions and that all conditions are considered. Special attention must
be paid to exceptional cases. The merge points and decision boxes of a flowchart
are especially important places to check.

Errors in Coding

A *coding error* is one that is distinct from the earlier errors described, in
that it is introduced in the coding of statements and not sooner. A logical error
may be coded as drawn and subsequently detected in the coding, but since the
flowchart contained the error, we cannot consider it a coding error. Coding errors
can be classified into three categories: syntax, structural, and transcription.

Syntax errors involve the use of an improper form of the statements in the
language. Usually the compiler, during compilation, detects syntax errors and
prints *diagnostics*. Some FORTRAN diagnostics on syntax errors are these:

1. An illegal symbol was used. (There may be too many characters, the first
   character may be a digit, etc.)
2. An arithmetic expression is mixed, i.e., it contains both integers and
   floating-point numbers illegally.
3. An error in the use of parentheses was made. (A left or right parenthesis
   may have been omitted.)
4. An illegal character is present. (Sometimes the presence of certain characters is illegal; this is common in FORMAT statements.)
5. Two arithmetic operators appear in sequence.

Structural errors are not concerned with the structure of a single statement;
such errors are syntax errors. They are rather concerned with the interaction of
two or more statements or with the manner in which the statements are structured
to form the program. Sometimes the compiler can give diagnostics on these.
Examples:

1. The DIMENSION statement for a subscripted variable is omitted.
2. Two or more statements have the same label.
3. A referenced statement is omitted or is unnumbered.
4. Control cannot pass to at least one statement in the program. (This is
   not an error itself, but is clearly indicative of one.)
5. A variable appearing on the right side of an equals sign or in an output
   statement was not previously (in terms of flow-of-control sequencing)
   assigned a value.
6. A transfer occurs to within a DO-loop from outside the loop.

Certain other structural errors cannot be detected by any compiler, for they
are legal though incorrect. The error might be detected by the compiler indirectly,
for it might lead to a diagnostic for a different error. Some examples of these

structural errors are the following:

1. Omission in the program of one or more operations or flowchart boxes in the problem.
2. The improper setting of loop specifications, as the initial value, increment, and terminal value.
3. The use of an improper format for reading or writing data.
4. The storage of information in locations where needed data are located. (This occurs when a variable is assigned a new value before the older value is utilized.)
5. Failure to allow for sufficient space in allocating space, in a DIMENSION statement.
6. Omission of a data-type declaration.
7. Control sent to the wrong statement.

A common source of error involves *transcription*. A given symbol, for example, such as LCNTR, must be copied to a coding form and then keypunched onto a card. It may appear in the program as LNCTR and not be detected readily. Other transcription errors include the use of a different symbol, as 'J' for 'I', in one or more places, and the interchange of two (probably similar) symbols, as 'ARRAYA' for 'ARRAYB'. Transcription errors may be due to the keypunch operator, so a printed listing of the program deck, made from the punched cards, should be compared with the original coding list.

Physical Errors

Errors involving the handling of the deck or use of associated program listings are termed *physical errors*; they have nothing directly to do with the programming task. Examples are these:

1. Omission of data cards.
2. Interchange of cards within a deck of programs.
3. Interchange of the several programs within a deck of programs.
4. Reference to an outdated program listing when checking a program deck.

Such errors can be decreased or eliminated if care is taken in the handling of decks. Often a programmer saves a sequence of listings in order to note progress in debugging. If this is done, all listings and decks should be properly marked, preferably with dates of generation. Better still, obsolete material should be discarded.

Machine Errors

Since no machine can perform indefinitely without malfunctioning, machine errors occur, though they are relatively rare. If a program, after running, yields an incorrect result, one may suspect the computer, but since that source of error is the rarest, all other possibilities should be considered first. If the computer has malfunctioned, a rerun of the program will yield a different (though not necessarily correct) result. It is also possible for the machine to have a bug in its hardware, such as a misplaced wire. Such bugs are even rarer than a malfunction, for rigorous tests usually eliminate them. Reruns when hardware bugs are present yield the same results.

Errors in the Data

The data supplied to a correctly written program must also be correct, if the program is to calculate the correct results. The data may be in error: The format may be wrong or the values given may be illegal or out of range. If the format is incorrect, numbers will be interpreted as having wrong values and results may then be nonsensical. It is important to check to see that format statements agree with the data format as supplied.

Very often a program is written to accept only a limited range of values of the data. For example, if a program computes the factorial of a given number, numbers like 100 and 200 cannot be accepted. In the case of an assembler, not all sequences of letters up to five or six characters can be accepted as operation codes (the assembler's data); 'XYZ' just won't do. Thus, checks must be made upon data as supplied to a program. The checks to be made will, of course, depend on the problem at hand. The safest approach to take in coding is to consider everything that can go wrong with the data and ways to check these possibilities. It is helpful if the program prints comments on the erroneous data, indicating the errors involved. A thorough check for errors, however, is time-consuming to code and to execute. It is not unusual for error checks on the data to occupy a significant portion of the total extent of the program.

Errors in Computation[1]

By *computation errors* we mean those errors that result from the use of approximations made in the method used to solve a problem or by the limitations inherent in the computer. These errors fall into four classes.

Measurement errors are introduced when numbers are used for physical quantities. No physical quantity can be measured precisely, and the number used to represent its value must be somewhat in error. Although such errors are unrelated to the programming problem, they may, if not processed properly, grow to destructive proportions. For that reason, one must have a knowledge of the nature of measurement errors.

Formulation errors arise when approximate methods are used to solve problems. An integral is usually evaluated as a sum, but the sum is only an approximation, and an error is introduced. As more and more terms are used in the sum, this error can be reduced to as small a value as desired. This is true of formulation errors; they can be made arbitrarily small, if there is no limit on the number of steps to be performed.

Truncation errors are similar to formulation errors in that they occur when a mathematical process is approximated on the computer. They result from the use of a finite sum as an approximation to an infinite sum. For example, a trigonometric function can be represented as an infinite series. In a computer, only a finite number of terms may be used; the error due to dropping the others is a truncation error. These errors can also be made as small as desired by taking enough terms.

Roundoff errors arise because of limitations imposed by fixed-length computer words. In a 32-bit word, no more than 31 bits of a signed number can be retained, unless double-precision arithmetic is used. The term *rounding* describes the process of introducing an error in the value of quantity because of the finiteness of a word into which it is stored. The process occurs during storage of a real number and during every operation upon it. If a programmer is aware of the way in which roundoff errors accumulate in a particular program, he may be able to construct his coding to minimize them. His goal is to structure a given problem so that the operations of addition, subtraction, multiplication, and division are performed in a manner that reduces accumulated roundoff error to a minimum. We shall consider roundoff errors in some detail in the following section.

EXERCISE

1. Consider each of the types of error in this section. Indicate how their occurrence can be minimized.

11.2 ROUNDOFF ERRORS

The Size of Roundoff Errors

The error involved in rounding depends upon the size of the word used to store a number, and whether storage is accomplished by placing the closest value that will fit (true rounding) or by dropping excess bits or digits. We shall always assume the former here. An *absolute error* is the difference between the true value of a quantity and an approximation to it. *Relative error* is the ratio of absolute error to the true value of a quantity.

Consider a word which has f bits in which to store the fractional part of a floating-point number. We shall consider only floating-point arithmetic because most arithmetic processes except for counting are performed in this mode. The relative error in the rounded stored number may be as large as one part in 2^f, though on the average will be smaller. This can be seen as follows. The maximum absolute error in any word is $\frac{1}{2}$ in the last bit stored, ignoring consideration of the exponent. For example, the fraction 0.110101 (in binary) may represent any value in the range from 0.1101001 to 0.1101011. We shall assume that all floating-point numbers are normalized, so that fractions always are at least 0.5 (in decimal). Most floating-point arithmetic operations yield a normalized result. The worst relative error occurs, then, when the fraction is the smallest, i.e., exactly 0.5 or 0.1_2. An error of $\frac{1}{2}$ in the fth bit has an absolute value of $2^{-(f+1)}$ and a relative value of $2^{-(f+1)}/2^{-1}$ or 2^{-f}, as stated above.

The best case occurs when the fraction is just under 1.0, i.e., $0.1111\ldots_2$, where the maximum relative error is very nearly one-half of the above, or $2^{-(f+1)}$. Average errors are likely to be half of the two maxima computed, and the overall average error is approximately the mean of these errors, i.e., $1.5 \times 2^{-(f+2)}$.

A similar analysis is possible with decimal machines. The maximum error in rounding is again $\frac{1}{2}$ in the last digit, or $\frac{1}{2} \times 10^{-(f+1)}$. The worst case occurs when the fraction is 0.1_{10}; the maximum absolute error is then $\frac{1}{2} \times 10^{-f}$. The best case occurs when the fraction is $0.999\ldots$, whence the relative error is $\frac{1}{10}$ of the worst case.

Errors in Arithmetic

We have thus far merely considered errors in the storage of numbers. In addition to these errors, we must contend also with errors that result from arithmetic operations. We shall now look at the manner in which these errors combine with roundoff errors and the way in which they propagate through processing in a computer.

Assume that two quantities, a_t and b_t, are to be stored in memory. If a and b are the values actually stored, and δ_a and δ_b are the absolute errors in a and b, then

$$\delta_a = a_t - a$$
$$\delta_b = b_t - b$$

Relative errors are given by

$$r_a = \frac{\delta_a}{a} = \frac{a_t - a}{a}$$

$$r_b = \frac{\delta_b}{b} = \frac{b_t - b}{b}$$

Relative errors ought to be computed using true values (a and b) but usually only the approximate values are known and so must be used.

Consider addition. The error in the sum of a and b is

$$\delta_{a+b} = (a_t + b_t) - (a + b)$$
$$= (a + \delta_a + b + \delta_b) - (a + b)$$
$$= \delta_a + \delta_b$$

Similarly, the error due to subtraction is

$$\delta_{a-b} = \delta_a - \delta_b$$

Using similar methods, the errors due to multiplication and division can be found to be

$$\delta_{a \times b} = a\delta_b + b\delta_a$$

$$\delta_{a/b} = \frac{b\delta_a - a\delta_b}{b^2}$$

if we ignore the small product $\delta_a \delta_b$ and if $\delta_b/b \ll 1$. Besides these errors, which result as arithmetic is performed, we must take into account the fact that additional errors β_i result as these computed results are stored. These roundoff errors must be added to the computational errors given above:

$$\delta_{a+b} = \delta_a + \delta_b + \beta_1$$

$$\delta_{a-b} = \delta_a - \delta_b + \beta_2$$

$$\delta_{a \times b} = a\delta_b + b\delta_a + \beta_3$$

$$\delta_{a/b} = \frac{b\delta_a - a\delta_b}{b^2} + \beta_4.$$

The relative errors associated with these operations can be computed. Consider addition; since

$$r_{a+b} = \frac{\delta_{a+b}}{a+b}$$

$$r_a = \frac{\delta_a}{a}$$

$$r_b = \frac{\delta_b}{b}$$

we can write, substituting these in the expression for δ_{a+b},

$$r_{a+b} = \frac{ar_a}{a+b} + \frac{br_b}{a+b} + \alpha_1$$

Also, we can derive

$$r_{a-b} = \frac{ar_a}{a-b} - \frac{br_b}{a-b} + \alpha_2$$

$$r_{a \times b} = \frac{ab(r_a + r_b)}{a+b} + \alpha_3$$

$$r_{a/b} = \frac{b\delta_a - a\delta_b}{b^2(a+b)} + \alpha_4$$

where the α's are the relative errors introduced by storing any result. Since round-off errors may be of either sign, maximum errors are computed by considering those signs that maximize the errors.

As an example of the propagation of errors during the evaluation of an algebraic expression, consider the following:

$$A = ax + b$$

The relative errors in the result is given by:

$$r_A = \frac{ax\left[\dfrac{ax(r_a + r_x)}{a + x}\right] + \alpha_5}{ax + b} + \frac{br_b}{ax + b} + \alpha_6$$

This is derivable from the formulas above. Note that multiplication is performed first; the error in roundoff is α_5; then addition is performed and the error in roundoff is α_6. (The labeling of the α's is arbitrary, so a sequential numbering is used.)

To compute actual errors, assume that the variables in the expression have these values:

$$a = 75, \qquad b = 60, \qquad x = 2$$

Further, assume that all roundoff errors are the same and equal to R; then $r_A = 4.8R$. Thus, the roundoff error in each variable propagates in this simple expression as an error almost five times as large.

Let us consider another case, that of summing N numbers. First, consider the summation of four numbers:

$$S = b_0 + b_1 + b_2 + b_3$$
$$= (((b_0 + b_1) + b_2) + b_3)$$

where the second form is used to illustrate the manner of summation. Let the relative errors in these numbers be r_0, r_1, r_2, and r_3, and let α_k be the roundoff error at the kth summation. We can write

$$r_S = \left[\left(\frac{r_0 b_0}{S_1} + \frac{r_1 b_1}{S_1} + \alpha_1\right)\frac{S_1}{S_2} + \frac{r_2 b_2}{S_1} + \alpha_2\right]\frac{S_2}{S_3} + \frac{r_3 b_3}{S_3} + \alpha_3$$

which is obtained by using the relative-error formulas and the fact that $S_1 = b_0 + b_1, S_2 = b_0 + b_1 + b_2$, etc. Multiplying this out and noting that

$S = S_3$, we can write

$$r_S = \frac{1}{S}(r_0 b_0 + r_1 b_1 + \alpha_1 S_1 + r_2 b_2 + \alpha_2 S_2 + r_3 b_3 + \alpha_3 S_3)$$

$$= \frac{1}{S}\sum_{k=0}^{3} r_k b_k + \frac{1}{S}\sum_{k=1}^{3} \alpha_k S_k$$

Generalizing, the error propagated by summing the N numbers $b_0, b_1, b_2, \ldots, b_{N-1}$, with relative error r_k in b_k and relative roundoff error α_k at the kth addition, can be written as

$$r_S = \frac{1}{S}\sum_{k=0}^{N-1} r_k b_k + \frac{1}{S}\sum_{k=1}^{N-1} \alpha_k S_k$$

Let us examine this last formula carefully. We see that the relative errors each have two components. The first of these is the sum of the relative errors in each number as stored; this component has the same value regardless of the manner of summation. The second component, which is due to the errors caused by summation, on the other hand, has a value determined by the way in which the numbers are summed. If we assume that all α_k are the same, equal to α, this component has the value

$$\frac{1}{S}\alpha \sum_{k=1}^{N-1} S_k$$

which is a factor times the sum of the successive partial sums. Thus, numbers added early effect the error component more than numbers added late. This indicates that the summation should be formed first on the smaller numbers.

To illustrate, assume values for the N numbers. Let these be $0, 1, 2, 3, \ldots, 9$ where $N = 10$. If all roundoff errors are assumed equal to R, then $r_A = 43R$. On the other hand, let the numbers be $9, 8, 7, \ldots, 0$, i.e., the sum numbers in decreasing order of size. Then, if all roundoff errors equal R, $r_A = 74.2R$.

We conclude the following:

1. The propagated errors in a lengthy arithmetic process may be many times the individual roundoff errors in the quantities being processed.
2. If, in particular, a sum of positive numbers is being formed, summation should proceed monotonically, starting with the smallest numbers and proceeding toward the largest.

It must be noted, in all fairness, that the relative errors computed in the last two examples are exaggerated. The assumption was made that all errors were the same, whereas in fact they cannot be. In addition, some of the errors will be negative (probably about half will be), so the accumulation of errors will cause some balancing. The result is that total errors will be much less than calculated.

The Problem of Zero

Although roundoff errors in numbers always cause problems to a greater or lesser degree, the problem of zero causes much trouble. The reason is that zero is so common a number, and the tendency is to assume that zero occurs exactly with no roundoff error. As an example, consider the inversion of a 2 by 2 matrix:

$$\begin{bmatrix} x_1 & x_2 \\ x_3 & x_4 \end{bmatrix}$$

The inverse exists if and only if the determinant is nonzero; the determinant is $(x_1x_4 - x_2x_3)$. In a program that computes the inverse, the zero test must be made. The statement

    IF (X1*X4 - X2*X3) ...

will fail to serve correctly unless the expression in the parentheses is exactly zero when it should be. The exact decimal values X1 = 0.3, X2 = 0.9, X3 = 0.1, and X4 = 0.3, when stored in a binary machine, do not yield zero when substituted in the IF statement, though they would appear to do so. Rarely, in fact, will zero be computed here, so inversion may always take place. The solution here is to compare the expression to a small number, say 0.00001. We can summarize by saying that zero is really no more of a computational problem than any other number, but programmers may make it so, carelessly.

EXERCISE

1. Perform an analysis, of the type given in the text, on these expressions:
   (a) $W = ax^3 + by^2$
   (b) $X = \sqrt{x^2 + y^2 + z^2}$
   Assume that $a = 50$, $b = 40$, $x = 75$, $y = 100$, and $z = 125$.

11.3 DEBUGGING

The Process

Debugging involves identifying the errors or *bugs* inadvertently introduced into a program during its writing. Bugs are detected by a test of the program when correct answers are not obtained by the program; at least one error must be present.

We may ask, "If we can determine correct answers manually so as to check programs, why do we need the computer?" The point has some merit, but it really serves to emphasize the importance of checking a written program in a known manner, i.e., by using data which will be processed to yield results that can be readily checked manually. Only through a carefully selected set of test data, checking the program under a wide variety of situations, can the programmer gain confidence in his coding. We also should note that in many problems, even when true data are supplied, the answers can readily be checked by hand. Among these problems are scanning and extracting routines and sorting programs.

Having detected the presence of at least one error, how can we identify it (or them)? In the last section, sources of errors was discussed. We should check each of those points in the program writing process where errors may have been introduced. Once we are satisfied that our analysis and flowchart are correct, we must then turn to the code itself, wherein are usually imbedded the great majority of errors.

Locating coding errors is a difficult task, one that follows no prescribed rules for all situations. During a programmer's development, he will, of course, make many errors. Sometimes errors will be repeated but with diminishing frequency. He undoubtedly feels that sooner or later he will have made all the errors he can, as often as he can, and that no more will remain. Somehow, this never seems to be the case. Bugs take on such a wide variety of forms that attempts to lay out a well-defined approach for their elimination or avoidance fail badly, for they are never comprehensive enough.

Despite this discouraging viewpoint, we can define a general approach that, in the long run, is most often used in one form or another. If we could accomplish the following, then we would always be able to locate and identify all bugs: Examine all words in memory after the execution of each operation in the program. (By "operation", we mean the function embodied in an executable program statement. Thus, if a statement is executed 100 times we imply 100 examinations of the data.) This method will clearly work, for each operation somehow modifies the data, and final results are obtained by a sequence of operations that successively modify data to its ultimate form. By examining the effects of each operation, we can see where the program went awry, and why.

This technique, however, is totally impractical. In any reasonable situation, there are hundreds, thousands, or perhaps millions of operations executed. There may be hundreds or thousands of words of data. The amount of information that would have to be examined is almost always prohibitively large.

What, then, can we do? If we do not debug at all, we examine only the computed results at the end of the program's run, whether that "end" be premature or not. (The program may stop short of its intended operations.) We must effect a compromise. We must examine the contents of *some* of the data at *some* of the operations in the program. We cannot look at everything all the time, nor can we usually discover anything by looking only at answers at the end.

The essence, then, of the debugging problem is the selection of those points in the program and those data to be chosen for study. Usually, selecting the data follows readily upon selection of the points, for the data are referenced in the statements selected. We shall examine this selection process in some detail.

Program Dumps

A *dump* is a printout of the contents of selected memory locations and may comprise one block (a sequence of words), several blocks, individual words, or a combination of these. Dumps are of two types. *Snapshot dumps* supply information that exists at specified points in the program; these are of interest to us here. *Post-mortem dumps* supply information available at the conclusion of a run and usually include all data in memory. In the paragraphs following, "dump" refers to snapshot dump.

Some computer installations have special provisions for executing dumps within a program. Many such facilities supply output in numeric form, i.e., essentially in machine language, as in Figure 11.1. Numbers are printed there in octal form. The first line represents machine instructions (on the GAMMA 70), while the other lines represent integers. It is clear that such a dump is difficult to read. The dump may be requested in octal-location form:

2200   SNAP   Ø,500,577

which means, "Print a dump of the block from locations 500 through 577, when control passes to location 2200."

1000 2200   2000 2000   2100 4270   2400 0001   1100 2000

. . .   .

0000 2671   0001 2760   0002 2245   0002 0376   0002 5540
0003 0000   0005 2701   0005 2007   0007 2323   0010 0110

Fig. 11.1.   An octal dump.

If an algorithmic language, such as FORTRAN, is used, the dump request should be in that same language, or nearly so. Further, the output should be appropriate to the types of data being printed. In other words, one should be able to write, e.g.,

WRITE,   (ARRAY(J), J = 1, 10)

A format probably ought to be given, but it would be more convenient if it were not required. Some processors provide "formatless" output, where the format need not be stated. It is clear that, in the above statement, the location of ARRAY must be known to the dumping routine.

Statements such as the WRITE statement above can, of course, be included within the source program at appropriate points. What are appropriate points? Generally a desirable place for a dump is at the conclusion of a segment of the program. Such a dump serves as a check on the correctness of the segment jump completed, provided it is known that all prior segments are correct. Logically, dumps should be requested after each segment in sequence, and thus we proceed until errors are removed from each of the segments.

It is important to note where dumps are requested. If the request is made within a loop, there may be far too much information printed. On the other hand, if a dump within a loop is desired, *conditional* dumping can be realized by a statement like this:

    IF   (I .LE. 4) WRITE . . .

where 'I' is the index in the loop, incremented by unity each cycle. In this case, three dumps only would be given, the first three times through. More complex conditions are possible too. For example, suppose a dump every third time through the loop was desired. This statement accomplishes this:

    IF   (I/3*3 − I .EQ. 0) WRITE . . .

The expression 'I/3*3 = I' equals zero only when $I = 3, 6, 9, \ldots$, because of the effects of division on integers.

When might one only want to dump every nth time through a loop, where n might be 3, 10, or 100? In an interation problem, examination of all values might be tedious, whereas examination of every 10th or 100th set of values might be more revealing of a source of trouble. Perhaps an error occurs when some quantity, say X, becomes small. We might then write

    IF   (X .LT. .0001) WRITE . . .

The variations are clearly endless.

As noted, the precise manner in which dump statements are inserted (where, what variables, what conditions) will depend upon the problem and the nature of the errors. We try to "zero in" on errors, eliminating some possible sources of trouble with each succeeding run. For it is most likely that debugging will occupy a sequence of runs, with different dump requests included each time. Experience with certain types of problems helps far more than a list of rules for dumping. In order to facilitate removal of dump statements when they are no longer needed, such statements can be punched on differently colored cards.

Run-Time Diagnostics

A number of the commonly available subroutines written for use in mathematical problems have been coded to provide written diagnostics when certain errors occur, thus aiding the debugging process. For example, a routine that extracts the square root of a number should initially check to see if the supplied argument is negative. It might print a comment such as this:

SQRT RØUTINE GIVEN NEGATIVE ARGUMENT: −44.980

The value of the argument, while not directly involved in the error at hand, may be of interest to the programmer. A similar situation evokes this comment from an arcsine routine:

ARCSIN RØUTINE ARGUMENT ØUT ØF RANGE: 1.568

Some processors include within the compiled program information on the subscript range called for (by a DIMENSIØN statement) and also include coding to check to see if the subscript ever exceeds this range. If so, the comment is:

ARRAY LISTQ: SUBSCRIPT ØUT ØF RANGE

where LISTQ is the array in question. Tests for such situations are, however, very time-consuming, though during debugging phases execution time is not critical. It is helpful if, after a program is debugged, this feature can be eliminated. Diagnostics are also sometimes provided by the computer. For example, these comments may be provided:

NØ DATA ØN INPUT FILE
DIVISIØN BY ZERØ ATTEMPTED
ØVERFLØW ØCCURRED IN ADDITIØN

The monitor prints these comments, upon the setting of certain failure indicators. The computer here has detected that (1) no further data appear on the input file although a "read" statement was executed; (2) a division where the divisor was zero was attempted; (3) as the result of addition, a number larger than the capacity of a word was produced. Often, the programmer may indicate that, despite the division error or overflow, the program shall continue, ignoring those errant operations.

REFERENCES

1. The problems one runs into in performing computation on computers are treated in these books:
   Richard W. Hamming, *Calculus and the Computer Revolution*, Houghton Mifflin Co., 1968, Chapters 1 and 2.
   Richard V. Andree, *Computer Programming and Related Mathematics*, John Wiley & Sons, Inc., 1967, pp. 205–222.

12 DATA STRUCTURES

We turn our attention in this chapter to a consideration of the ways in which data may be stored in core memory. In all problems, considered in previous chapters, the data were stored in individual words, in linear arrays, or in two-dimensional arrays. There are many different ways to structure data in core memory, and we shall consider some of these now.

Let us consider at least three characteristics of data supplied to computer programs. First, data may have an inherent structure which we may want to retain in computer memory. Second, the entries in data are often variable in size; some entries may be perhaps ten times as long as other entries in a set; to allow the maximum size for each entry would be highly wasteful of space. Third, when information is retrieved from a collection of data, requests may imply particular means for structuring the data; were the data to be arbitrarily structured, retrieval of information might be very time-consuming. Consideration of these three characteristics forces us to consider different means for structuring data in a computer.[1]

12.1 DATA STRUCTURING

Definitions

The manner in which data are stored in a given situation, i.e., the format used, is termed the *data structure*. The information stored in such a structure is called a *data set*, *data base*, or *data bank*.

Data storage refers to the process of placing data received into a data structure. The program that accomplishes this clearly requires information on the nature of the structure involved. In examples later in this chapter, we shall see how this "knowledge" is built into the program. *Data retrieval* refers to the opposite process, that of removing data from a structure so that it can be processed, printed, or otherwise treated. This process must also take into account the nature of the data structure.

The Need for Structures

Let us consider in some detail the reasons for utilizing data structures before we examine the forms that they take. The primary reason is that the data for a programming system has intrinsic structure, and processing is efficient if a data structure in a computer honors that intrinsic structure. Reference was already made to this concept in Section 8.2. In a two-dimensional array of numbers, the location in the array of a particular item, say b_{ij}, is significant; the array would be different if b_{23} and b_{25} were interchanged, for example. As another example, consider a complex electronic system. Most likely it is organized into bays of equipment, with several chasses to each bay, several circuits in each chassis, and several components in each circuit. In both instances, it is vital that the interrelationship of the elements of data, present in the information supplied, is retained in some form in the computer.

A second reason for considering data structuring results from data size variability. In a collection of information about students, for example, part of the information might concern miscellaneous items (awards won, clubs joined, jobs, etc.) A great deal of variation might exist among students' records. Data structuring must consider such variations and allow for expansion and deletion of such items as well, if space is to be efficiently used. Little concern for structuring might lead to allowing constant amounts of space for all students, probably resulting in much wasted space.

A third major consideration is the manner of information retrieval from a data structure. If the data are not organized in the computer in a way that permits relatively fast access in the manner desired, much time can be wasted. Consider again the electronic system. If we wished to know which components comprised the audio amplifier circuit on chassis 8 of bay C, we can obtain this information quickly if the data structure follows the system structure as described above, for we need only search the named circuit. However, if we wanted to know how many capacitors there were in the system, a search of all circuits in all bays would be required. Structuring the data to accommodate information retrieval needs is clearly very important.

There is yet a fourth reason for concern over structuring data. If a system of programs is to be developed, a standardized data structure eases the communication problem among these programs. Defining a structure defines the standard, upon which the data in all programs to be developed can be based. This approach leads to consistency and compatibility. It tends to lead to a modular or segmented approach to program development which, as we have seen, is an efficient way to develop computer programs. In Chapter 8 (on subroutines), the importance of standards among calling sequences was stressed; the same concept can be extended to data structures.

One other point must be made. If we are to consider fully the storage of computer-based information, then magnetic tapes, disks, drums, and the like must be examined. In the present chapter, we shall concern ourselves only with structures in core memory, for problems there are simpler. In this case, we can assume that any memory word is accessible as any other, which eases the problem of structure design. In Chapter 14, Data Management, other storage media will be studied.

Data management, mentioned briefly in Section 8.2, is a much broader concept than data structuring, for it is concerned with many aspects of file creation, storage, retrieval, and editing. Before a file can be utilized, however, it must be described. This is the structuring problem. The files of interest here, as we noted, are located in core memory, and we are referring to them here as data bases. The management of data in more general files is also a topic for Chapter 14.

In the succeeding sections of this chapter, various methods of structuring data are examined. We begin with simple structures and proceed to others more complex.

12.2 LINEAR ARRAYS

Complete Arrays

The simplest data structures are linear arrays. In such arrays, which may be of any dimension (though usually no greater than three), we may use the indexing notation of algorithmic languages. Unless we are at the end of an index range, we find the "next" item at any point by increasing the index by one. Thus we process elements $A(I)$, where I is 1, 2, 3, 4, ..., N, by running through values of I. After $A(N)$ is reached, we are done. Consider a two-dimensional array. We process elements $A(1, J)$, where J is 1, 2, ..., M. After $A(1, M)$ is reached, we proceed to $A(2, 1)$, ..., modifying the first index by unity. Alternatively, we may process $A(I, 1)$, $I = 1, 2, ..., R$. The operation of processing through all entries in a linear array is thus quite straightforward, for it involves simple modification of indices.

The FORTRAN programmer is not usually concerned with where in memory element $B(I, J, K)$ is located, but it may be of interest to write a formula for expressing such locations. In FORTRAN IV, elements of arrays are stored in increasing addresses, with the first (leftmost) index varying most rapidly. That is, the memory sequence for an array $A(i, j)$, of dimensions $m \times n$, is the following (in increasing addresses):

$$A(1, 1), A(2, 1), A(3, 1), ..., A(m, 1), A(1, 2), A(2, 2), ..., A(m, 2), ...,$$

$$A(1, n), A(2, n), ..., A(m, n)$$

In other words, the array is stored by columns, the entries of a column being in adjacent locations. In general, the element $A(i, j)$ is located at

$(j - 1)m + i - 1$ locations beyond the first element, $A(1, 1)$, which is located in the base address (BA). The base address is considered as the address of the array. Thus we can write

$$L(A(i, j)) = BA + (j - 1)m + i - 1$$

which expresses the mapping of the array into a linear memory sequence; recall that $L(x)$ is the location of x. This formula is of interest if we want to know where each element is located, as in examining a memory dump.

If a programmer writes an expression such as 'A(2, 5)' or 'A(i, j)' the compiler will generate code with appropriate address fields to permit proper memory access. The compiler, in other words, performs the mapping. The programmer thus need not be concerned with the mapping. In the first of these two expressions, the mapping is accomplished at compilation, for the exact location is known; e.g.,

$$L(A(2, 5)) = BA + 4m + 1$$

and m is known from the DIMENSIØN statement. On the other hand the mapping for the second expression, which is more general, can only be partially accomplished at compilation. We can rewrite the earlier expression:

$$L(A(i, j)) = BA - m - 1 + (jm + i)$$

where the expression in parentheses must be calculated during program execution, since i and j are not known until then. We shall not concern ourselves here with the manner in which this is done.

A similar analysis can be performed for three-dimensional arrays:

$$L(A(i, j, k)) = BA + (k - 1)lm + (j - 1)l + i - 1$$

where the array is dimensioned $l \times m \times n$.

Because linear arrays are so common in mathematical problems, compilers process then directly, given a DIMENSIØN statement, as described. Other data structures are not so readily handled.

In Example 10.7 a two-dimensional array FIELD was considered. To the compiler, this array had two dimensions. To the programmer, however, the array was one-dimensional, for each element in the array was a character string which occupied a sequence of words (i.e., an array to the compiler). In FORTRAN, array elements are normally thought to occupy one word each, when programmer-oriented arrays match in dimensionality compiler-oriented arrays. However, when elements require two or more words each, the two arrays will differ by one in dimensionality. Both character strings and double-precision numbers require more than one word per entry.

Semi-Arrays

The term *semi-array* refers here to what is approximately half a square array. More specifically, it means all the entries on and below the main diagonal of a square array, the entries labeled in Figure 12.1, for example. A semi-array is useful if space is in short supply, when the balance of the entries in a square array can be discarded. This would be the case if the array were symmetric. An example is the table of mileages that often appears on a map; the distance from city A to city B is the same as the distance from city B to city A. The advantage of a semi-array lies in its space utilization, but a disadvantage exists as well. Compilers do not generate code appropriate to semi-arrays, so that special effort is required to reference their entries.

A_{11}				
A_{21}	A_{22}			
A_{31}	A_{32}	A_{33}		
A_{41}	A_{42}	A_{43}	A_{44}	
A_{51}	A_{52}	A_{53}	A_{54}	A_{55}

Fig. 12.1.   A semi-array.

We shall consider the storage of a semi-array to be by *rows*, i.e., in this order in memory (for an $m \times m$ semi-array):

$$A(1, 1), A(2, 1), A(2, 2), A(3, 1), \ldots, A(3, 3), A(4, 1), \ldots,$$

$$A(4, 4), \ldots, A(m, 1), \ldots, A(m, m)$$

$$L(A(i, j)) = BA + \tfrac{1}{2}i(i - 1) + j - 1$$

Note that we previously considered arrays stored by *column*.

Consider now the problem of accessing $A(i, j)$. Let us store all entries in successive locations in a one-dimensional array B of size $(m + 1)/2$. We cannot use the usual notation 'A(I, J)' to reference entries, because the compiler cannot compile correct references to 'A(I, J)'. Instead, we must compute a new index, which we call k, for the array B:

$$k = \tfrac{1}{2}i(i - 1) + j - 1$$

Then $B(k)$ is the required entry. Let us generalize the problem.

Example 12.1. Write a program segment that prints the Nth row of a semi-array A, which is stored linearly in array B.

Since we wish to print a complete row, indexing is desirable. We wish to print the entries $A(N, 1), A(N, 2), \ldots, A(N, N)$. Since the index i in the expression above is constant (and equal to N), we evaluate part of the expression for k outside a DØ-loop, and evaluate the balance (involving j) within the loop:

```
      K1 = N*(N - 1)/2 - 1
      DØ 10 J = 1, N
      K = K1 + J
   10 WRITE (6,100) B(K)
```

Example 12.2. Write a program segment that sums the *m* rows of a semi-array *A*, stored in array *B*, placing the sums in the one-dimensional array *C* (of size *m*).

   This code is a direct extension of Example 12.1. An extra loop is placed around the loop above; the outer loop index is I, which runs from 1 through *m*.

```
      DØ 10 I = 1, M
      K1 = I*(I − 1)/2 − 1
      C(I) = 0
      DØ 10 J = 1, I
      K = K1 + J
   10 C(I) = C(I) + B(K)
```

EXERCISE

1. Derive a formula for the location of element (i, j) in the following memory storage schemes:
   (a) A semi-array of size $m \times m$ stored by columns.
   (b) A square of elements comprising the outermost elements of a square matrix.
   (c) The complement to case (b), i.e., all the interior elements of a square matrix.

12.3 IRREGULAR ARRAYS

   We have allotted a specific amount of space for all arrays considered thus far, in all problems. The amount of space allotted for an element was either the precise size of each array element or an upper bound for that size. For example, in Example 10.7, it was assumed that each card field required no more than 16 words (15 characters plus a count) and that there were no more than 20 fields. Thus, 320 words were allocated for these fields. Since all fields were supplied on one card, no more than 80 words (exclusive of counts) were actually needed. Furthermore, no fields greater than 15 characters are permissible, because of the allocation per field. A different scheme for space allocation can be devised to improve storage efficiency.

   We have thus seen that the following case demands special space allocation treatment: data elements with varying size, particularly when wide variations are likely. These elements might be alphanumeric strings, variable arrays of integers, etc. The special treatment should take this variation into account and avoid the waste of space in unused portions of arrays. The solution is to utilize precisely as much space as is needed for each array element.

   If we arrange to allocate exact amounts of space for such arrays, we must access each element "by hand", i.e., with special code, as was required with semi-arrays. Furthermore, now we do not know in advance (i.e., at the time of coding) the extent of each element. If the character strings of Chapter 10 are the data, then size counts are present in the strings, but this is available only during execution.

Another point with variable elements is that we cannot readily locate a given entry, once it has been stored. A very useful device for this purpose is a *reference table* (or *index table*) which lists the locations of all array entries present (i.e., the locations of the first words of these entries).

Figure 12.2 depicts the use of a reference table for an array C; the reference table is itself a one-dimensional array RT of size m, where m is the maximum number of elements in C. The arrows starting at dots in RT represent the locations of the elements c_i which are stored in RT. Such "arrows" are called *pointers* in programming.

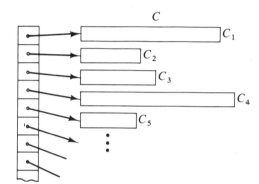

Fig. 12.2.   An irregular array
with reference table.

Since the object here is to conserve space, the entries c_i will be stored in sequence in memory. For this purpose a single, one-dimensional array will be used; let us call it T. Its dimension is M, the maximum total size of the array. We see that we are freed of the need to specify the upper bound of each entry c_i, but we must indicate an upper bound on the total size. In the general case, where there are several variable arrays, we still need only utilize a single one-dimensional array.

It is more convenient to store within RT the *indices* of the array T that locate variable entries, rather than absolute memory locations, since indices are readily accessible within the program. Such an arrangement permits the program to be callable as a subroutine since all references are local within the subroutine.

Let us consider an example now that illustrates the manner in which variable arrays may be constructed and utilized.

Example 12.3 Write a program segment that reads cards containing alphanumeric strings (one string per card), trims them by deleting trailing blanks, allocates precisely enough space to accommodate each string, and establishes a reference table. The input data are terminated by a blank card.

The allocation problem is handled quite simply. After each card is read into array CARD and trimmed, it is stored in the array T. The initial index value is, let us say, I, set as the result of storage of the last string (or set to 1, initially). The final index value is given by $I + m$, where m is the character count of the string (and $m + 1$ is the total entry length). The storage operation is executed by moving the string, one character at a time, into T, the index on T running from I to $I + m$. The value m is located in CARD(1). After each card is read, the index I must be increased by $m + 1$ so that the array T is ready to receive the next card, $m + 1$ words beyond the previous. In this way, just enough space is allocated for each string.

To generate the reference table, we need only store values of I in RT. These values are the initial index values for T as entries are made to T.

The program:

```
C    IRREG
         DIMENSIØN RT(100), T(5000), CARD(80)
C    INITIALIZE RT INDEX, T INDEX.
         N = 1
         I = 1
C    READ, TRIM A STRING.
      5  CALL READST(CARD)
         CALL TRIM(CARD)
C    CHECK FØR BLANK CARD (ZERØ CØUNT).
         IF (CARD(1) .EQ. 0) STØP
C    MAKE ENTRY IN REFERENCE TABLE.
         T(N) = I
C    MØDIFY RT INDEX.
         N = N + 1
C    CØMPUTE TERMINAL INDEX FØR STRING.
         K = I + CARD(1)
C    INITIALIZE STRING INDEX.
         M = 1
C    STØRE STRING IN ARRAY T.
         DØ 10 J = I, K
         T(J) = CARD(M)
     10  M = M + 1
C    RESET I INDEX FØR NEXT CARD.
         I = I + CARD(1) + 1
C    RETURN FØR NEXT CARD.
         GØ TØ 5
```

With entries in array T, it is of course now necessary to be able to extract specified entries. To fetch the nth entry and store it in ENTRY, the following coding is used:

```
C    FETCH PØINTER TØ ENTRY.
         I = RT(N)
C    CØMPUTER TERMINAL INDEX ØF ENTRY.
         K = I + T(I)
C    INITIALIZE "ENTRY" INDEX AND FETCH ENTRY.
         M = 1
         DØ 20 J = I, K
         ENTRY(M) = T(J)
     20  M = M + 1
```

The statement 'K = I + T(I)' should be explained. I is a pointer to the desired entry, the *value* stored in the reference table. Thus, T(I) is the first word of that entry, the character count.

12.4 LINKED LISTS

Concepts

We have seen that very often the linear nature of computer storage is inappropriate for the data of many problems. Special data structures require special treatment of memory, so that those structures take on the form of the data stored.

In the several structures considered in this chapter, we had to answer these questions: (1) Where is the *next* item? (2) Where is the *i*th item? In order to make efficient use of space when we have irregular arrays, we cannot use memory so that the next item is in the next address—or the address k locations beyond this one, where k is a constant. We cannot use memory so the *i*th item is i locations or $k \times i$ locations from the start.

Because we could not so locate the desired items, a reference table was required, with pointers to the items in the array. The reference table, however, *was* simply structured. In that table, items are linearly placed, so we can take advantage of a simple addressing scheme anyway, and fetch pointers which in turn are used to fetch items.

Let us now, however, consider a variation on the examples in the last section. Let the strings be stored in memory in the order they are read but consider the case where the strings are to be processed not in that order, but in another, according to some rule. Consider the following example.

An array of alphanumeric strings is to be processed. Associated with each string is an identification (ID) number. The strings are to be processed subsequently in increasing value of their ID numbers. The strings, as received, are not ordered but are given arbitrarily.

A storage scheme somewhat like the last one is needed, but the reference table must be replaced by a flexible list of pointers whose order changes as new entries are received. If we had thousands of strings, it would be inefficient to move the table pointers to accommodate new entries in numeric order. Instead, entries will be logically inserted into the existing list but not physically inserted. This means that pointers point always to items in ID-number sequence, even though the strings are in arbitrary order.

Consider Figure 12.3(a). The reference table RT has been made a $2 \times m$ array. A second set of pointers, one per string c_i, has been added. The last new pointer word is set to zero, to indicate the end of the table RT. Now m extra words are required, but flexibility has been added. Now the entries in RT can be logically separated to accommodate entries, without any physical displacement of old entries. Examine Figure 12.3(b). Entry c_5 was found to belong logically after c_2 and before c_3. To accommodate this, the fifth RT entry was logically inserted into

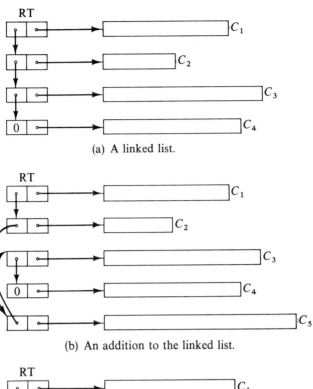

(a) A linked list.

(b) An addition to the linked list.

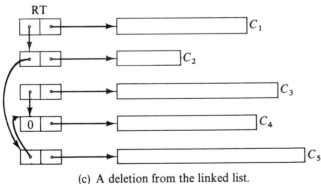

(c) A deletion from the linked list.

Fig. 12.3.   A linked list.

the list, following c_2, by adjusting pointers as shown. The pointer from c_2 to c_3 was replaced by one to c_5, and c_5 was given a pointer to c_3.

The processing of strings follows the sequence of pointers; the strings are accessed through the outgoing pointers from RT. We see that the two sets of pointers are used in different ways. The sequence formed by the intra-RT pointers is termed a *linked list*. It is useful not because the c_i entries are irregular (a linear RT will suffice for that), but because of the need to make insertions in the list without moving all existing entries. We see that, at any point, the *next* entry is obtained by the pointer. The *i*th entry in the list must be obtained by starting at the beginning and by counting as pointers are encountered.

We should note that other changes can readily be effected in the linked list. We may delete an item, as shown in Figure 12.3(c) where string c_3 was deleted from the configuration of (b). This is accomplished simply by changing the c_5 pointer so it points to c_4 rather than to c_3. The c_3 string is still physically present, but it cannot be reached by sequencing through the linked list. Other variations on RT modifications can readily be imagined.

Building Linked Lists

Example 12.4. Write a program segment LLIST that reads cards with alphanumeric strings (one per card), trims them, allocates space, and establishes a linked-list RT based on ID number. ID numbers are given as four-digit fields in columns 77 to 80 on each card. Processing is to be in increasing ID-number order, and strings are supplied in an arbitrary order. Assume there is no duplication of ID numbers.

Since we order RT entries by ID number, we must allow space for the storage of ID numbers. It is most convenient to store these in RT itself, because then those numbers can be quickly located. Thus, we allocate a third word per RT entry, so each entry is a triplet, as shown in Figure 12.4. For simplicity, let us assume RT is a one-dimensional array.

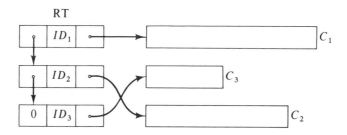

Fig. 12.4.   RT triplet entries.

Let us consider the code in sections. First, we develop the code to read strings and store them in the main array T. Array RT is initialized here, but discussed subsequently. We will later see why the RT index is initialized to 2.

```
C    LLIST
     DIMENSIØN T(5000), CARD(77), RT(300)
C    INITIALIZE T, RT INDICES.
     I = 1
     N = 2
C    READ A STRING, TRIM.
     READ (5, 100), (CARD(J), J = 2, 77), ID
```

```
100   FØRMAT (76A1, I4)
      CARD(1) = 76
      CALL TRIM(CARD)
C   CHECK FØR BLANK CARD.
      IF (CARD(1) .EQ. 0) STØP
C   CØMPUTE TERMINAL INDEX FØR STRING.
      K = I + CARD(1)
C   INITIALIZE STRING INDEX.
      M = 1
C   STØRE STRING IN ARRAY.
      DØ 10 J = I, K
      T(J) = CARD(M)
10    M = M + 1
```

The next step is entry of the triplet (next-pointer, ID, string-pointer) into the reference table RT, which is to be a linked list. It is easiest to visualize this by considering the general case. Let us assume that an ordered linked list already exists, into which we must now add a new entry, in the proper place (ordered by ID). We must know where the list begins, and must "anchor" the list to a known word. Let us choose RT(1) as that origin; it will always contain a pointer to the first triplet.

Initially, the first triplet is located in RT(2) through RT(4), but a later ID may precede this one, so that RT(11) through RT(13), e.g., may be first. Thus, a fixed origin, such as RT(1), is essential. After a number of entries have been made, the storage picture in RT is as in Figure 12.5. Shown are entries k' and k, which are in sequence. Entry names are RT indices; hence entry k' is in location RT(k'), and entry k is in location RT(k). To make a new entry in RT, the current ID value is to be compared with the ID's already in RT, in their order of appearance in the list. As soon as the ID is found to be less than an ID value in the list, the location for the current entry is determined: It belongs immediately prior to that last entry checked. This is depicted in the loop in Figure 12.6. The initial value of k' is 1, since the "entry" preceding the new location is the starting point initially. The initial value of k is RT(1), the pointer to the first entry. As long as ID is greater than RT($k + 1$), an ID value, we search

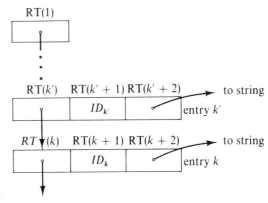

RT(1)

RT(k')   RT($k' + 1$) RT($k' + 2$)   → to string
           $ID_{k'}$ entry k'

RT(k)   RT($k + 1$) RT($k + 2$)   → to string
           ID_k entry k

Fig. 12.5.   Entries in RT.

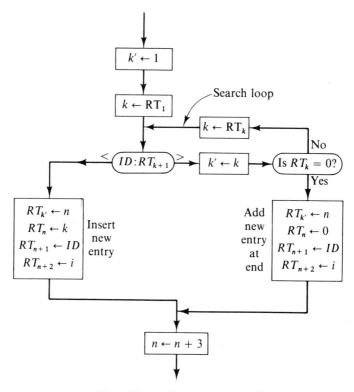

Fig. 12.6.   Adding new entry to RT.

through the list, setting k each time to the value of the pointer to the next entry, i.e., $RT(k)$, and setting k' each time to the last pointer, i.e., to the old value of k. If $RT(k)$ is zero, the current ID value exceeds all ID values in the list, and the entry must be made at the end of the list.

When ID is less than $RT(k + 1)$, it is necessary to insert the current entry between entries k' and k. This is accomplished in the box labeled "insert new entry" in Figure 12.6. We should note that the value of n is the index of the first available (un-used) location in RT. Initially $n = 2$, since R(2) is the start of entries. For that reason, the RT index, n, is set to 2 at the start. The statements in the box have these meanings:

$RT_{k,+1} \leftarrow n$:   Reset the "next-pointer" of entry k' to the location of the new entry, which begins at $RT(n)$.

$RT_n \leftarrow k$:   Set the "next-pointer" of entry n to the entry to follow it in sequence, entry k.

$RT_{n+1} \leftarrow ID$:   Enter the ID value in its place in entry n.

$RT_{n+2} \leftarrow i$:   Set the "string-pointer" of the new entry ("entry n"); i is the pointer to the new added string in array T.

When it is necessary to add the entry at the end of the list, i.e., when $RT(k)$ is zero, the box labeled "add new entry at end" is executed. Its statements are the same as the other box considered, except that RT(n), the next-pointer word, must be set to zero, indicating the new end of the list.

After each entry is made, the RT index must be increased by 3, to locate the next entry three locations beyond the last. Finally, a test must be made to see that RT does not overflow; it can accommodate only 99 entries in this program, although the limit is arbitrary. Also, a test ought to be made on overflow of T. Both overflow tests have been omitted from the flowchart, but appear in the code, which is shown below. KK represents k'.

```
C    INITIALIZE THE SEARCH.
     KK = 1
     K = RT(1)
C    CØMPARE ID VALUES.
  20 IF (ID .LE. RE(K+1)) GØ TØ 40
C    SET KK.
     KK = K
C    TEST FØR END ØF LIST.
     IF (RT(K) .EQ. 0) GØ TØ 50
C    SET K.
     K = RT(K)
     GØ TØ 20
C    INSERT NEW ENTRY.
  40 RT(KK) = N
     RT(N) = K
     RT(N+1) = ID
     RT(N+2) = I
     GØ TØ 60
C    ADD NEW ENTRY AT END.
  50 RT(KK) = N
     RT(N) = 0
     RT(N+1) = ID
     RT(N+2) = I
C    MØDIFY RT INDEX.
  60 N = N + 3
```

A few comments on the array RT are appropriate. It might seem more reasonable at first to define RT as a two-dimensional array with one dimension equal to 3. If this were done, however, it would be more involved to set pointers into RT(k), i.e., to set the next-pointers. It would be necessary to calculate the pointers, taking into account the current values of two RT indices, performing arithmetic on them. A one-dimensional array eliminates this problem, though addressing RT entries may seem a bit awkward in this scheme.

Other Linked Structures

It is frequently useful to be able to return to the starting point of a linked list. With the linked list described, there is no way of doing this, since all pointers are directed forward. If, however, we replace the zero used as an end indicator by a pointer to the start of the list, we form a loop which is called a *ring*. Figure 12.7 illustrates this modified structure.

It is sometimes very useful to be able to go backwards in a linked-list structure. After a particular item is processed, its predecessor may have to be reprocessed for some reason. A *doubly-linked list* is valuable in this instance; it is depicted in Figure 12.8. Each triplet has been replaced by a quadruplet, a four-word entry. The extra word contains a backward pointer to the preceding entry. If the pointers close on themselves, as in Figure 12.7, the structure is a doubly-linked ring.

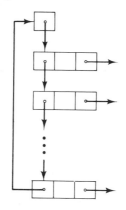

Fig. 12.7.   A ring structure.

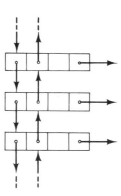

Fig. 12.8.   A doubly-linked list.

EXERCISES

1. Compare simple one-dimensional arrays to linked lists. List advantages and disadvantages to each type of data storage.

2. What advantages (and disadvantages) do doubly-linked lists have over simple linked lists?

3. How, in a qualitative way, should the processes described in the text for simple linked lists be modified for doubly-linked lists?

* * * * * *

4. Write a program to find and to print the *n*th entry in a linked list. Assume this call:

   CALL   FIND(LØC,N)

   where LØC is the location of RT(1) and N contains *n*.

5. Write a program that searches for the entry associated with a given ID number and prints the ID and the entry. Assume this call:

   CALL   FINDID(LØC,ID)

   where LØC is the location of RT(1) and ID contains the ID.

6. Write a program to combine two linked lists, that is, place one after another to form a single one. Assume the call:

CALL CØMBIN(LISTA,LISTB)

where LISTA and LISTB are the header locations, RT(1), of the two given lists.

7. Write a program segment that prints each string (maximum size: 76 characters) in sequence, ordered by ID number, on doubly-spaced lines, with an appropriate title. List 25 strings to a page and number pages sequentially.

8. Modify the code in Example 12.4 to create a ring structure instead of a linked-list structure.

12.5 TREES

Tree Structure

Linked-list structures help us around the problem of maintaining an ordered sequence of entries without the difficulties of moving entries in memory as additions and deletions are made. A linked list permits memory to be organized not sequentially, as internally addressed, but in any manner we wish, provided the data are to be stored in a simply connected chain.

If the data of interest are structured naturally in a manner that calls for branching at several levels, with separate paths to be followed under appropriate circumstances, then the linear nature of a linked list is unsatisfactory. Consider the data structure implied in Figure 12.9. The structure is composed of *nodes*, the heavy dots with labels, and *branches*, the lines interconnecting the nodes. Implied is that, at any node, the data are organized so that a search may take one of several paths. The shape of this structure gives its name, a *tree*, for it resembles a tree (inverted) with branches. Labeling the nodes in this tree reflects their interrelationship. For example, the nodes one reaches directly from the primary node a are a_1 and a_2; the nodes one reaches directly from node a_1 are a_{11} and a_{12}. In

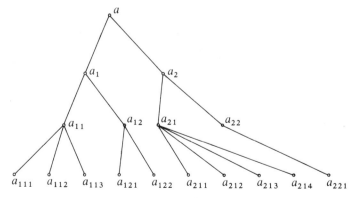

Fig. 12.9.   A treelike structure.

general, to name the several nodes one reaches directly from a given node, the subscripts '1', '2', ..., are appended to the given node's name. In this way, we can see that node a_{214} must be reached by paths 2, 1, and 4 from the primary node, if paths from a node are numbered in sequence, left to right.

Some data are naturally structured like the tree of Figure 12.9. As an example, consider the electronic system mentioned earlier in this section. We can assume the following structure:

    Electronic system
        Bay
            Chassis
                Circuit
                    Component

This sequence of indented terms implies that each line is a level one lower than the line above. A typical system might appear as follows if completely specified:

    Electronic System XYZ
        Bay 1
            Chassis 1.1
                Circuit 1.1.1
                    Component 1.1.1.1
                    Component 1.1.1.2
                Circuit 1.1.2
                    Component 1.1.2.1
                    Component 1.1.2.2
                    Component 1.1.2.3
                Circuit 1.1.3
                    Component 1.1.3.1
            Chassis 1.2
                Circuit 1.2.1
                    Component 1.2.1.1
                     :
                     :

        Bay 2
            Chassis 2.1
                Circuit 2.1.1
                Component 2.1.1.1
                Component 2.1.1.2
                 :
                 :

                Circuit 4.6.3
                    Component 4.6.3.1
                    Component 4.6.3.2
                    Component 4.6.3.3

The naming convention at each level is clear: Use one more integer in the string comprising the name for each level down from the top, and label in sequence within one level. This is a similar notation to that used in the tree in Figure 12.9 and reveals the similarity between a tree and the structure given above.

Details

There are many different ways to build tree-like data structures. We shall develop a series of such structures, each more complex than the preceding, and consider several operations that we would want to perform on them.

Initially, let us focus our attention on a node, pictured schematically in Figure 12.10. The node, a_2, has four branches leaving it, labeled to match the nodes that they precede: b_{21}, b_{22}, b_{23}, and b_{24}. The node is shown to have pointers to the branches, representing the manner in which storage is allocated to these items.

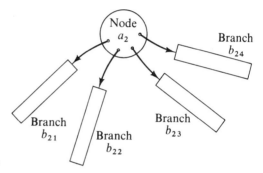

Fig. 12.10.   A node, with branches.

If a search is executed for a data item in a particular branch, a search for the location of the desired branch is required. To indicate the location of a branch, the branch name (or number) must be stored in the node. As a result, the node consists of a table of branch names and pointers to branches, i.e., a reference table as described in the last section.

If the number of branches leaving a node is no greater than a fixed amount, a simple reference table can comprise the node, as shown in Figure 12.11. Here branches are assumed to be variable in length, as with irregular arrays. There need not be k branches present at all times, however. Zero pointers can indicate missing branches. The n_i are the names of the branches; when a particular branch is sought, its name is found in the reference table, which then indicates the location by the associated pointer. Shown also is n_0, the name of the node.

Next we can look at the inclusion of nodes that these branches point to. Figure 12.12 diagrams the structure with these additions. Note that the branches have pointers to nodes. Since each branch points to but one node, one pointer suffices. The details of the structure are shown in Figure 12.13, where pointers to nodes are shown as the first entry in the branches. Clearly, the search for a node is very simple, since its pointer's location is known.

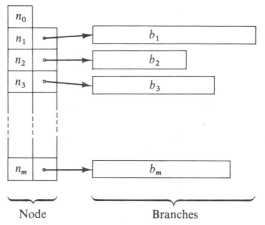

Fig. 12.11.   Details of a node.

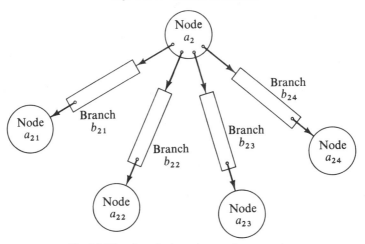

Fig. 12.12.   A node, branches, and more nodes.

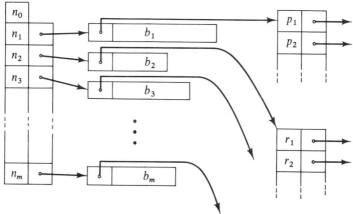

Fig. 12.13.   Details of the structure.

Tree Structure Operations

In the last section, on linked lists, some attention was paid to the problem of building structures. We may note that, in the cases of the tree structures of this section, the building procedures are quite similar to those studied. Consequently, we shall focus attention on another aspect of structuring, that of searching for branches. The searching problem is the key to structure manipulation, for the prime reason for designing and using a particular structure is to permit efficient storage and retrieval operations. Initially, we shall consider the search for a particular branch in the structure just described. We then shall generalize that structure to more complex forms, and also we shall generalize the search procedure by requesting more information.

In identifying a node or branch, both in supplying one as input to a subroutine and in returning one as output, a pointer is used. We shall refer to nodes and branches together as *blocks*. Generally, these areas will be carved out of a large array (cf. array T in Example 12.3), and a pointer to the array locates a block. This concept is embodied in the examples that follow.

Example 12.5. Write a subroutine SRCHB1 (<u>s</u>ea<u>rch</u> for <u>b</u>ranch) that locates a named branch in a given node.
The call is of the form

CALL SRCHB1(nptr,bname,bptr)

where <u>nptr</u> is a pointer to the node, <u>bname</u> is the branch name, and <u>bptr</u> is a pointer returned that points to the sought branch.
The program is the following:

```
      SUBRØUTINE SRCHB1(NPTR,BNAME,BPTR)
      CØMMØN ST(5000), M
      INTEGER NPTR, BNAME, BPTR
      MM = 2 * M
C     CØMMENCE SEARCH THRØUGH MØDE.
      DØ 20 J = 1, MM, 2
      IF (ST(NPTR + J) .EQ. BNAME) GØ TØ 30
   20 CØNTINUE
C     HERE IF NAME NØT PRESENT.
      BPTR = 0
      RETURN
C     HERE IF NAME PRESENT.
   30 BPTR = NPTR + J
      RETURN
      END
```

The CØMMØN variables, ST and M, are the total array out of which all blocks are built and the number of branches leaving a node, respectively. The pointers

NPTR and BPTR are *relative* pointers, having values relative to the start of ST; i.e., they are indices in that array. The search proceeds by incrementing J by 2, since names are stored in the node in alternate locations. The index of ST in the IF statement, 'NPTR + J', successively locates the branch names in the node. Note that the subroutine returns a zero pointer (BPTR) if the given branch name is not present.

The structure considered permitted nodes of fixed size ($2k$) only, but a more general structure would allow nodes of varying sizes. We have already discussed the advantages of such an approach. To accomplish this, we replace the simple reference table by a ring. In this way, we reap the advantages of both rings (or linked lists) and trees. Figure 12.14 shows this generalized form. We can consider the search procedure now required.

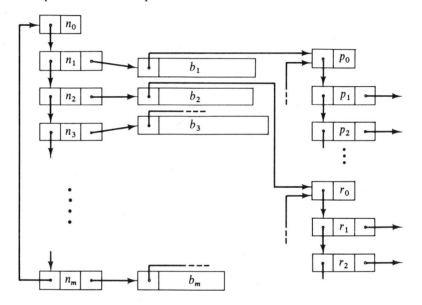

Fig. 12.14.   Details of ring-and-tree structure.

Example 12.6. Write a modified search subroutine SRCHB2 that locates a named branch in a given ring-structure node.

The call is again of the form

CALL SRCHB2(nptr,bname,bptr)

The program is the following:

```
SUBRØUTINE  SRCHB2(NPTR,BNAME,BPTR)
CØMMØN  ST(5000)
INTEGER  NPTR, BNAME, BPTR
C    INITIALIZE  SEARCH  INDEX.
     J = ST(NPTR)
```

```
C    CØMMENCE SEARCH THRØUGH NØDE.
  10   IF (ST(J+1) .EQ. BNAME) GØ TØ 30
C    SET INDEX TØ NEXT NAME.
       J = ST(J)
C    TEST FØR END ØF RING-STRUCTURE NØDE.
       IF (J .NE. NPTR) GØ TØ 10
C    HERE IF NAME NØT PRESENT.
  25   BPTR = 0
       RETURN
C    HERE IF NAME PRESENT.
  30   BPTR = J + 2
       RETURN
       END
```

This program is similar to SRCHB1, except that the search proceeds through the linked list by fetching pointers to the following names. The index J here is set relative to the start of the array ST, in contrast to the index J in SRCHB1, where J was set relative to the start of the node.

A common structure retrieval problem is that of locating a given branch somewhere in a tree, beginning the search from the top node. It is possible for branches in different paths to have the same name. This does not lead to ambiguity as long as two branches at the same level, i.e., leaving the same node, never have the same name. In general, a search may be made for a particular branch at any level if the sequence of names of successive branches from the top node is given. For example, if we wanted branch b_{3546}, we can give the sequence 'b_3, b_{35}, b_{354}, b_{3546}'. This would not seem necessary, because the subscripting here is redundant, but if we consider symbolic names, the full request is reasonable. In a personnel file, e.g., we might ask for a subfile (treated as a branch) as 'PERSNL, PAYRØL, 65880, SALARY'. This might mean, "in the PERSNL file, in its PAYRØL subfile, locate the man whose payroll number is 65880 and obtain his salary".

Example 12.7. Write a subroutine SRCHBS (search for branches) that locates a named branch in a tree, beginning the search from the top node. The branch is identified as a sequence of the branch names in its path from the top.
The call is of the form

CALL SRCHBS(bnames,bptr)

where bnames is an array containing the series of branch names with a count of those names as its first entry, and bptr is a pointer returned to the sought branch. The array of given branch names is assumed to be no longer than 20.
The program is the following:

```
SUBRØUTINE SRCHBS(BNAMES,BBPTR)
CØMMØN ST(5000)
```

```
      INTEGER BNAMES(20)
C   FETCH BRANCH CØUNT, SET NØDE PØINTER.
      N = BNAMES(1) + 1
      NPTR = 1
C   CØMMENCE SEARCH FØR SUCCESSIVE BRANCH NAMES.
      DØ 20 I = 2, N
      CALL SRCHB2(NPTR,BNAMES(I),BPTR)
      IF (BPTR) 20, 30, 20
C   HAVING BRANCH PTR, SET NØDE PTR.
   20 NPTR = ST(BPTR)
C   HERE AFTER BRANCH NAMES ARE EXHAUSTED.
      BBPTR = BPTR
      RETURN
C   HERE IF CØMPLETE GIVEN LIST NØT PRESENT.
   30 BBPTR = 0
      RETURN
      END
```

Since this search begins at the top node, NPTR is initialized to zero, assuming the top node is located at the start of ST. Note that SRCHB2 is used once for locating each branch name in the given array, after a node in the path is located. No search is required, as noted earlier, to locate the single node pointed to by a branch; statement 20 accomplishes this. If BPTR is ever set to zero, then one name in the given set of branch names is absent, and the search is ceased.

Sometimes information at one level of a tree structure is common to other information at that level or, less commonly, to information at a different level. Consider the electronic system mentioned, part of which formed the basis of study in the last section. Suppose a particular component was present in a number of circuits within the system. This is in fact a most likely situation. It is also possible that a given circuit is present in several chassis within the system. In these cases, there is no need to structure the data as a tree; instead, we can *merge* lower levels to utilize the fact of commonality of data within the structure. This situation is illustrated in Figure 12.15, which can be compared to Figure 12.9. Here, element a_{12} is common to higher level elements a_1 and a_2. Similarly, elements a_{112} and a_{113} are common to a_{11} and a_{12}. We note that there are six lowest-level elements, but that there are eight *instances* of lowest-level elements.

The use of a merged tree saves space, since repetition of information is avoided. This structure has essentially the same properties as if its branches were not merged.

The physical structure of a merged tree is similar to that of a tree; in fact, they are the same structure except for the duplication of pointers in branches to nodes. Some of these pointers may be the same as others.

We shall discuss one further problem associated with trees in general, applying its solution to a merged tree. That problem consists of listing the members

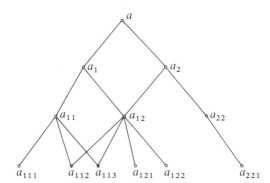

Fig. 12.15.   A merged-tree structure.

of all paths from the top node of a given tree. These paths are to be described by naming all blocks comprising them. To this point we have not assigned names to nodes, but we shall do that here.

A simple circuit AMPL is shown in Figure 12.16; it consists of three sub-circuits EARLY, MID, and LATE. These subcircuits have a total of nine components, but there are only three distinct types of components. The structure of the circuit data is shown in Figure 12.17 as a merged tree. Note that the distinct components are RES, CAP, and IND, which represent three electrical parts one might select from a catalogue.

The nine specific components of the circuit appear in the branches at the second level. These branches represent *specific* instances of the three catalogue components, containing information on their specific use. For example, these branches may contain information on the location of components, as indicated by x–y coordinates, terminal locations, etc. Thus 'R1' is a specific case of a component (resistor) of type RES. The branches at the lowest level, labeled VALS, COSTS, and MFG, represent specific traits of component RES. Thus, VALS may contain data on values in ohms, tolerances, and power ratings; COSTS may contain data on unit cost, cost per 100, and cost per 1000; and MFG may contain data on manufacturer's name and address. In the same way, the lowest-level branches under CAP and IND contain similar data. The duplication of branch names at this level poses no problem, as long as retrieval requests include the node name.

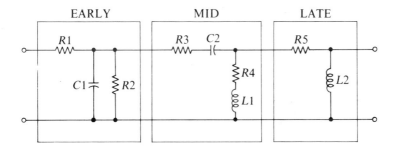

Fig. 12.16.   Circuit AMPL.

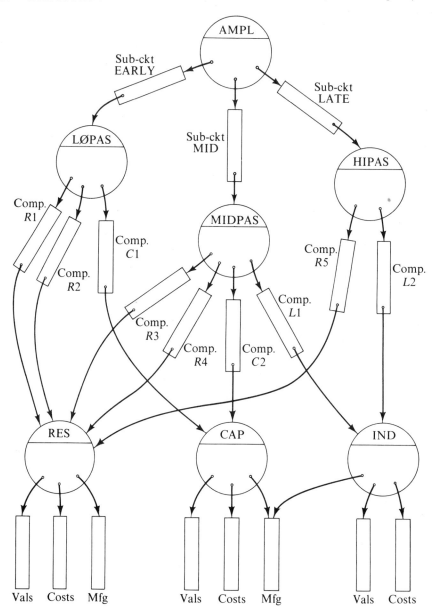

Fig. 12.17. Circuit data structure.

Note the merging at the structure bottom. The implication is that the same manufacturer supplies both CAP and IND components.

A similar analysis applies to the branches at the top and the nodes they point to. EARLY, MID, and LATE are specific subcircuit names, while LØPAS,

MIDPAS, and HIPAS are subcircuit type names. These subcircuits might each appear more than once in a circuit.

In general, we can say that nodes represent types of elements in the circuit, such as subcircuits and components. Branches represent specific instances of those types. The storage of data in this tree is consistent with this philosophy.

We shall discuss one further problem associated with trees in general, applying its solution to a merged tree. That problem consists of listing the numbers of all paths from the top node of a given tree. These paths are to be described by naming all blocks in each. In the circuit data structure just considered, the list of all paths (excluding the final branch) is the following:

```
EARLY,LØPAS,R1,RES
EARLY,LØPAS,R2,RES
EARLY,LØPAS,C1,CAP
MID,MIDPAS,R3,RES
MID,MIDPAS,R4,RES
MID,MIDPAS,C2,CAP
MID,MIDPAS,L1,IND
LATE,HIPAS,R5,RES
LATE,HIPAS,L2,IND
```

Before we consider the method whereby these paths are traced, we must first turn our attention to a new concept.

Push-Down Lists

If we contemplate the problem of searching a tree for all its paths, we realize that information on the current path being traced must be saved. We need this information because after going down one path, we must be able to trace our way back up to locate the next path. In the tree structure, as described, there are only pointers down the tree. Having reached a final node or branch, there is no way to go up the tree to locate the next final node or branch, using just the pointers in the tree. What we can do instead is keep a list of the names of the blocks traversed. However, since we do not know directly where blocks are located in memory, we could store pointers to them, since these pointers are direct references to these blocks. But we still have a problem, for we would rather know where the *next* block is located, so if we store pointers to the block pointers themselves, we are close to saving the very information we need.

If we consider Figure 12.14, which describes the ring-and-tree data structure discussed above, we see that a list of the pointers in the node rings to the next node entries is the list of interest. These pointers are shown as bold arrows in Figure 12.18. This set of pointers "define" a path. If it is saved in a list, we can retrace our steps back to a sufficiently high node and then trace the next path. It is clear, as successive paths are traced, that entries near the end of the list will be frequently

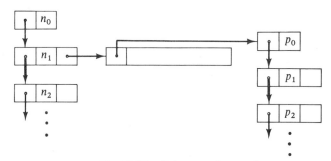

Fig. 12.18.   Pointers to be saved.

modified as, e.g., the several branches from the lowest-level node are followed in successive path tracings. Higher-level entries in the list change less frequently. These pointers saved are in effect pointers to the branches that follow. In this sense, the list entries are as shown in Table 12.1. "List(i)" means contents of the list for the ith path. The table thus shows a time history of the list contents.

TABLE 12.1   LIST ENTRIES, IN SUCCESSION

List(1)	List(2)	List(3)	List(4)	List(5)
EARLY	EARLY	EARLY	EARLY	EARLY
R1	R1	R1	R2	R2
VALS	COSTS	MFG	VALS	COSTS

The list described is an example of a *push-down list*. Such a list is of quantities stored at one end and, as used, are deleted from that same end. New entries are made and removed in time. In this way, the push-down list acts as a temporary repository for items. It has been likened to a tray holder in a cafeteria, which is both loaded and unloaded from the top. Such a holder has the characteristic that it pops up as fewer trays are loaded, giving equal access to the last tray. In like manner, a push-down list offers equal access to the last entry made, using a pointer to that entry.

Tree Searching

Having studied push-down list concepts, let us now apply their use to the problem described earlier, that of searching a tree for all paths from the top node.

Example 12.8. Write a program PATHS that prints all paths of a given tree (which may be merged), printing these paths by listing the nodes and branches in each.

The tree structure shown in Figure 12.18 is that described earlier. The top (first-level) node is named n_0. First-level branches are $(b_i; i = 1, m)$; their names are $(n_i; i = 1, m)$. The second-level nodes are named $(p_{i0}; i = 1, k)$. Second-level branches are $(c_{ij}; i = 1, m; j = 1, l)$; their names are p_{ij}. The third-level nodes are q_{ij0}. Finally, the third-level branches are d_{ijk}; their names are q_{ijk}.

A three-level tree is considered here. After flowcharting the procedure for such a tree, we shall generalize the method to trees of any level.

We shall use a push-down list (PDL) to store pointers to "next branch names" and to nodes. We require the former in order to trace our way back up the tree as described earlier. We require the latter in order to check on ring completion. From Figure 12.19, we can readily see that in order to determine when a ring has been completely searched, we can compare pointers to next branch names with pointers to node names. In the top node, the pointer after name n_m points to node n_0, as does the top pointer at the left. Thus, the PDL will serve two purposes.

An early observation that we can make is that the path searching problem is highly repetitive. As we go down in level, the search technique remains the same. Let us consider the search at one level. The symbol $P(x)$ means "a pointer to x". The steps in the search at the second level are these (i was given a value from the previous step):

1. Set $j = 1$.
2. Place p_{ij} in the output list.
3. Place $P(p_{i,j+1})$ in PDL.
4. Fetch c_{ij}.
5. Place $P(q_{ij0})$ in the PDL.
6. Place q_{ij0} in output list.

The "output list" is the list of node and branch names in a path, to be printed. The symbol $p_{i,j+1}$ is the branch name following the current name. If we follow these six steps, we find that the search proceeds from pointer from a branch b_i to the pointer from a branch c_{ij}, thereby covering one level. A complete flowchart appears in Figure 12.20. "OL" is the output list. This is the first version of our flowchart.

In the center box of Figure 12.20, the path is printed, where "PRINT OL" appears. In this box, note that the procedure differs from the other boxes. This is true because there is no need to continue searching for pointers. The path is at an end. At the end of each nested loop, the index $(i, j,$ or $k)$ is increased by one and the next path out of a node is searched. Following this, there is a test to see if the ring has been checked to its end. As noted, this test involves comparing two pointers.

Once all three levels have been traversed, the PDL contains these items:

(a) $P(n_0)$.
(b) $P(n_{i+1})$.
(c) $P(p_{i0})$.
(d) $P(p_{i,j+1})$.
(e) $P(q_{ij0})$.
(f) $P(_{i,j,k+1})$.

Of these items, (a), (c), and (e) are pointers to nodes, used for testing for the ends of rings, while items (b), (d), and (f) are pointers to "next branch names".

It is now necessary to translate the flowchart of Figure 12.20 into a form more nearly resembling a computer program. We shall assume all space for the data structure is located in a linear array ST (storage). If such an array is used, we actually need only a single index, which will be I. All references at all levels can be made through I. Consider the six steps again. First, we assume I is set so that it points to the start of

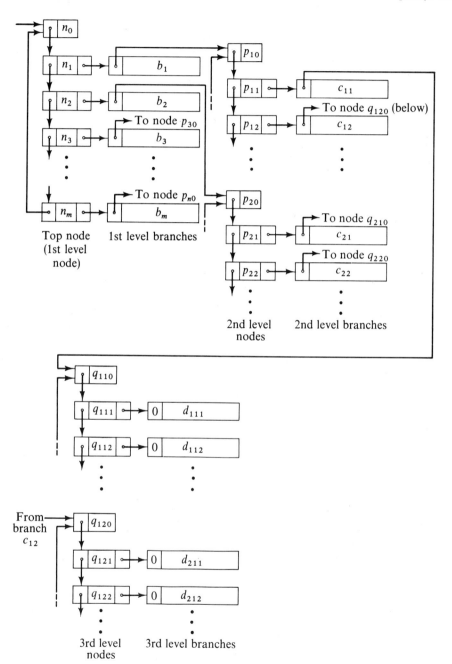

Fig. 12.19. Details of a tree.

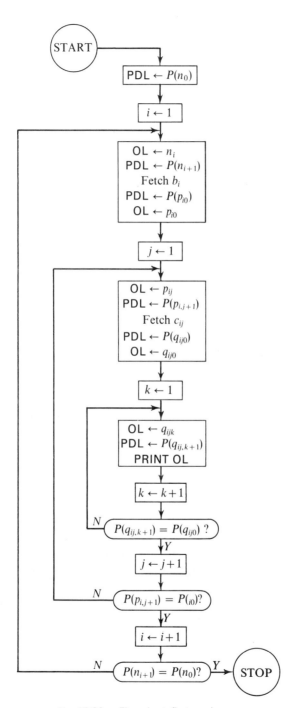

Fig. 12.20.   Flowchart, first version.

the node containing p_{io}, for some i. In other words, ST(I + 1) contains p_{io}. This corresponds to the start of the six steps. These steps are translated into the following:

1. I ← ST(I)
    (I now points to p_{i1}; this is an initialization step.)
2. OL ← ST(I + 1)
    (Place p_{ij} in OL.)
3. PDL ← ST(I)
    (Place $P(p_{i,j+1})$ in PDL.)
4. I ← ST(I + 2)
    (I now points to c_{ij}.)
5. PDL ← ST(I)
    (Place $P(q_{ij0})$ in PDL.)
6. I ← ST(I + 1)
    (I now points to q_{ij0}.)
6A. OL ← ST(I + 1)
    (Place q_{ij0} in OL.)

The reader can follow the pointer manipulations by examining Figure 12.19. The above list should be compared to the earlier list of steps; note that two steps (6 and 6A) replace the earlier step 6. A complete revised flowchart appears in Figure 12.21. The subscripts on 'PDL' refer to entry labels, given above as (a) through (f). Running from the top of the chart to the bottom, we note that these subscripts increase and then decrease, reflecting the nature of the PDL operation. Even in inner loops, these subscripts vary in this manner, as they should.

One other point should be noted. The steps involving adding information to OL and PDL must be modified to reflect the manner in which information is added to an array in memory. Let J and K represent indices in the PDL and OL arrays, respectively. Now, using FORTRAN notation, we write:

1. I = ST(I)
2. ØL(K) = ST(I + 1)
    K = K + 1
3. PDL(J) = ST(I)
    J = J + 1
4. I = ST(I + 2)
5. PDL(J) = ST(I)
    J = J + 1
6. I = ST(I)
6A. ØL(K) = ST(I + 1)
    K = K + 1

Now we are ready to generalize the problem to any number of levels. Our notation already permits this, for we are using a single index in the array ST. Initially, I, J, and K must all be set to 1. Since $P(n_0)$ is in ST(1), we can also initialize PDL(J) to 1, if J = 1, and then add 1 to J, for consistency.

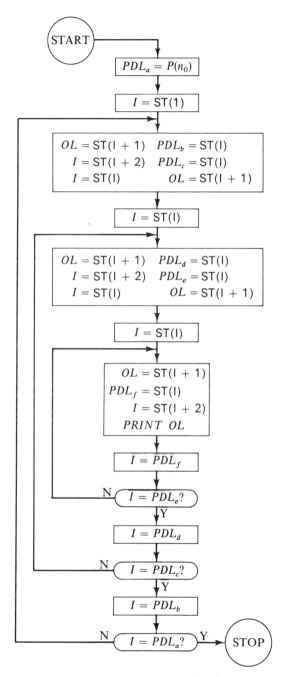

Fig. 12.21. Flowchart, revised version.

The case of different treatment of the lowest level must be considered. To test for that level, we can check ST(I) for zero after step 4, for at that point I points to a branch. ST(I) is then the pointer to the next node; if this is zero, there is no next node. In that event, we wish to print OL and initialize its index (K) again.

Finally, we must note that to progress "up" PDL, as shown in the lower portion of Figure 12.21, index J must be decremented properly. The final flowchart, in FORTRAN notation, for any number of levels, is shown in Figure 12.22.

Some further explanation of this final flowchart should be given, for it has a peculiar appearance. It contains three loops, not nested. Two of these loops actually cross each other. Let us consider each loop in turn.

The "descending loop" (so marked in Figure 12.22) is traversed as a path is traced from upper to lower levels in the tree. It is traversed as many times in succession as there are levels in a path from the last node whose ring is processed prior to the path. Thus, if we rise to a node, move one position around its ring, and drop three levels in tracking the next path, the descending loop is traversed three times. There is no corresponding loop in Figure 12.21, for it represents the variability in the number of loops present.

The "ring loop" is traversed whenever a ring is traced by moving along it to the next branch pointer. The system can traverse this loop for all levels of the tree, but traverses it m times in succession if a ring has m branch pointers. Just prior to looping back in the flowchart, the index I is set to the next branch pointer by the statement 'I = PDL(J)'.

The "ascending loop" is traversed whenever there is a rise in level, i.e., whenever one ring is completed. At this point, the PDL index is decreased by 2, and a test is made to see if we have popped up to the very top of PDL and are done. If not, the system loops back to reset I at the start of the next higher-level ring and thereupon the ring loop processing commences. As with the descending loop, there is no corresponding loop in Figure 12.21.

The program corresponding to the procedure is as follows; statement numbers correspond to boxes in Figure 12.22.

```
C    PATHS
C    A PRØGRAM TØ PRINT ALL THE PATHS ØF A TREE
C    STRUCTURE, STARTING FRØM AN INITIAL NØDE.
     INTEGER ST(5000), PDL(100), ØL(100)
C    INITIALIZE PØINTERS.
     I = 1
     J = 1
     K = 1
C    MAKE FIRST ENTRY IN PDL.
     PDL(J) = 1
     J = J + 1
C    INITIALIZE STRUCTURE PTR FØR FIRST BRANCH NAME.
  10 I = ST(I)
C    ENTER BRANCH NAME IN ØL, PTR TØ NEXT NAME IN PDL.
  20 ØL(K) = ST(I+1)
     K = K + 1
```

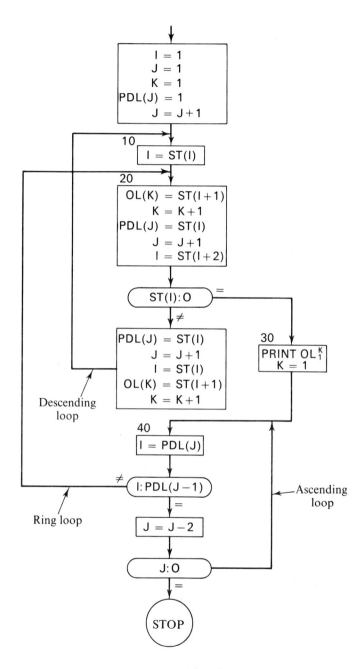

Fig. 12.22.   Final flowchart.

```
            PDL(J) = ST(I)
            J = J + 1
C    SET STRUCTURE PTR FØR BRANCH.
            I = ST(I+2)
C    TEST TØ SEE IF BRANCH IS AT BØTTØM LEVEL.
            IF (ST(I) .EQ. 0) GØ TØ 30
C    IF NØT, ENTER PTR TØ NEXT NØDE IN PDL.
            PDL(J) = ST(I)
            J = J + 1
C    SET STRUCTURE PTR FØR NEXT NØDE, ENTER NØDE IN ØL.
            I = ST(I)
            ØL(K) = ST(I+1)
            K = K + 1
            GØ TØ 10
C    PRINT ØUTPUT LIST (ØL).
     30     PRINT (6,100) (ØL(M), M = 1, K)
            K = 1
C    RESET STRUCTURE PTR TØ NEXT BRANCH NAME IN RING.
     40     I = PDL(J)
C    CHECK FØR END ØF RING.
            IF (I .NE. PDL(J-1)) GØ TØ 20
C    IF SØ, MØDIFY PDL INDEX (PØP UP), TEST FØR END.
            J = J - 2
            IF (J .NE. 0) GØ TØ 40
            STØP
    100     FØRMAT (10(1X,A4))
            END
```

EXERCISES

1. What other problems or systems have information that is treelike in the manner of the electronic system described?

2. Assume that information has been organized as a tree. What happens if it is desired to extract some data not so structured? As an example, consider the electronic system; suppose we want to have a list of all capacitors on in all circuits.

3. What are the consequences of having branch 234 of a tree be the same as branch 235? The same as branch 24?

4. Show how an algebraic expression can be structured as a tree by giving examples.

5. What are some push-down lists in everyday life and in engineering?

* * * * * *

6. Write a subroutine ADDBR that adds a given branch to an existing tree structure of the form given in this section (Figure 12.14). The call:

CALL ADDBR(tree,branch)

where <u>tree</u> is the structure to be added to, and <u>branch</u> is a pointer to an array whose contents are to be added.

7. Write a subroutine DELBR that deletes a named branch from a given tree. The call:

CALL DELBR(tree,branch)

8. Write a subroutine CKMERG that determines whether or not two named branches are the same branch in a merged tree. The call:

CALL CKMERG(tree,bran1,bran2)

where <u>bran1</u> and <u>bran2</u> are the two branches to be checked.

REFERENCE

1. The following book has a very thorough discussion of data structures (or "information structures"):

Donald E. Knuth, *The Art of Computer Programming*, Vol. 1, "Fundamental Algorithms," Addison-Wesley Publishing Co., 1968, pp. 228–463.

13 STORAGE ALLOCATION

When space in computer memory is used for data arrays or data structures, we say that the space has been *allocated* for that purpose. In this chapter we consider the problem of storage allocation in a manner that resembles our treatment of data structuring in the previous chapter. In a computer program that processes data within a multi-dimensional array, the data can be referred to by simple subscripting. When the data are complex in format, however, special treatment of the structuring problem must be given. By the same token, space for arrays can be simply allocated by a DIMENSIØN statement, while in complex situations, the allocation of space must be handled in a special way. It is to this task that we direct our attention here.

13.1 TYPES OF STORAGE ALLOCATION

Static Allocation

Space may be allocated for a program by the programmer as he writes the code. The space assigned is set aside for a specific purpose for the duration of program execution. This is *static* storage allocation. As an example, if a 10 × 10 array is required, this statement

```
DIMENSIØN B(10,10)
```

might be used. This is a command to the compiler to set aside 100 locations in memory permanently for array B. That space may not be used, under normal circumstances, by any other data in the program. Even after the space is no longer needed, it remains allocated for B, though it might be needed by another array.

If core memory were limitless, all space could be allocated in this manner. However, in many large problems, space may be quickly used up if it is so allocated. Several schemes are available for reclaiming this space; these are discussed shortly. We need only add here that in small problems, such as most of those considered in this book, we need not be at all concerned with reuse of space.

Dynamic Allocation

Another approach to memory utilization is to allocate space during the running of a program; this is termed *dynamic* storage allocation. Here, when space is required for a task, a call to an allocation subroutine (an *allocator*) is made, with an indication of the amount of space required. Regardless of the nature of the data structure, space is almost always allocated in blocks of consecutive words in memory. The tree structure of Section 12.5, e.g., might be allocated one node or branch at a time. Space is usually allocated from a single large array, as from ST in the section mentioned.

After space has been dynamically allocated, it may be given up or made "free" or "available" once again. Such space can then be used by other data, as required. Thus, only as much space as needed at a given time need be in active use. The allocator at all times keeps track of the amount of space in use and of the amount available yet to be used.

We can summarize the characteristics of dynamic storage allocation as follows:

1. An executing program makes a call to the allocator, indicating the required space. Usually, a memory location is also supplied as a parameter; the allocator then returns a pointer in this location to the allocated space.
2. The allocated space is then used by the program until no longer needed.
3. The program makes a second call to the allocator, indicating that the space is no longer needed. The allocator then frees the space.

There are many techniques for performing dynamic allocation, but all are based on these three simple concepts. Several points concerning dynamic allocation can be made.

1. BLOCK MOVEMENT. The allocator supplies blocks, as called for by the executing program, of the size specified. In some instances, it may be essential that such blocks never be moved. In the case of space allocated for a subroutine, these might be entry points. In the case of data, these might be memory references. On the other hand, sometimes blocks may be moved. If several blocks were allocated, and an earlier one were freed before a subsequently allocated block were freed, then under some circumstances the freed space could best be reused if the later block were moved back in memory. We shall consider this possibility later. If blocks are moved, addressing them is somewhat of a problem. References are usually indirectly made through words that are fixed in memory.

2. BLOCK LOCATION AND SIZE. It is necessary that the allocator retain information of the location and size of each allocated block. If this information were lacking, the allocator could not then reclaim the space for future use. Location and size information may be stored in a variety of ways.

3. FREEING BLOCKS. When the main program calls the allocator, stating that an allocated block is no longer needed, the allocator may either immediately place that block into its pool of available space, or it may simply mark the space as "free" and do nothing else until the space is needed.

4. REUSING SPACE. If freed space is immediately incorporated into available memory, perhaps by moving together all still-used blocks, then each newly allocated block is taken from the first available memory locations after the active blocks. On the other hand, if freed blocks are simply marked but not immediately used, the allocator may attempt to create, from freed blocks, a block of the proper size. The approach taken may depend upon the need to retain all allocated blocks at fixed locations. The single block of available space, located after all active blocks, will be called the *pool*.

5. LIST STRUCTURES. If all memory is allocated to linked lists, then the allocation scheme may be quite different. In such instances, blocks might all be of fixed size and relatively small, each block containing one or two pointers and perhaps a few words for data. Treatment of such blocks is generally different from treatment of large, variable-sized blocks.

We shall consider these several aspects of the dynamic storage allocation problem by studying three allocation schemes. First, we shall assume blocks can be moved and that all freed space will immediately be reclaimed. Second, we shall assume that blocks cannot be moved and that they are merely marked upon being freed. Third, we shall consider a list-structure allocation scheme that involves four-word memory blocks.

EXERCISES

1. The static storage scheme implied in the use of DIMENSIØN statements can be utilized for dynamic allocation. In qualitative terms, how can this be done?

2. Give examples of problems where dynamic storage allocation is important.

3. Block movement in storage allocation was discussed. In what kinds of problems could blocks be moved? When should they not be moved? What are the consequences of moving blocks?

13.2 ALLOCATION WITH MOVABLE BLOCKS

The Structure

The first allocation technique assumes that movable blocks are to be allocated. All blocks will be allocated from a large one-dimensional array called

ASPACE. A reference table of pointers to the starting locations of all allocated blocks will be used; it is called BTABLE. It has several two-word entries, equal in number to the maximum number of blocks allocated at one time; this number is fixed. Aside from containing pointers to the allocated blocks, each entry contains the size of the allocated block.

A set of pointers, a BTABLE entry, and an allocated block A are shown in Figure 13.1. The pointer to block A is located in the calling program in a location named A. Actually, as can be seen in the figure, the pointer to block A is really a pointer to the A-entry in BTABLE. At any given time, some previously assigned areas in ASPACE may be free, so that there may be free entries in BTABLE. We assume here that the entries in BTABLE are never moved. As a result, the pointers from the calling programs need never be changed.

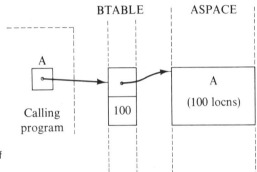

Fig. 13.1.   Allocation of block A.

After several blocks are allocated, the situation may be as shown in Figure 13.2, where blocks A, B, and C are still active. The spaces for A, B, and C are 100, 75, and 50 locations, respectively. Each BTABLE entry has a pointer to an area allocated. Each entry also has a size count. There is also a FREE two-word block, with a pointer to the first free word (in the pool) and a count of the space available. Finally, BPTR points to the first free entry in BTABLE.

Allocation Subroutine

The call for allocated space is

CALL ALLØC1(name,size)

where name is a variable name in the calling program, and size is the requested allocation size. After return from ALLØC1, name contains a pointer to the BTABLE entry. As an example, block A was allocated by this call:

CALL ALLØC1(A,100)

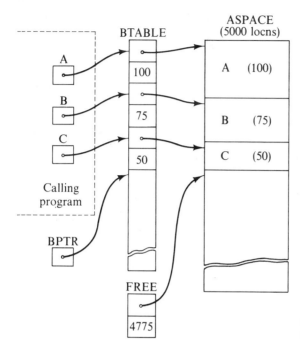

Fig. 13.2.   Allocation of several blocks.

A flowchart of the allocation procedure appears in Figure 13.3. Box numbers refer to program statements. These are the steps:

1. An index j is initially set by BPTR. If j is then greater than the size of BTABLE (i.e., S_b), no allocation can take place.
2. A test is made, using FREE(2), to see if there is sufficient space for the request. If there is, the allocation is made by properly setting pointers: "name ← j" sets <u>name</u> so it points to BTABLE; "BTABLE(j) ← FREE(1)" sets the pointer in BTABLE to the new block; "BTABLE $(j+1)$ ← size" enters the size in BTABLE; the last two statements in Box 30 update the FREE entries.

The ALLØC1 program is the following:

```
      SUBRØUTINE ALLØC1 (NAME,SIZE)
      CØMMØN BTABLE(200), FREE(2), BPTR
      INTEGER J, BTABLE, BPTR
C     INITIALIZE INDEX J.  TEST FØR BTABLE EXHAUSTIØN.
      J = BPTR
      IF (J .LT. 200) GØ TØ 20
10    NAME = 0
      RETURN
```

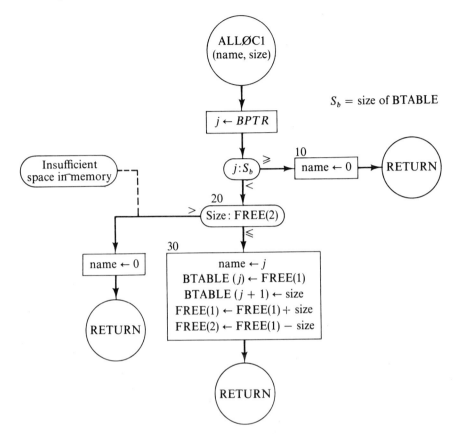

S_b = size of BTABLE

Fig. 13.3.   ALLØC1 subroutine.

```
C    TEST FØR SUFFICIENT SPACE.
  20 IF (SIZE .LE. FREE(2)) GØ TØ 30
     NAME = 0
     RETURN
C    ALLØCATE SPACE.
  30 NAME = J
     BTABLE(J)   = FREE(1)
     BTABLE(J+1) = SIZE
     FREE(1) = FREE(1) + SIZE
     FREE(2) = FREE(2) - SIZE
     RETURN
     END
```

It is important to note just how ALLØC1 is used. Prior to its entry, BPTR and FREE pointers are established. At the first allocation, both BPTR and FREE(1) contain 1, which means they "point" to BTABLE(1) and ASPACE(1), respectively. At later allocations, BPTR and FREE(1) contain higher values. In addition, FREE(2) will initially contain 5000 and later contain smaller counts. Note that the ASPACE array is not mentioned in ALLØC1.

After allocation, <u>name</u> contains a pointer to ASPACE, i.e., a numeric value (the index) from 1 to 5000. We have not considered how the allocated block is to be used, but we can see that to refer to the block, the established pointers must be used. Reference will be made, e.g., to 'BTABLE(A)' to get the pointer to ASPACE (if A is the allocated block) and then ASPACE itself. These operations, however, are part of block processing routines and do not directly concern us now.

Freeing Subroutine

The call for freeing an allocated area is

    CALL   FREE1(name)

We need only name the block to be freed; the BTABLE entry contains the size information.

Freeing a block involves moving all blocks still allocated back so that the freed space is effectively pushed into the pool. To accomplish this, all blocks beyond the one to be freed are simply moved back in memory an amount equal to the size of the freed one; pointers in BTABLE must be moved to reflect this

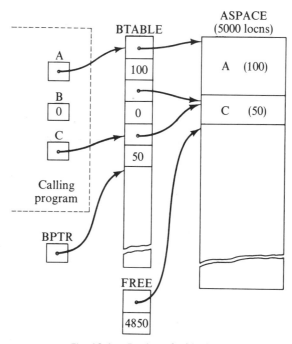

Fig. 13.4.   Freeing of a block.

change. As an example, suppose block B in Figure 13.2 is freed. The result is shown in Figure 13.4. Note that block C was moved back 75 locations, forcing the 75 words formerly in block B into the pool. The pointer in BTABLE used by B is still present, but it is "dead", as indicated by the zero size in the next word; this does not affect any future allocation of space. Figure 13.5 shows the FREE1 sub-routine. Initially, index j is set by the given name, which points to BTABLE. Then, name is set to zero. The movement of all blocks beyond the freed one is accomplished as follows: the ASPACE array, from the index value given by BTABLE(j) + BTABLE($j + 1$) to the index value given by FREE(1) − 1, is moved back the

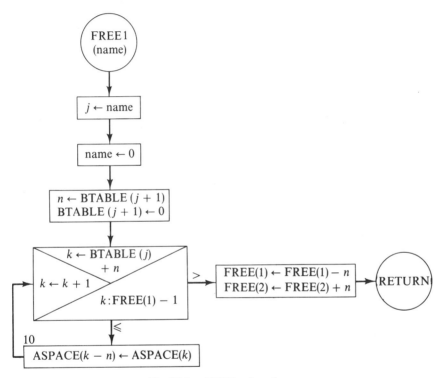

Fig. 13.5.   FREE1 subroutine.

number of locations given by BTABLE(j +1). In other words, the initial word in the areas to be moved is n locations beyond the first word of the freed block, where n = size of that block. The final word is, of course, the one just prior to the pointer in FREE(1). The distance moved is n. Finally, the FREE block entry pair must be updated.

The FREE1 subroutine is the following:

```
SUBRØUTINE FREE1(NAME)
CØMMØN ASPACE(5000), BTABLE(200)
INTEGER J, BTABLE, BPTR
```

```
C   INITIALIZE INDEX, ZERØ NAME, FETCH BLØCK SIZE.
    J = NAME
    M = BTABLE(J+1)
    BTABLE(J+1) = 0
C   MØVE THE ACTIVE BLØCKS BEYØND FREED BLØCK.
    KINIT = BTABLE(J) + N
    KFIN = FREE(1) - 1
    DØ 10 K = KINIT, KFIN
 10 ASPACE(K-N) = ASPACE(K)
    FREE(1) = FREE(1) - N
    FREE(2) = FREE(2) + N
    END
```

EXERCISES

1. Modify the ALLØC1 subroutine to indicate which return was used in a given case: the one that indicates insufficient BTABLE size or the one that indicates insufficient ASPACE size.

2. The dead entries in BTABLE represent wasted space. How can the ALLØC1 (and possibly FREE1) routine be modified to make use of these locations?

13.3 ALLOCATION WITH NONMOVABLE BLOCKS

The Structure

The second allocation scheme to be considered assumes that blocks, once allocated, are not moved as long as they remain active. When blocks are freed, their space is marked and used as appropriate for subsequent allocations. As before, all blocks are allocated from a large array, BSPACE. A reference table BTABLE will be used. The same pointer scheme as before can be used here, pointers in BTABLE pointing to the starts of allocated blocks, with some modification as given below.

We have noted that, in this method of allocation, we may not move blocks. Thus, as some blocks are freed, the available space for future allocations may consist of several disconnected memory areas. We therefore must mark the freed blocks. Let us again assume a two-word entry per allocated block, in BTABLE. A pointer in the calling program can point directly to a block, because the block will not move. The second word in the BTABLE entry will be used in two ways. First, the sign of this word will be set '+' if the associated block is allocated and set '−' if the block is freed. Second, the rest of the word will contain the size of the allocated block. Even after a block is freed, its size will remain in the word. Figure 13.6 illustrates a situation where three blocks, A, B, and C, were allocated as before. A count CNT indicates the number of allocated blocks in use. BEGPTR and ENDPTR contain pointers to the start and end of the pool. Jointly they serve the same purpose as the two-word FREE array in the last case.

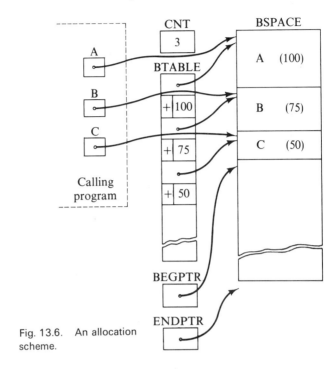

Fig. 13.6.   An allocation scheme.

Allocation Subroutine

The call for allocated space is as follows:

CALL ALLØC2(name,size)

A flowchart of the procedure is shown in Figure 13.7. Initially, size is compared with the available space, ENDPTR − BEGPTR. If there is sufficient space, a block is allocated; these are the steps:

1. CNT is increased by one.
2. Both name and the next entry, BTABLE(2*CNT − 1), are set to have pointers to the new space entered.
3. The size is entered into the next BTABLE entry.
4. BEGPTR is reset to the remaining free area, being increased by size.

This procedure is, however, only an initial version, for it does not take into account the presence of marked, freed blocks.

Now we must consider the possibility that some blocks may be freed and that free spaces exist between still active areas. In contrast to the earlier allocation

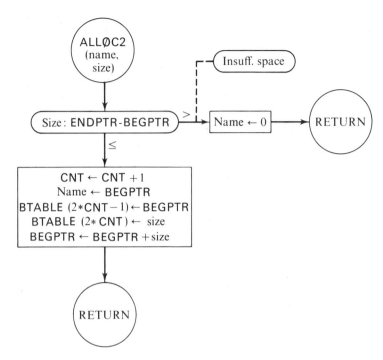

Fig. 13.7.   An ALLØC2 subroutine (initial version).

scheme of Section 13.2, those free spaces cannot be moved and consolidated into one free area. We must search through all free areas, checking to see if any is large enough to accommodate the current request, and if not then use the pool.

It is necessary to search for available space by examining BTABLE entries. We note that in BTABLE we look for entries where (1) the second word is negative and (2) the number in that word is nonzero. In other words, the second word contents (as a number) must be less than zero. Having found such an entry, we check on the size of the free block. If that size exceeds or equals the requested size, part or all of that space can be used. The balance (if there is any) must be accounted for by the establishment of a new entry in BTABLE with a pointer to it, the size of it, and an indication that the block is free.

The revised ALLØC2 subroutine appears flowcharted in Figure 13.8. Box 1 does indexing during the search for available space. Box 2 checks for the proper value in the second word in a BTABLE entry. Box 3 checks for a fit; the absolute value of the entry word is checked against _size_. Box 4 is encountered if the free space is larger than needed. A search is then made for a free entry in BTABLE, starting at the beginning of that table. Boxes 4 and 5 are involved in that search. If there is no room for a new BTABLE entry, the whole free space is used. In box 6 the new BTABLE entry is established. This action is illustrated in Figure 13.9. Adding _size_ to the first word of the existing BTABLE entry creates a new pointer

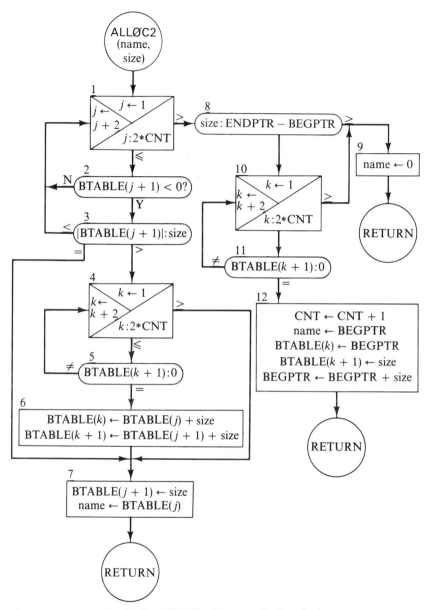

Fig. 13.8.   ALLØC2 subroutine (final version).

<u>size</u> location later in memory, thus pointing to a block smaller than the original
free block by that amount. Adding <u>size</u> to the second word of the entry *reduces*
the size by the allocated amount, for the sign in that second word is ' − '. Figure
13.9 shows this process. There a 500-word block was found for use by a 350-word
allocation request.

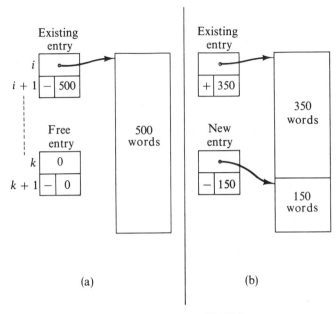

Fig. 13.9.   Creating a new BTABLE entry.

The entry that refers to the allocated block must be set. By storing <u>size</u> in the second word, in box 7, the sign is set '+' and the allocation is nearly complete. If the available space exactly matches the requested size, boxes 4 through 6 are bypassed, but box 7 applies anyway. Additionally, the pointer from the calling program is set.

The remaining task is to test for sufficient space in the pool, pointed to by BEGPTR. That size is ENDPTR − BEGPTR; the test is done in box 8. A search must be made in BTABLE for room for an entry; this is done in boxes 10 and 11. Finally, in box 12, if space is found, the entry is created, the pointer from the calling program is set, and BEGPTR is increased by size.

The ALLØC2 subroutine is the following:

```
      SUBRØUTINE ALLØC2(NAME,SIZE)
      CØMMØN BTABLE(200), CNT, BEGPTR, ENDPTR
      INTEGER J, K, BTABLE, BEGPTR, ENDPTR
C     SEARCH FØR SPACE IN FREED AREAS.
      JFIN = 2 * CNT
   1  DØ 21 J = 1, JFIN, 2
   2  IF (BTABLE(J+1) .LT. 0) GØ TØ 21
   3  IF (ABS(BTABLE(J+1)) − SIZE) 21, 7, 4
  21  CØNTINUE
C     NØT SUFFICIENT SPACE IN FREED AREAS.  TRY PØØL.
   8  IF (SIZE .LE. ENDPTR−BEGPTR) GØ TØ 10
```

```
C    PØØL ALSØ TØØ SMALL.
   9  NAME = 0
      RETURN
C    PØØL HAS ENØUGH SPACE.
  10  DØ 22 K = 1, JFIN, 2
  11  IF (BTABLE(K+1) .EQ. 0) GØ TØ 12
  22  CØNTINUE
C    NØ SPACE IN BTABLE FØR NEW ENTRY.
      NAME = 0
      RETURN
C    MAKE NEW ALLØCATIØN.
  12  CNT = CNT + 1
      NAME = BEGPTR
      BTABLE(K) = BEGPTR
      BTABLE(K+1) = SIZE
      BEGPTR = BEGPTR + SIZE
      RETURN
C    HAVE A SPACE IN A FREED AREA, LARGER THAN NEEDED.
   4  DØ 62 K = 1, JFIN, 2
   5  IF (BTABLE(K+1) .EQ. 0) GØ TØ 6
  62  CØNTINUE
C    NØ SPACE IN BTABLE FØR NEW ENTRY.
      GØ TØ 70
C    MAKE NEW BTABLE ENTRY.
   6  BTABLE(K) + BTABLE(J) + SIZE
      BTABLE(K+1) = BTABLE(J+1) + SIZE
C    SET BTABLE ENTRY PRØPERLY FØR NEW BLØCK ALLØCATED.
   7  BTABLE(J+1) = SIZE
      NAME = BTABLE(J)
      RETURN
      END
```

Freeing Subroutine

The call for freeing an allocated area is

CALL   FREE2(name)

as before. The freeing procedure here differs from the previous one primarily because no active blocks are moved. We need only set the sign of the second word in the affected BTABLE entry to '−' and zero the pointer in <u>name</u>. As an example, the result of freeing block B is shown in Figure 13.10. Note that the entry in BTABLE for block B is unchanged, except for the introduction of the '−' sign. For consistency, all BTABLE entries can be zeroed and alternate signs set '−' prior to any allocation.

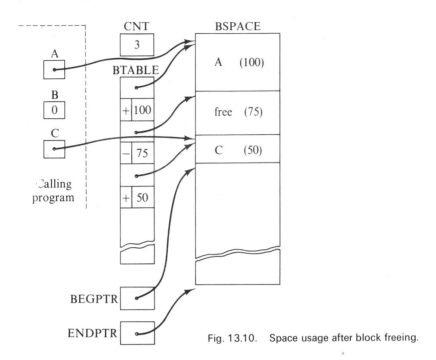

Fig. 13.10.   Space usage after block freeing.

Another operation should take place, for efficient use of freed space. It may happen that two adjacent allocated blocks are both freed. In that event, their space may be combined without affecting any other blocks. Figure 13.11 shows this situation, where blocks B and C were both freed, but a fourth block D had previously been allocated. This condition should be checked for, and the two adjacent spaces combined, as shown in Figure 13.12. We replace the two entries in BTABLE by a single entry, with a pointer to the start of the combined block, and add a new total size of that block equal to the sum of sizes. The signs remain '−', and the unused entry is otherwise set to zero in both words. That second entry space is now available for use as another BTABLE entry for a future allocation. We note that in general the entries in BTABLE may not be adjacent, even though their associated blocks may be.

Since it is possible that the freed block may be the last allocated in memory, just above the pool, this should be considered. This is true if the sum of the pointer in the associated entry and the size of the freed block equals the contents of BEGPTR; this equality implies that the block is just prior to the pool. Then, BEGPTR can be reduced by that size, and the final available space increases by that size.

The flowchart of the FREE2 subroutine appears in Figure 13.13. S_b is the size of BTABLE. Boxes 1 and 2 involve a search through BTABLE for the pointer to the block <u>name</u>. This is necessary because the pointer in the calling program is to the block, rather than to BTABLE as previously. There is a matching pointer

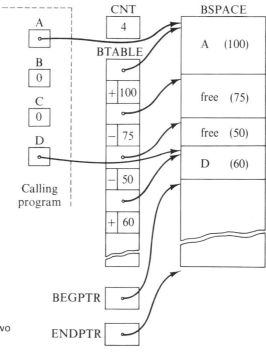

Fig. 13.11. Freeing two adjacent blocks.

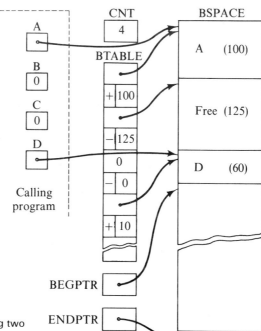

Fig. 13.12. Combining two adjacent free blocks.

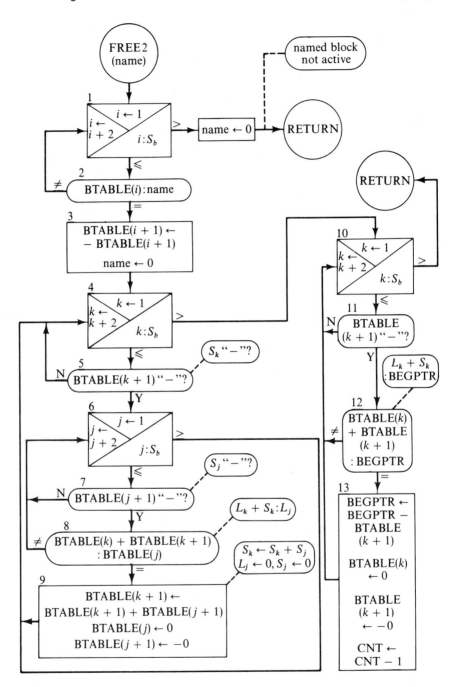

Fig. 13.13.   FREE2 subroutine.

in BTABLE, which is here sought. There is an error exit for the case of a name given not matching an allocated block. In box 3 the sign of the second word in the block entry in BTABLE is set ' − ', and the allocated size remains. Also, the pointer in name is set to zero. At this point the freeing operation is complete. However, we have noted that adjacent blocks should be combined.

We can now test for adjacent blocks as follows. Let L_A be the location of block A (i.e., the pointer to block A) and S_A be the size of A. Let L_B and S_B have similar meanings for block B. If

$$L_A + S_A = L_B$$

then A and B are adjacent, with B following A. (Note that the BTABLE entries for A and B need not be adjacent.) In this case, the B entry should be freed (the two words set to 0 and −0), and the A entry should be modified so that $S_A + S_B$ replaces S_A in the second word. Boxes 4–9 perform this combination. Each entry (index k) is compared with each other entry (index j), the match described above being sought. Note that subscripts (j) and (k) refer to L-entries, while subscripts ($j + 1$) and ($k + 1$) refer to S-entries. This process could be made somewhat more efficient by testing only if either index k or index j had the value i (the index of the entry just deleted).

A check for the case of the freed block's lying just above the pool is needed. We check to see if $L_A + S_A =$ BEGPTR. Boxes 10–13 check for this condition and eliminate an entry if appropriate. In this case, CNT is decreased by one.

The FREE2 subroutine is the following:

```
      SUBRØUTINE FREE2(NAME)
      CØMMØN BTABLE(200), CNT, BEGPTR, ENDPTR
      INTEGER J, K, BTABLE, BEGPTR, ENDPTR
C     SEARCH FØR PØINTER TØ NAMED BLØCK IN BTABLE.
    1 DØ 20 I = 1, 200, 2
    2 IF (BTABLE(I) .EQ. NAME) GØ TØ 3
   20 CØNTINUE
C     NAME GIVEN NØT AN ACTIVE BLØCK.
      NAME = 0
      RETURN
C     MARK BLØCK AS FREED AND DELETE REFERENCE.
    3 BTABLE(I+1) = −BTABLE(I+1)
      NAME = 0
C     TEST FØR ADJACENT FREED BLØCKS.
    4 DØ 40 K = 1, 200, 2
    5 IF (BTABLE(K+1) .GE. 0) GØ TØ 40
C     HAVE ØNE NEGATIVE ENTRY.
    6 DØ 30 J = 1, 200, 2
    7 IF (BTABLE(J+1) .GE. 0) GØ TØ 30
```

```
C    HAVE SECØND NEGATIVE ENTRY.
     8  IF (BTABLE(K) + BTABLE(K+1) .EQ. BTABLE(J)) GØ TØ 9
    30  CØNTINUE
C    CAN CØMBINE FREED AREAS.
     9  BTABLE(K+1) = BTABLE(K+1) + BTABLE(J+1)
        BTABLE(J) = 0
        BTABLE(J+1) = -0
    40  CØNTINUE
C    TEST FØR FREE AREA JUST ABØVE PØØL.
    10  DØ 50 K = 1, 200, 2
    11  IF (BTABLE(K+1) .GE. 0) GØ TØ 50
    12  IF (BTABLE(K) + BTABLE(K+1) .NE. BEGPTR) GØ TØ 50
C    HAVE FREE AREA JUST ABØVE...CØMBINE
    13  BEGPTR = BEGPTR - BTABLE(K+1)
        BTABLE(K) = 0
        BTABLE(K+1) = -0
        CNT = CNT - 1
    50  CØNTINUE
        RETURN
        END
```

EXERCISES

1. Modify the ALLØC2 subroutine to indicate the type of failure occurring when it is impossible to allocate the requested block.

2. The process of checking for two adjacent freed areas in FREE2 (boxes 4–9 in Figure 13.13) can be made more efficient if testing for the condition is done only if either index j or index k has the value i (the index of the entry of the block just freed). Rewrite FREE2 to do this.

13.4 ALLOCATION WITH LINKED LISTS

The Structure

The third allocation scheme to be considered applies to a special structure, a linked list, studied in Chapter 12. For simplicity, we shall assume the following: (1) four-word blocks are used throughout the structure, linked to each other by pointers to head locations of other blocks (addresses of the initial words in the blocks); (2) the list structures only have forward pointers to succeeding blocks, these pointers occupying the fourth word of each block; (3) to permit branching, a dual pointer system is used, the third and fourth words of a block *both* being used as pointers to different succeeding blocks. Free space, from which blocks are allocated, comprises a simply linked list of four-word blocks, so set initially. When a block is freed, it is added immediately to the free list by moving pointers only; no blocks are ever moved, either during allocation or freeing. Figure 13.14 illustrates a structure composed of blocks and pointers; also shown is the free list of linked blocks, called the "available space list" (ASL). All allocated space is taken from a large linear array CSPACE.

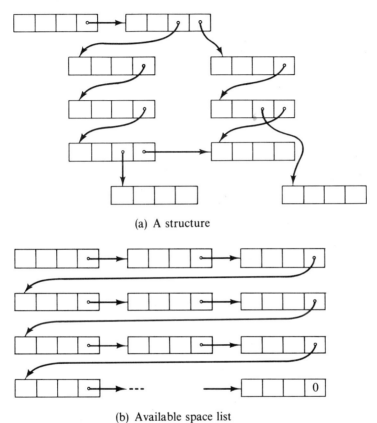

(a) A structure

(b) Available space list

Fig. 13.14.   A data structure.

The pointers within the data structure are of no concern to the storage allocator; they are established by the calling program that merely asks for blocks as required. The allocator merely supplies the four-word blocks, returning a pointer to head words to the calling program. The freeing subroutine, being given such a pointer, merely returns the block to the ASL.

Allocation Subroutine

The call for an allocated four-word block is

CALL ALLØC3(name)

No size is given because allocated blocks are fixed in size. The effect of a call to the allocator is shown in Figure 13.15: (a) shows the configuration before allocation, while (b) shows the configuration afterwards. A word in memory, BEGPTR, points to the head of the ASL, so that the allocator can refer to and allocate a block. Another word, ENDPTR, points to the last block in the ASL. Blocks are not marked as allocated or free; their absence or presence in the ASL determines their status. The blocks in the ASL are initially sequentially located in memory, but after several are allocated and freed, they may be randomly linked; this is irrelevant in general for linked lists (cf. Section 12.4). In Figure 13.15, once block A has been allocated, there is still a residual pointer in the block to the ASL. This is unimportant, since BEGPTR now points to the block beyond block A. The calling program will utilize the block as required, overwriting that pointer.

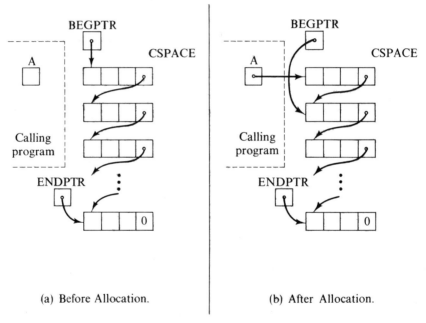

(a) Before Allocation.   (b) After Allocation.

Fig. 13.15.   Allocation of a block.

A flowchart of ALLØC3 appears in Figure 13.16. The procedure, as we can see, is quite simple. First, a test must be made to see if any space is left in the ASL, in CSPACE. Once the last block has been allocated, BEGPTR contains zero. This can also be seen in Figure 13.15, where the new value of BEGPTR is taken from the last word of the block just allocated; in the case of the last block in the ASL, this value is zero. Thus, the test for space is a zero test of BEGPTR. Following this, if space is left, <u>name</u> is set to the value of BEGPTR, i.e., a pointer is established to the first block in the ASL. Then, the pointer located in the last word of the newly allocated block is moved to BEGPTR.

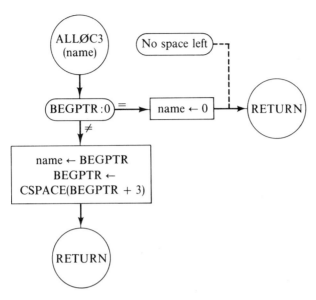

Fig. 13.16.   The ALLØC3 subroutine.

The ALLØC3 subroutine is the following:

```
      SUBRØUTINE ALLØC3(NAME)
      CØMMØN CSPACE(5000), BEGPTR, ENDPTR
      INTEGER BEGPTR, ENDPTR
      IF (BEGPTR .EQ. 0) GØ TØ 10
C     HAVE A BLØCK TØ ALLØCATE.
      NAME = BEGPTR
      BEGPTR = CSPACE(BEGPTR+3)
      RETURN
C     NØ SPACE REMAINING.
   10 NAME = 0
      RETURN
      END
```

Freeing Subroutine

The call for freeing a four-word block is

CALL FREE3(name)

After a block is freed, it is to be added to the ASL. Figure 13.17 shows the situation after block A of Figure 13.15 is freed, assuming no other blocks were allocated. The freeing subroutine is also quite simple, but one special case must be specially considered. That case occurs when no space remains in the ASL. In that situation, BEGPTR is zero, and ENDPTR points to the last block allocated; the value of ENDPTR is actually irrelevant in this case.

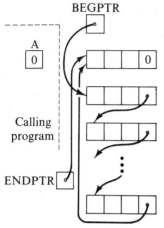

BEGPTR

A
0

Calling
program

ENDPTR

Fig. 13.17.   Freeing of a block.

The flowchart for FREE3 appears in Figure 13.18. Initially, a test is made for zero BEGPTR. If that word is zero, then both BEGPTR and ENDPTR are caused to point at the word being freed. Additionally, the last word of the freed block is set to zero, as required. Finally, name is set to zero, as always. If, on the other hand, there was at least one block in the ASL previously, the procedure is different. The last word in the ASL, which is zero, is set to point where name points, thus adding a new link to the linked list. In addition, ENDPTR is set to point where name points. Then, as with the special case, the new last word in the ASL is set to zero, as is name. Since the last three statements in each rectangular box of the flowchart are identical, the procedure can be simplified, as reflected in the following, the FREE3 subroutine:

```
        SUBRØUTINE FREE3(NAME)
        CØMMØN CSPACE(5000), BEGPTR, ENDPTR
        INTEGER BEGPTR, ENDPTR
        IF (BEGPTR .NE. 0) GØ TØ 20
  C     HERE IF NØ SPACE AT START.
        CSPACE(ENDPTR+3) = NAME
        GØ TØ 30
  C     HERE IF SPACE AT START.
    20  BEGPTR = NAME
  C     CØMMØN SEQUENCE ØF CØDE.
        ENDPTR = NAME
        CSPACE(ENDPTR+3) = 0
        NAME = 0
        RETURN
        END
```

EXERCISES

1. Write a subroutine CØMBIN to combine two separate available space lists. The call:

   CALL CØMBIN(list1,list2)

   where list1 and list2 are the two lists; return one pointer to the combined list, which is then called list1.

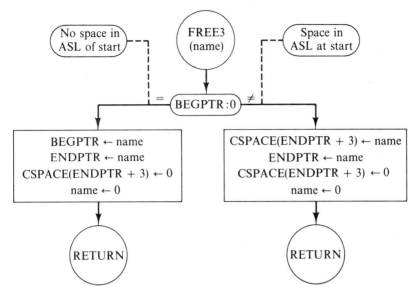

Fig. 13.18.   The FREE3 subroutine.

2. Write a subroutine to realize the branching blocks shown in Figure 13.14. These blocks have two pointers each; two are shown in that figure. The call:

   CALL BRANCH(brname)

   where brname is the location of the block to become a branch. The available space list is to provide both appended blocks.

14 DATA MANAGEMENT

In earlier chapters, much attention was paid to the problems of defining and manipulating data. After all, computer operation is based upon such processes. Specifically, Chapter 9 was concerned with input-output processes; Section 9.5 dealt with files of information. Chapter 12 considered the various ways in which data might be structured in core memory. Chapter 13 described a related process, that of allocating core memory space for structures. The present chapter rounds out the picture by extending the structuring concepts of Chapter 12 to the kinds of files introduced in Chapter 9. In short, we now take up the problem of structuring files.

We go farther than mere structuring considerations here, however; we also deal with the several problems involved in storage and retrieval of data from files. We shall see how this problem is related to several encountered earlier. We will broaden the scope of data processing to include auxiliary memory.

14.1 PURPOSE AND SCOPE

A Definition

The term *data management*, as defined here, involves the storage, maintenance, and retrieval of information in machine-readable form, through the use of computers. "Machine-readable" information can be read by computer, as can magnetic tape or disk, for example. This definition only partially describes the scope of "data management"; a reading of this chapter will much more clearly provide the scope.[1]

Data management problems for in-core data structures certainly exist; we have studied many of them in Chapters 12 and 13. When we consider auxiliary memory, however, the problems multiply considerably, for the physical characteristics of the storage device and storage medium must be considered. In auxiliary memory, all units of data (such as 32-bit words) are not equally accessible as in core. Part of the data management function is to take physical characteristics into account. We shall use the word "file" to refer to collections of data in auxiliary memory, as opposed to collections of data in core.

Functions

A number of well-defined functions of a data management system can be described; many of these shall be described in Section 14.3. We will list them here and briefly describe each of them.

A preliminary task is the definition of a file. By this is meant the designing of the file, taking into account the physical structure of the storage device, and the structure of the data. When a file is defined, rules for storage and retrieval are implied.

Information storage is a function of major importance. In order to have a file to process and utilize, it is necessary to create it, i.e., to store information in it. The storage function is performed according to the rules defined for this purpose, mentioned in the last paragraph.

Once a file is created, it is necessary to be able to process the data within it. Every process involves, to a lesser or greater extent, a search of all or part of the file. Thus, we can list a searching function next. Whether we wish to extract information from a file or add more to it, or whether we wish to change stored information or completely reorder it, it is necessary that specific entries in the file, somehow identified, be located. Thus the searching function, auxiliary to most user-oriented functions, is one that must be available.

Files are commonly created but once and maintained over long periods of time. The editing or maintenance function involves making new additions to, changes in, and deletions from an existing file. In a broad sense, one can even consider the initial creation as a special case of file addition, addition to a null file. Editing tasks are performed so often that we must consider the means whereby editing can be both convenient and efficient.

Finally, if files are to be useful collections of data, information must be retrieved from them. The retrieval function takes many forms, including the generation of a small list of items meeting certain selection criteria on demand, as well as lengthy comprehensive reports prepared on a regular basis. If retrieval is done frequently, operating efficiency here, too, is vital.

Consequences

We now explore briefly the consequences of establishing a computer-based data management system. We may note initially that the usual advantages that accrue from computer utilization in any problem area exist here. Additionally, there are other points to note that come about because of the particular nature of data management. This approach to information organization and utility provides a service to other programs, that of managing their data, and so provides these special benefits.

Utilization of data management system implies a standardization of file structures, over the areas in which the system is used. Sometimes, a wide group of users will make use of a particular file. If the data management system is used to create and process the file, by its nature it will produce a standard structure. Programs that do not even utilize the data management system to process data in the file can be written with a knowledge of the structure.

A related aspect of the interrelationship of separate computer programs is their communication. Large programming systems must be written in small segments, as we have seen, and the problem of communication, i.e., of transferring data among them, is critical. Programs that jointly use the same data management system can be more efficiently combined because the system provides standard ways of transmitting data. These data can be transmitted between programs as readily as between a program and a file.

Finally, we point out what is almost obvious: that a data management system makes practical the use of a large collection of data, highly organized in a manner suitable to a given problem. Very early in this text, in Chapter 1, we noted that one reason for the use of computers to solve problems was their ability to provide rapid access to large amounts of information. It is this point we now re-emphasize, adding now the features that data management provides.

As we study in some depth the specific data management functions we shall realize in what specific ways the above-mentioned benefits are the consequences of the systems described.

EXERCISES

1. Give examples of machine-readable information and information in other forms. Why is the former more useful?
2. Files are common in many aspects of business. Consider an ordinary filing system that a small business might maintain, and describe the several functions of file processing, as listed.

14.2 FILES

Review

In Section 9.5, we studied files of information in relation to input-output processes. Here we shall review that material before going on to other file concepts. The files considered were limited to magnetic-tape files for simplicity; in this section we shall examine disk files as well. Three classes of files were studied; (a) *scratch files* are temporary files, created during computer runs and not used afterwards; (b) *input files* are read during computer runs; they may be permanent files created by earlier program runs and represent collections of data stored for a period of time; (3) *output files* are written during program runs; they usually become input files for the future.

With respect to FORTRAN, a system input tape (or file) and system output tape (or file) were identified; these files supplied programs and their data as input, and they supplied the results of computations as output. Special tape designations ('5' and '6') are used for these files; other designations are used for other files of the three types described above.

Those files are but special cases of the files to be studied here. They are all sequential, i.e., each record follows the one before in sequence. To retrieve the ith record, it is necessary to read the previous $i - 1$ records. If a data structure other than this linear one is desired, it must be imbedded within the sequence in the manner that a structure is imbedded in linearly-addressed core memory. The significant difference between a core structure and a magnetic-tape structure, however, is the random accessibility of the former; magnetic tapes must be written and read sequentially. We will study disks, which provide a far greater degree of randomness in accessibility.

Structure of Storage Devices

We shall examine several methods by which files may be organized, with consideration given to the physical nature of magnetic disks. Most storage media other than tapes have characteristics very similar to disks, so the study of disks is of general application. Attention must be paid to physical characteristics because they greatly influence file organization.

Let us briefly examine the structure of disk memory and its addressing scheme. A magnetic disk contains a series of concentric tracks, each of which contains information in magnetic bit positions, much in the manner of magnetic tape. A disk track contains about 30,000 bits of information. Thus, for a 30-bit word computer, approximately 1000 words of information can be stored on a track. Each disk contains about 200 tracks.

A disk storage unit contains a number of disks stacked upon each other, with about one-half inch spacing between them. Read-write heads on arms that pivot permit access to each of the tracks on each disk surface. Generally, two surfaces are available on each disk for storage. The read-write heads are physically linked so that they move in and out across the disk radius together. Thus, in any one of about 200 head positions, $2n - 2$ tracks can be read, if $n =$ the number of disks in a stack. (The uppermost and lowermost disk surfaces are not used for storage.)

A certain amount of time is required to move the stack of read-write heads from position to position, this time being dependent upon the distance moved. About 100 milliseconds is required in an average move. On the other hand, no significant time is required to go from track to track in one head position.

Consequently, all the $2n$ tracks in one such position can be considered as a unit of storage, the next-higher unit above a track itself. Such a unit is termed a *cylinder*, by its physical nature. The disk storage structure is depicted in Figure 14.1. If we assume that there are 11 disks in all, then each cylinder comprises 20 tracks or about 600,000 bits.

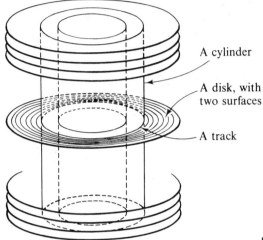

A cylinder

A disk, with
two surfaces

A track

Fig. 14.1.   A disk unit.

As a consequence of this structure, we can consider disk memory to be organized in the manner shown in Figure 14.2. There are NM strings of information, where N = the number of tracks in a cylinder, and M = the number of cylinders. In the disk unit assumed, $N = 20$ and $M = 200$. Each track is addressed by giving a cylinder address and a surface address.

One other aspect of disk addressing must be considered. The disk unit continually rotates at high speed, typically 2400 revolutions per minute (rpm). At that speed, 25 milliseconds are required per revolution. Each track must be read at its starting point, which is specially marked by the storage unit. Average access time, at 2400 rpm, is therefore 12.5 milliseconds.

The design of a particular data structure for disk unit must take into account three factors. First, the memory organization of the disk, as described above, is important, for it is not true that all information is equally accessible. The sizes of tracks, cylinders, and whole disk units, as well as the various access times, must all be taken into account. Second, the inherent structure of the data, considered in earlier chapters, is important. Third, the manner in which the data are to be processed is very significant. When data structures were considered in Chapter 12, only the second and third of these factors had to be considered.

Characteristics of Files

Chapter 9 contained several definitions pertaining to files. A *file* was defined as a set of ordered records; a first, next, and last record can be identified. A *record*

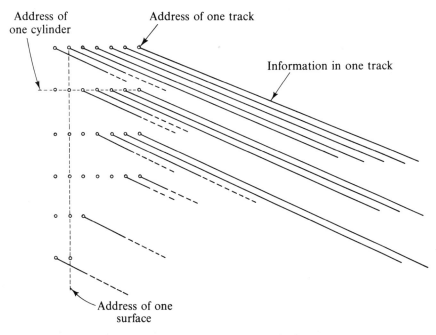

Fig. 14.2.   Disk unit memory organization.

was defined as a convenient unit of information, specifically that information read or written by the execution of a single input-output statement. A *field* was defined as the smallest part of a record that is addressed by a program.

It is useful to be able to give a symbolic name to each of the fields in a record, as was seen earlier. When a file is created, the several attributes of a field (size, type, value) can be given, along with its name. Subsequently, upon searching, only the name need be given. If there are many records of the same structure in a file, the field names apply to the same field positions in all the records.

Let us reexamine the file definitions in the light of the specific storage device now under consideration, the disk unit. The definition of a file still applies, but we now must impart an order to the tracks and/or surfaces of the disk. Clearly, within each track, records are ordered in sequence along the track. A set of tracks, however, has no such inherent order. If we imagine tree structures to be stored on disk, we realize that it is not necessary to consider all the records in all the tracks to be in a single sequence, because we can branch down different paths of the tree. We may only search a fraction of the records in the file for a particular one. However, if a complete search of the file is needed for some reason, all tracks must be searched in *some* order; that order imparts a total order to all records.

A record is now not conveniently defined by input-output statement execution. In the execution of a single disk read operation, an entire track may be read into core. Alternatively a specific record may be read. The track may contain several records. A record will now be redefined as a group of records that are some-how associated with one other, generally, by a common characteristic. For example, a record for an electrical part may contain fields with these items: part number, price, manufacturer, type of component, value, and rating. An important characteristic of a record, particularly within the kinds of files we are now con-sidering, is its *key*. The *key* is a field within the record that uniquely identifies the record. In the example above, the key would most likely be the part number. Frequently, a file is sorted on a key, to make a retrieval an easier task.

A file may have two keys. In the case of parts, these may be manufacturer and part number. Possibly, part numbers are not unique in the file, so both fields are required to identify a specific part uniquely. Or, alternately, it may be neces-sary to search the file in either of two ways, by part number or by manufacturer. If the file is sorted, it is sorted first on one key (say, manufacturer) and then, within the same manufacturer, by part number. Table 14.1 illustrates part of such a file.

TABLE 14.1 RECORDS OF A FILE SORTED ON TWO KEYS

ABC MANUFACTURING	56908	...
ABC MANUFACTURING	67909	...
ABC MANUFACTURING	75252	...
ABC MANUFACTURING	80222	...
BRØWN CØMPUTING CØ.	9005	...
BRØWN CØMPUTING CØ.	10554	...
BRØWN CØMPUTING CØ.	22222	...
...	...	...
...	...	...

A record key (or keys) is used to locate a record within a file. Alternatively, a record may be sought by its contents. For example, in the parts file, we may wish to examine all resistors having values between 500 and 1000 ohms. Now, unless resistors are separately grouped within the file and sorted by value, all records must be examined. The record keys are of no help in this instance.

When a file must be searched frequently for nonkey fields, an additional file, a *cross-reference file*, can be created. Its records are sorted by values of those fields. For example, resistors may be sorted by value, as suggested. In such cases, these additional records may be incomplete to save space, but then reference must be made also to the main file. Usually the second reference is made by a key extracted from the cross-reference file.

Methods of File Organization and Access

Files may be organized in two general manners. In a *sequential file*, the keys of physically adjacent records are in ascending or descending order. In other words, the file is sorted as described previously. In a *random file*, keys of physically adjacent records have no simple relationships. As we shall see, there may be a definite relationship among adjacent keys in a random file, but it may be quite complex.

The ideally organized file achieves the optimum balance between performance and storage utilization. More specifically, the output is achieved in a minimal time, the available storage area is utilized to the maximum, and data are accessible by a variety of keys or field contents. Clearly, depending upon storage medium, data structure, and manner of requests for processing, some compromises are required in file design.

There are several methods of file access, i.e., methods of locating records in a physical storage device. Four methods are described here; these are the serial, indexed, direct, and indirect access methods.

In *serial access*, every record is scanned until the required record is found. This method applies only to sequential files. Since a file must then be searched from start to finish, this approach is slow. If magnetic tapes must be used, however, only this method can be used.

In *indexed access*, a record is located by reference to one or more indices. A table is required; it contains keys given in order, with associated record addresses. A key is given, from which a record address is determined from the table. In this approach, only the required section of the file need be searched, so accessing is fast. On the other hand, there is the disadvantage that the table must be maintained along with the file.

In *direct access*, the record key is converted to an address in a track, which locates the record. Specifically, the key is divided by the number of records in a track: The quotient is the track address, and the remainder is the record position in the track. Alternatively, the quotient may be a combined surface and track address pair. In this method, each record has a unique address (hence the name *direct*), and records are of fixed-length and must have numeric keys. A direct-access device (disk, drum, etc.) is used, and the file is sequential. Direct access is very fast and no index is required, but because of fixed-length and numeric-key requirements, applications may be limited.

In *indirect access*, the record location is determined by computing the storage address from the key. The computation compresses the range of keys to a smaller range of addresses. The result is to have some keys with the same address; these are called *synonyms*. The synonyms lead to storage problems that can be handled by randomizing techniques, considered in the next section. The file is used in a "random" way and records are of fixed length.

There are *combined-access* methods, incorporating features from each of two access methods. In *indexed-serial access*, one or more indices are used to locate the address of a small part of the physical device; records in this part are then accessed serially. This method is the most important of the several described. If we consider the memory organization depicted in Figure 14.2, we can see its applicability there. Two indices can be used to supply the surface and track addresses. Then, the records in each track can be accessed serially. The given key is sought in the index table, from which the two addresses are determined.

In *indexed-direct access*, an index is used to locate the starting address of a range of records. Then, as in direct access, the key is converted to a specific track access, relative to the start of the range of records for the index.

Storage Randomized

Direct access is very fast, for a simple computation converts a record key into its physical address in a file. If record keys within the set of records are uniformly distributed over the range of key values, this method is very efficient in space utilization. For example, assume that a file of student records is stored in order of identification number, and that all such numbers in a range are used. Then, direct access yields an optimal space utilization, under the added assumption that all student records are fixed in size.

On the other hand, if the record keys are nonuniformly distributed, as a file of parts keyed by part number might be, space will be unevenly used. If the distribution is very uneven, there may be very poor use of space. As an example, assume that part numbers are six digits long and that there are 5000 parts in a file. Then, 5000 records may suffice; assume 50 tracks of 200 records each are available. However, only 5000/1,000,000 or 0.5 percent of the possible part numbers are used. The distribution may be very uneven. If direct access techniques are used, the part number would be divided by 50 (the number of available tracks). The result may be that a very large fraction of all records would be assigned to one track. In this case, many keys would be converted to the same physical location, resulting in synonyms, as described earlier. Since no more than one record can be stored at one location, other means for converting keys to locations are required.

The indirect access method, as mentioned, involves using special computations to compress the range of keys into the range of available locations. More specifically, an attempt is made to take random keys and convert these to a uniformly distributed set of storage locations. Because even with such techniques, there is a chance for duplication of addresses, a somewhat larger area is allocated than is strictly required. Thus, in the example above, 10,000 records can be stored in the 50 tracks, while only 5000 records are actually stored. The more space made available, the less likely duplication (synonyms) will occur, but the greater the cost in storage.

One solution to these problems is to use *randomizing* techniques. These techniques are used to transform a set of keys into a set of addresses with approximately uniform distribution. The transformation appears to be random because there is usually no simple relationship among keys in adjacent locations in storage; the keys appear to be randomly stored.

In a simple randomizing method, the value of the key, if it is numeric, is processed arithmetically. For example, the center four digits may be squared; then the result may be centrally truncated to four digits, which become the storage address. Consider part number 563894. The square of the center four digits is 6389^2 or 40819321. The center four digits of this number, 8193, become the record address. This particular scheme works if the given part numbers are distributed such that this transformation yields uniformly distributed addresses. Note that these computed addresses each become a pair of addresses: a surface address and a track address.

There are more complex methods that attempt to make uniform the storage addresses. Some of these involve an analysis of some or all of the digits in the keys. Generally, the digits chosen are those that are already most uniformly distributed over the 10 possibilities. The effect of the computation is an expansion of the key range to very large virtual addresses. However, high-order address digits are dropped, so that the effect is that of rapidly cycling through addresses. This results in a more uniform assignment of addresses through the actual addresses. Another aspect of this approach is the fact that the sum of the digits under consideration is the prime factor in determining the computed address. The sum of the digits of random numbers generally tends to provide a more uniform distribution of values than the numbers themselves.

File Structure

We have considered the various ways in which files may be organized and accessed. Let us consider files in somewhat greater detail now. Generally, a file contains a number of sections, only a few of which may be accessed over a given period of time. Consider a student file, ordered by identification number (ID number). If ID numbers are assigned to students chronologically, perhaps in the order in which they register, then all the members of one class will have ID numbers within a specific range. (A few spare numbers would probably be reserved for students transferring into the school partially through their college careers.) Thus, it might be that numbers are assigned as follows:

Seniors:	45577–45687
Juniors:	45688–45800
Sophomores:	45801–45904
Freshmen:	45905–46018

If frequently only data for one class at a time were to be processed, then four separate sections of the file should be created. Such sections are termed *subfiles*, though each is in effect a file itself. When it is known that one class subfile is to be accessed, the search can proceed directly on that subfile. If, on the other hand, an ID number is given, the table above would be referenced initially to determine the subfile of interest. The separate tracks of a disk unit make ideal physical divisions for use as subfiles, provided subfiles are small enough to fit within single tracks. If not, then groups of tracks can serve as subfiles.

Another concern in file structure is the format of individual records. For example, if the student-record file (last studied in Section 9.5) is again considered, each record will have such information as: name, class, major, number of courses, information on each course, weighted average, five top grades, and an indication of whether the student qualifies for the honor society. Since the number of courses completed is variable, it is necessary either to have records of fixed length or to include a count of the size of the records. In order for the records to be accessed from the file, information must be available on their format. Using the FORTRAN conventions for format specification, we can describe the record format as follows:

(7A4,A2,I2,A4,I3,n(A4,7A4,A2,F1.0,F3.0,A3),F4.1,5F5.0,A1)

where n is the number of courses the student has taken. This format specification was derived from the FØRMAT statements in Example 9.2; the specifications used to skip fields on punched cards (e.g., '2X') were deleted, for they are unnecessary.

We saw, in Section 9.2., that greater flexibility can be built into a program if the data format can be supplied during program execution. We can achieve this if the specification given above is stored in the file itself. It might be stored in a separate subfile and always be read before the data records are accessed. There is the following very definite advantage to this approach. After a file is created, and many programs have been written that access the file, it is possible to change the record format with impunity, as long as the format specification is changed accordingly. The coding in the programs that use the file require no changes at all. Files that incorporate the format specifications are sometimes termed *self-formatted files*.

The power of this approach can be enhanced if other information is added to the file. Each field in a record can be given a symbolic name. The added information might be stored in a form such as this:

(NAME(A30),CLASS(I2),MAJØR(A4),NUMBER(I3),n(CØURSE(A4),
   TITLES(A30),CREDS(F1.0),GRADES(F3.0),TERMS(A3),
   WAVER(F4.1),TGRADS(5F5.0),QUAL(A1))

Now the file-reading program, when reading the format information also reads field names and stores them in a table. Subsequently, a program calls for the values of these fields by name only. The programmer need not know where specific fields are located in the records. In other words, he may list the variables in any order in an input-output statement. The term *dictionary* is sometimes used to refer to the list of format information given above.

EXERCISES

1. The problem of searching a tree for a particular branch was studied in Section 12.5. Imagine that searching had to be linear, as on a tape, rather than random. About how many times as slow would this kind of searching be?

2. Consider the three factors that affect the design of a data structure (under "Structure of Storage Devices"). Specifically, how do these factors affect the structure designed? Consider several cases.

3. Describe a cross-reference file for a parts file. Refer to Table 14.1.

4. Give specific details for each type of file access method described in the text (under "Methods of File Organization and Access"). Choose small files as examples.

$$* \quad * \quad * \quad * \quad * \quad *$$

5. Consider a personnel file of 5000 persons, with each person's data in one record of 20 words. Individuals are organized by department (40 to a department) and then by division (5 departments to a division).
   (a) Design a physical file, on one surface of the disk organized for rapid access by department. Consider indexed access.
   (b) Design a physical file, organized for rapid access by age or length of service of an individual. Consider direct access.

6. Any file is likely to grow in time. Modify the files designed in Exercise 5 to allow for the growth of each department to double the size given, yet retain a certain measure of efficiency.

7. Consider one further complexity. Allow department sizes to vary from 20 to 100, yet retain efficient use of disk space.

8. Would combined access methods be of value in these files? If so, redesign the files on this basis.

14.3 BASIC FILE PROCESSES

General

Several data management file-processing functions were briefly described in Section 14.1. We shall consider them here in greater detail, illustrating their operation by a specific example. The student-record processing problem of earlier chapters will be studied once again. A file for this information will be created, and the several file processes will be coded.

The Data

Let us review the data that we have defined on student records. A student identification (ID) number will be included for each student as a record key; all references to the file will be assumed made via that key. We shall group all the data on one student into one record; the separate parts of the record are called *subrecords*. The card formats, as used in the past, are the following, which have one new item (the ID number) for each student:

One card:

Columns 1–30:	student's name (alphanumeric)
Columns 31–32:	student's class (integer)
Columns 35–38:	major subject (alphanumeric)
Columns 40–45:	student's ID number (integer)

One card:

>   Columns 1–3:   number of grades or courses (integer)

Several cards, one per course:

>   Columns   1–4:   course number (alphanumeric)
>   Columns 7–36:   course title (alphanumeric)
>   Column   38:   number of credits (floating point)
>   Columns 40–42:   grade (floating point)
>   Columns 44–46:   term taken (alphanumeric)

In the files created in Example 9.2, other information was added, but this was not present in the punched cards. The added information was computed by the program that created the file.

   Now let us consider the file records. We assume the file is binary, as described in Section 9.5. Each record comprises an integral number of words, the equivalent of the space in core memory required for the data. A "word" on disk is a sequence of bits, equal in number to the size of a core memory word. The sequence of subrecords for a student is the following:

One subrecord:

>   Word   1:   student's ID number
>   Words 2–9:   student's name
>   Word   10:   student's class
>   Word   11:   major subject
>   Word   12:   number of grades

Several subrecords, one per course:

>   Word   1:   course number
>   Words 2–9:   course title
>   Word   10:   number of credits
>   Word   11:   grade
>   Word   12:   term taken

One subrecord:

>   Word   1:   weighted average
>   Words 2–6:   five top grades

For simplicity, we shall omit the data on whether a student qualifies for the honor society. The code is much simpler as a result.

Disk Commands

   Let us consider the design of a disk file for the information. We assume the following disk unit: It has 200 cylinders, 20 surfaces, and holds 1000 words in each track. There are thus 20 tracks per cylinder, numbered from 0 to 19. The cylinders are numbered from 0 to 199. Words in each track are addressed from 000 to 999. The following statements are used for disk input-output:

(a) CALL SEEKTR(cylinder,track)

   CALL SEEKRC(cylinder,track,loc,size)

where cylinder is the cylinder address, track is the track address, loc is the word location in a track, and size is the size of the record. If loc and size are not given, as in the first case, the start of the track is located and the entire track is accessed.

The seek subroutines locate a track or record and perform no input-output.

(b) READ (3) list-of-variables

   WRITE (3) list-of-variables

where list-of-variables is the usual list associated with READ and WRITE statement; file 3 is the disk unit.

The seek subroutines, given the addresses and location specified, position the read-write heads and activate the proper one. They cause the proper track or record to be read into a buffer within the operating system, so that the following READ or WRITE statement can then be used as normal.

This imaginary manner of reading and writing disk is similar to actual techniques used. SEEK instructions position read-write heads, though in a somewhat different manner.

File Access

Let us consider the size of the records. The maximum number of courses a student might take is about 40, though we might allow a maximum of 50. Thus, the record for one student has $12 + 50(12) + 6$, or 620 words, approximately. The average record might be $12 + 20(12) + 6$, or 260 words, approximately.

If we allow the maximum space for each record, only one record can be placed on a track. If there are 2000 students, 2000 tracks or 100 cylinders, one-half of the disk unit, are required. On the other hand, if we allocate space for records so that none is wasted, we can place about four records on a track, requiring 500 tracks or 25 cylinders, one-tenth of the unit. Let us examine both approaches.

First, consider a direct access method. Assume that ID numbers are assigned in sequence, as students register. If, at a given time, all active numbers fall within a narrow range (with possible gaps), then direct access can be used. For example, suppose all active numbers lie in the range 024570 to 028400, a range of 3830. Then track 0 on cylinder 0 can hold record 024570, track 1 can hold record 024571, etc. In other words, records are assigned in sequence by ID number to the available tracks. The 2000 records, over a range of 3830 ID numbers, would require as many tracks, with almost half the space unused. The key, the ID number, gives the record position directly, as follows:

1. Subtract 24570 from the ID number (which sets record 024570 into the first record position).

2. Divide the result by 20; the remainder gives the track number; the quotient gives the cylinder number.

As an example, consider record 026692. Subtracting 24570 gives 2122; thus the record is in the 2122th record position in the unit. Dividing 2122 by 20 gives 106 with a remainder of 2. Thus, record 026692 is on track 2 of cylinder 106.

This direct-access method is clearly fast; no searching is required. The key is quickly converted to give all addressing information required. However, much space is required for much is wasted. The unused record positions and unused subrecord positions involve more space than the used areas. When the upper ID number is too large, all the records would have to be moved down, provided the total range of active ID numbers can fit in the unit. Thus there is an advantage (speed) and a disadvantage (wasted space) in this approach.

Now let us consider indexed access. We set up a table containing the ID numbers, which are keys, the record locations, and record sizes. The locations are given as cylinder and track addresses and word locations. For example, part of the table might appear thus:

ID Number	Cylinder	Track	Loc.	Size
024570	005	03	001	280
024571	081	10	490	215
024572	157	19	778	145

The record location would be supplied to a SEEK call along with the size, so that the desired record can be extracted.

The table itself must be stored as a series of records in the file. The record might have this format: five words, each containing one of the items on a line in the table as shown above. Thus, 2000 records on students would require 10,000 words for the table, which fills eight tracks. This space is 2 percent of the space needed for the 2000 records themselves (500 tracks).

Another table is required in this file. Since records occupy differing amounts of space, a disk storage allocator is required. The status of each track in the unit must be stored in a table so that the allocator can determine where space is available. This problem is discussed in the next section, below.

Data Storage

The data to be stored have been defined; i.e., record structure has been given. Two approaches to file design for the student-record processing problem have been described. Now we shall consider the task of actually storing the information in the file. The storage program can be used both to create a new file from a set of cards and to add a new student record to an existing file.

In the direct-access method, storage is simple enough. A record is written on disk in the track corresponding to the ID number. The storage program is given here; for simplicity, program declarations and the coding to determine qualification for the honor society are omitted. Refer to Example 9.2 for these details.

```
C    STREC4
C    DIRECT-ACCESS STØRAGE.
C    THIS PRØGRAM READS STUDENT DATA ØN CARDS
C    AND STØRES THEM ØN A DISK FILE.
C
C    START NEW PAGE.
   10   WRITE (6,100)
  100   FØRMAT (1H1)
C    READ A STUDENTS RECØRD AND PRINT IT.
        READ (5,101) NAME, CLASS, MAJØR, ID
  101   FØRMAT (7A4,A2, I2, 2X, A4, I6)
        WRITE (6,102) NAME, CLASS, MAJØR, ID
  102   FØRMAT (8H0NAME: 7A4,A2, 8H CLASS: I2,
      1       8H MAJØR: A4, 9H ID-NØ: I6)
        CLASS = CLASS − 68
C    READ NUMBER ØF GRADES, THEN GRADES.
        READ (5,103) NUMBER
  103   FØRMAT (I3)
        WRITE (6,1030) NUMBER
 1030   FØRMAT (19H0NUMBER ØF CØURSES: I3)
        DØ 11 I = 1, NUMBER
        READ (5,104) CØURSE(I), (TITLES(I,J), J = 1,8),
      1       CREDS(I), GRADES(I), TERMS(I)
  104   FØRMAT (A4, 2X, 7A4,A2, 1X, F1.0, 1X, F3.0, 1X, A3)
        WRITE (6,1040) CØURSE(I), (TITLES(I,J), J = 1,8),
      1       CREDS(I), GRADES(I), TERMS(I)
 1040   FØRMAT (A4, 4X, 7A4,A2, 3X, F1.0, 3X, F3.0, 3X, A3)
C    MØVE GRADES TØ ANØTHER ARRAY.
        DØ 50 K = 1, NUMBER
     50 TGRADS(K) = GRADES(K)
C    DETERMINE STUDENT AVERAGE.
        CALL WAVER1(AVER)
        WRITE (6,105) AVER
  105   FØRMAT (23H0CØURSE GRADE AVERAGE: F4.1)
        CALL BSØRT(5)
        WRITE (6,106) (GRADES(I), I = 1,5)
  106   FØRMAT (25H0THE FIVE TØP GRADES ARE: 5F5.0)
C    CØMPUTE THE TRACK NUMBER FRØM THE GIVEN
C    ID NUMBER. "LØWNUM" IS THE LØWEST ID NUMBER
C    TØ BE STØRED IN THE FILE.
        RECØRD = ID − LØWNUM
```

```
      CYLIND  =  RECØRD/20
      TRACK  =  RECØRD  -  CYLIND*20
C   STØRE RECØRD ØN DISK.
      CALL SEEKTR(CYLIND,TRACK)
      WRITE (3) ID, NAME, CLASS, MAJØR, NUMBER,
     1     (CØURSE(I), TITLES(I,J), J = 1,5),
     2     CREDS(I), TGRADS(I), TERMS(I), I = 1,
     3     NUMBER), AVER, (GRADES(I), I = 1,5)
      GØ TØ 10
      END
```

The following notes apply to this program:

1. This program supplies a printout of all the information stored in the file, in contrast to Example 9.2.
2. The grades, originally in GRADES, must be copied into another array (TGRADS) because the subroutine BSØRT records the entries in GRADES and the single WRITE routine at the end would supply incorrect data.
3. The long list of variables in the final WRITE statement corresponds to the fields of the single disk record for a student. No FØRMAT statement is needed since the file is binary.

In the indexed-access method, the storage problem is complicated by the fact that space must be found. The following scheme will be adopted. The first track that has sufficient space to store the record will be used. A table is needed that lists all track numbers and the space unused in each at the time of search. The space used is indicated by a number that indicates the first free word in a track. Space will be used so that all active space in a track is packed from the start, as in the first allocation scheme in Section 13.2. For simplicity here, let all tracks in the table (called TRSTAT) be numbered 0000 through 3999. Thus, track 0000 is actually track 0 of cylinder 0, track 0001 is track 1 of cylinder 0, ..., track 3999 is track 19 of cylinder 199. We can refer to these new numbers as whole track numbers (WTRACK in the program). The beginning of the table might appear as follows:

Whole Track Number	First Free Word
0000	579
0001	730
0002	000
0003	980

Here, track 0000 has 421 free words, track 0001 has 270 free words, track 0002 is entirely free, and track 0003 has 20 free words. This table requires two words per track status, or 8000 words in all; this requires eight additional tracks.

The storage technique is the following:

1. Search the track-status table (TRSTAT array in core) for the first track with sufficient space for the record. (Note that the table must previously be read from the file into core.)
2. Store the record in that track, updating the track-status table.
3. Enter into the index table (INDEX array in core) the entries required to locate the record subsequently.

The storage program is similar to the last one, as far as reading cards is concerned. The code is identical through statement 106. The code that actually locates available space and stores the record will be needed by other routines and so is developed as a subroutine (called DSTØRE, for disk store). The program:

```
C    STREC5
C    INDEXED-ACCESS METHØD.
C    THIS PRØGRAM READS STUDENT DATA ØN CARDS
C    AND STØRES THEM IN A DISK FILE.


     106  FØRMAT (25H0THE FIVE TØP GRADES ARE: 5F5.0)
          CALL DSTØRE
      GØ TØ 10
      END
```

Note that the subroutine call has no arguments. All pertinent information is stored in CØMMØN, i.e., the variables to be stored and the tables. The subroutine is the following:

```
      SUBRØUTINE DSTØRE
C    DETERMINE THE SIZE ØF THE RECØRD.
      SIZE = 12 + 12 * NUMBER + 6
C    SEARCH FØR A TRACK WITH ENØUGH SPACE.
      DØ 10 I = 1, 4000, 2
      IF (SIZE .LE. 1000 - TRSTAT(I,2)) GØ TØ 30
   10 CØNTINUE
C    HERE IF NØ SPACE.
      . . .
C    HERE IF SPACE
   30 WTRACK = TRSTAT(I,1)
      CYLIND = WTRACK/20
      TRACK = WTRACK - CYLIND*20
      LØC = TRSTAT(I,2)
      CALL SEEKRC(CYLIND,TRACK,LØC,SIZE)
```

```
        WRITE (3) ID, NAME, CLASS, MAJØR, NUMBER
      1       (CØURSE(I), TITLES(I,J), J = 1,5)
      2       CREDS(I), TGRADS(I), TERMS(I), I = 1,
      3       NUMBER), AVER, (GRADES(I), I = 1,5)
C    UPDATE TRSTAT.
        TRSTAT(I,2) = TRSTAT(I,2) + SIZE
C    MAKE ENTRY TØ INDEX TABLE.
        INDEX(K,1) = ID
        INDEX(K,2) = CYLIND
        INDEX(K,3) = TRACK
        INDEX(K,4) = LØC
        INDEX(K,5) = SIZE
        GØ TØ 10
        END
```

Note that TRSTAT is a 4000 × 2 array; each two-word entry consists of a track number and a word pointer. The INDEX table is a 2000 × 5 array, as suggested earlier. K is a pointer in that table to the first available entry; K must also be stored on the file. The WRITE statement is the same as previously.

File Searching

There are several operations in file processing that require that the file be searched for a specific record. Among these are file retrieval and file maintenance. Before we consider them, let us examine the manner of searching our disk file, which might be organized in one of two ways. The search requires locating a specific record, given its key (ID number).

In the case of direct access, the search is simple. Given the ID number, we need only subtract the quantity LØWNUM to obtain the track number, thus locating the record.

In the case of indexed access, a search must be made of the index table (on the file). Assuming a subroutine DSRCH (<u>d</u>isk <u>s</u>ea<u>r</u>ch), coded below, the code to read a record into core, given the ID number, is the following:

```
C    GIVEN AN ID NUMBER, READ RECØRD INTØ CØRE.
        CALL DSRCH (ID,CYLIND,TRACK,LØC,SIZE,K)
        CALL SEEKRC(CYLIND,TRACK,LØC,SIZE)
        READ (3) . . .
```

The READ statement includes the same list of variables given earlier, in WRITE statements. The index K is returned for it is sometimes needed (as will be seen); it points to the entry in array INDEX corresponding to the record read.

The subroutine is the following:

```
        SUBRØUTINE DRSCH(ID,CYLIND,TRACK,LØC,SIZE,K)
        CØMMØN . . .
```

```
C     GIVEN AN ID NUMBER, LØCATE THE RECØRD.
      DØ 20 K = 1, 2000, 2
      IF (ID .EQ. INDEX(K,1)) GØ TØ 40
   20 CØNTINUE
C     HERE IF NØ RECØRD WITH GIVEN ID.
        . . .
C     HERE IF RECØRD IS LØCATED.
   40 CYLIND = INDEX(K,2)
      TRACK = INDEX(K,3)
      LØC = INDEX(K,4)
      SIZE = INDEX(K,5)
      RETURN
      END
```

Data Retrieval

A file is created and organized in a particular manner so that retrieval of data is efficient. If a request is made for the printing of a specific record identified by ID, then all that need be done is to search for the record and to print it. The search methods described above would be used, followed by a seek call, a read statement, and a write statement.

More commonly, however, retrieval is somewhat different. In the first place, retrieval may be requested by other than ID number. A record may be requested by student name, e.g., "Print the record of James R. Browning." If the file is organized by ID number as key, the index table is useless. A search of all the records is required. If requests in this form are very common, another table can be established which contains student names and ID numbers or record positions. Since ID numbers are shorter (one word each) than record positions (four words each in an indexed file), the former probably would be used. In any event, this approach requires more space in the file. Specifically, since a name requires eight words, 9×2000 or 18,000 additional words (18 tracks) are needed. Nonetheless, it pays to have this extra information if retrieval by name is common.

Note that if retrieval by name is to be allowed, there must be full understanding of the precise format of the name, unless the search procedure can interpret many forms. For example, consider these forms, all referring to the same student:

JAMES R. BRØWNING
JAMES R BRØWNING
BRØWNING, JAMES R.
BRØWNING JAMES R

Another common variation of the retrieval request is one given conditionally. One may ask, e.g., for all students with averages that exceed 85.0, or for all students who live in New England who are studying physics. Such requests are usually made by statements such as the following:

```
PRINT FILE 'STUDENT' IF 'AVERAGE' .GT. '85.0'
PRINT FILE 'STUDENT' IF 'STATE' .EQ. 'R.I.' .ØR.
   'ME.' .ØR. 'N.H.' .ØR. 'VT.' .ØR.
   'MASS.' .ØR. 'CØNN', IF 'MAJØR' .EQ. 'PHYS.'
```

The two *queries* (as they are termed) request the printing of all records in file 'STUDENT' (as we assume our file is named) meeting the given conditions. 'AVERAGE', 'STATE', and 'MAJØR' are the names of fields in the records. (Our own files do not include addresses, but clearly they could.) In order to specify the condition "who live in New England" it would presumably be necessary to list all six New England states, as shown, since it is unlikely that New Englanders would be explicitly listed in the file.

Queries may be quite complex, with conditions that require parentheses for proper expression. We have already studied the hierarchy in FORTRAN of relational operators such as "and", "or", and "not". The rules of precedence would apply here, and parentheses might be required in some cases. The file processing system must be able to scan the query statements and establish proper file testing procedures. Queries are usually given not as statements within a program, but rather as commands in the manner of operating system control cards.

The manner in which a file is queried plays an important role in designing its structure. If retrieval is always by ID number, the file organizations described earlier for direct and indexed access are appropriate. In these organizations, retrieval is as fast as can be. Also, if retrieval is by student name, the use of an additional table (already described) makes retrieval almost as fast.

On the other hand, if retrieval is by *content*, i.e., retrieval occurs if field values meet stated conditions, then in general the entire file must be searched, i.e., every record must be examined. If it is known that most queries are going to be of a certain type, say by course average, then the file can be organized accordingly. The direct-access file probably would not be used in this case, but the indexed-access file offers some possibilities for improvement. The file can be sorted by averages, i.e., students with averages over 94 might be in one cylinder, students with averages over 92 but not exceeding 94 might be in another, etc. Sorting within a cylinder is not likely to be of any particular advantage. This approach requires extra planning, for now there will have to be space set aside in each cylinder to allow for growth of the several groups. The index table is of the same form as previously, but entries to tracks of the records are made selectively.

One can see, from the several retrieval considerations given here as well as others imagined, that optimal file organization is a complex process. Many factors must be taken into account. Among these are the physical nature of the files and the nature of retrieval. Another factor is the inherent structural nature of the data. There may be a hierarchy of information that must be retained, although in the case of the student data, this is not true.

File Maintenance

Invariably, any given computer file requires maintenance, i.e., it requires being kept up to date. The maintenance, or editing, task usually comprises three types of operations: data insertion, data deletion, and data modification. The *data insertion* task is similar to data storage, treated earlier, but we shall make a distinction between them. By data storage we mean the adding of records on new students to the file; by data insertion we mean the addition of new data to an existing record. *Data deletion* involves the deletion of information in the file, either part or all of a record (or records). Finally, *data modification* is concerned with changing the values of specified fields of records. We shall consider each of these maintenance tasks in some detail.

Data Insertion

We shall consider one specific data insertion task, that of adding information on the latest courses that a student has taken. This information is supplied:

One card:

    Columns 7–12:   student's ID number
    Columns 13–15:   number of new courses

Several cards, one per course, in the same format as given earlier.
We shall see shortly why columns 1 through 6 are left blank.

The procedure for insertion is the following:

1. Read the ID number and the number of new courses.
2. Read into core the "old" student record (the one existing in the file).
3. Read the new course data, adding these to the array already in core. Increase the number of courses to the new amount.
4. Write the revised, "new" record on the file.

Step 1, however, shall not be included in the subroutine given below. The information is, for the present, assumed to be in core memory.

The program, for the direct-access method:

```
        SUBRØUTINE INSRTD
        CØMMØN . . .
C    READ ØLD RECØRD INTØ CØRE.
        RECØRD = ID − LØWNUM
        CYLIND = RECØRD/20
        TRACK = RECØRD − CYLIND*20
        CALL SEEKTR(CYLIND,TRACK)
        READ (3) . . .
```

```
C    READ NEW CØURSE DATA.
         DØ 5 I = 1, NEWNUM
     5   READ (5,202) CØURSE(NUMBER+I),
     1       (TITLES(NUMBER+I,J), J = 1,8),
     2       CREDS(NUMBER+I), GRADES(NUMBER+I),
     3       TERMS(NUMBER+I)
C    UPDATE NUMBER ØF CØURSES.
         NUMBER = NUMBER + NEWNUM
C    WRITE NEW RECØRD ØN FILE.
         CALL SEEKTR(CYLIND,TRACK)
         WRITE (3) . . .
         RETURN
         END
```

The same string of arguments given previously applies to the disk READ and WRITE statements. In the case of the latter, the index limit NUMBER has an increased value. Note that the card READ statement uses "NUMBER+I" as the subscript, in order that the new data be located immediately following the old data in the several arrays.

The program, for the indexed-access method:

```
         SUBRØUTINE INSTRI
         CØMMØN . . .
C    READ ØLD RECØRD INTØ CØRE.
         CALL DRSCH(ID,CYLIND,TRACK,LØC,SIZE,K)
         CALL SEEKRC(CYLIND,TRACK,LØC,SIZE)
         READ (3) . . .
C    READ NEW CØURSE DATA.


C    UPDATE NUMBER ØF CØURSES.
         NUMBER = NUMBER + NEWSUM
C    WRITE NEW RECØRD ØN FILE.
         CALL DSTØRE
         RETURN
         END
```

The sequence of code headed by "READ NEW CØURSE DATA" is the same as in subroutine INSRTD.

Data Selection

Occasionally it is necessary to delete a record from a file. In the case of our student file, this would be true if a student graduated or transferred to another school. Records would be kept in an inactive file, but the disk file would be purged of such records. In the case of the direct-access file, deletion is a simple matter. A record to be deleted would simply be blanked; perhaps the ID-number field would be set to zero. Upon attempted retrieval of a deleted record, then, a diagnostic could be given.

In the case of the indexed-access file, deletion can be equally simple. An entry in the index table can be eliminated, so that subsequent searching for a deleted entry leads to a failure and a diagnostic. However, if no attempt is made to reuse the freed space, as with a space-freeing routine, there may eventually be insufficient space. Let us consider packing all records in a track, once a record has been deleted, as in subroutine FREE1 of Section 13.2.

The following steps are involved in deleted a record and freeing the space used by it:

1. Given the ID number, locate the record to be freed, using DSRCH.
2. Move back all records in the track that follow the record to be freed; move them an amount equal to the freed space.
3. Modify entries in INDEX so that the locations of all moved records are correctly given.
4. Modify the entry in TRSTAT so that the available space in the track is correctly given.

The subroutine is the following:

```
      SUBRØUTINE DELETI
C     THIS RØUTINE FREES THE SPACE IN A TRACK USED
C     BY A NAMED RECØRD (IDENTIFIED BY "ID") AND
C     ADJUSTS ENTRIES IN TABLES INDEX AND TRSTAT.
      DIMENSIØN BUF(1000)
C     LØCATE RECØRD TØ BE FREED.
      CALL DRSCH(ID,CYLIND,TRACK,LØC,SIZE,IND)
C     MØVE RECØRDS FØLLØWING ... FIRST, READ RECØRDS INTØ CØRE.
      CALL SEEKRC(CYLIND,TRACK,LØC+SIZE,1000-LØC-SIZE)
      READ (3) BUF
C     SECØND, READ RECØRDS BACK ØN DISK, MØVED BACK.
      CALL SEEKRC(CYLIND,TRACK,LØC,1000-LØC-SIZE)
      WRITE (3) BUF
C     MØDIFY "INDEX" TABLE.  FIRST, SET SIZE ØF
C     RECØRD DELETED TØ ZERØ.
      INDEX(IND,5) = 0
C     SECØND, CHANGE LØCS. ØF ALL RECØRDS IN TRACK
C     THAT WERE MØVED.
      DØ 30 I = IND, 2000
      IF (CYLIND .NE. INDEX(I,2)) GØ TØ 30
```

```
      IF (TRACK .NE. INDEX(I,3)) GØ TØ 30
      INDEX(I,5) = INDEX(I,5) − SIZE
  30  CØNTINUE
C   MØDIFY "TRSTAT" TABLE
      WTRACK = CYLIND + TRACK*20
      DØ 40 I = 1, 4000
      IF (WTRACK .EQ. TRSTAT(I,1) GØ TØ 44
  40  CØNTINUE
      RETURN
  44  TRSTAT(I,2) = TRSTAT(I,2) − SIZE
      RETURN
      END
```

The following remarks apply to this subroutine:

1. The array BUF is used as a temporary buffer to contain the records in core read from the track.
2. The arguments in the SEEKRC calls are chosen to effect the required shift within the track; e.g., location "LØC+ SIZE" is the location of the record immediately following the deleted record.
3. The statement just before statement 30 causes the location entries to be decreased by SIZE, reflecting the fact that records are moved by that amount in the track.

Data Modification

One other task involved in using a file is that of modifying existing records in the file. Generally, this process involves changes in specified fields. We shall consider only two simple possible changes, that of changing a student's name (perhaps as the result of a marriage) and that of changing his major subject.

The changes shall be supplied as follows on a card:

Columns 7–13:   student's ID number
Columns 14–19:   name of field affected;
           "NAME" for name field,
           "MAJØR" for major-subject field
Columns 20–49:   new value of the field:
           30 characters or less for name,
           four characters for major.

The subroutine, for direct access:

```
      SUBRØUTINE MØDIFD
      CØMMØN ...
      DIMENSIØN VALUE(5)
```

```
            DATA TNAME/4HNAME/TMAJØR/4HMAJØ/
C   READ CHANGE, CARD.
            READ (5,404) ID, FIELD, VALUE
C   READ IN RECØRD AFFECTED.
            RECØRD = ID - LØWNUM
            CYLIND = RECØRD/20
            TRACK = RECØRD - CYLIND*20
            CALL SEEKTR(CYLIND,TRACK)
            READ (3) ...
C   IDENTIFY FIELD AFFECTED.
            IF (FIELD .EQ. TNAME) GØ TØ 20
            IF (FIELD .EQ. TMAJØR) GØ TØ 30
C   HERE IF ERRØR IN FIELD NAME.
            . . .
C   HERE IF NAME IS GIVEN.   CHANGE NAME.
      20  DØ 22 I = 1, 5
      22  NAME(I) = VALUE(I)
            GØ TØ 50
C   HERE IF MAJØR IS GIVEN.   CHANGE MAJØR.
      30  MAJØR = VALUE
            GØ TØ 50
C   WRITE MØDIFIED TRACK ØN FILE.
            CALL SEEKTR(CYLIND,TRACK)
            WRITE (3) ...
            RETURN
            END
```

The subroutine, for indexed access, is very similar. (Compare the similarities and differences in INSRTD and INSRTI.) DSRCH and DSTØRE are used for searching for the affected record and storing the modified record.

An Editing Program

Now that editing subroutines have been developed, let us consider a general editing system that accepts edit cards of the several types and acts upon them.

We shall allow three types of edit cards. Prior to 'insertion cards', this card shall be required: 'INSERT' punched in columns 1 through 6. The form of the insertion cards was given in the section Data Insertion.

Prior to 'deletion cards', this card shall be required: 'DELETE' punched in columns 1–6. The form of deletion cards is the following: the ID number is punched in columns 1–6.

Prior to 'modification cards', this card shall be required: 'MØDIFY' punched in columns 1–6. The form of modification cards was given in the section Data Modification.

Following is a set of edit cards as an example:

```
ɩNSERT
         045856   5
         M104  ELEMENTS ØF  MECH  ENGG            3   88  F69
         P106  PRØGRAMMING  TECHNIQUES            3   93  F69
         E106  ENGLISH – LITERATURE  15TH  C.     3   90  F69
         S200  MECH  ENGG  SHØP                   1   85  F69
         Y103  PHYSICS – ØPTICS                   4   96  F69
DELETE
         045599
         045589
MØDIFY
         047001  MAJØR  PHYS
         047888  MAJØR  CHEM
         049860  NAME   GREEN, MRS.  KAREN  R.
END
```

Note that each group of cards of one type is located after one of the *identifying cards* (with INSERT, DELETE, or MØDIFY) and before either another of these cards or the END card. Thus each group is delimited and identified. The number of *command cards* of each type is variable, although the number of course cards must be given on the first card of a student's set among insertion cards.

The flowchart in Figure 14.3 shows the structure of the editing procedure, assuming an indexed access method. The first card is read and, depending upon its type, control passes to one of three parts of the procedure. Then another card is read and, depending upon its type, control passes to one of three parts of the procedure. Then another card is read; this card will be an actual editing card (insertion, deletion, or modification card) so control passes to one of these subroutines: INSRTI, DELETI, or MØDIFI. Then, the next card is read. The process repeats until an identifying card is encountered, in which case control passes once again to the appropriate part of the procedure. The END card is always checked for, to indicate the end of the edit process.

We must examine certain features of this procedure and of the command cards format, before we go on to coding. Consider first the card formats, summarized here. Fields are shown by column numbers, below which in parentheses appear the format specifications for them. Field names are also given. The formats are these:

	Columns 1–6	Columns 7–12	Columns 13–15
Insertion:	(blank)	(I6)	(I3)
		ID-number	Number of courses
Deletion:	Columns 1–6	Columns 7–12	
	(blank)	(I6)	
		ID-number	

	Columns 1–6	Columns 7–12	Columns 12–17	Columns 20–49
Modification:	(blank)	(I6)	(A4)	(7A4,A2)
		ID-number	Field name	Field value

Since we allow cards to be distributed as given earlier, it is necessary to check each card, as it is read, to see if it is a command or an identifying card. For that reason, the format statement to be applied to each of the formats above must also apply to the identifying cards. Hence, columns 1 through 4 are also read as "A4", and the ID-number field is located in columns 7 through 12.

Consider now the procedure, as flowcharted in Figure 14.3. It might appear more reasonable for each edit subroutine to do the reading of command cards of its type. It is, in fact, more reasonable but because of the rule that cards are distributed as illustrated, the card reading must be performed outside the subroutines. Again, each card, as read, must be checked for both command and identifying types. This is most easily done outside subroutines.

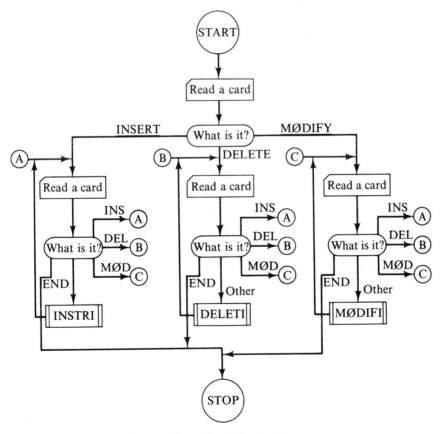

Fig. 14.3.   Edit program.

We should note that we could simplify the procedures described above by using other rules for supplying editing information. If an END card (or its equivalent) were required after each type of command card, then the blank field on the command cards could be eliminated, and the reading of command cards could be done inside subroutines. A decision on which approach to choose had to be made; the choice is almost arbitrary, being a personal style preference.

The edit program is the following:

```
C    EDIT
     CØMMØN . . .
     DATA INSERT/4HINSE/DELETE/4HDELE/
     DATA MØDIFY/4HMØDI/END/3HEND/
C    READ THE FIRST CARD AND TEST IT.
     READ (5,501) CARD
501  FØRMAT (A4)
     IF (CARD .EQ. INSERT) GØ TØ 1
     IF (CARD .EQ. DELETE) GØ TØ 2
     IF (CARD .EQ. MØDIFY) GØ TØ 3
C    HAVE "INSERT" CARD.
  1  READ (5,502) CARD, ID, NEWNUM
502  FØRMAT (A4, 2X, I6, I3)
     IF (CARD .EQ. INSERT) GØ TØ 1
     IF (CARD .EQ. DELETE) GØ TØ 2
     IF (CARD .EQ. MØDIFY) GØ TØ 3
     IF (CARD .EQ. END) GØ TØ 99
     CALL INSRTI
     GØ TØ 1
C    HAVE "DELETE" CARD.
  2  READ (5,503) CARD, ID
503  FØRMAT (A4, 2X, I6)
     IF (CARD .EQ. INSERT) GØ TØ 1
     IF (CARD .EQ. DELETE) GØ TØ 2
     IF (CARD .EQ. MØDIFY) GØ TØ 3
     IF (CARD .EQ. END) GØ TØ 99
     CALL DELETI
     GØ TØ 2
C    HAVE "MØDIFY" CARD.
  3  READ (5,504) CARD, ID, FIELD, VALUE
504  FØRMAT (A4, 2X, I6, 1X, A4, 2X, 5A6)
     IF (CARD .EQ. INSERT) GØ TØ 1
     IF (CARD .EQ. DELETE) GØ TØ 2
     IF (CARD .EQ. MØDIFY) GØ TØ 3
     IF (CARD .EQ. END) GØ TØ 99
     CALL MØDIFI
```

```
        GØ TØ 3
C    HAVE "END" CARD.
  99  STØP
     END
```

It can be seen readily that this program does nothing more than read cards, test cards, and transfer control. This is reasonable, for the editing system has been segmented into three subroutines that perform actual editing. The main program is an "executive" program. Many systems are designed in this manner.

The Several File Processes

We can briefly summarize this section's material by listing the processes studied within it. First, the nature of the data was discussed and its format defined. Secondary, disk commands of a simplified type were described. Third, the physical units were described, with associated structure and capacity. Finally, the actual computer processes were programmed, one at a time. These included data storage, file searching, and file maintenance. In the last case, an editing procedure was fully discussed and coded. In more general situations, each of these tasks would require much more analysis and development. What we have done here is to consider a simplified problem and to develop the required programming for each phase. This material, though simplified, represents the actual tasks involved in designing a data management system for the computer.

EXERCISES

1. Compare the direct access and indexed access methods for the student file under discussion. Consider space used, space wasted, access time, and other pertinent factors.

2. The K index in the DSTØRE subroutine is a CØMMØN variable. What other coding is required (in a calling program) to update and store this index?

3. Complete the coding of the STREC4 subroutine by supplying declarations and statements regarding the honor society.

4. If the range of ID numbers were greater than the number of tracks (4000), how would the direct access method have to be modified?

*   *   *   *   *   *

5. Decide what should occur in the DSTØRE subroutine if there is no space available for storage of a record. Insert code in the appropriate place in that subroutine.

6. As in Exercise 5, insert code in the DSRCH subroutine to handle the case where no record exists with the given ID number.

7. Some computer systems do not permit access of a particular portion of a disk track, unless there are physical record marks on the disk. Thus, the SEEKRC

subroutine followed by a READ statement would not work. Write a subroutine READRC to perform the task. The call:

CALL   READRC(cylinder,track,loc,size,buffer)

where the first four arguments correspond to those of SEEKRC, and <u>buffer</u> is the core buffer read into. Assume the existence of the SEEKTR subroutine.

8. Write a subroutine MØDIFI, to match MØDIFD, which was alluded to.

9. The possibility of using extra END cards to set off several types of command cards for the edit program was mentioned. Assume that such cards are used, i.e., that insertion cards start with 'INSERT' and end with 'END', for example. What changes would occur in the flowchart (Figure 14.3) and in the programs as a result?

10. Develop a program for handling file queries. This problem has these aspects:
    (a) Develop an algorithm for handling Boolean expressions that represent queries, as the examples given (under "Data Retrieval"). Consider only expressions that do not require parentheses: for example, this is allowed:

$$p \text{ ØR } q \text{ AND } r$$

while this is not:

$$(p \text{ ØR } q) \text{ AND } r$$

    (b) Write a subroutine to analyze such expressions and extract fields. Since this is a complex process, assume a fixed format for the expressions.
    (c) Write a subroutine to retrieve a record and test it to see if given conditions (in the query) are met.
    Put all this together in a unified meaningful way.

REFERENCES

1. This book deals with the general problem of information retrieval, with emphasis on the use of computers in this area:

Charles T. Meadow, *The Analysis of Information Systems*, John Wiley & Sons, Inc., 1967.

The following series has several articles on data management and related topics:

Carlos A. Cuadra, editor, *Annual Review of Information, Science and Technology*, John Wiley & Sons, Inc., each year since 1966.

15 PROGRAM DESIGN AND DEVELOPMENT

All the preceding chapters of this book have dealt with various aspects of writing computer programs. Many different aspects of program design, many techniques useful in programming, and many different kinds of problems were examined in detail. In this final chapter, we shall summarize the steps involved in program design and development.

When a large complex system of programs is to be designed and built, there are many more steps involved than when a single simple problem is to be written. In order to illustrate the steps in a meaningful way, two actual problems will be considered. The steps described here will be applied, as appropriate, to these problems.

15.1 DEVELOPING A PROGRAM

Why Program Design?

In nearly all of the problems studied in this book, there is certainly no need for "program design", whatever that term might mean. Certainly, the term has not yet been defined, yet its name implies that a certain amount of planning, related to the nature of the parts of the program, is required. When we write a program that reads a set of numbers, sorts them in a particular way, and then computes their sum, we need only draw a flowchart and start coding. Design? It's hardly even worth a thought.

On the other hand, if we consider the problem that has been given a great deal of attention in this book, the processing of student records, it is clear that much planning and design is needed. As the programs for this problem were developed, over several chapters, more and more planning and designing was done and more capabilities were implemented in the coding. This system is hardly even close in size to some of the most complex programming systems that have been developed.

Program design is required in order that all aspects of the problem, the data structure, and the program structure are carefully considered and planned for mutual interaction prior to actual coding. Unless this is done, it is likely that the program will not be complete in scope nor accurate in all parts. It may be difficult to check out and even more difficult to extend and modify in the future. More specifically, at least four direct benefits can be realized by proper program design:

1. A more complete understanding of the problem to be solved will result, for all of its factors must be considered: its scope, its data, the desired results.
2. Program modularity, which is so desirable, is more easily developed.
3. Documentation becomes easier to realize or is even directly abetted.
4. Careful planning tends to lead to fewer errors in programming.

The Steps in Program Design and Development

Listed below are the steps involved in program development. To state that these are "the" steps in program development is perhaps presumptious, because the process of designing a program is somewhat individualistic. Furthermore, it depends so greatly on the nature of the problem, the manner in which it is written, etc. Nonetheless, it is instructive to examine these steps, applying those appropriate to a particular problem. Another point to note is that while these steps are listed here in what is essentially chronological order, sometimes several steps are performed at one time. Sometimes one step listed below another is performed before it. Most commonly, parts of a program or system of programs may proceed far down the list while others remain at early steps until a later time. In short, the list is at best an approximation of most of the steps one will perform on a complex programming design problem.

DEFINITION OF THE PROBLEM. This is obviously the first step in any program development. It may be done rather easily, as in most problems in this text, or it may take weeks of study. Under problem definition, we can list the following: (1) a statement of the problem, in precise terms; (2) definition of the goals sought for the program and of the purposes of the program; (3) description of the data, including data structure and the ranges, volume, format, and accuracy of the data.

PROGRAM STRUCTURE PLANNING. In planning the structure of the program, it is necessary to perform these steps: (1) selection of a method; (2) consideration of the computing environment, which influences the method selected; (3) selection of program emphasis, where one or two of several specific approaches to programming are selected.

PROBLEM ANALYSIS. Aside from the obvious step, (1) analysis of the problem, considered early in the book, there are associated other tasks: (2) flowcharting; (3) development of program structure, i.e., restructuring the analysis in computer terms; (4) design of the data structure (in core memory); (5) design of the file structure, if one is to be used; (6) design of input and output formats, which consider the user and the way he will interact within the program; (7) design of a language, a medium of communication with the program.

WRITING THE PROGRAM. This step is what most of the book is about; it is the task of converting an analyzed problem into statements or instructions in a programming language. The task is eased if certain approaches are taken.

TESTING AND CHECKING. This step is necessary for insuring that the program does what it has been designed to do. All conceivable ranges of data must be applied to the problem, if its validity is to be believed.

DOCUMENTATION. This final task serves the purpose of recording the purpose, techniques, and use of a program for users and future developers.

In the succeeding sections, these steps are examined in detail. To illustrate them, two specific examples are studied.

15.2 DEFINITION OF THE PROBLEM

Scope

In this section, we consider these steps:

1. Statement of the problem.
2. Definition of goals.
3. Description of the data.

Statement of the Problem

The starting point in program development is a complete and accurate statement of the problem. The importance of this cannot be overstressed, for these reasons:

1. The problem statement defines the scope and purpose of the program, needed for a realistic appraisal of the effort involved.
2. The statement makes clear both to the programmer and the person for whom the job is being done precisely what the problem is to be solved.

A misstatement or misunderstanding here can invalidate all work on the program.

A computer program, as we have seen, must be explicit in all respects. Every possibility must be accounted for, and all possible actions to be taken must be coded.

The following must be supplied about the problem: (1) a statement of what information is given; (2) a statement of what answers are wanted; (3) if applicable, a statement of how accurate the results must be; (4) the precise manner in which data are supplied; (5) the precise manner in which the answers are to be produced.

The first problem we shall consider in these sections, by way of illustration, is a fairly simple one. It can be developed as a single program. The problem is the following:

> Determine the amount of time necessary to complete the payments of a home mortgage, at a given interest rate for a given unpaid principal balance, if fixed monthly payments are made.

The problem, as stated, might be presented to a program designer, who would then be asked to develop specific requirements on the data supplied and the answers to be given. These might be developed as follows:

Given: Initial date (month and year) after which payments are to be made; unpaid principal balance; interest rate; monthly payment.

Results: For each succeeding month, the separation of the monthly payment into interest and equity (reduction in unpaid balance); unpaid balance at the end of each month; date of the last payment; total interest to be paid. The first two items are to be printed optionally.

The second problem considered is more complex. It is one we have already studied fairly extensively, the student record processing problem. Here we shall outline and describe in some detail the development of the system used to solve that problem. The system described will be broader than that studied, but the development will be less detailed, for much of it has already been covered. The problem is the following:

> Develop a computer-based system for the storage, maintenance, and retrieval of all the student records for a college.

This problem, as defined, might be given as an initial statement of the kind of system required. Obviously, it is only a beginning, for it is necessary to specify in great detail what is to be done. A study of the needs for such a system require much study. We shall here, at each step in this problem, indicate the kind of information needed, but details shall be omitted.

A more detailed statement of the problem might be the following:

The file: The information in each record, which shall contain the information on one student, is as follows: ID number, name, class, major, courses, etc. Some of the fields may be variable in number, such as data on courses taken.

Updating the file: As students register, new records for them are to be established in the file. As terms end, new data on completed courses shall be added to the file. Also, as required, information in the file shall be changed. As students graduate, their records are to be deleted.

Reports to be supplied: At the end of a term, a summary for each student is to be printed, after new grades are added to the file. Each summary report is to contain the results of the most recent term's courses, as well as the student's average for the term and for his college career.

In both of these problems, the problem statement has been given. The details of the problem definition, given by a fuller statement of what functions the programs are to perform and what data are to be supplied and produced, are given next. It is not always necessary, of course, to make this distinction among the parts of the problem definition.

Definition of Goals

Under the heading "definition of goals", we include a more specific statement of what the program is to accomplish. Very often, a subroutine merely processes data and one cannot point to any "goals" beyond the problem statement. For example, a subroutine to sort 1000 numbers does just that and no more. More commonly, however, the scope of a programming system is quite broad and it could encompass dozens of functions. A decision must be made on which functions will be provided. The decision is based on time availability, manpower availability, and whatever limitations the computer and compiler impose. Certain functions may be invaluable and so must be performed "at any price", while others may simply be "nice to have". Clearly, the cost of programming enters the picture.

The usage of the program must be considered. If a system is to be in constant use over many years, as a payroll system might be, the extra effort in coding all conceivable functions may be worthwhile. If the system is to attempt to cover many different types of problems, as a data management system might, the same might be true. If the reverse is true, if usage is to be brief and narrow in scope, goals must correspondingly be foreshortened.

Some thought must be given to the purposes of the proposed system. It is needed to save time, to save cost, to improve the efficiency of operation of a process, etc? Will it provide capabilities impossible to achieve otherwise? Answers to such questions aid in program design.

The mortgage problem statement need not be extended any further. The problem is simple enough that no additional goals need be given. If this program were to become part of a larger system concerned, say, with financial management, then more might be said on system goals. We shall, however, exclude this possibility here.

The student-record problem statement can be extended in the following ways:

1. These tasks are to be performed: New records are to be added, fields are to be added to existing records, fields in specific records are to be modified, and records are to be deleted.
2. The file can be queried, ranges of values being given on specific fields in the file of records. Selected information is thus to be printed.
3. New fields are to be added as desired, i.e., fields with new information are to be created for all records. These might include information on honors received, campus activities, salary earned, etc.
4. The indexed access method of file structure is to be used for flexibility and inefficient use of space. Disk memory is to be used.
5. Special reports, such as lists of students with averages exceeding 90.0, are to be produced as required. The ability to define these reports according to any desired format shall be included.

These tasks are to be performed to provide rapid access to files, providing information quickly when needed. The main purpose is thus high speed of response. A secondary goal, however, is to provide more accurate maintenance of records at lower cost.

Description of the Data

Before any specific planning of the program and the algorithms to be used can be performed, it is necessary to have a description of the data. Specifically this means: (1) the data to be supplied, (2) the data structure to be used in core in the program, (3) the file structure to be used as a permanent store, and (4) the data to be printed as output. The structure of the data, the range of values, the volume of the data, and the precision of the data all must be considered. Included within the description of the structure are the logical links between portions of the data, if any, and the nature of each of the fields and records in the files. It is not always necessary for all of this information to be known at this point; some of it may be provided later. However, if all can be supplied here, the program development is more easily accomplished.

The following applies to the mortgage problem:

Input data: Each set of data, corresponding to one sequence of payments to completion, comprise these items: initial date (month and year), unpaid balance, interest rate, and monthly payment. Additionally, there is to be given some indication of whether a monthly summary is to be printed for each payment.

Output data: For each data set, the input data shall be printed, with (optionally) a list of monthly summaries, including the date, the interest payment that month, the equity payment that month, and the new unpaid balance. The total interest paid is to be printed.

Range of data and results: The following limits apply:

Unpaid principal: $99999.99
Monthly payment: 999.99
Monthly interest: 999.99
Monthly equity: 999.99
Total interest: 99999.99
Interest rate: 9.99%
Payment period: 99 years, 11 months

Accuracy: Compute all amounts to within $0.01.

The following information applies to the student-record problem:
Data cards: Fields on each card.
File records: Fields in each record.
File organization: Indexed access, with ID numbers as keys in a reference table, with cylinder, track, and location addresses and record sizes.
Volume of data: Records for 2000 students are to be provided.
This information is incomplete, but earlier specifications for this problem (in Section 14.3) apply here, except for additional fields that might be added.

We can sum up this section by noting that these examples have now been essentially completely defined as far as their statement is concerned. The purposes, tasks, and data define the problem, permitting programming to commence. In any large system, of course, many minor decisions are required during programming that further define the problem, but these must be deferred because in truth one cannot know everything about a problem at the start. The scope of a system changes, sometimes narrows and sometimes broadens, as the realization develops of what is involved in coding. Sometimes there is incomplete information at the start, yet programming must commence because of time pressures. Eventually the missing information must be supplied. In short, these techniques apply when possible, but are really guidelines rather than firm rules.

At this point, it is appropriate to pause and insert one very important step, one that is sometimes overlooked: A serious examination of the question of whether a computer solution to the problem at hand is the correct approach. Although computers are wonderful machines and their use is probably limited most by programmers' imaginations, still there are many problems that may best be solved by manual means, by use of a desk calculator, by other business machines than the digital computer, or by a combination of these. The steps listed here to this point ought to provide the basis for a decision on this matter, although further information is required as well. Other questions to be asked are these: What will the programming and debugging jobs cost? Do we have the talent to do the programming? Do we have the computers required or can we afford them? Have similar jobs been done already on the machine that can be adapted to these needs?

How much is improved efficiency and/or decreased time to solution worth (in dollars)? There will be further questions in particular cases.

In summary, it should not be a foregone conclusion that programming a computer is the best way to solve a problem. With these warnings, we can proceed to other steps (some of which might be needed to help in this consideration).

15.3 PROGRAM STRUCTURE PLANNING

Scope

In this section, we consider these steps:

1. Selection of a method.
2. Consideration of the computing environment.
3. Selection of program emphasis.

Selection of a Method

The problem of selection of an algorithm has been given consideration in Chapter 2. We can list a number of factors that must be taken into account when a method is chosen:

1. The problem to be solved.
2. The nature of the data for the problem.
3. The characteristics of digital computers (and of the computer at hand, in particular).

The most important criterion for algorithm selection is the nature of the problem to be solved. Very often, this is all that matters, and other considerations are relatively insignificant. There is little to be said here on this point, for every problem merits its own analysis, perhaps quite apart from most other problems. We will only note that there are problems involving arithmetic and algebra, involving the ordering of items according to some rule, involving manipulating strings of characters, involving simulation of processes, involving searching of lists or files, and so on. The methods used in each case clearly must reflect the problem to be solved. While the problem itself ranks as the most important influence on choice of a method, little can be said about it of a general nature, so we move on to other criteria.

Any program must process data, which as we have seen may exist in a variety of forms, some quite complex. The method selected for solution may have to take into account the form of the data. The entries in a matrix, for example, may be given as a two-dimensional array, one word to be allotted per entry. Alternatively, if nearly all entries are zero, the matrix may be given as a set of triplets: $(i, j,$ value). Methods for processing will probably be different, for the same data would be represented differently. The data as supplied ought to be conveniently structured, and might have to be restructured for efficient processing. This possibility too must be considered.

Since problems of interest here are to be solved on the computer, the characteristics of digital computers in general, as well as of the particular computer available, must be considered. Among the characteristics of interest are these:

1. The finiteness of internal memory and the different sizes and accessibility of auxiliary memory devices.
2. The finiteness of memory words in most computers.
3. The set of instructions available in most computers and the statement types available in languages.
4. The automatic indexing feature.

FINITENESS OF MEMORY. In the examples considered in this book, no thought was given to memory size because only hundreds of items of data were involved. We can extend some of the problems, however: We might have to search 50,000 numbers for the largest one, or we might have to analyze 200 pages of alphanumeric text (with perhaps 400,000 characters). We cannot fit all these data into core memory, so our methods have to be modified.

If the problem at hand involves large amounts of data, little can be done to avoid the use of auxiliary memory, unless the data can be processed in small batches. Perhaps, for example, we can analyze the 200 pages of text by processing a page at a time. This is satisfactory if no page needs to be processed a second time after others are processed. If auxiliary memory is required, the capacities and accessibilities of each available type must be considered. The method of solution must take these into account in such instances.

FINITENESS OF WORDS. We have already seen the effect of the finiteness of words on roundoff. The algorithm selected should be one that does not rely upon extremely high accuracy at any stage of processing. Double-precision arithmetic is available in some computers, but it adds to processing time. Double precision can be stimulated by programming but at a great cost in running time. In many problems, word size is not critical. An example is the set of programs written for alphanumeric string manipulation. Accuracy is not at issue, so finiteness of words is not either.

INSTRUCTION SETS AND STATEMENT TYPES. In this book, we have given little thought to the instructions available on computers, except for our brief considerations of the GAMMA 70. Instructions typically involve input-output, arithmetic, shifting of bits, testing on several criteria, moving data around in memory, and indexing. Machine-language symbolic coding must take such instructions into account, while algorithmic programming involves the set of statements available in the language. FORTRAN permits the evaluation of formulas, the testing on various complex criteria (for truth or falsity), and little else. Thus problems involving other processes may fit awkwardly into the FORTRAN context. Simple string manipulation can be resolved into a sequence of decisions and as such fits in fairly well. The algorithm selected to solve a problem can most efficiently be coded if it matches the language well. Since a wide variety of programming languages is not always available, the programmer is often forced to use a particular one. In that event, his algorithm choice is more restricted.

AUTOMATIC INDEXING FEATURE. This feature of digital computers has not been described explicitly, but its function can be appreciated by a consideration of the utility of subscripting in algorithmic languages. Since indexing is so common in problem solving, compilers are designed to allow such operations to be easily performed:

```
DØ 40 I = 1, 100
        .
        .

SUM = SUM + A(I)
        .
        .
```

Reference to each element in the array A is facilitated if each constituent memory word can be rapidly addressed. Computers are so built, with automatic addressing facilities wired in the equipment. Consequently, an algorithm that processes data that are linearly arrayed generally proceeds rapidly.

We can summarize most of the material just covered by pointing out that the method selected should match both the characteristics of the problem and of the computer being used (including its language) to solve it. (In this respect, the method differs from a "manual" one, which need only match the problem.) A perfect match in both instances is likely to result in an efficient, fast-running program. Rarely, however, is this the case. The greater the deviation at either end, the greater is likely to be the difficulty in coding and debugging the procedure selected and the worse the efficiency of operation.

Let us consider a method to solve the mortgage problem. To determine the length of time required to complete the payments of the mortgage balance, we must compute the interest charge and equity amount each month. Then this equity is subtracted from the unpaid balance to yield a new balance. This process is repeated until the balance is paid in full. This is an iterative process which ends when the unpaid balance falls below the monthly payment. Summarizing, we have these steps:

1. Compute monthly interest and equity payments.
2. Determine new unpaid balance.

3. Compare new balance to monthly payment; if balance exceeds payment, return to step 1; otherwise, stop.

Matching the method to the problem and the computer (with a language) is a simple task here. The steps listed follow directly from the problem. Since we are merely computing a few variables at every step and need only retain a limited number for future steps, we cannot run out of space. If several payment periods are to be computed, we must allocate space for the results for the final summary; there still will be no space problem if less than a thousand or so cases are treated.

Considering the student-record problem next, we note first that the problem to be solved is basically one of information structuring, storage, and retrieval, with certain associated auxiliary tasks. The method selected considers the data to be structured into sections (stored on tracks), individually addressable, from which sequential retrieval is performed. The method is not significantly influenced here by the nature of the problem, but rather by the nature of the data and the storage medium for the data. The data comprise many records, linearly related (through an ID number), each with a set of fields. Physical properties of the disk used for storage lead to a further breakdown into subregions, the tracks. A knowledge of the capacities of the tracks leads to a decision on how many records to store per track and to a particular storage allocation scheme. The method selected has already been analyzed in detail, in Chapter 14. Such considerations as finiteness of memory and of individual words are irrelevant here.

The Computing Environment

As thought is given to the manner in which a problem is to be programmed, one must consider the environment within which the programming must be done. This includes the following factors:

1. The computer.
   (a) Its core memory size (or that part of it readily available to one program).
   (b) Its operating system and the functions the system performs for the programmer.
   (c) Its set of instructions (if assembly language is to be used).
   (d) Its type (i.e., scientific, business; binary, decimal; fixed-word length, variable-word length; etc.).
2. Auxiliary memory.
   (a) The types available (drum, disk, tape, etc.).
   (b) The capacities, access speeds, structure, and cost of each type.
3. Programming languages.
   (a) The types of problems each handles.
   (b) The set of statements in each.

Sometimes, at a computer installation, there is little choice among all these factors, especially if the installation is small. Generally, however, a programmer has choices that range over most of if not all the factors above.

Consider the mortgage problem. It is a small one, requires virtually no memory space for data, and is a numerical problem. There is little need for much decision among the factors listed; FORTRAN (or another algebraic language) is the obvious choice.

Consider the student-record problem. The primary concern is over auxiliary memory, for this is a data management problem that makes use of a file. In the analysis in Chapter 14, disk was selected because of its accessibility and structure. No consideration was given to cost, but this must be taken into account. Magnetic tape is considerably cheaper than disk, but is correspondingly less flexible in use. FORTRAN was used here as the language; again, any algebraic language is suitable. File processing is usually most efficiently done in assembly language, however, and this should be studied.

Selection of Programming Emphasis

Using a given algorithm, one can develop a program to solve a problem using a variety of ways to place emphasis, depending on the goals and purposes set down. Among these ways are the following:

1. The elapsed time, from start to finish, of the programming can be minimized.
2. The execution time of the program can be minimized.
3. The memory space required by the program can be reduced to a minimum.
4. The program can be written so that changes are easily made; the program's flexibility can be maximized.

Development of a program most likely will not emphasize only one of these goals; rather, two or three may be simultaneously sought. One goal may be foremost with a second close behind. Some goals tend to be mutually incompatible, as items 2 and 3. Let us consider these goals in some detail.

MINIMIZING DEVELOPMENT TIME. Sometimes it is most important that a program be completed as quickly as possible. There are several reasons for this. The results supplied by the program may be needed for some other work; there may be several programmers on a project whose work must be coordinated; schedules must be met; etc. There are various ways to achieve this goal, each blending an appropriate sequence of coding and debugging, which depends on the problem and the programmer. Another factor is the programming language used;

compiler languages are easier to code in, provided they match the problem, and so their use speeds development.

MINIMIZING EXECUTION TIME. This goal is always sought, but in most small programs it is of little consequence, for they run quickly in any event. Large systems, particularly when auxiliary memory is involved, present more critical situations, for one can so easily develop slow-running procedures. Extra effort is usually required to decrease the execution time of certain processes such as searching, looping, and input-output. In these instances, the effort is worthwhile if the process occurs frequently. Subroutines that are used many times should be fast to execute. One invariably has to trade development time for execution time, and the circumstances require careful consideration. Another common tradeoff is with space. An example here is the use of a computed table to which references can be made in lieu of frequent calculations. The price paid is the space of the table. If a compiler language is used, the generated code generally occupies up to twice the space required by equivalent "hand-coded" machine code. Here too is an example of a tradeoff.

MINIMIZING MEMORY SPACE. As noted above, this goal is often incompatible with that of fastest execution. Yet frequently one must make programs as small as possible. Small computers, usually used off-line by themselves or in conjunction with larger machines, sometimes severely restrict program size, so this goal becomes uppermost. One can always place "excess" programs and data in auxiliary memory, but often at considerable cost in time. The heavy use of subroutines can decrease overall memory requirements, as can "overlays", where programs are loaded into memory overwriting other programs no longer needed. As before, we should note that the use of a compiler language generates code that runs slower, often by a factor of two, than hand-produced code.

MAXIMIZING FLEXIBILITY. A degree of flexibility is certain to be needed in almost any program, for it is almost axiomatic that programs are changed and improved in time. What seem to be total requirements early in the development of a program are often found to be insufficient after the program has been in use awhile. People almost always ask for more information or for more functions to be performed by programs. Needs change, usually in an increasing manner. Unless a program has originally been designed to handle more situations and supply more results, major recoding may be required. Allowing for these changes, i.e., incorporating flexibility in programs, requires extra effort initially, but almost always this is worth it.

In summary, it is well to note that one rarely should carry any of these goals to extreme. It is not worth the effort to have a program be absolutely as small or as fast as possible. If the goal is nearly reached, this is good enough. Of course, this statement, like many given above, is general, and special situations merit their own analysis.

In the mortgage problem, most of the considerations described do not apply, for the problem is a small one. Most likely, the first goal, that of getting the program to work as quickly as possible, is likely to predominate. Program flexibility is always highly desired, and here too it would be considered. One might eventually want to know the effect, e.g., of increasing monthly payments, rather than having these payments be constant.

In the student-record problem, these points are likely to apply:

1. Getting the program working as quickly as possible is not the most urgent consideration, for a fairly large system is involved and its functions are broad and would evolve over a period of time.
2. Execution time is certainly a consideration that influences the file organization. On the other hand, the student file is likely to be processed relatively rarely, and then with bunched operations at the end of each term. Execution time is not too critical, for the file is relatively small and at worst can be processed quickly.
3. Memory space is not a problem, since only a few records at a time will be in core.
4. Program flexibility is very important here, for most systems of this type seem to grow almost without limit in capability. Any file structure that is designed must be expandable readily to include new fields in existing records and new kinds of records.

The system, as designed in this book, is reasonably flexibly designed. In the indexed-access approach, record sizes can readily grow, though it means (as it must) that each record individually must be read into core, added to, and stored back on disk. The storage allocation scheme permits this. If new fields or record types are added, the several input-output subroutines require recoding, but most other statements are not affected. If new processing is to be performed, then of course new statements are required.

15.4 PROBLEM ANALYSIS

Scope

In this section, we consider these steps:

1. Analysis of the problem.
2. Flowcharting.
3. Development of program structure.
4. Design of data structure.
5. Design of file structure.
6. Design of input and output formats.
7. Design of a language.

Analysis of the Problem

The analysis of a problem proceeds with this underlying theme: that it is necessary to translate the original statement of the problem into a computer program written in a specific language. If the language selected accepts mathematical formulas (as does FORTRAN), then formulas to be coded must be developed in the analysis. If a more detailed analysis is required because of the language, that must be done. Analysis can, of course, stop short of these goals. If it does, however, the final translation into code may be more difficult and more subject to error.

There are no standard notations or schemes for analysis. A recommended procedure is to use a decimal-digit breakdown of steps. Thus, we might initially write steps 1, 2, 3, and 4. Upon further breakdown, the steps may be numbered thus:

1.
  1.1
    1.1.1
    1.1.2
  1.2
    1.2.1
    1.2.2
    1.2.3
  . . . .

In the analysis of the problem, computer restrictions, listed earlier, must be recalled and kept in mind. Errors due to roundoff are always a possibility in arithmetic operations, so the analysis should proceed to minimize these errors. Finiteness of words and total high-speed memory must also be considered. Much of the worry over these matters may have already been taken care of in the selection of a method, but since arithmetic details are usually deferred to the analysis, continued concern is advised.

We repeat the steps in the mortgage problem:

1. Compute monthly interest and equity payments.
2. Determine new unpaid balance.
3. Compare new balance to monthly payment; if balance exceeds payment, return to step 1; otherwise, stop.

One other operation is required in this iteration: a tally of the number of elapsed months.

Let

I = monthly interest charge
R = interest rate (as a decimal fraction)
P = old unpaid balance of principal

P' = new unpaid balance
E = equity payment in month
M = monthly payment
T = total interest prior to current payment
T' = total interest to date

Then

$$I = \frac{R \times P}{12}$$

$$T' = T + I$$

$$E = M - I$$

$$P' = P - E$$

Additionally, we shall keep track of the date, so that we can determine the total period payment. Let us maintain two values, the month and the year of the last payment. Although this is not necessary for the calculation of the payment period, it is required for the monthly summary. If that summary were not to be provided, a simple count of the number of elapsed months would suffice.

Let

m = month of the year
y = year

Then the calculations of the new month (m') and new year (y') are these:

If $m < 12$, $m' = m + 1$, $y' = y$

If $m = 12$, $m' = 1$, $y' = y + 1$

To terminate the calculations, it is necessary to test the new balance at the end of each month's calculations. As soon as that balance fails to exceed the monthly payment, one final payment (of that balance) is made.

The detailed analysis below includes input-output operations for completeness:

1. Read m, y, P, R, M, S.	Read data. ($S = 0$ if monthly summary is to be printed; $S = 1$ otherwise.)
2. Print m, y, P, R, M.	Print data with appropriate text.
3. If $PR/12 \geqslant M$, print error comment and stop.	Check to see if interest charge equals or exceeds monthly payment.

4. $T \leftarrow 0$ Initialize T. Retain initial date.
   $m_0 \leftarrow m$
   $y_0 \leftarrow y$

5. Check value of m: Modify the date. Note that an
   5.1. If $m < 12$, $m \leftarrow m + 1$ initial month "exceeding 12" is
   5.2. If $m \geq 12$, $m \leftarrow 1$, $y \leftarrow y + 1$ taken as "12".

6. $I \leftarrow (P \times R)/12$ Compute interest charge.

7. $T \leftarrow T + I$ Compute interest to date.

8. $E \leftarrow M - I$ Compute equity payment.

9. $P \leftarrow P - E$ Compute new unpaid balance.

10. If $S = 0$, print m, y, I, E, P.   If requested, print monthly summary.

11. If $P > E$, go to step 5; otherwise,   As long as balance exceeds
    go on.   monthly payment, iterate.

12. Print "Last payment is made";   Exit from loop.
    if $S = 1$, print current date also.

An analysis of the student-record problem will not be given here because it appears in Chapter 14. Analysis to the depth given above for the mortgage problem is not quite appropriate, since most of the processing in the student problem is input-output. In the above problem, the processing was almost entirely numerical.

Flowcharting

Flowcharting is part of analysis, providing in graphic form what has been developed in text form. Flowcharts are certainly not always required, but in complex procedures the pictorial form helps a programmer visualize program structure. We have already said much about the value of flowcharting.

The flowchart of the mortgage problem appears in Figure 15.1.

Development of Program Structure

The primary consideration here is the identification of segments and subroutines in the program. A *segment* (or *module*) is any distinct portion of the program that can be considered largely independent of other portions. Segments are independent to the extent that they accept a set of data for processing and transmit results to the next segment. Segmentation implies identification of chronologically executed portions, as opposed to subroutinization which refers to the development

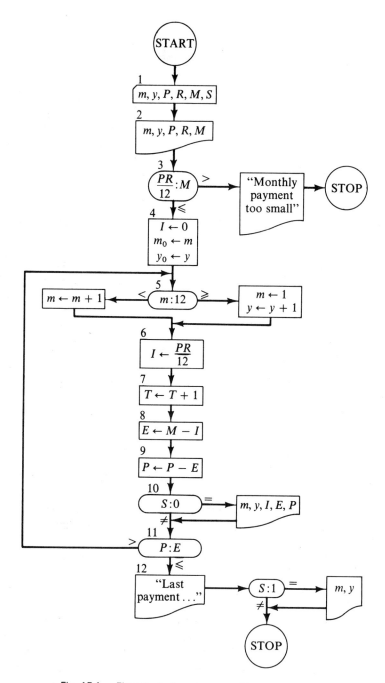

Fig. 15.1.   Flowchart of mortgage problem.

of isolated processes used throughout a program. If a programmer codes and checks out each module in turn, errors that develop can more readily be traced, for they are most likely to belong to the latest segment.

There is another reason for the identification of program modules: Their use provides flexibility and interchangeability. If, for example, a sorting module is developed within a program and it is subsequently found that a better algorithm exists, a new module can be used to replace the old. Alternatively, in a given programming system, a user can be given a choice among several modules at a point in the processing. This choice would be appropriate if the programming system has been designed to handle a variety of situations. One module may be preferable to another, though both do the same job, because the situation is different.

Subroutines have been explored in depth in Chapter 7, and little more need be added here. In program development, one must consider (1) what subroutines are already available for use, and (2) what new subroutines might be developed. Generally those processes that are frequently used in essentially the same form are candidates for subroutines. Each procedure must be individually examined.

The mortgage problem is simple enough not to require consideration of segments or subroutines. More likely, the program would itself be developed as a subroutine, given arguments such as principal sum, interest rate, and monthly payment. It then might become part of a system of programs on financial management.

In Chapter 7, a study was already made of what processes might be developed as subroutines for the student-record problem. Three subroutines were identified: to compute a weighted average of grades, to sort, and to find the smallest of a set of numbers. These were chosen because they are common processes and conceivably might be useful in a number of problems. If this problem were extended to perform other data management tasks on the student records, undoubtedly many other subroutines would be developed.

Design of Data Structure

In earlier sections of this chapter, attention was given to the nature of the data supplied to a program for processing. The term *logical structure* refers to the character of the data as supplied, implying inherent relationships among the data, as when some items are subordinate to others in a hierarchy. The task is to decide how memory shall be used to store this information for efficient processing. In Chapter 12 this problem was extensively studied. The term *physical structure* refers to the structure within the computer. It is somewhat independent of the logical structure, being machine-oriented, but is related to it.

Once again, the mortgage problem is so simple that one need not give any thought to anything resembling a "structure". The data are read, some computation is performed, and answers are supplied. The data are stored as a few constants in memory.

The same is largely true in the student-record problem, except that linear arrays are used for the data on each student in memory. This is a convenience for indexing only and there is no structure beyond this. The same is not true of the file, of course, as noted below.

Design of File Structure

File-structure design is very similar to core-structure design, in that "logical data" must be converted into "physical data". The difference lies in the nature of the memory devices involved. In the core design, the problem is simpler, for all words in core are equally accessible. In the file design, however, this is not true. We have seen how disk memory is organized; a hierarchy of memory units is available. File design must take this into account and the assignment of data to the file reflects this consideration.

The student-record problem was developed largely with a disk unit in mind, as noted earlier in this chapter. The manner of storage became the most important task, since the problem is one essentially in data management. The details of this design were given in Chapter 14.

Design of Input and Output Formats

The input data have been described and defined earlier, but before a program can read them, a specific format must be designed. Generally, this format applies to data on punched cards. Considerations here center about ease of key-punching, ease of reading by the programmer, and ease of interpretation by the computer. The format might be fixed, which makes programming easier, or variable, which generally makes keypunching and human reading easier.

The formats below apply to the data for the mortgage problem:

Input data: Each set of data is placed on each card:

Columns 1–2:   initial month

Columns 4–5:   initial year

Columns 7–14:   unpaid balance, XXXXX.XX (no '$')

Columns 16–20:   interest rate, .XXXX (decimal fraction)

Columns 22–27:   monthly payment, XXX.XX (no '$')

Column 29:   '0' if monthly interest, equity, and balance are to be printed
                 '1' if not

Format of results: Results are to be printed. For each data set (one card), the results shall appear as follows:

(New page)
INITIAL DATE IS XX–XX   (month; year)

```
UNPAID BALANCE ØF PRINCIPAL = $XXXXX.XX
INTEREST RATE = X.XX PERCENT
MØNTHLY PAYMENT = $XXX.XX
DATE   INT.     EQUITY  BALANCE
XX–XX  XXX.XX   XXX.XX   XXXXX.XX
```
(One line of above form for each month until principal is
no more than one month's payment; single-spaced)
```
THE LAST PAYMENT IS THEN MADE.
TØTAL INTEREST PAID = $XXXXX.XX
```

If the option of column 29 is exercised, the series of single-spaced monthly results
is suppressed and the next line reads

```
THE LAST PAYMENT IS THEN MADE IN XX–XX      (month; year)
```

The summary of results appears as follows:

(New page)
```
A SUMMARY ØF RESULTS IS THE FØLLØWING ...
INITIAL DATE  UNPAID PRINCIPAL  INT. RATE  MØNTHLY PAYMENT
```
(Above line, continued):
```
                    LAST PAYMENT  TØTAL INTEREST  PAYMENT PERIØD
```

Below these headings, centered under each, the following item formats:

```
XX–XX  $XXXXX.XX  X.XX PCT.  $XXX.XX  XX–XX  $XXXXX.XX
                  XX YRS.,  XX MØS
```

The format of punched cards for the student-record problem was given in
detail in earlier chapters.

Design of a Language

In most cases, the programming language used for coding a procedure is the
only language that is of concern to a programmer. Certainly this is true in the case
of the mortgage problem. However, sometimes it is insufficient for more data to
be supplied to a program, because the data are structurally complex or because
the operations to be performed are complicated. Some commands may also be
required that accompany the data, identifying, defining, or otherwise directing their
use. These commands require design; the design leads, in effect, to a "language",
the subject of this section. A common example of this language is the set of control
cards that is used with an operating system. These commands do not constitute
programming statements nor a procedure to be executed, but rather identify a
sequence of operations to occur.

In the student-record problem, we encountered an example of such commands that formed a language. The queries, described in Section 14.3, form a language for data retrieval. One statement, given there, was this one:

    PRINT FILE 'STUDENT' IF AVERAGE .GT. '85.0'

This statement resembles English and is an example of command language. It was designed to be easy to use and yet be precise in form. A data management system typically will have a variety of statements of this type.

15.5 WRITING THE PROGRAM

Scope

The subject of program writing (or *coding*) has been treated at length in this book. We shall here merely discuss several approaches and attitudes that, if pursued, ease the burden of coding and testing. These are as follows:

1. Development of data tests.
2. Inclusion of test points.
3. Saving of intermediate results.
4. Use of commentary.
5. Preparedness for errors.

Development of Data Tests

Although the input data presumably has been correctly supplied, the possibility exists that erroneous data will be supplied to a program. This must be allowed for in coding by the inclusion of tests on the data as read. If, e.g., a particular item must not exceed 48, a test as follows might be appropriate:

    IF (ITEM .GT. 48) GØ TØ 99

where statement 99 cuts the job, prints an error comment, or takes other such action. A check on the volume of data might also be needed to insure that allocated space for data is not exceeded. (A related problem is the overflow as the result of computations within the program. This should also be checked.)

If thorough tests on data are made, the code required for this can approach or even exceed the code required to solve the problem. Some moderation is required, although if absolute accuracy is vital, large amounts of testing must be present.

The main point to keep in mind is that any program, no matter how complex or comprehensive, is designed intentionally or otherwise to handle properly a specific range of data values and volume. Data testing should be designed to account for instances where the range is exceeded.

In the mortgage problem, tests for these conditions can be included:

1. A month exceeding '12'.
2. A rate exceeding whatever is a legal or reasonable limit, such as 12.00 percent.
3. A monthly payment exceeding whatever is a reasonable amount, such as $1000.

Item 1 is an absolute check, for the month cannot exceed "12". Items 2 and 3 are relative checks, because any values here are theoretically possible, but certain reasonable limits exist.

In the student-record problem, there are many more possibilities for error, because the supplied data are much more numerous. Some error conditions are these:

1. A class not equal to '69', '70', '71', or '72'.
2. A major subject not in list of majors.
3. An unreasonable number of courses.
4. An illegal course number or title.
5. An illegal course grade.

Inclusion of Test Points

As a check of each program segment, it is desirable to include a check point at its conclusion. Such a point may provide a printed comment concerning the success or failure of the program at that point.

The comments printed may be statements of fact about conditions:

```
ESTIMATES ARE DIVERGING
CØUNTS DISAGREE
ARRAY IS EXCEEDED
PART 5 CØMPLETED
```

The first comment is printed when an iterative process diverges, revealed by the sequence of computed estimates for the proper answer.

The second comment is printed when a check fails. The check is made of an accumulated count of entries in a list against an original count.

The third comment is printed when an allotted array is about to overflow with new data.

The fourth comment is printed when Part 5 is completed. A more useful comment might be one printed only on the successful completion of Part 5.

The comments printed might also be numerical statements. Samples of the data generated at a point might be printed. Examples:

```
25 ITERATIØNS WERE MADE.
THE FIRST 2 ELEMENTS ARE .3452E + 02 AND  − .3329E + 02.
THE ESTIMATED ERRØR IS  + .000026.
```

In this manner, both desirable and undesirable conditions can be indicated. They can be scattered throughout the program to indicate its progress. Very often, examination of the sequence of comments can tell at a glance the most likely place where trouble might exist.

When the program is working satisfactorily, it is a simple matter to delete these check points, since they will usually no longer be needed. If, however, it seems desirable to retain some or all for a while, it does little harm and may do much good to leave them in. It is advisable to retain them even after it is believed that the program is in "production".

Saving of Intermediate Results

If a program performs large amounts of computation, final results rarely supply an understanding of the procedure. It helps considerably if intermediate results are available for this purpose. Study of these results provides greater insight into the operation of the procedure. This added information aids in at least two other ways. First, it is usually invaluable in debugging when no "final" results are computed. Examination of the information often turns up sources of error. Second, in the case of a very long program run, execution may have to be cut before completion. Intermediate results can sometimes be used to restart the program at an intermediate point.

Intermediate results, if small in volume, can simply be left in core if a dump can later be used to read them. Alternatively they can be printed, or they can be stored in auxiliary memory for later study. The choice among these approaches depends on the volume of data involved and the availability of dumping and storage facilities.

Use of Commentary

When a procedure has been fully analyzed and possibly flowcharted, the translation to code is straightforward. There may be a one-to-one correspondence between steps in the analysis and statements or sequences of statements in the program. If, after a program has been developed, it is necessary to read and interpret the code, one can compare analysis to code to aid in understanding the latter. As we have already noted, this is almost certain to be done, for almost any program in frequent use is modified.

An efficient way to aid future study of a program is to include within the program itself enough commentary (on the analysis) to permit the listing to provide the whole story. In this way, comments appear physically adjacent to the code they represent. It is difficult to overestimate the importance of including comments within program listings. Very often only listings are readily available while other documentation is either nonexistent or less accessible. It is valuable to see explanations of code next to the code itself. Although it is often troublesome to include comments, the effort more than pays for itself later. One important point to note, however, is that commentary is useless if it is not updated as code is changed. When modifications are made in the program, appropriate modifications must be made in the comments.

The mortgage problem is coded here. Commentary, labeled to match the steps in the analysis given earlier, is included.

```
C    VARIABLES AND DECLARATIØNS.
C        PRØGRAM VARIABLES VS. ANALYSIS VARIABLES ...
C            MØ  = SMALL M
C            YR  = Y
C            PRIN = P
C            RATE = R
C            MPAY = CAPITAL M
C            SUPP = S
         INTEGER MØ, YR, SUPP, MØINIT, YRINIT, MØS, YRS,
         REAL PRIN, RATE, MPAY, TØTCH, CHRG, EQUITY
C
C    1.0  READ DATA CARD (SUPP = 1 TØ SUPPRESS MØNTHLY
C         SUMMARY)
         READ (5,100) MØ, YR, PRIN, RATE, MPAY, SUPP
   100   FØRMAT (I2, 1X, I2, 1X, F8.2, 1X, F5.4, 1X, F6.2, 1X, N1)
C    2.0  WRITE DATA READ.
C    2.1  START NEW PAGE.
         WRITE (6,201)
   201   FØRMAT (1H1)
C    2.2  PRINT MØNTH AND YEAR AT START.
         WRITE (6,202) MØ, YR
   202   FØRMAT (16HØINITIAL DATE IS  I2, 1H- I2)
C    2.3  PRINT INITIAL UNPAID BALANCE.
         WRITE (6,203) PRIN
   203   FØRMAT (35HØUNPAID BALANCE ØF PRINCIPAL IS = $ F6.3)
C    2.4  PRINT INTEREST RATE, AFTER CØNVERTING TØ PERCENT.
         PRATE = RATE * 100
         WRITE (6,204) PRATE
   204   FØRMAT (17HØINTEREST RATE = $ F4.2, 8H PERCENT)
C    2.5  PRINT MØNTHLY PAYMENT.
         WRITE (6,205) PAY
   205   FØRMAT (19HØMØNTHLY PAYMENT = $ F6.2)
C    2.6  TEST "SUPP".  IF NØNZERØ, SUPPRESS SUMMARY BY MØNTHS.
         IF (SUPP .NE. 0) GØ TØ 27
         WRITE (6,206)
   206   FØRMAT (32HØDATE    INT.   EQUITY BALANCE)
    27   WRITE (6,207)
```

```
    207  FØRMAT (1H )
  C
  C   3.0  CHECK ØN SIZE ØF MØNTHLY PAYMENT.
         IF (PRIN*RATE/12. .GT. MPAY) GØ TØ 40
         WRITE (6,300)
    300  FØRMAT (29H0MØNTHLY PAYMENT IS TØØ SMALL)
         STØP
  C
  C   4.0  INITIALIZE "TØTCH" (TØTAL CHARGE, INTEREST TØ DATE).
  C        SAVE INITIAL DATES.
     40  TØTCH = 0
         MØINIT = MØ
         YRINIT = YR
  C
  C   5.0  CØMPUTE NEW DATE . . . INCREASE "MØ" BY 1, UNLESS IT
  C        EQUALS 12, WHENCE SET TØ 1 AND INCREASE "YR" BY 1.
         IF (MØ .EQ. 12) GØ TØ 56
         MØ = MØ + 1
         GØ TØ 60
     56  MØ = 1
         YR = YR + 1
  C   6.0–9.0  CØMPUTE INTEREST CHARGE, TØTAL INTEREST TØ
  C            DATE, MØNTHLY EQUITY PAYMENT, NEW UNPAID
  C            BALANCE.
     60  CHRG = RATE * PRIN / 12
         TØTCH = TØTCH + CHRG
         EQUITY = MPAY – CHRG
         PRIN = PRIN – EQUITY
  C
  C   10.0  IF "SUPP' IS ZERØ, PRINT SUMMARY . . . DATE, INTEREST
  C         CHARGE, EQUITY PAYMENT, NEW UNPAID BALANCE.
         IF (SUPP .NE. 0) GØ TØ 110
         WRITE (6,1000) MØ, YR, CHRG, EQUITY, PRIN)
   1000  FØRMAT (1H I2, 1H– I2, 2X, F6.2, 2X, F6.2, 2X, F8.2)
  C
  C   11.0  CHECK FØR END ØF ITERATIØN . . . CØNTINUE LØØPING AS
  C         LØNG AS UNPAID BALANCE EXCEEDS MØNTHLY PAYMENT.
    110  IF (PRIN .GE. MPAY) GØ TØ 50
  C
  C   12.0  PRINT TERMINAL STATEMENT AND, IF "SUPP" IS NØNZERØ,
  C         ADD DATE.
    120  WRITE (6,1200)
   1200  FØRMAT (30H0THE LAST PAYMENT IS THEN MADE)
         IF (SUPP .EQ. 0) GØ TØ 130
```

```
      WRITE (6,1201) MØ, YR
1201  FØRMAT (1H+ 30X, 3HIN I2, 1H− I2)
      END
```

Preparedness for Errors

Errors that occur during coding are usually far more numerous than the programmer expects, be he novice or expert. They occur so frequently that it is necessary to code expecting them at every possible point in the program. If one codes with the expectation that a program bug may occur anywhere, the coding will tend to be written so that bugs can be more readily detected.

15.6 TESTING AND CHECKING

Manual Checking

Although this is often overlooked, it is necessary at the start to be certain that the problem is stated clearly. An analysis proceeds, all possibilities that may arise in the procedure must be considered. It is vital to see that the analysis is accurate and complete before proceeding to coding.

Despite all the care that might have been taken prior to writing down instructions, errors will manage to find their way into code. While there are several ways to detect and remove errors, the first step should be a careful examination of the instructions or statements written down.

Coding should be compared with the analysis and flowchart, to see if they match. All operations within individual boxes should be compared with their respective coding sequences. Decision points are especially important. If a new flowchart is drawn from the coding and found to match the original flowchart, drawn from the analysis, an excellent check is provided on the coding. If it is possible for a second person to draw this new flowchart, probably a better check results, since he will not tend to make the same errors as the programmer. A verbal explanation of the analysis and coding to a second part is another good way to check.

Finally, an instruction-by-instruction study of the coding, though tedious, may uncover more errors. Regardless of where errors are made in the program-writing process, they will eventually show up in the code (unless there are canceling errors) and can be caught there. This check thus must keep both the problem (and its analysis) and the programming language (and the computer) in mind. This is proposed as an objective check on the instructions themselves: Do they not only solve the problem but are they consistent within themselves and do they obey the rules of the language?

The question of manual checking does not end with the initial computer run. In fact, at every point in the debugging process, the programmer must answer this question either explicitly or implicitly: Shall I further check the coding by hand or shall I now turn to the computer and debugging aids to help? It is a hard question to answer at times and always takes into account the style of the programmer.

In Chapter 11, a detailed study was made of many sources of and types of errors. Suffice it to say that those errors should be avoided, if possible.

Use of Test Data

Before a program can be considered correct, it must be thoroughly checked. This is done by the application of test data, data that are representative of what will be encountered by the program when it is actually used in a problem. Generally such data ought to be simple, at least initially, so that hand calculations can be used where appropriate as a check. For example, if we have written a program to solve for the unknowns in a set of linear algebraic equations, the test data might consist of a set of three equations' coefficients. To make the hand-checking process even simpler, we can begin with a set of solutions and then write equations that will yield the assumed results. The resulting equations are satisfactory for checking purposes.

A check on all possibilities of the flow of control in a program is essential. Every path in the program should be traversed with a variety of data. Once normal test data have yielded successful results, revealing the absence of gross errors, variations on the data should be used to check out unusual situations. The broad aspects as well as the fine details of a program can be tested in this way. Extreme cases, such as one-cycle loops or no-cycle loops, must be considered; frequently these simple situations, particularly the zero case, are overlooked.

The test data must be carefully chosen, as this example illustrates. Consider the expression

$$X = (Y - .235)(Z + 1.33)^3$$

where the constants are known only approximately. If '.235' is really '.239', the values of Y near this value will lead to large errors. Thus, values of Y in that range should be used. On the other hand, if the value $Y = .235$ was chosen, the effect of the term in Z is masked completely. In any event, if the originator of a problem is not its programmer, test data should be chosen by the former, since he presumably has more knowledge of the supposed performance of the program.

Finally, continued use of a program using actual data tends to prove out a program. Yet, it is surprising how common it is that a program can be used dozens or even hundreds of times with success, only to fail when an "unusual" set of data is used. In truth, it is rare that the data are unusual; rather, it is that the program was not checked out in sufficiently many different situations. Bugs that show up in such circumstances are almost always very difficult to unearth. They are the bane of the programmer's existence.

15.7 DOCUMENTATION

The process of documentation refers to the writing of the purpose, the description, the use, and the methods of a program. Ideally, a documented program stands by itself, so that it can be used by anyone and so that it can be modified by someone experienced with the techniques used. Such a person should be able, from the description given, to understand enough about the coding to change it as needed. It is poor practice to assume, as many persons do, that the writer will forever be available to make changes.

Documentation should include the following: the purpose of the program, the method used to solve the problem (in general terms), capabilities and restrictions, computer environment required (including peripheral devices used, program language used, and the operating system used), input requirements, output results, diagnostic and error-detection facilities, flowcharts in appropriate detail, and a complete program listing. For the purposes of usage alone (not coding modification), the following can be deleted: flowcharts, the listing and, possibly, the method. However, these should be available readily, as in a program library.

Sometimes the very format of a computer program listing serves a purpose in documentation and explaining the structure. This can be taken advantage of in a FORTRAN listing, where blank spaces can be freely used. A fairly simple way for this to be done is to indicate nestings of DO loops, as in the following:

```
        DØ 20 I = 1, N
          SUM = 0.
          DØ 10 J = 1, N
            IF (J − I) 5, 10, 5
            SUM = SUM + A(I,J)*X(J)
10          CØNTINUE
20        X(I) = (B(I) − SUM)/A(I,I)
```

Similar indentations can be utilized to reveal other aspects of program structure.

If we use a program written by someone else, we want to know just how it was tested—using what kind and scope of data. This tells us how applicable it is to our situation, or what its probability of success is. These items should also be incorporated into the documentation.

15.8 PROGRAM STYLE

What is it?

If computer programs are developed according to the plan given in these sections, they will have imparted to them something loosely called "style"—that is, good style. Good program style is desirable, for reasons we shall shortly see. But what is style?

Computer programs are more than procedures written in programming languages for solving problems. They are also documents for future reference, they are educational media for instruction on coded algorithms, and they are used for further development of better programs. If programs serve these purposes well, they are more valuable than if they merely act as coded procedures. Good program style will make them more valuable.

A program has good style if it has these traits: a logical structure, abundant commentary, consistency in all respects, mnemonic symbols, labels that match analysis steps, modularity, and subroutinization. Not all of these traits are required for satisfactory style, and certainly there may be others in special instances. However, if most or all are present, programs will have a desirable style and so be useful beyond their originally intended use.

LOGICAL STRUCTURE. The structure of a program, as embodied in source statements, should make apparent sense. For example, if a test is performed that has five outcomes, it is more reasonable to list the code for each outcome in some sensible order, as by increasing values of a test parameter. It is reasonable because a reader expects it this way; another scheme may lead to confusion. It makes sense to place all frequently used code together, with exceptional cases treated near the end of the program. Allocated space for data should be done with a pattern, not randomly. These are some examples of *logical* (i.e., *reasonable* or *expected*) program structure.

ABUNDANT COMMENTARY. Mere volume of commentary does not add style or any particular aid to the reader. However, many facts can be placed in listing comments. We have seen some examples in this book. Commentary can be extended to include all information one might expect in full documentation, but that may be going too far. Most important items are these: explanations of the several steps in the program, identification of variables when required, identification of the calling sequence when the program is a subroutine, and information about results. Full details on these items can be located elsewhere.

CONSISTENCY. Of probably the greatest aid to an understanding of code is the consistent use of module types and sizes, variable names, comments, types of decisions, and program structure in general. Not many procedures are thoroughly consistent, but to the extent that they (and their programs) are, understanding of them is improved.

MNEMONIC SYMBOLS AND MEANINGFUL LABELS. If the names of variables and arrays are mnemonic, they are to an extent self-defining. The use of 'VECTØR' rather than 'VEC' or 'V' is desirable, although it takes longer to write and keypunch. Even the alternatives are better than 'A' if the prime trait in the variable is that it is a vector (or *the* vector). If labels match flowchart box numbers or steps in an analysis, programs are easier to follow, for they can be related to these earlier procedural forms.

MODULARITY. Modularity is not only beneficial in program development, as we have seen in these sections, but its use makes clearer the parts of a procedure. We think more easily about a complex process if its steps are well-defined. We then need only study one step at a time to understand the system as a whole.

SUBROUTINIZATION. The use of subroutines parallels the use of program modules, helping both the programmer and the reader. Subroutine calls, as noted, form a stylized language, particularly if arguments are selected and ordered in a logical manner.

Another characteristic of certain computer programs is that called *elegance*. Like style, the concept is elusive. It generally refers to the "clever" or "sophisticated" way in which a process is coded, using techniques that are not apparent on cursory examination. Elegant techniques often save time and space, and they frequently use statements or instructions originally intended for other purposes. Mention is made here of program elegance with a caution: Its use generally precludes flexibility; if an extension of the coded process is called for, the elegant approach usually cannot do the job. Such a technique must therefore be used with care.

Why Use it?

Having seen what good program style entails, we can readily see why it ought to be present. Its main purpose is to offer clarity for readers of program listings. It offers help not only in understanding code, but in developing it, for the programmer too can forget many details in a large program. Future modifications are more easily made. Documentation itself is simplified—if it needed at all beyond what has been included in program commentary. In summary, we close with the thought that if all programs were written to serve as tutorial material for their own understanding, they would probably contain that which constitutes good programming style.

INDEX